Global Issues
Politics, Economics, and Culture

Fourth Edition

RICHARD J. **PAYNE**

Illinois State University

Boston   Columbus   Indianapolis   New York   San Francisco   Upper Saddle River
Amsterdam   Cape Town   Dubai   London   Madrid   Milan   Munich   Paris   Montreal   Toronto
Delhi   Mexico City   São Paulo   Sydney   Hong Kong   Seoul   Singapore   Taipei   Tokyo

Senior Acquisitions Editor: Vikram Mukhija
Editorial Assistants: Beverly Fong, Isabel Schwab
Marketing Managers: Wendy Gordon, Lindsey Prudhomme
Production Manager: Fran Russello
Full Service Project Management: Chitra Ganesan/PreMediaGlobal
Creative Art Director: Jayne Conte
Cover Illustration/Photo: © Veer Images
Printer and Binder: Courier Companies, Inc.

Library of Congress Cataloging-in-Publication Data
Payne, Richard J.,
  Global issues : politics, economics, and culture / Richard J. Payne.—4th ed.
     p. cm.
  Includes index.
  ISBN-13: 978-0-205-85459-2
  ISBN-10: 0-205-85459-1
  1. Globalization—Textbooks. 2. World politics—Textbooks. I. Title.
  JZ1318.P39 2013
  303.48'2—dc23

                                        2011050350

2 3 4 5 6 7 8 9 10—CRK—16 15 14 13

PEARSON

ISBN-13: 978-0-205-85459-2
ISBN-10: 0-205-85459-1

To Elaine Cook Graybill
and
Alyson Sue McMillen

BRIEF CONTENTS

Contents   v
Preface   xi
Maps   xviii

CONTENTS

PREFACE

Persistent and sustained popular revolts against entrenched political patriarchs and oppressive regimes across the Middle East and North Africa are the pivotal development of the twenty-first century. They mark radical transitions to democracy in a region widely perceived to be resistant to political change and respect for individual freedom and human rights. Change in Egypt and Syria, in particular, has profound global political implications. Israel, the United States, Iran, and Turkey are forced to alter deeply entrenched foreign policies as democratic governments in the Middle East change the status quo on many issues, including the Palestinian-Israeli conflict. These revolutionary developments were influenced by significant demographic changes, widespread poverty and inequality, government corruption and repression, declining economic opportunities in the wake of the global financial and economic crisis, declining public trust in government institutions, and the growing power of global communications. These uprisings clearly demonstrate that social networks are enhancing citizen participation in domestic and global affairs, challenging traditional practices of government secrecy and control in general, and opening up a new period of greater transparency in domestic and international relations.

The global financial and economic crisis accelerated profound shifts in power in the international system. While the United States remains the leading power, emerging market countries such as China, India, and Brazil are diffusing power. This power shift is reinforced by the growing participation of nonstate actors and individuals in international relations. Emerging powers have their own interests and agendas, even as solutions to global issues require more global cooperation. These new realities are forcing leading states to adopt multilateralism and to cooperate more with other states and nonstate actors to achieve their goals. Enforcing the no-fly zone restrictions in Libya in 2011 showed America's recognition of shifting global power. The United States relinquished its preeminent military role to France, Britain, and NATO.

States, the foundation of international relations, emerged relatively recently from fundamental technological, religious, economic, political, and cultural changes. The forces of globalization are now profoundly altering international relations, weakening the virtual monopoly of power enjoyed by states, strengthening nonstate actors and intergovernmental organizations, and eroding all forms of hierarchical organizations. Revolutions in technology, especially in communications, directly challenge traditional approaches to international politics. WikiLeaks' publication of government secret documents on the Internet underscores that point.

Globalization intertwines the fates of states, intergovernmental organizations, nonstate actors, and individuals to an unprecedented degree. Wars, which have been a primary concern for states and traditionally the focus of international relations, also have changed. Globalization has made traditional warfare less likely and unconventional wars more prevalent. America's longest war is not with another state but is instead against nonstate actors, especially al-Qaeda and the Taliban. Although Osama bin Laden, widely viewed as the embodiment of global terrorism, was killed by U.S. Special Forces in Pakistan on May 1, 2011, the end of the war on terrorism is not in sight.

My decision to write this textbook was strongly influenced by the need for a comprehensive, accessible, and student-oriented introductory textbook for undergraduates that focuses specifically on global issues. This text concentrates on global issues that students around the world are passionate about because they are directly related to the forces of globalization that are integral components of their lives. The issues discussed in this book are both primary global concerns and those in which students have shown great interest. This book's pedagogical features are based on classroom experiences that demonstrate how to help students understand complex concepts, develop critical-thinking skills, and engage in problem solving.

NEW TO THIS EDITION

All chapters have been substantially revised and updated to reflect current developments. Each chapter concludes with a detailed case study on a current global issue. Included are case studies on democratic transitions in the Middle East and North Africa, the growing power of emerging markets, the war in Afghanistan, government corruption in India, food security and the global food crisis, the impact of the global financial crisis on Ireland, and the earthquake and tsunami in Japan. Also new are annotated suggested readings at the end of each chapter and an expanded index to help students find key terms. Additional features of each new chapter include

- Chapter 1, "Challenges of Globalization": transitions to democracy and the rise of emerging market countries; the impact of social networks on global affairs; the power of young people to effectuate political and cultural change in the Middle East and elsewhere
- Chapter 2, "The Struggle for Primacy in a Global Society": the rise of China and the decline of the United States; domestic economic challenges to America's global power, especially budget deficits
- Chapter 3, "Human Rights": the global response to the treatment of Libyan civilians; evolving perceptions of a common humanity due to communications and migration; human rights of homosexuals
- Chapter 4, "Promoting Democracy": global implications of recent democratic revolutions; the roles of generational change and the Internet in transitions to democracy
- Chapter 5, "Global Terrorism": counterterrorism laws, such as the Patriot Act; the killing of Osama Bin-Laden; domestic terrorism
- Chapter 6, "Weapons Proliferation": developments in nuclear weapons programs, including the New START treaty; the proliferation of small arms; weapons and terrorism

- Chapter 7, "The Global Financial Crisis": continuing fallout from the crisis, including a global power shift from the G-7 to the G-20
- Chapter 8, "Global Trade": global companies and the promotion of equality; currency wars and global trade; emerging market economy countries
- Chapter 9, "Global Inequality and Poverty": poverty as a factor in popular uprisings; the global recession and foreign aid; growing inequality in the United States, Germany, and India; hunger and malnutrition
- Chapter 10, "Environmental Issues": indigenous peoples and the environment; new efforts to prevent deforestation; climate change and natural catastrophes
- Chapter 11, "Population and Migration": the Romanies in France; new refugees from countries with democratic revolutions; population growth in the developing world contributing to global power shifts; China reexamining one-child policy
- Chapter 12, "Global Crime": war, ethnic conflict, and crime; government corruption; piracy on the Somali coast and gangs in Central America
- Chapter 13, "The Globalization of Disease": cholera in Haiti and Congo fever in India
- Chapter 14, "Cultural Clashes and Conflict Resolution": increasing conflicts between states and nonstate actors; attempts to resolve ethnic conflict in Iraq and Sudan

FEATURES

Global Issues: Politics, Economics, and Culture is based on ten philosophical components that are interwoven into each chapter and throughout this book in order to provide students with:

1. A clearer understanding of how the powerful forces of economic, financial, cultural, political, environmental, and military globalization are affecting governments, nonstate actors, and individuals.
2. A deeper awareness of the growing inability of governments, nonstate actors, and individuals to neatly compartmentalize problems within countries outside broader global developments.
3. An appreciation for the complexities of global problems and their interdependence.
4. A broader sense of the global issues and problems in developing countries.
5. A historical background to many global issues that enables students to see continuity and change in human experiences.
6. A deeper awareness of how globalization is profoundly challenging the state-centric emphasis that dominates international relations and world politics.
7. A foundation for more advanced courses on globalization and global affairs.
8. An understanding of basic concepts and theories and an ability to evaluate and apply them to real-life events and problems.
9. An ability to think critically, develop independent judgment, and sharpen intellectual curiosity and imagination.
10. A recognition of the power of individuals, including students, to have a positive impact on global problems.

The text is composed of fourteen chapters, each focusing on a specific topic and related subtopics. The global issues covered in this book are widely regarded to be of critical importance by both the global community and instructors. In addition to providing instructors with the flexibility to stimulate student participation, the range of issues allows sufficient time during a semester to cover each chapter and to incorporate various pedagogical approaches. Instructors will have enough time to review for exams, administer at least three exams, and allow students to present research papers and other projects. This book can be easily supplemented with subscriptions to publications such as the *New York Times*, the *Washington Post*, the *Wall Street Journal*, the *Economist*, or *Foreign Affairs*, enabling students to obtain more current examples of the global issues discussed in these pages.

As a comprehensive introduction to global issues for students from different academic disciplines, *Global Issues* is written in a style that makes information very accessible. A more conversational writing style engages students, encourages them to relate what they read to global developments and their own lives, facilitates the development of analytical skills, and makes it easier for them to engage in discussions. Above all, it attempts to present a clear, straightforward discussion of interesting and important global issues without obscuring their complexity.

- **Chapter Introductions** The introduction provides a brief overview of the main points in the chapter, tells students what is covered, and provides examples of controversial issues included in the chapter to stimulate students' interest in the material.
- **Current Examples** Consistent with the decision to adopt an accessible writing style, I have included many brief and current examples of global issues throughout the book. These examples make global issues more immediately relevant for students and encourages them to develop a concrete understanding of specific problems.
- **Historical Background** Each chapter provides practical historical background information to give students an understanding of the issue's broader context.
- **Cross-Referenced Issues** Chapters are cross-referenced to help students see the interrelatedness and interdependence of global issues. For example, by reading Chapter 10, "Environmental Issues," students will explore the impact of economic globalization on the environment and culture as well as the relationships among environmental issues, global and domestic inequality, economic development, migration, cultural conflicts, and the spread of infectious diseases.
- **Maps and Photographs** Maps help to put issues in context and enable students to better grasp essential points discussed in the text. Carefully selected photographs portray specific developments and capture students' attention.
- **Tables** Tables throughout the book help students understand important points discussed in the text.
- **Boldfaced Key Terms and Definitions** These are designed to draw students' attention to definitions, concepts, key terms, and main points. Stressing their importance reinforces the point that they are the building blocks of the chapter.
- **Marginal Glossaries** Small boxes in the margins define key terms and give students a quick reference to important definitions and concepts.

- **End-of-Chapter Summaries**   These provide a brief review of the chapter. They focus students' attention on major points and help them to improve their comprehension and retention of the information.
- **End-of-Chapter Questions and List of Key Terms**   These questions and key terms are designed to improve students' retention of information, stimulate discussions in study groups, and help students prepare for exams.
- **Annotated Suggested Readings**   A list of suggested readings is included at the end of each chapter to familiarize students with scholarly literature and to help them gain additional information.
- **Index**   This listing allows students to quickly find key terms, concepts, names, and subjects discussed throughout the text. Many students find the index especially helpful when reviewing for exams.

SUPPLEMENTS

Longman is pleased to offer several resources to qualified adopters of *Global Issues* and their students that will make teaching and learning from this book even more effective and enjoyable. Several of the supplements for this book are available at the Instructor Resource Center (IRC), an online hub that allows instructors to quickly download book-specific supplements. Please visit the IRC welcome page at **www.pearsonhighered.com/irc** to register for access.

MySearchLab   For over 10 years, instructors and students have reported achieving better results and better grades when a Pearson MyLab has been integrated into the course. MySearchLab provides engaging experiences that personalize learning, and comes from a trusted partner with educational expertise and a deep commitment to helping students and instructors achieve their goals. A wide range of writing, grammar and research tools and access to a variety of academic journals, census data, Associated Press newsfeeds, and discipline-specific readings help you hone your writing and research skills. To order the print text with MySearchLab, use ISBN 0-205-23152-7.

Passport   Choose the resources you want from MyPoliSciLab and put links to them into your course management system. If there is assessment associated with those resources, it also can be uploaded, allowing the results to feed directly into your course management system's gradebook. With MyPoliSciLab assets like videos, mapping exercises, *Financial Times* newsfeeds, current events quizzes, politics blog, and much more, Passport is available for any Pearson political science book. To order the print text with Passport, use ISBN 0-205-23151-9.

Pearson MyTest   This powerful assessment generation program includes multiple-choice questions, true/false questions, fill-in-the-blank questions, matching questions, and essay questions for each chapter. Questions and tests can be easily created, customized, saved online, and then printed, allowing flexibility to manage assessments anytime and anywhere. Available exclusively on the IRC.

LONGMAN ATLAS OF WORLD ISSUES (0-205-78020-2) From population and political systems to energy use and women's rights, the *Longman Atlas of World Issues* features full-color thematic maps that examine the forces shaping the world. Featuring maps from the latest edition of *The Penguin State of the World Atlas*, this excerpt includes critical thinking exercises to promote a deeper understanding of how geography affects many global issues.

GOODE'S WORLD ATLAS (0-321-65200-2) First published by Rand McNally in 1923, *Goode's World Atlas* has set the standard for college reference atlases. It features hundreds of physical, political, and thematic maps as well as graphs, tables, and a pronouncing index.

THE PENGUIN DICTIONARY OF INTERNATIONAL RELATIONS (0-140-51397-3) This indispensable reference by Graham Evans and Jeffrey Newnham includes hundreds of cross-referenced entries on the enduring and emerging theories, concepts, and events that are shaping the academic discipline of international relations and today's world politics.

RESEARCH AND WRITING IN INTERNATIONAL RELATIONS (0-205-06065-X) With current and detailed coverage on how to start research in the discipline's major subfields, this brief and affordable guide offers the step-by-step guidance and the essential resources needed to compose political science papers that go beyond description and into systematic and sophisticated inquiry. This text focuses on areas where students often need help—finding a topic, developing a question, reviewing the literature, designing research, and last, writing the paper.

ACKNOWLEDGMENTS

I am deeply indebted to many students who made significant contributions to this collaborative and interdisciplinary project. Feedback from students in my Global Issues courses over the years has been invaluable and has contributed to making the book accessible to other students. I am also indebted to many research assistants, especially Yu Bo, Lara Saba, Brian Zednick, Janet Schultz, Natalie Mullen, Anthony DiMaggio, Nadejda Negroustoueva, Lindsay Barber, Meaghan Gass, Jake Owen, and Vanda Rajcan.

I am grateful to many colleagues who read the manuscript, made useful suggestions, and shared their insights. I would like to thank Michele Ganschow, Jamal Nassar, and Cherie Valentine of the Department of Politics and Government at Illinois State University; Laura Berk of the Department of Psychology at Illinois State University; Kelly Keogh of Normal Community High School; Carole J. Cosimano of the Illinois Humanities Council; Michael Edward Allison of the University of Scranton; Mikhail Alexseev of San Diego State University; Lindsey Back of Morehead State University; Eric Budd of Fitchburg State College; Brad T. Clark and M. Dawn King of Colorado State University; Mark E. Denham and Richard F. Weisfelder of the University of Toledo; Erich Frankland of Casper

College; Mark Haas of Duquesne University; Barbara Hufker of Webster University; Sabrina Jordan of Bethune-Cookman University; Robert King of Georgia Perimeter College; Mark Martinez of California State University at Bakersfield; Daniel McIntosh of Slippery Rock University; Anjana Mishra of Florida International University; Luis Antonio Payan of the University of Texas at El Paso; George Quester of the University of Maryland; Timothy Russell of the University of Memphis; Houman Sadri of the University of Central Florida; Tom Schrand of Philadelphia University; Mark Schroeder of the University of Kentucky; Boyka Stefanova of University of Texas–Austin; Bill Sutton of Southern Maine Community College; Marjorie K. Nanian of Schoolcraft College; and Thomas J. Volgy of the University of Arizona.

I would also like to thank Michele Ganschow for her invaluable assistance, as well as Kay Stultz of Institutional Technology Service; and Eric Stano, Toni Magyar, Lindsey Prudhomme, Beverly Fong, and Vikram Mukhija at Pearson Longman. Above all, I am especially indebted to Jason C. F. Payne for helping me with the chapter on the global financial crisis and to Elaine Cook Graybill for her support, insights, and suggestions throughout the process of writing this book.

RICHARD J. PAYNE

MAPS

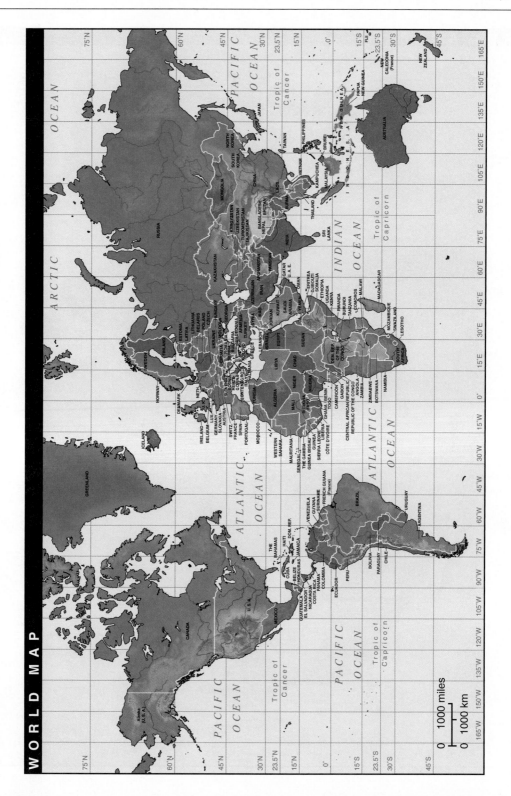

NORTH AMERICA

SOUTH AMERICA

80°W · 70°W · 60°W · 50°W · 40°W · 30°W

Caribbean Sea

10°N

Barranquilla

Maracaibo
Barquisimeto · Valencia

VENEZUELA · **GUYANA**

Medellín · **SURINAME**

Bogotá · Georgetown · Paramaribo

Rio Orinoco · Cayenne

COLOMBIA · **FRENCH GUIANA (France)**

0° · 0°

ECUADOR

Quito · *Rio Negro* · Marajó Island · Belém

Gulf of Guayaquil · Guayaquil · *Amazon Basin* · Fortaleza

Rio Amazon · Manaus · *Amazon R.*

Teresina

Rio Madeira

PERU · *Rio Juruá* · *Rio Purus* · **BRAZIL** · Recife

10°S · Lima · *Rio Tapajós* · *Rio Xingu* · 10°S

Lake Titicaca · *Rio São Francisco*

Mato Grosso Plateau · Salvador

BOLIVIA · Brasília

La Paz · Goiânia

Sucre · *Rio Araguaia* · Belo Horizonte

20°S · 20°S

CHILE · **PARAGUAY** · Campinas · Rio de Janeiro

23.5°S · *Tropic of Capricorn* · São Paulo · Cabo Frio · *Tropic of Capricorn* · 23.5°S

Asunción · Curitiba

Rio Paraná

PACIFIC OCEAN

Atacama Desert · **ARGENTINA** · Porto Alegre

30°S · Cerro Aconcagua · 30°S

Santiago · Rosario

Pampas · **URUGUAY**

Buenos Aires

Montevideo

Andes Mountains

40°S · 40°S

Isla Grande de Chiloé · *Gulf of San Matías*

ATLANTIC OCEAN

Valdés Peninsula

Patagonia · *Gulf of San Jorge*

Taitao Penninsula

50°S · 50°S

Strait of Magellan · **FALKLAND ISLANDS**

Tierra Del Fuego · Port Stanley · **SOUTH GEORGIA ISLAND**

0 —— 500 miles

0 —— 500 km

70°W · 60°W · 50°W · 40°W · 30°W

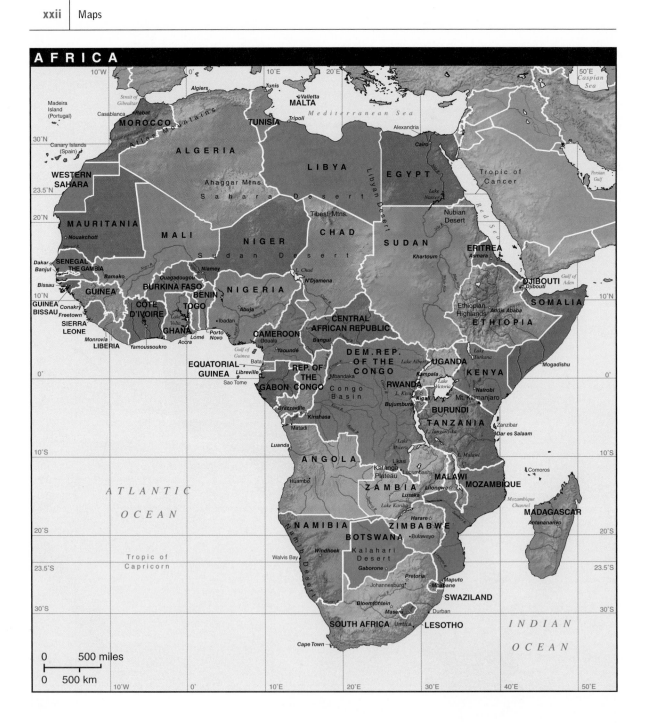

EUROPE

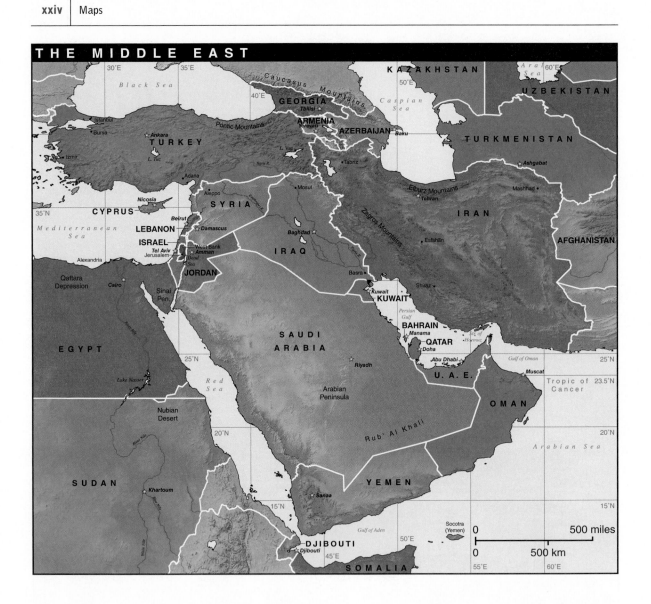

THE MIDDLE EAST

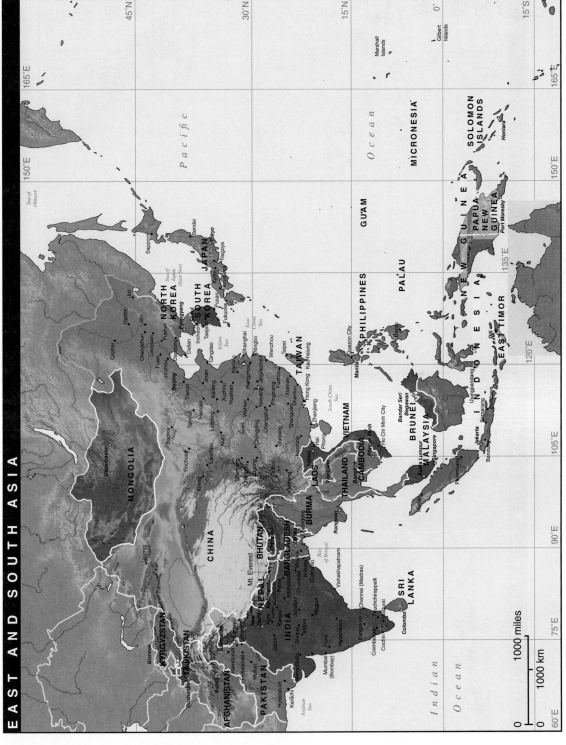

EAST AND SOUTH ASIA

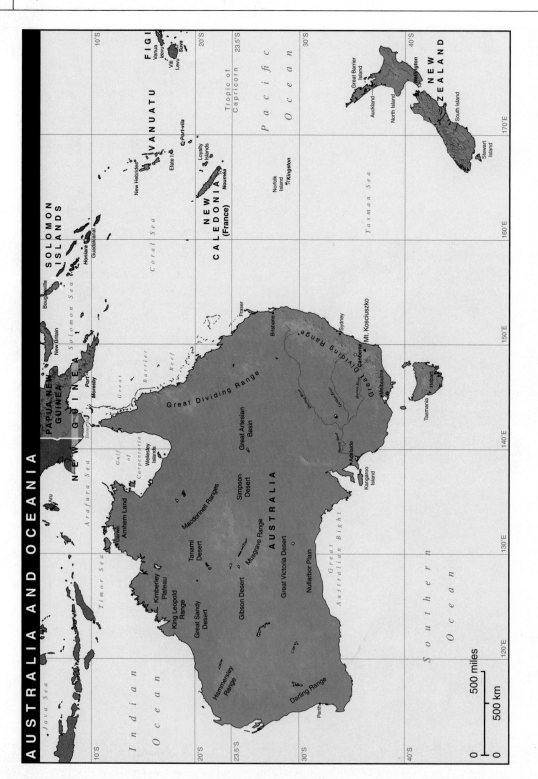

AUSTRALIA AND OCEANIA

Global Issues: Challenges of Globalization

A growing worldwide interconnectedness in the age of globalization has weakened the ability of authoritarian governments to control their citizens. Egypt exploded with joy when pro-democracy protesters ended President Hosni Mubarak's three-decade rule.

INTRODUCTION

Revolutions in technology, transportation, and communication and the different ways of thinking that characterize interdependence and globalization are exerting pressures on nation-states that strengthen them in some ways but weaken them in others. States that played leading roles in international affairs must now deal with their declining power as global power is more diffused with the rise of China, Brazil, India, and other emerging market countries. Global communications, including social media, pose significant challenges to states. The publication of hundreds of thousands of secret government documents on the Internet by WikiLeaks in 2010 undermined the traditional practice of states to safeguard their secrets and to control information available to their citizens and others. Social networks such as Facebook and Twitter were instrumental in spreading popular revolts in favor of achieving democratic transitions in Tunisia, Egypt, Libya, and Syria, and throughout the Middle East and North Africa.

Globalization—especially economic, financial, cultural, and environmental globalization—has spawned debates around the world. These debates illustrate both the significant resistance to and the widespread acceptance of globalization. Although some aspects of globalization are embraced as positive, others are rejected as destructive to cultures, the environment, and political and economic institutions, especially in poorer countries.

This chapter examines the economic, political, and cultural aspects of globalization. Like all the chapters in this book, it demonstrates how politics, economics, and culture are intricately linked in an increasingly complex global society. It also examines the causes of globalization, various forms of globalization, periods of globalization, and the debates about globalization. Given the significance of religion in global affairs, the chapter concludes with a detailed case study on challenges facing the Catholic Church.

international relations ■ The relations among the world's state governments and other actors

Peace of Westphalia ■ The treaty that concluded the Thirty Years' War in 1648

state ■ A legal and political unit that must be internationally recognized, be politically organized, and be a populated geographic area that has sovereignty

sovereign ■ The ability of a state to be independent and free from the control of another state

FROM INTERNATIONAL RELATIONS TO GLOBAL ISSUES

International relations is concerned with the interaction of states. The modern state emerged in Western Europe in 1648, following the Peace of Westphalia, which ended thirty years of war among various groups of princes and between political leaders and the Catholic Church. International relations, international politics, and world politics, which are all closely related, focus on states as the main actors. States are often referred to as nations, and most students of international relations use the terms *states* and *nations* interchangeably. They also use the term *nation-state*. The terms *state* and *nation* are related, but they are not exactly the same. A state is essentially a political unit composed of people, a well-defined territory, and a set of governing institutions. It is regarded as sovereign. This means that it is recognized by other states as having the exclusive right to make its own domestic and foreign policies. In other words, it is an independent actor in world politics. The United States is composed of diverse populations and is based on primarily an ideology. All states have ideologies, or systems of values, beliefs, and ideas. A nation is generally defined as a group of people who have strong emotional, cultural, linguistic, religious, and historical ties. The two concepts have become linked in everyday usage, and many scholars and practitioners of international relations use the term *nation-state* to capture this linkage.[1] International relations focuses on three main questions:

1. What are the contexts in which states operate, and how do these contexts shape or influence the decisions governments make?
2. What are the major objectives and interests of states in international politics, and what strategies do they employ to achieve them?
3. How are the choices made by states explained?[2]

At the heart of these questions is the concept of power. Power is defined as the ability to get others to do things they would not ordinarily do or to behave in ways they would prefer to avoid. Central to an understanding of international relations is the view that the interactions among countries are characterized by a struggle for power.[3] This emphasis on states as the dominant, almost exclusive, actors in world politics is referred to as the state-centric model.

All fields of study are concerned with theories. The general purpose of a theory is to describe, explain, and predict how humans behave or how things work in the real world under certain circumstances. A theory is generally defined as an orderly, logical, integrated set of ideas or statements about human behavior or things in our environment. All theories provide conceptual frameworks and simplify complex realities.

PLURALISM AND INTERDEPENDENCE

A theory marking the transition from traditional international relations to global issues is that of pluralism and interdependence. Although this approach views states as the most important actors in world politics, it takes nonstate actors (i.e., organizations that are not formally associated with governments) into consideration. Its main concern is with how human activities are intertwined and interconnected across national boundaries. New and far-reaching forces of globalization are having such profound effects on the world that how we approach international relations must also be significantly transformed. James N. Rosenau and Mary Durfee have concluded that "daily occurrences of complex and uncertain developments in every region of the world are so pervasive as to cast doubt on the viability of the long-established ways in which international affairs have been conducted and analyzed."[4] The rapid proliferation of states as well as nonstate actors, revolutions in technology and communications, the growing sophistication and global views of many ordinary citizens, and the changing nature of conflicts are all contributing to the complex environments in which we live.[5] State failure and the inability of governments to effectively address a wide range of global issues reinforce this transformation of international relations.

The violence and threat of violence that accompanied the emergence of modern states led to the pervasive emphasis on military power as the highest priority of states. The fear of losing territory or being eliminated was very real.

---

ideology ■ A system of values, beliefs, and ideas

nation ■ A group of people who identify as a political community based on common territory, culture, and other similar bonds

state-centric model ■ The view that world politics is dominated almost exclusively by state actors

theory ■ Predicts how humans behave or how things work in the real world under specific circumstances

nonstate actors ■ Organizations that are not formally associated with governments and play a crucial role in setting the international agenda

It is estimated that 95 percent of the state-units in Europe at the beginning of the sixteenth century have been destroyed or combined to make other countries.[6] The devastating effectiveness of military force and the development of nuclear weapons that threaten the extinction of most of the world make countries extremely reluctant to use military force.

In addition to terrorism, there are other nontraditional threats to national security. Economic competition, the global financial crisis, population growth and migration, organized crime, drug trafficking, environmental problems, poverty, inequality, the globalization of diseases, piracy, and ethnic conflicts are among the threats to security. Recognition of these threats is strengthening the concept of human security in an increasingly global society. Human security is viewed as being linked to challenges that human beings face every day, most of which are not primarily related to military power. The concept of human security focuses on seven categories of threats.[7] They are

human security
■ A concept of security that deals with the everyday challenges humans face that don't involve military issues

- Economic security (an assured basic income)
- Food security (access to an adequate supply of food)
- Health security (access to basic health care)
- Environmental security (access to clean water, clean air, etc.)
- Personal security (safety from physical violence and threats)
- Community security (safety from ethnic cleansing and genocide)
- Political security (protection of basic human rights and freedoms)

The growing complexity of our world is generally viewed as giving rise to a new period in international relations, or postinternational politics.[8] This transition is characterized by greater attention to interdependence and globalization, and a stronger emphasis on global politics in particular and global issues in general. Global politics refers to political issues and activities by states and nonstate actors that extend across national boundaries and that have implications for most of the world. But the concept of global politics inadequately portrays how economic, cultural, environmental, and demographic factors, among others, are creating a global society with global norms (i.e., a set of basic values that are increasingly common to human societies). This book focuses on global issues. Stressing global issues indicates a recognition of how globalization intertwines many aspects of human activities and how essential it is to adopt an interdisciplinary approach in order to understand our world and its impact on our daily lives.

global politics
■ Political issues and activities that have implications for most of the world

global norms ■ A set of basic values that are increasingly common to human societies

global issues
■ Encompass traditional international relations and worldwide politics

Generational change is profoundly influencing global issues. Young people have grown up in a world characterized by globalization. Their perceptions and access to communications technologies challenge many traditional concepts and practices in relation to states.

THE GROWTH OF THE MODERN STATE

humanism ■ A system of thought that centers on human beings and their values, capacities, and worth

The state emerged over several centuries through struggles for power among institutions, groups, and individuals with military, economic, cultural, religious, and political interests. As we will see, the power of ideas played a pivotal role in the process. The spread of humanism—with its emphasis on the study of ancient Greek and Hebrew texts, which concentrated on the Bible—strengthened individualism and critical thinking. Humanism was accompanied by the Renaissance, which evolved in Italy in the fourteenth century and marked the transition from the Middle Ages to modern times. Like humanism, the Renaissance concentrated on the individual, self-consciousness, creativity, exploration, and science. The combination of ideas, technological developments, ambition, the quest for freedom, and the constant struggle for power radically altered accepted practices, institutions, and patterns of authority. Because the Catholic Church was the dominant institution in Western Europe following the decline and fall of the Roman Empire, it was inevitably the target of those advocating change. Challenges to the Catholic Church were strengthened by the development of technology, namely, the printing press. Johann Gutenberg (1397–1468) invented the printing press around 1436.

As the Church's influence eroded, queens, princes, and kings in Europe attempted to enhance their own power by promoting national consciousness and territorial independence. They were assisted in their efforts to consolidate their secular authority within their territories by the Protestant Reformation. This does not mean that European royalty emerged with an antireligious character. In fact, a clear separation of church and state within European countries is still a subject of debate today. This religious transformation was gradual. The most outspoken critic of the Catholic Church was Martin Luther (1483–1546), a professor of theology at the University of Wittenberg who had been motivated to act by the campaign for selling indulgences (i.e., pardons of temporal or secular punishment due to sin) in Germany.[9] European monarchs also formed alliances with merchants to weaken the Catholic Church and the Holy Roman Empire. Small political units made it extremely difficult to engage in profitable trade and other economic transactions beyond their limited boundaries. Larger, unified political systems were beneficial to businesses because of uniform regulations and fewer taxing jurisdictions, and the enhanced ability of larger areas to enforce the laws. These economic interests coincided with the various monarchs' desire to collect more taxes in order to acquire military technology and build larger armies.

Traveling through Europe, one notices that many towns are dominated by old castles. These castles symbolized not only military strength but also the political and economic independence of local barons. Refinement of cannons and the availability of gunpowder enabled Europe's kings and queens to effectively challenge barons and others and to consolidate their power over increasingly larger areas. Between 1400 and 1600, large numbers of the smaller political entities lost their independence.[10] An excellent example of how Europe's monarchs strengthened internal control as they tried to weaken the power of the Catholic Church is provided by England's King Henry VIII in 1534. Named Defender of the Faith in 1521 for his strong support of the Catholic Church, the king clashed with Rome when he decided to divorce his first wife, Catherine of Aragon, on the grounds that she could not produce a son. Instead of retreating after being excommunicated by the pope, King Henry VIII persuaded England's Parliament to make him Protector and Only Supreme Head of the Church and Clergy of England, thereby creating the Anglican Church. The king ignited the spark of English nationalism and increased his own economic, political, and religious power.

Religious, cultural, political, economic, and technological developments ultimately led to the outbreak of the Thirty Years' War in 1618. The German

Renaissance ■ The humanistic revival in Europe of classical art, architecture, literature, and learning

Johann Gutenberg ■ (1397–1468); German inventor of the printing press

Martin Luther ■ (1483–1546); German theologian and Reformation leader

Protestant princes, who also fought each other, were allied with France, Sweden, Denmark, and England against the Holy Roman Empire, represented by the Hapsburgs of Spain and the Catholic princes. The Hapsburgs, also concerned about maintaining their own power, often clashed with each other.[11] The Thirty Years' War had devastating consequences for Germany. Two thirds of the population perished, and five sixths of the villages in the empire were destroyed. Those who survived experienced great hardship.[12]

SOVEREIGNTY

Pressures for change that spread across Europe were accompanied by the formulation of new philosophies. The interaction of the power of ideas and change is demonstrated by Jean Bodin (1530–1596) and his major contribution to the modern idea of sovereignty. Bodin was a French social and political philosopher and lawyer. During the last half of the sixteenth century, France was experiencing severe disorder, caused primarily by conflicts between Roman Catholics and the Huguenots (i.e., French Protestants who were followers of John Calvin). Bodin believed that order could be restored through a combination of greater religious tolerance and the establishment of a fully sovereign monarch. In his *Six Books on the Commonwealth* (or state), Bodin stressed that the state, represented by the king, was sovereign.

Universal Catholic laws that governed Europe were replaced by international law. Leaders and scholars realized that states also needed a system of rules and norms to govern their interaction and to establish order and predictability. This view was articulated by Hugo Grotius (1583–1645). Grotius was a Dutch lawyer, author, and strong advocate of natural law, and is regarded as the father of international law. Grotius stressed that sovereign states were governed by natural law because they were composed of human beings who were ruled by nature and because it was in the interest of sovereign states to support an international legal system. A second component of the new international system was diplomacy. Diplomats, their possessions, and their embassies were regarded as extensions of sovereign states and accorded extraordinary legal protections. A third component of the system for maintaining international order was the balance of power, which attempted to prevent a state or group of states from becoming strong enough to dominate Europe. Finally, the new international system would rely on common cultural values and family connections to avoid disorder.[13]

There has always been a gap between the ideal of sovereignty and the actual realization of sovereignty. There are four types of sovereignty:

1. *International legal sovereignty*, which focuses on the recognition of a state's independence by other states and respect for its territorial boundaries.
2. *Westphalian sovereignty*, which focuses on the exclusion of other states from the affairs of the government that exists within a given territory.
3. *Internal or domestic sovereignty*, which refers to the rights of the government or formal organization of political authority within a state to exercise a monopoly of power over social, economic, political, and other activities within its borders.

Jean Bodin
■ (1530–1596); French social and political philosopher and lawyer

Huguenots
■ French Protestants who were followers of John Calvin

international law
■ An international system of rules created to govern the interaction of states and to establish order

Hugo Grotius ■ (1583–1645); Dutch lawyer, author, strong advocate of natural law, and the father of international law

4. *Interdependence sovereignty*, which reflects the realities of globalization. It is concerned with the ability of governments to control or regulate the flow of people, money, trade, environmental hazards, information, and ideas across national boundaries.[14]

The Decline of Sovereignty

Information and technological revolutions and the ease of international travel are contributing to the erosion of a state's control over its population as well as to the decline of citizens' identification with the state, two of the key components of sovereignty. Social networks enable individuals to interact globally. The Internet has eroded secrecy of all kinds, including government secrecy. Although most governments continue to exert significant influence over their domestic economies, many governments are perceived as "mere salesmen, promoting the fortunes of their own multinational corporations in the hope that this will provide a core prosperity that keeps everyone afloat."[15]

THE EUROPEAN UNION: REDEFINING SOVEREIGNTY

European states are voluntarily relinquishing some of their sovereignty to achieve political and economic objectives. European leaders redrew the map of Europe by extending the fifteen-member European Union (EU) eastward to include twelve additional countries, most of them former Communist bloc countries. This unprecedented European expansion created a new Europe that has a population of 491 million and the world's largest economy. The Euro is the common currency of most countries in the EU. The general view is that European countries are modifying their sovereignty on a scale not seen since the Emperor Charlemagne tried to unify Europe twelve hundred years ago.[16] Many Europeans began to believe that excessive sovereignty and nationalism were leading causes of wars that engulfed the Continent and destroyed the most basic aspects of security and independence. This was especially the case in World War II. Statesmen such as Jean Monnet and Robert Schuman of France and Paul Henri Spaak of Belgium were visionaries who believed that a united Europe, in which traditional sovereignty would be redefined, was essential to preserving peace and security and preventing another European holocaust. The basic idea was that controlling coal and steel (materials essential for war) would ultimately result in the reconciliation of Europe. France and Germany, the two principal antagonists, would combine their coal and steel production. In 1957, France, Germany, Italy, Belgium, the Netherlands, and Luxembourg signed a treaty that led to the creation of the Coal and Steel Community, the first major European institution. The Europeans signed the Treaty of Rome in 1957, which established both the European Economic Community and the European Atomic Energy Community (EURATOM). Since then, in many areas of political and economic life, power has been gradually transferred from the state level to the European Union and its various institutions.[17] For example, the European Court of Justice has powers that are similar to those of the U.S. Supreme Court.

euro ■ Common European currency established by the European Union

Jean Monnet ■ French statesman and distinguished economist

Robert Schuman ■ French prime minister after World War II who proposed the Schuman plan for pooling the coal and steel resources of Western Europe

Paul Henri Spaak ■ Foreign minister of Belgium who was elected first president of the General Assembly of the United Nations

Treaty of Rome ■ Established the European Economic Community as an economic alliance

European Court of Justice ■ A judicial arm of the European Union, based in Luxembourg

THE RISE OF NONSTATE ACTORS

Nonstate actors, or nongovernmental organizations (NGOs), are not formally associated with states or the authority structures of states, although they often cooperate with the government to achieve their goals. Transnational NGOs operate across national boundaries and have achieved significant influence in world affairs. Their wide range of activities have led many observers to conclude that their emergence is almost as important as the rise of the nation-state.

There are several types of NGOs. These include

Economic organizations, such as transnational corporations;
Advocacy organizations/, such as Greenpeace and Amnesty International;
Service organizations, such as the International Red Cross and Doctors
    Without Borders;
Transnational terrorist organizations that seek to undermine governments;
    and
Transnational criminal organizations that focus on profiting from illegal
    activities.

With the exception of terrorist and criminal NGOs, nonstate actors have played *four main roles* that are generally accepted by states and international governmental institutions:

1. *Setting Agendas:* NGOs often force national policymakers to include certain issues on their agendas.
2. *Negotiating Outcomes:* NGOs work with governments and business groups to solve global problems.
3. *Conferring Legitimacy:* Organizations, such as the World Bank, and transnational corporations derive legitimacy from the support or approval of various NGOs.
4. *Making Solutions Work:* Many governments and intergovernmental organizations rely on NGOs to implement their decisions in areas such as humanitarian relief and economic development.[18] Two of the oldest and most significant nonstate actors are the Catholic Church and transnational corporations.

The Catholic Church

On the streets outside the Palazzo Montecitorio, where the lower house of Italy's Parliament meets, crowds gathered to participate in a historic event on November 14, 2002. Pope John Paul II was scheduled to address eight hundred lawmakers and national leaders, including Prime Minister Silvio Berlusconi. Given the fact that Italy is predominantly Catholic, you are probably wondering why such an address would be significant. The pope's speech marked the first time a head of the Catholic Church had ever made an appearance in the Italian Parliament.[19] Much of Italy, unlike the rest of Europe, continued to be ruled by popes until the middle of the nineteenth century. In 1871, Italy was largely free of control by the papal authorities, and popes were deprived of almost all their land. A compromise between the Vatican and the Italian government was reached in 1929, when the

Lateran Treaty, negotiated with Benito Mussolini, the Italian dictator and leader of the Fascist movement, was signed. The Italian government recognized Vatican City as fully sovereign and independent, and the Vatican recognized the Italian government.

The Vatican has voiced strong opinions on social, economic, political, and military issues, especially under the leadership of Pope John Paul II. For many years the Catholic Church strongly opposed Communism and reached out to Catholics in Poland and other Communist bloc countries in an effort to undermine Communist rule. Pope John Paul II, a native of Poland, played a major role in the fall of Communism in Eastern Europe. But the pope also criticized the West for its extreme materialism and individualism, as well as for its tolerance of poverty and inequality in the developing countries. The Catholic Church condemned the proliferation of nuclear weapons in the United States, Russia, and other countries and opposed America's military action against Iraq. But as the case study shows, the Catholic Church is facing its own challenges.

Transnational Corporations

A multinational corporation (MNC) is generally defined as a national company that has many foreign subsidiaries. These subsidiaries are basically self-contained, making what they sell in a particular country, buying their supplies from that country, and employing that country's citizens. Transnational corporations are structurally different from MNCs. A transnational corporation is organized as a global entity. Although selling, servicing, public relations, and legal matters are local, planning, research, finance, pricing, marketing, and management are conducted with the world market in mind.[20] Companies were instrumental in the conquest and settlement of North America, India, Southern Africa, and elsewhere. The British East India Company was, in effect, the government of British-controlled areas of India for a long time. The Dutch West India Company was granted a charter that allowed it to make agreements and alliances with leaders of conquered areas, to construct fortifications, to appoint and discharge governors, to raise armies, to provide administrative services, and to maintain order.[21]

INTERDEPENDENCE AND GLOBALIZATION

Interdependence in world affairs, as it is in private life, involves mutual dependence and cooperation. This means that what happens in one place usually has consequences elsewhere. A war in Iraq, for example, drives up the price of gas at your neighborhood gas station. Countries rely on each other for raw materials, security, trade, and environmental protection. Their fates are intertwined, and they share a sense of mutual vulnerability, although some states are clearly more vulnerable than others in some areas. At the heart of the concept of interdependence is reciprocity.[22]

Globalization refers to shrinking distances among the continents, a wider geographic sense of vulnerability, and a worldwide interconnectedness of important aspects of human life, including religion, migration, war, finance, trade, diseases,

Lateran Treaty ■ A compromise between the Vatican and the Italian government

Benito Mussolini ■ Italian Fascist dictator and prime minister from 1922 to 1943

British East India Company ■ Established under a royal charter of Queen Elizabeth I for the purposes of spice trading; it launched British rule of India.

Dutch West India Company ■ Trading and colonizing company, chartered by the States-General of the Dutch Republic in 1621 and organized in 1623

interdependence ■ A political and economic situation in which two states are simultaneously dependent on each other for their well-being

globalization ■ The integration of markets, politics, values, and environmental concerns across borders

drugs, and music. Globalization implies a significant and obvious blurring of distinctions between the internal and external affairs of countries and the weakening of differences among countries. Although globalization is generally regarded as the Americanization of the world, America itself was, and continues to be, profoundly shaped by the forces of globalization.[23]

CAUSES OF GLOBALIZATION

The causes of globalization are inseparable from the human desire to explore, to gain greater physical and economic security, to be creative and curious, and to move from one place to another. The movement of large numbers of people from one part of the world to another over a relatively short time was facilitated by improvements in transportation. Canal building, the development of navigational equipment (such as the compass), the ability to construct stable oceangoing vessels, and the development and improvement of railways helped to speed up migration. Improved transportation also made it easier to conduct trade over long distances and to colonize new areas.

Cold War ■ The hostile relations between the two superpowers, the United States and the Soviet Union, from 1945 to 1990

Advances in military and medical technologies have also driven globalization. The ability to mount a cannon on a ship gave a country a decisive advantage over its opponents and also allowed the countries possessing them to expand commerce and to acquire territories. Perhaps nothing reminds us more about our interdependence than nuclear weapons and other weapons of mass destruction. Our security is still greatly determined by the ability of nuclear powers to preserve the strategic balance and to prevent the use of nuclear weapons. Our sensitivity to how military weapons link our fates was heightened during the Cold War (i.e., the competition between the United States and the Soviet Union that occurred after World War II).

Demographic changes marked political transformation when President Hosni Mubarak was brought down in Egypt. Graffiti on a Tahir Square barricade shows the impact of young people using social networks on transitions to democracy.

We have entered into an age of uncertainty heralded in by the use of both conventional and unconventional weapons by terrorist organizations.

As Table 1.1 indicates, commerce and finance provided the foundation for many of these advances. A major cause of globalization is financial market expansion. The availability of finance encouraged more economic interactions, innovation, entrepreneurship, and the development of new technologies. As Chapter 7 demonstrates, the global financial crisis affects nearly all aspects of globalization. New technologies made it easier to conduct trade, migrate, conquer territories, and resist diseases. These new technologies have now spread around the world, speeding up innovation and strengthening competition.

Global communications have been facilitated by the spread of the English language around the world during an earlier period of globalization. America's dominant technological, economic, military, and cultural position in the world helps to reinforce the centrality of English in all aspects of global life. Roughly half of the world's population has access to some combination of cell phones and the Internet, enabling people to communicate within and across national borders.[24] The communications revolution is regarded as the major cause of globalization because it directly affects economic, financial, military, cultural, environmental, and criminal globalization.

financial market expansion ■ The global expansion of national markets

TABLE 1.1

Periods of Monetary Expansion and Globalization

Period	New Technologies and Commercial Applications
1807–1844	Extensive canal building, railway boom, steam power used in manufacturing, improved machine tool design, invention of McCormick's reaper, commercial gas-lighting, and development of the telegraph
1851–1873	Advances in mining, railways and shipping, and rapid growth of corporations
1881–1914	Increased productivity in Europe and the United States, improvements in steel production and heavy chemical manufacturing, first power station, spread of electricity, development of the internal combustion engine, and developments in canning and refrigeration
1922–1930	Commercialization of automobiles and aircraft, spread of artificial fibers and plastics, new electrical appliances invented, and telephone ownership grows
1960–1973	Development and application of transistor technology, advances in commercial flying and shipping, and the spread of telecommunications and software
1985–Present	Rapid growth in computer memory and information processing, advances in biotechnology and medical technologies, and commercial use of the Internet

Source: Michael Pettis, "Will Globalization Go Bankrupt?" *Foreign Policy*, No. 126 (September/October 2001), 56–57.

FORMS OF GLOBALIZATION

Among the most important forms of globalization are (1) economic and trade globalization, (2) financial globalization, (3) political globalization, (4) military globalization, (5) cultural globalization, (6) environmental globalization, and (7) criminal globalization. Although we will discuss each of these forms separately, they cannot be neatly separated from each other in the real world.

Economic Globalization

economic globalization ■ Free trade, open markets, and competition in the world economy

Economic globalization may be defined as the intercontinental exchange of products, services, and labor. This form of globalization has a long history and has intensified with the emergence of new technologies and their diffusion to major parts of the world. MNCs have been instrumental in globalization of both production and distribution networks. Consumers worldwide use similar products made by the same corporations. Economies around the world develop greater capability to produce and export goods as they obtain capital, technology, and access to distribution networks. As trade increases, competition intensifies, leading to lower prices and the elimination of companies that cannot effectively compete in the global market.[25]

Economic globalization also includes the movement of people and the exchange of ideas. The most innovative companies encourage the formation of global teams that operate across national borders. Multinationals usually have training camps that help to create a common corporate culture. Engineers from India, Japan, Germany, Australia, and elsewhere who work for Hewlett-Packard, for example, work with their American counterparts in Los Gatos, California. Economic globalization has also stimulated the development of global cities, such as New York, London, Tokyo, Shanghai, Hong Kong, Milan, Sidney, Zurich, and Chicago. Companies put their headquarters in major cities to take advantage of the services of lawyers, accountants, consultants, and advertising firms. The implications of economic globalizations were obvious following the 2011 earthquake and tsunami that destroyed business and ports in Japan and damaged a nuclear power plant, releasing significant amounts of radiation. Many products could not be shipped to or from Japan.[26]

Financial Globalization

Terrorist attacks on the World Trade Center and the Pentagon on September 11, 2001, sent shock waves through financial markets worldwide, painfully demonstrating direct linkages among American, European, Asian, and Latin American economies. The financial world reacted in a synchronized manner, with each market that opened the day following the attacks falling precipitously in the first few minutes. A flood of sell orders inundated the Tokyo Stock Exchange, delaying the opening and pushing the benchmark Nikkei index down 6 percent. All of the major stock markets declined dramatically in the week after the terrorist attacks, as Figure 1.1 shows.

Financial problems spread across the world almost instantaneously, reflecting how revolutions in telecommunications and computers have linked financial institutions. The financial crisis of 2008 and 2009 reflected this reality. Similarly, the earthquake and tsunami that caused widespread destruction in Japan in 2011 caused the Nikkei (the Japanese stock market) to fall by 12 percent. The G-7

STOCK INDEXES	PERCENTAGE CHANGE
Britain	- 2.7%
S. and P. 500	**- 4.9**
Canada	- 5.9
Argentina	- 6.8
Nasdaq	**- 6.8**
Dow Jones ind. avg.	**- 7.1**
Spain	- 7.6
Japan	- 7.7
France	- 8.5
New Zealand	- 8.8
Australia	- 9.0
Germany	- 9.3
Hong Kong	-10.5
Brazil	-11.6
Italy	-11.9
South Korea	-13.3
Mexico	-14.7
Singapore	-14.8
Thailand	-18.1

FIGURE 1.1

Financial Market Response to Terrorists'
Attack on September 11, 2001

Source: The *New York Times,* 18 September 2001, C3

(the seven leading industrialized countries) intervened to prevent the yen, the Japanese currency, from rising too much against other currencies.[27]

Four basic developments drive financial globalization, leading to the expansion and deepening of global finance. The first is the *consolidation of financial institutions* in most countries. Local banks were, until about two decades ago, largely locally owned and operated. The second development is the *globalization of operations*, which is evident everywhere as banking conglomerates extend their reach by forming strategic alliances with similar institutions in different countries. The third development is the emergence of *new technologies* that are familiar to all of us. Money moves across national boundaries at the touch of a button. The fourth development is the *universalization of banking*. Growing competition in financial markets, the increasing irrelevance of national borders, and the increasingly complex relationships among businesses have contributed to a blurring of bank and nonbank financial services.[28]

Other forms of globalization have strengthened financial globalization. When the British Empire stretched across much of the world, the British pound became the strongest and most desirable currency. As British power receded, America rose to international prominence and the U.S. dollar became the leading global currency. In 1944, the United States, Britain, and other countries held a conference at Bretton Woods, New Hampshire, to determine the international financial order. The conference established the Bretton Woods System, which required the currencies of other countries to have an exchange rate fixed to the dollar, with the dollar fixed in terms of gold at $35 an ounce. This arrangement gave the United States significant influence over the international money supply.

The Bretton Woods System set up the World Bank (also known as the International Bank for Reconstruction and Development) to help stimulate Europe's economic recovery after the devastation of World War II. It also created the International Monetary Fund (IMF) to implement the rules of the international financial system and to help countries experiencing short-term balance-of-payment and liquidity problems. IMF loans, which now go primarily to developing countries, are given with certain conditions attached (e.g., reducing government spending, eliminating trade barriers, cutting social subsidies, devaluing currencies, and removing artificial barriers to foreign investment). As Europe recovered, and as the Soviet Union and other countries deposited their dollar holdings in Western European banks, European banks receiving deposits in dollars simply kept them instead of changing them into the national currencies. The practice resulted in the growth of Eurodollar funds. Large U.S. budget deficits—caused partly by the Vietnam War, domestic inflation, and the practice of many American companies of depositing their foreign currency earnings in European banks—weakened the U.S. dollar and strengthened the Eurodollar. These developments eventually contributed to the collapse of the Bretton Woods System. On August 15, 1971, President Richard M. Nixon decided that the dollar no longer was to be freely convertible into gold, thereby ending fixed exchange rates. Furthermore, large financial surpluses accumulated by oil-exporting countries as a result of the quadrupling of oil prices by the Organization of Petroleum Exporting Countries (OPEC) in 1973 increased the liquidity of international banks. These financial institutions had approximately $50 billion to recycle through the world economy. Given the failure of global institutions to effectively deal with contemporary challenges such as financial instability, fluctuating commodity prices, and the diffusion of global economic and political power, currency reforms are viewed as essential.[29] In 2011, European countries using the euro grappled with their responsibility to shore up or bail out failing banks and nations in the "euro zone." The world watched as euro zone countries dealt with questions of integration of European Union countries, ultimate survival of the euro, and potential repercussions to the global economy.

Political Globalization

Political globalization is characterized by the acceptance of states, the relative power of states, the proliferation of international and regional organizations composed of states, and the spread of nonstate political actors. The competition that dominated relations between the United States and the Soviet Union during the Cold War is an example of political globalization. Most of the emphasis on political globalization is concentrated on the spread of multilateral institutions. These are organizations composed of many states pursuing common objectives and include international intergovernmental organizations (IGOs), such as the United Nations, the European Union, the Organization of American States, and the British Commonwealth.

Many policies that were once considered to be primarily of local or national concern are now global, which suggests the strengthening of policy interdependence. In other words, national policies of one country are intertwined with those of other countries, and many national problems can be solved only through global cooperation. States form international regimes to cope with problems generated by complex interdependence. Regimes are essentially institutions designed to regulate the behavior of their members. The basic goal is to establish orderly and predictable interactions to secure the interests of those participating in these international institutions. At the heart of most international regimes is the concept of global governance, which refers to collective actions taken to establish international institutions and norms to deal with national and global issues.[30]

Military Globalization

Military globalization is characterized by extensive as well as intensive networks of military force. This includes both the actual use of force and threats to use violence. The most obvious example of military globalization is the nuclear age and the proliferation of weapons of mass destruction. The balance of terror created by nuclear weapons threatens the future not only of the countries that have them but also of all human existence on the earth. *Military globalization is demonstrated by several developments in modern history.* These include

1. The *competition among European powers and territorial expansion* that resulted in the colonization of Asia, Africa, and the Americas;
2. The emergence *of international alliances and international security regimes*, such as the Concert of Europe and the North Atlantic Treaty Organization (NATO);
3. The *proliferation of weapons and military technologies worldwide*; and
4. The creation of global institutions to deal with military issues, such as the nuclear nonproliferation regime.[31]

Cultural Globalization

As we will discuss in Chapter 2, cultural influences usually accompany the expansion of economic and military power. In other words, cultural globalization—which involves the exchange of food, music, people, products, ideas, and technology across national boundaries—has very deep roots. Few people in Europe stop to think that potatoes came from South America, and few Americans realize that their cattle came from Europe and their corn came from Mexico. The spread of ideas, technology, and products from China and other parts of Asia through the Middle East to Western Europe profoundly influenced the development of Western civilization. Imagine America without Christianity. Christianity, like Islam, originated in the Middle East and later spread across the world. Although cultural globalization is often equated with Americanization, it is a very complex development.[32] Sports, which have generally been associated with nationalism, are one of the most obvious and emotional aspects of cultural globalization. World Cup soccer (football), watched by billions of people around the world, demonstrates the global passion for sport.

multilateral institutions ■ Organizations composed of many states pursuing common objectives

policy interdependence ■ National policies of one country are intertwined with those of other countries

international regimes ■ International institutions designed to regulate the behavior of their members

global governance ■ Collective actions taken to establish international institutions and norms to deal with national and global issues

military globalization ■ Networks of military force that operate internationally

cultural globalization ■ The spread of one culture across national borders

Environmental Globalization

Visitors to Boston generally observe that extremely valuable land in the center of the city has been preserved as a public park. The Boston Common was originally used by the city's residents as a place where their cattle could graze. When discussing the environment, it is useful to think of our planet as a common. We are all affected by what happens to it, and the problems can be solved only through the cooperation of the global community. Environmental globalization focuses on the interdependence among countries in relation to problems such as global warming, the spread of infectious diseases, air and water pollution, deforestation, the loss of biodiversity, and threats to endangered species.

environmental globalization ■ The interdependence of countries to work together to solve environmental problems

Criminal Globalization

Terrorist attacks in the United States on September 11, 2001, represented an extreme form of criminal globalization and diminished the attention given to less dramatic but almost equally dangerous transnational criminal activities. The terrorists used the instruments of globalization to achieve their objectives. Criminal globalization is the intercontinental spread of global crime and its impact on governments and individuals. As Chapter 12 shows, criminal globalization includes transborder crimes, such as drug trafficking, money laundering, prostitution, alien smuggling, arms trafficking, piracy, and counterfeiting. National boundaries have never been effective barriers to the conduct of transnational crimes. As globalization has expanded, criminal organizations have deepened and widened their activities. Furthermore, globalization has imposed on governments certain burdens, such as smaller public budgets, decentralization, privatization, deregulation, and an open environment that is more conducive to criminal globalization.[33]

PERIODS OF GLOBALIZATION

Because globalization is a process that advances and retreats, and that is more intense at some points than at others, it is artificial to divide it into distinct periods. However, for discussion, we can identify *five waves of globalization* in the constant sea of change that defines human experience.

The *first wave of globalization* is as old as human civilization. For more than five thousand years, human beings from different places have interacted, mostly through trade, migration, and conquest. Globalization was occurring long before the language of globalization came into existence.[34]

The *second wave of globalization* is closely associated with the Western European conquest of Asia, Latin America, and Africa and the spread of capitalism to these areas. This wave of globalization continues to influence developments within and among societies today. Dependency theorists view this period of globalization as being profoundly influential on global politics and trade.

dependency ■ Belief that industrialized countries benefit from the present capitalist economic system at the expense of poor countries

The *third wave of globalization*, which began around 1870 and declined around 1914, was marked by breakthroughs in technological development, the global production of primary commodities as well as manufactured products, and mass migration. Less-expensive transportation costs, the switch from sails to steam power, the development of railways, the availability of capital, and the re-duction of trade barriers combined to fuel global economic growth. Vast areas of land in North America, Argentina, Australia, and elsewhere were cultivated, and agricultural products were exported. The production of primary products led to the demand for labor. In addition to the Africans and others who were already providing labor, about 60 million Europeans migrated to North America and Australia to work on farms. Argentina, Australia, New Zealand, and the United States became some of the richest countries in the world by exporting primary commodities and importing people, institutions, capital, and manufactured products.[35] This explosion of global activities was followed by a retreat into nationalism from 1914 to 1945. World War I was followed by the Great Depression and a wave of protectionism, led by the United States. America attempted to protect its economy by enacting the Smoot-Hawley Tariff Act in 1930, a move that led to retaliation abroad. Between 1929 and 1933, U.S. imports fell by 30 percent and exports fell by almost 40 percent.[36]

Smoot-Hawley Tariff Act ■ Act that brought the U.S. tariff to the highest protective level in the history of the United States

The *fourth wave of globalization*, from 1945 to 1980, was spurred by the re-treat of nationalism and protectionism and the strengthening of internationalism and global cooperation, led by the United States. The removal of trade barriers was selective, but institutions—such as the World Bank, the IMF, and the General Agreement on Tariffs and Trade (GATT)—were formed to encourage global trade and development. Many developing countries, relying on the exports of primary commodities, continued to be marginalized and disadvantaged in the global economy. This period of globalization was characterized by both cooperation and conflict. Efforts to encourage nations to work together in the United Nations were weakened by the rivalry between the United States and the Soviet Union. Although the economic aspects of globalization are usually emphasized, the most important form of globalization during this period was military globalization, dominated by the constant threat of a nuclear war between the superpowers.

The *fifth wave of globalization*, which is the current period, is characterized by unprecedented interdependence among nations and the explosive growth of powerful nonstate actors.

RESISTANCE TO GLOBALIZATION

Overall, many countries, groups, and individuals who resist globalization do so because they equate it with Westernization in general and Americanization in particular. Many see such problems as global inequality and conflict as direct results of globalization. However, much resistance to globalization comes from France and the United States, two countries that play a pivotal role in the process of globalization.

France's opposition to globalization is strongly linked to its desire to retain control over its borders and to preserve its culture. Although France has been instrumental in creating European organizations that clearly diminish national sovereignty, it also sees a weakening of sovereignty as a factor that facilitates the invasion of France by immigrants, most of whom are Muslims from North Africa. France also resists globalization because it perceives it as an Anglo-Saxon threat to the French cultural model, which is portrayed as a "high-brow" culture of philosophers, fine dining, and intellectual films. Globalization is equated with the "low-brow" uniformity of American culture—fast food, bad clothing, and, even worse, sitcoms.[37] Globalization is also seen as promoting American individualism. France, on the other hand, values a strong centralized government that can provide essential benefits for the people as a whole. Consider America's resistance to globalization. On several fronts, Americans are increasingly embracing a view of sovereignty that rejects participation in a number of international regimes. Many American intellectuals and policymakers defend American institutions from the encroachment of international institutions.[38] At a more general level, many regard globalization as a threat to their jobs, wages, and culture.

DEBATING GLOBALIZATION

There is disagreement about the extent to which globalization exists. The *three dominant positions* in this debate are assumed by (1) the hyperglobalizers and transformationalists, (2) the weak globalizers, and (3) the skeptics and rejectionists. The *hyperglobalizers and transformationalists* see profound changes in the international

The Catholic Church is a nonstate actor with significant influence in world affairs. Saudi Arabia's King Abdullah Bin Abdulaziz Al Saud met with Pope Benedict XVI at the Vatican to discuss religious freedom in Saudi Arabia, an issue in the relationship between the Catholic Church and the Arab kingdom.

CASE STUDY | Challenges Facing the Catholic Church

The Catholic Church, the oldest and most widely known and powerful global nonstate actor, predated the rise of the modern state in Western Europe and continues to exert tremendous influence in global affairs and in the lives of more than a billion people worldwide. While the Catholic Church remains largely conservative and is the epitome of traditionalism and hierarchy, globalization is undermining traditional and hierarchical institutions everywhere and transferring power from centralized authority to individuals and groups. Cultural globalization, especially America's culture of secularism, is changing values globally and challenging old ideas and behavior. Patriarchal institutions including the Catholic Church confront global demands for gender equality and the growing number of women in leadership positions in virtually all areas of society. The global information age empowers individuals with communications technologies that weaken secrecy and strengthen demands for transparency and the free flow of ideas and information globally. Furthermore, generational change and globalization have combined to transform how people think about a wide range of issues over which the Catholic Church exerted almost unquestioned authority. Since the 1960s, there has been profound social change, with individuals embracing autonomy and freedom of choice. Finally, the Catholic Church has weakened itself by its own behavior, especially pervasive sexual abuse of children and blatant attempts to cover it up and protect abusers from prosecution, while condemning as immoral behavior which many Catholics regard as normal.

The Catholic Church has also been weakened by its traditional opposition to artificial contraceptives, despite use by most Catholics. Opposition to using condoms during an AIDS pandemic has created moral dilemmas for the Catholic Church. Faced with unrelenting criticism, Pope Benedict XVI said that condoms could be used by male prostitutes to prevent the spread of AIDS. As we will discuss in Chapter 13, the global community strongly encourages the use of condoms to prevent AIDS and other infectious diseases.

Compared with its decline in Western Europe, the Catholic Church is expanding in the developing world due to population growth. But, Catholicism is also being challenged by Pentecostalism and evangelical Christianity, which are more egalitarian, less hierarchical, and less doctrinal. As Scott M. Thomas observes, globalization is making religion more pluralistic. Religion is increasingly becoming a matter of choices and is no longer imposed or taken for granted by prevailing cultures.[40] Evangelical Protestantism has eroded Catholicism in predominantly Catholic areas such as Latin America, especially in Central America. Less than half the Christians in El Salvador, Nicaragua, and Belize are Catholic. Sexual abuse scandals and economic growth have weakened the Catholic Church in Ireland, where more individuals are embracing traditional Celtic priestless religions.[41] Fewer young people are joining the Catholic priesthood, and successful lawsuits have forced many Catholic churches into bankruptcy in the United States.

How can the Catholic Church respond to these fundamental challenges? One solution is to promote transparency and to assist in the prosecution of priests, bishops, and others who sexually abuse the most vulnerable members of society: children. Another approach could be to transform its message to deal with the realities of a globalized world without sacrificing its core beliefs. But the Church must also change itself and become less rigid. As societies become better educated and more scientific, both women and men reject traditional and subordinate roles assigned to women. The Catholic Church will have to give women equal opportunities. We saw that the growth of states in Western Europe challenged the Church. The modern forces of globalization are also transformative. Traditional institutions will have to face contemporary realities.

system, such as the erosion of sovereignty and the weakening of nation-states, a borderless economy that integrates people everywhere in the global marketplace, and the emergence of new forms of social and economic organizations that challenge traditional states. The *weak globalizers* argue that this increased internationalization is not altering the world to the extent claimed by the hyperglobalizers and transformationalists. States remain sovereign, and people around the world, while living in the "global village," continue to jealously guard their own huts. Finally, the *skeptics and rejectionists* basically argue that globalization is largely a myth that disguises the reality of the existence of powerful sovereign states and major economic divisions in the world. National governments remain in control of their domestic economies as well as the regulation of international economic activities. National governments determine the nature of global interactions. Inequality continues to fuel nationalism, and, instead of cultural homogenization, the world is dividing into cultures that remain suspicious of each other.[39]

At another level is the debate about the nature and impact of globalization and whether it is temporary or reversible. Some groups see globalization as homogenization, whereas others view it as promoting diversity and greater tolerance of differences. Many nonstate actors view globalization as conducive to their efforts to improve social conditions, protect the environment, and promote democracy. By removing restraints on people's movement, globalization is perceived as instrumental in giving to the individual the power to choose. People are free to shape their identities, pursue an education anywhere in the world, and upgrade their standard of living. On the other side, critics of globalization focus on how cultural homogenization imposes Western values on others and destroys their traditions, religious beliefs, identities, and sense of community and belonging. Many believe that globalization is a threat to national sovereignty and autonomy. Environmentalists, for example, believe that globalization contributes to environmental degradation, and labor unions contend that globalization lowers wages and creates greater inequality.

SUMMARY AND REVIEW

This chapter discussed the foundations of international relations and provided a general view of how interdependence and the forces of globalization are creating serious challenges to governments as the almost exclusive major actors in world politics. It examined how technological, economic, social, political, and philosophical developments in Europe contributed to the rise of the modern state, the concept of sovereignty, the system of relations among states, and the decline of the Catholic Church as the dominant political and cultural institution in Europe. It illustrated how political, economic, and cultural forces contributed to the rise of the modern nation-state and how they continue to be integral components of contemporary globalization. We looked at interdependence and globalization. Just as interdependence plays a role in our private lives (e.g., most of us do not grow the food we eat), it also plays a role in world affairs. Globalization creates more obvious and extensive webs of interdependence. The causes of globalization can range from social issues (e.g., migration) to technological advances (e.g., in fields such as communication and transportation) to economic issues (e.g., market expansion). The major forms of globalization are (1) economic and trade, (2) financial, (3) political, (4) military, (5) cultural, (6) environmental, and (7) criminal. Finally, we discussed the five historical waves of globalization and the current debate that exists between groups that have resisted it and those that have been more accepting of it.

KEY TERMS

international relations   2
Peace of Westphalia   2
state   2
sovereign   2
ideology   3
nation   3
state-centric model   3
theory   3
nonstate actors   3
human security   4
global politics   4
global norms   4
global issues   4
humanism   4
Renaissance   5
Johann Gutenberg   5
Martin Luther   5
Jean Bodin   6
Huguenots   6
international law   6
Hugo Grotius   6
euro   7
Jean Monnet   7
Robert Schuman   7
Paul Henri Spaak   7
Treaty of Rome   7
European Court of Justice   7

nongovernmental organizations
   (NGOs)   8
Lateran Treaty   9
Benito Mussolini   9
British East India Company   9
Dutch West India Company   9
interdependence   9
globalization   9
Cold War   10
financial market expansion   11
economic globalization   12
Bretton Woods System   14
World Bank   14
International Monetary Fund (IMF)   14
Eurodollar   14
Organization of Petroleum Exporting
   Countries (OPEC)   14
political globalization   14
multilateral institutions   15
policy interdependence   15
international regimes   15
global governance   15
military globalization   15
cultural globalization   15
environmental globalization   16
dependency   16
Smoot-Hawley Tariff Act   17

DISCUSSION QUESTIONS

1. What roles do nonstate actors play in international relations?
2. This chapter discusses the five waves of globalization and provides examples of globalization for each time period. What are some additional examples of globalization within some of these periods?
3. "Interdependence is the foundation of society." What does this mean? How does it relate to the concept of globalization?
4. Discuss how advances in technology have contributed to globalization. What are some of the new problems we face because of these advances?
5. What are some of the arguments made against globalization? Do you agree or disagree with any of these arguments? Explain.

SUGGESTED READINGS

Bremmer, Ian. *The End of the Free Market.* New York: Portfolio, 2010. The financial crisis has undermined America's promotion of free market capitalism.

Hufbauer, Gary Clyde, and Kati Suominen. *Globalization at Risk.* New Haven, CT: Yale University Press, 2010. Discusses trade, migration, finance, and other aspects of globalization. Argues that globalization has improved lives around the world.

Muldoon, James P., et al., eds. *The New Dynamics of Multilateralism.* Boulder, CO: Westview Press, 2010. Emphasizes the ongoing shift away from the state-centric model and focuses on multilateral forums and nonstate actors.

Toft, Monica Duffy, et al. *God's Century.* New York: Norton, 2011. Religion is growing in significance in global politics due to greater independence of religious groups from governments and revolutions in communications.

ENDNOTES

1. Richard J. Payne and Jamal R. Nassar, *Politics and Culture in the Developing World* (New York: Longman, 2011), 8–9.
2. K. J. Holsti, *International Politics: A Framework for Analysis* (Upper Saddle River, NJ: Prentice Hall, 1995), xi.
3. Hans Morgenthau, *Politics Among Nations* (New York: Knoff, 1948), 23.
4. James N. Rosenau and Mary Durfee, *Thinking Theory Thoroughly* (Boulder, CO: Westview Press, 2000), 48.
5. James N. Rosenau, *Along the Domestic-Foreign Frontier: Exploring Governance in a Turbulent World* (Cambridge: Cambridge University Press, 1997), 58–60.
6. Richard Rosencrance, "Trade and Power," in *Conflict After the Cold War*, ed. Richard K. Betts (New York: Longman, 2002), 281.
7. Roger Thurow, "The Fertile Continent," *Foreign Affairs* 89, No. 6 (November/December 2010), 103.
8. Rosenau and Durfee, *Thinking Theory Thoroughly*, 47.
9. Charles W. Kegley and Gregory A. Raymond, *Exorcising the Ghosts of Westphalia* (Upper Saddle River, NJ: Prentice Hall, 2002), 30.
10. James Lee Ray, *Global Politics* (Boston: Houghton Mifflin, 1998), 165.
11. Richard Cavendish, "The Treaty of Westphalia," *History Today* 48 (November 1998), 50–52.
12. Carlton Hayes, *A Political and Social History of Modern Europe* (New York: Macmillan, 1921), 231.
13. Geoffrey Stern, *The Structure of International Society* (London: Printer, 2000), 78.
14. Stephen D. Krasner, *Sovereignty* (Princeton, NJ: Princeton University Press, 1999), 4.
15. William Greider, *One World, Ready or Not: The Manic Logic of Global Capitalism* (New York: Simon and Schuster, 1997), 24.
16. "Germany's Economy," *Economist*, 5 February 2011, 17.
17. Richard Rosencrance, "Bigger Is Better," *Foreign Affairs* 89, No. 3 (May/June 2010), 44.
18. Parag Khanna, *How to Run the World* (New York: Random House, 2011).
19. Frank Bruni, "John Paul Makes First Papal Address to Italy's Parliament," *New York Times*, 15 November 2002, A3.
20. Matthew Bishop, "Multinationibles." *Economist*, 1 January 2011, 25.
21. Marina Ottaway, "Reluctant Missionaries," *Foreign Policy*, No. 125 (July/August 2001), 45.

22. Robert O. Keohane and Joseph S. Nye, *Power and Interdependence* (Boston: Little, Brown and Company, 1977).

23. David Held et al., *Global Transformations* (Stanford, CA: Stanford University Press, 1999), 28; and James H. Mittelman, *The Globalization Syndrome* (Princeton, NJ: Princeton University Press, 2000), 15.

24. Eric Schmidt and Jared Cohen, "The Digital Disruption," *Foreign Affairs* 89, No. 6 (November/December 2010), 75.

25. Nancy Birdsall and Francis Fukuyama, "The Post-Washington Consensus," *Foreign Affairs* 90, No. 2 (March/April 2011), 48.

26. David Jolly, "Long Pause for Japanese Industry Raises Supply Concerns," *Miami Herald*, 18 March 2011, 1B.

27. Turo Fujioka and Mayumi Otsuma, "G-7 Intervenes to Arrest Yen's Appreciation," *Miami Herald*, 19 March 2011, 1B.

28. Thomas Balion and Angel Ubide, "The New World of Banking," *Finance and Development* 37, No. 2 (June 2000), 41.

29. Held et al., *Global Transformations*, 202, and Aaditya Mattoo and Arvind Subramanian, "From Doha to the Next Bretton Woods," *Foreign Affairs* 88, No. 1 (January/February 2009), 17.

30. Mark Malloch Brown, *The Unfinished Global Revolution* (New York: Penguin Press, 2011).

31. Josef Joffe and James W. Davis, " Less Than Zero," *Foreign Affairs* 90, No. 1 (January/February 2011) 8.

32. Robert O. Keohane and Joseph S. Nye, "Globalization," *Foreign Policy*, No. 118 (Spring 2000), 107.

33. Toby Miller et al., *Globalization and Sport* (London: Sage Publications, 2001), 11–12.

34. Moises Naim, "The Five Wars of Globalization," *Foreign Policy*, No. 134 (January–February 2003), 30.

35. Mittelman, *The Globalization Syndrome*, 18.

36. Paul Collier and David Dollar, *Globalization, Growth, and Poverty* (New York: Oxford University Press, 2002), 25.

37. Collier and Dollar, *Globalization, Growth, and Poverty*, 27.

38. Kishore Mahbubani, "The Case Against the West," *Foreign Affairs* 87, No. 3 (May/June 2008), 111.

39. Peter J. Spiro, "The New Sovereigntists," *Foreign Affairs* 79, No. 6 (November/December 2000), 9.

40. Scott M. Thomas, "A Globalized God," *Foreign Affairs* 89, No. 6 (November/December 2010), 98.

41. "The Void Within," *Economist*, 7 August 2010, 20.

The Struggle for Primacy in a Global Society

A country's militar
show of dominanc

INTRODUCTION

One of the most discussed global issues is the rise of China and the decline of the United States. Throughout history great powers—such as Rome, Spain, and Britain—have gone through growth and decline, through competition and internal weakness. Power transition theory, which is an offshoot of cycle theories, stresses that the distribution-of-power changes in countries will rise and fall. Dominant countries are often referred to as great powers, hegemonies, superpowers, or states that enjoy primacy in the international system. Often, these terms are used interchangeably. They generally refer to the ability of a country or a small group of countries to have extraordinary influence over the behavior of the other states.[1]

When there are several hegemons, dominant states, or great powers, the international system is defined as being multipolar. An example is the international system that existed before World War II, when the United States, Britain, France, Germany, Japan, Italy, and the Soviet Union were considered great powers. Following World War II, there were clearly two dominant countries: the United States and the Soviet Union. The new structure was bipolar. The disintegration of the Soviet Union created a unipolar world, dominated by the United States.

A dominant country exercises significant power, has few potential rivals, and leads an international system that benefits other powerful countries. Below the dominant countries are great powers, which help to maintain the international system. Then there are regional powers. But most countries are at the bottom of the pyramid of power.[2] Power is now diffused. It is viewed as resembling a three-dimensional chess game. On the top chessboard, military power is essentially unipolar. Here is where the United States dominates. Power is multipolar in the middle, where leading players are the United States, China, Western Europe, and Japan. Nonstate actors are on the bottom board.[3]

This chapter examines the nature of power, factors that influence the rise and fall of nations, and the strategies countries use to maintain their dominant position. It focuses on the United States and China and concludes with a case study on challenges facing China.

power transition theory ■ Stresses that the distribution-of-power changes in countries will rise and fall

hegemons ■ The leading country in an international system

multipolar ■ The international system that includes several hegemons, dominant states, or great powers

bipolar ■ The international system that includes two hegemons, dominant states, or great powers

unipolar ■ The international system that has only one hegemon, dominant state, or great power

POWER AND LEADERSHIP

Central to the rise and fall of dominant nations is the concept of power. Power is generally understood as the ability to get others—individuals, groups, or nations—to behave in ways that they would ordinarily try to avoid. *Power capabilities* are usually determined by economic strength, military strength, and political effectiveness. *Elements of power* include a country's geographic area and location, its population, and its natural resources. Other elements of power are intelligence capabilities, the quality of national leadership, the level of educational and technological achievement, the openness of the political system, the character of the people, transportation and communication capabilities, ideology, and the appeal of a country's culture (generally referred to as "soft power").[4]

power ■ The ability to get others—individuals, groups, or nations—to behave in ways that they ordinarily would not

GNP ■ Measures the total market value of all goods and services produced by resources supplied by residents and businesses of a particular country, regardless of where the residents and businesses are located

GDP ■ Measures the total market value of all goods and services produced within a country

power conversion ■ The capacity to change potential power, as measured by available resources, into realized power, which is determined by the changed behavior of others

structural leadership ■ The possession of economic resources, military power, technology, and other sources of power that enable a small group of countries to shape the international system

institutional leadership ■ The ability to determine the rules, principles, procedures, and practices that guide the behavior of members of the global community

situational leadership ■ The ability to seize opportunities to build or reorient the global system, apart from the distribution of power and the building of institutions

Economic power is often seen as the foundation of military and political power. It is measured in terms of the gross national product (GNP) or the gross domestic product (GDP). The GNP measures the total market value of all goods and services produced by resources supplied by the residents and businesses of a particular country, regardless of where those residents and businesses are located. The GDP measures the total market value of all goods and services produced within a country. Military power is often the most visible and impressive manifestation of national power.[5] As we will discuss, a major challenge for great powers is to maintain a balance between economic strength and military might. Too much emphasis on the military often weakens the economy, and ultimately the military itself.

A nation's strength goes beyond simply possessing the various resources that are sources of power. Countries, like individuals, must be skilled at converting these resources into effective influence. Power conversion is defined as the capacity to change potential power, as measured by available resources, into realized power, which is determined by the changed behavior of others.[6] Knowing what resources to use, when, and how will also affect the exercise of power. Certain factors—such as globalization, domestic support for policies, and the willingness of citizens to support activities associated with international primacy—must also be considered.

An important component of power is leadership. Leadership is the ability to persuade others to behave in certain ways, to shape their interest, and to influence their thinking. Leadership implies a capability to get others to cooperate to achieve particular objectives.[7] At the foundation of leadership is the ability to get others to follow. Leadership can be structural, institutional, or situational. Structural leadership is derived largely from the control of economic resources, military power, technology, and other sources of power that enable a small group of countries to shape the international system. Structural leadership is often augmented by institutional leadership: that is, the ability to determine the rules, principles, procedures, and practices that guide the behavior of members of the global community. Institutions provide order and predictability and allow the dominant power to exercise control. Finally, situational leadership is primarily the ability to seize opportunities to build or reorient the global system, apart from the distribution of power and the building of institutions. Often, this kind of leadership is associated with a specific individual.[8]

THE RISE AND FALL OF GREAT POWERS

States generally expand because of *threats* and *opportunities* in their international system. States fear power vacuums because rival states are likely to take advantage of them if they fail to act. Weaker states tend to gravitate toward a rising power and to move away from a declining power.[9] Failure to demonstrate strength causes a bandwagoning effect, which benefits the rising power. Population pressures influence the rise of great powers. Population growth puts pressure on available domestic resources. To address this problem, countries will venture across oceans or land boundaries to obtain raw materials, markets for their products, and living space for their people. Uneven economic growth enables some countries to enhance their power while other countries decline.

Urbanization has usually been associated with freedom and innovation. Urban areas attract diverse groups of people with differing ideas. They also improve the wealth-generating, administrative, and political capabilities of a rising power. The efficient functioning of great cities depends on a commitment to tolerance, freedom, and trust. These characteristics, in turn, attract more talent, wealth, innovation, and technology to cities. Trust, for example, is essential for commercial transactions as well as for mundane, routine interactions. Cities such as London and Amsterdam attracted refugees from religious intolerance and persecution. During the seventeenth-century religious wars, Protestants and Jews migrated to Amsterdam and other Dutch cities that were more tolerant of religious diversity.[10]

Geography is another factor that influences the rise and fall of great powers. Britain and the United States have benefited from their geographic location and, in the case of the United States, its continent-size territory. They are not located in the middle of warring states, and they usually refrained from getting involved in other nations' conflicts until it was to their advantage to do so. They could fight in other countries and avoid destroying their own. Their geography also enabled them to concentrate resources on internal consolidation, which ultimately increased their power vis-à-vis other states.

War, which played a crucial role in making states, has been a major factor in the rise and fall of great powers. It usually increased the power of some nations at the detriment of others. Even when countries emerged victorious from war, some were so weakened that the countries that had avoided major damage rose to the top. An example is Britain after World War II: It experienced declining power as America's global dominance grew. Historically, war has been instrumental in strengthening patriotism and nationalism. Historically, Britain went to war against France and Spain to engender cohesion among England, Scotland, Wales, and Ireland.

Many great powers decline because of hubris (i.e., excessive pride) and imperial arrogance. They tend to overestimate their power and expand their military power so much that they ultimately erode their economic base. In other words, believing that their power is virtually limitless, they allow a gap to grow between their global ambitions and the resources they have to fulfill those ambitions. This disparity is referred to as the Lippmann Gap because Walter Lippmann clearly articulated the problem as early as 1943; Paul Kennedy, writing in the late 1980s, referred to this problem as imperial overstretch.[11] Taking resources away from domestic programs for military activities abroad often leads to the unraveling of domestic political cohesion.

population pressures ■ The pressure on resources that leads countries to expand beyond their boundaries

uneven economic growth ■ A factor that enables some countries to enhance their power while that of other countries declines

hubris ■ A term used to stress the dangers of excessive pride and arrogance

Lippmann Gap ■ The disparity between the global ambitions of countries and their resources to fulfill those ambitions

imperial overstretch ■ The disparity between the global ambitions of countries and their resources to fulfill those ambitions

STRATEGIES FOR MAINTAINING POWER

Leading powers, facing challenges from rising countries, adopt several strategies to preserve their position in the international system. *Democratic enlargement* is a prominent strategy in this effort. Potential challengers are restrained when they internalize the values, beliefs, and norms articulated by the dominant power. The

United States, for example, has emphasized spreading democracy. But the dissemination of values and beliefs by great powers does not guarantee indefinite control, a reality that Britain had to face as India and other colonies demanded for themselves the rights enjoyed by people in Britain, including the right to self-government. Great powers also *build institutions to legitimize their control*. They articulate concepts of an international normative order, concepts that involve principles of order and change within the international system as well as normative claims about the role of the leading power within that order.[12]

Another strategy used to prevent rising powers from creating disorder in the international system is *offshore balancing*. Following Napoleon's final defeat in 1815, European powers created the Concert of Europe to maintain stability by preserving a relatively equal distribution of power among them. The main goal was to prevent one country from gaining so much power that it would dominate the others. *Balancing*—which basically means opposing the stronger or more threatening side in a conflict—can be achieved through efforts by individual states to strengthen themselves and by building alliances to preserve the balance of power.[13] Closely related to balancing is the strategy of containment, which attempts to prevent ambitious powers from expanding and destroying order and balance in the international system. When the Soviet Union marched through Eastern Europe and subjugated the countries there, the United States and its European allies responded by implementing a policy of containment.

Binding and engagement are also important state responses to rising powers. The European Union (EU), as we have seen, has its origins in efforts by France and other countries after World War II to avoid the nightmare of another war in Europe by forming economic and political alliances with Germany, which had initiated the conflict. *Binding* aims at controlling the behavior of the rising or threatening country by embedding it into bilateral or multilateral alliances. By making the rising state a member of the alliance, dominant countries allow it to participate in decisions and to contribute to building the institutions that maintain the status quo. *Engagement* attempts to minimize conflict with a rising power and to strengthen those aspects of its behavior that are consistent with the status quo and the interests of the great powers.[14] Eventually the rising power will have too great a stake in preserving the international order to challenge it.

Concert of Europe ■ Created by European powers to prevent one country from gaining so much power that it would dominate the others

containment ■ A strategy that attempts to prevent ambitious powers from expanding and destroying order and balance in the international system

binding ■ Attempts to control rising states by embedding them in alliances

engagement ■ Efforts to minimize conflict with challengers

America

America's decision to launch a preemptive war against Iraq in March 2003 without broad international support and with significant domestic opposition to war demonstrated its power to ignore world opinion. Its awesome military power was evident in its "shock and awe" campaign against Iraq. However, although there was strong disagreement about America's decision to engage in a preemptive war, there was global consensus about America's military predominance. The wars in Iraq and Afghanistan weakened American power. Nevertheless, the strength of the U.S. military is unprecedented in the history of great powers. America spends roughly $700 billion on its military. That is more than the rest of the world combined. It spends three times as much on military research and development as the next six powers combined. America's economic might is also undisputed. With 5 percent of the world's population, the United States produces about a quarter of the world's GDP. Its economy is worth approximately $14.3 trillion. That is more than the economies of China, Japan, Germany, and France combined. The United States has a per capita income of around $47,000, compared to $6,000 for China. It has the best universities in the world, and its culture is dominant globally. Culturally, intellectually, scientifically, and politically, America dominates the global system.

America's emergence as the most powerful country in history was a complex and relatively gradual process. The United States, like previous civilizations, borrowed heavily from others and built on foundations created by others. America, in many ways, was a continuation of British society in the New World. The Pilgrims who arrived in 1620 on the *Mayflower* at Plymouth in Massachusetts were English people who brought English values and institutions with them. The United States utilized strategies very similar to those used by other great powers to achieve its dominant position. It also benefited from the protection of the Pacific and Atlantic Oceans and unthreatening neighbors on its borders. The expansion of the United States occurred over land through the acquisition of Native American territories. Similar to other great powers, America relied heavily on military force to expand and consolidate its power. Believing in the concept of manifest destiny, it eventually expanded its territory from the Atlantic to the Pacific. The Mexican-American War (1846–1848) resulted in America's acquisition of two fifths of Mexico's territory, including California and the present American Southwest, in the Treaty of Guadalupe-Hidalgo, which ended the conflict. However, the issue of slavery divided the United States into two warring factions, leading to the bloodiest war in American history. Even so, the American Civil War removed a serious obstacle to the United States' rise as a great power. In essence, the Civil War forged a common American culture and internal unification.[15]

Internal stability enabled the United States to concentrate on building its economy and broadening its interests. The Civil War produced advancements in American military organization and technologies. However, after the war the United States demobilized the army, scrapped over half its warships, and allowed the rest to rot. The government declined to remain ahead of other countries in construction of iron-clad steamships.[16] As a continental-size power, the United States remained largely preoccupied with domestic and regional affairs. Furthermore, America believed that it could be "a City on a Hill" and an example to other nations, albeit from a distance and without getting entangled in their problems. This proclivity toward isolationism has always been an essential component of American foreign policy. But isolationism also emanated from the reality that until the late 1880s America was far behind great powers such as Britain, France, Germany, Austria-Hungary, Russia, and Italy. In fact, when the Sultan of Turkey decided to reduce expenses in 1880, he closed Turkey's diplomatic missions in Sweden, Belgium, the Netherlands, and the United States.[17] Yet America's vast territory, abundant natural resources, spirit of freedom and innovation, ability to attract immigrants and investments, institutional stability, and cultural values contributed to its phenomenal growth in the 1880s. The United States became a leading producer of agricultural products, coal, iron, and steel. Its banking and manufacturing sectors surpassed those of the major countries. By 1890 the United States had decided to strengthen its navy to be competitive

manifest destiny ■ Jingoistic tenet that the U.S. expansion is reinforced through God's will

Mexican-American War ■ The war between Mexico and the United States (1846–1848) that resulted in the U.S. acquisition of two fifths of Mexico's territory, including California and the present American Southwest

with European navies. This development was fueled partly by America's imperial ambitions, evidenced by its conquest of the Philippines, Puerto Rico, and Guam and its increased influence in Cuba and Hawaii as a consequence of its victory in the Spanish-American War in 1898. By ending Spain's declining position in the Americas and the Pacific, the United States established itself as the hegemon of the Western Hemisphere, thereby achieving the objective of the Monroe Doctrine of 1823, namely, diminishing European involvement in the Americas.

Reluctantly, America began abandoning its policy of isolationism during World War I in response to dangers of war in Europe and indiscriminate German submarine warfare. President Woodrow Wilson accelerated the construction of military weapons and warships, drafted young men, and trained them to fight. World War I stimulated a rapid growth in the foreign-policy establishment and brought out a strong American commitment to free trade, the promotion of democracy, support for national self-determination, and an emphasis on international cooperation to achieve world peace through organizations such as the League of Nations. American power was applied to protect its growing interests abroad. The United States' rise to global prominence meant that it could no longer avoid entanglement in European affairs, a reality made clearer by World War II. President Franklin D. Roosevelt, even before Japan bombed the American fleet at Pearl Harbor on December 7, 1941, expressed an urgent need to strengthen the military. He created the U.S. Air Force in 1939 and a two-ocean navy in 1940. The military draft was reinstated, military cooperation with Britain was enhanced, and military assistance was extended to Britain, the Soviet Union, and China. America's entry into World War II unleashed unprecedented military growth. By the end of the war, the United States was indisputably the dominant global power. But the Soviet Union, especially after it acquired intercontinental nuclear weapons, also gained superpower status. As Table 2.1 shows, the major European powers and Japan, destroyed by war, declined. Figure 2.1 demonstrates the global reach of America's military power.

Spanish-American War ■ The war between Spain and the United States (1898)

Monroe Doctrine ■ The statement of U.S. policy made by President James Monroe in 1823 that resulted in diminished European involvement in the Americas

League of Nations ■ International alliance created in 1920 to promote international peace and security

Pearl Harbor ■ Bombed by Japanese submarines and carrier-based planes in 1941

▶ **TABLE 2.1**	
Great Powers from 1495 to Present	
Period	**Great Powers**
1495–1521	France, England, Austrian Hapsburgs, Spain, Ottoman Empire, Portugal
1604–1618	France, England, Austria, Spain, Ottoman Empire, Holland, Sweden
1648–1702	France, England, Austrian Hapsburgs, Spain, Ottoman Empire, Holland, Sweden
1713–1792	France, Great Britain, Austrian Hapsburgs, Spain, Sweden, Russia, Prussia
1815–1914	France, Great Britain, Austria-Hungary, Russia, Prussia/Germany, Italy, United States, Japan
1919–1939	France, Great Britain, Soviet Union, Germany, Italy, United States, Japan
1945–1989	Soviet Union, United States
1989–Present	United States

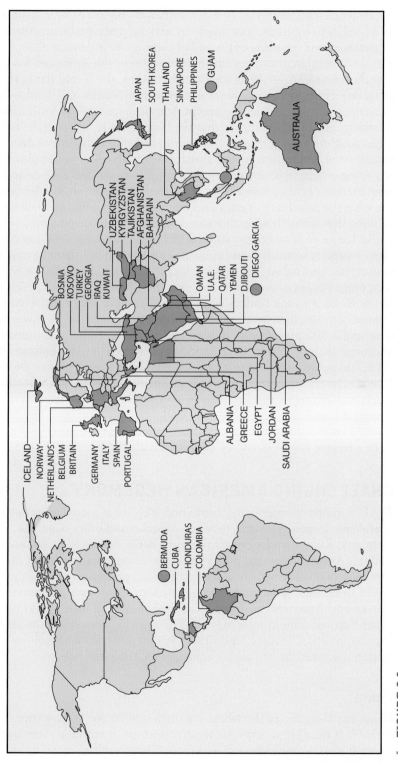

FIGURE 2.1
Location of U.S. Military Forces

America's hegemony or primacy rests not only on its dominant power but also on its ability to legitimize that power by making it acceptable to potential challengers in particular and members of the global community in general. Cooperation, integration, and multilateralism became cornerstones of the American-led postwar order. Certain institutions—such as the United Nations, the World Bank, the International Monetary Fund, and the General Agreement on Tariffs and Trade—benefited most countries and induced them to accept American leadership. Institutionalization and increasing globalization meant that the United States and other countries would be constrained to varying degrees and would embrace multilateralism and cooperation instead of unilateralism. As the global leader, America would play a major role in providing collective benefits or public goods (i.e., services such as security, stability, open markets, and economic opportunities). By doing so, the United States would minimize the possibility of envy and resentment that could escalate into the fear and loathing that spawn hostile alliances designed to balance power.[18]

public goods ■
Collective benefits, such as security, stability, open markets, and economic opportunities

In the Gulf War against Iraq in 1991, the United States' use of very sophisticated weapons stunned many countries and prompted them to upgrade their own military technologies. Ten years later, the war in Afghanistan was fought with even more advanced weapons. For example, American commandos using binoculars with laser range finders could spot distant enemy targets and relay the coordinates to satellite telephones or laptop computers in U.S. warplanes. Bombs weighing 2,000 pounds and guided by lasers and global positioning systems that improved their precision were dropped on targets in Afghanistan. Bombs weighing 4,700 pounds were used against Baghdad in the 2003 war. New technologies allowed American forces to detect heat, magnetic fields, and vibrations through as much as 100 feet of solid rock, and thermobaric weapons could be used to penetrate rock and concrete to destroy underground targets.[19] The Predator, an unmanned reconnaissance and surveillance plane that is controlled by a ground team from a remote location, can be equipped with Hellfire missiles to strike targets.

CHALLENGING AMERICAN HEGEMONY

The U.S. military superiority, combined with what many countries viewed as unilateralism, deepened fissures between America and other countries, such as France, Germany, Russia, and China. Instead of being perceived as promoting the global welfare, American foreign policy was increasingly seen as being preoccupied with narrowly defined American interests. Instead of consulting, Washington was perceived to be issuing demands and ultimatums. America's preference for a unipolar system and American global hegemony threatened other great powers, most of which favored a multipolar system. The growing consensus among foreign policy experts, political leaders, and others is that America's hegemony is over.[20] This section discusses the principal challenges to American power.

China

China has been one of the world's leading powers for at least four thousand years. China was once far superior to Western Europe in virtually every human endeavor. These historical achievements reinforce China's self-perception as a great power.

What impact does China's search for energy have on the global economy and China's foreign relations? Oil is extracted from tar sands at this Syncrude mine in Canada, which is a joint venture of China's Sinopec and other companies.

China's many contributions to human civilization, its population of more than 1.3 billion, its rapid economic growth, and the spread of its culture across continents combine to strengthen its view that it is entitled to play a major role in world affairs. Just as an individual's identity helps to influence his or her perception of his or her role in the world, a nation's identity is crucial in its determination of its global status. China's identity is that of a great power.[21] China has traditionally emphasized protecting its borders, fostering domestic integration and stability, and reducing regional threats.

But China is now widely viewed as a major challenger to America's dominance of the global system. It is using its financial power to acquire companies and gain access to much-needed natural resources. To obtain these resources, Chinese companies are forming partnerships and joint ventures in the United States, Canada, and Latin America. China has established strong economic ties with oil-producing countries in Latin America, the Middle East, and Africa. As the United States became preoccupied with wars in Iraq and Afghanistan, fighting global terrorism, and preventing nuclear proliferation in Iran and Korea, China strengthened its navy and increased its defense spending.[22] Both China's perception of its growing global power and America's perception of its loss of its dominant position in the international system, heightened by the global financial and economic crisis, combine to engender antagonistic relations between the two countries. Each country perceives the other as a threat to its power and ambitions.

China's economic growth has been spectacular since it implemented far-reaching economic reforms and improved relations with the United States in the 1970s. The economy has consistently grown by around 10 percent a year, even during periods when the American economy experienced recession. Even when most of the industrialized world experienced a severe economic recession due to the financial crisis, China's economic growth was roughly 7.2 percent. China's economic growth was spurred by deliberate and often draconian policies to reduce population growth, by the adoption of the free market, by increased privatization of the economy, by promotion of entrepreneurship, and by the efforts to attract foreign investments through the creation of special enterprise zones. In 2011, China had roughly $2.6 trillion in foreign exchange reserves. It overtook Japan to become the world's second-largest economy. It has vast dollar reserves and holds 22 percent of America's treasury debt. In other words, America is indebted to China.

Companies from around the world established subsidiaries in China to take advantage of low production costs as well as the growing Chinese market. Despite strained relations with Taiwan, which China claims to be part of its territory, many Taiwanese engineers and high-technology companies have moved to China to take advantage of business opportunities. China's own engineering and technological schools and universities are producing experts in information technology. China's economic might also enables it to convince leading global companies to transfer advanced technologies to it. Such advantages in technology improve China's economic competitiveness as well as its military capabilities. Faced with declining exports due to the global recession, China focused on increasing domestic investing and consumer spending.

Although largely preoccupied with regional security, especially the significant U.S. military presence in the area, China developed nuclear weapons as a deterrent to threats from the Soviet Union and the United States. In addition to acquiring advanced Russian military technology, China is making a concerted effort to build a new generation of nuclear-powered submarines that can launch intercontinental nuclear missiles. It is also modernizing its air force and reorganizing its army to enable it to be a mobile and technologically competent force able to fight limited wars under high-technology conditions. Growing perceptions of America's unilateralism and its willingness to use its military might reinforce China's determination to balance American power, especially in Asia. However, China is also careful not to jeopardize its strong economic links with the United States or its rapid economic development by allocating an overwhelming share of its resources to expanding its military.

Treaty of Friendship and Cooperation ■ Chinese-Russian alliance designed to challenge the U.S. framework for international security.

China is building alliances with Russia, symbolized by the Treaty of Friendship and Cooperation of July 2001, to challenge the American framework for international security. It is also strengthening relations with India and resolved the border dispute between the two countries. In July 2006 they reopened the Nathu La Pass, which was closed for forty-four years, to facilitate trade. With a third of the world's population, the alliance between China and India has the potential to significantly impact global affairs. China is India's largest trading partner, and there are numerous economic and investment ties between the two countries. During his visit to India in December 2010, Chinese Premier Wen Jiabao stressed the importance of cooperation between the two countries, and that if they work together, the twenty-first century will be the Asian century. The United States is strengthening its ties with India to counteract China's rise.

As we have seen, financial and economic power is widely regarded as the foundation of global political power. Countries whose economies suffer severe declines often experience a diminution of power. America's wars in Iraq and Afghanistan, the rapid decline of its manufacturing sector, huge budget deficits, and its reliance on borrowing from China and other countries to fund its expenditures have contributed to the relative increase in China's power. The financial crisis exposed America's vulnerabilities and raised serious questions about America's capitalism. China clearly perceives itself as the leading rising global power. Although China is unlikely to directly confront the United States for global leadership, its financial and economic strength has influenced it to demand greater recognition and influence in global affairs. China's rise, in contrast to America's decline, is also fueling Chinese nationalism and changing America's relationship with China. U.S. perceptions of and its responses to China play a crucial role in shaping relations between the two countries. If China is perceived as a military and economic threat rather than a competitor that also cooperates with the United States, a hostile relationship will be fostered. On the other hand, given the transformation of the international system in an information age that allows individuals to exert influence on international relations, cultural ties and increased understanding between the two countries could override threat perceptions. As the case study demonstrates, China will be restrained by many of its own problems.

THREATS TO U.S. POWER: EMERGING POWERS AND NONSTATE ACTORS

Emerging market economy countries pose challenges to America's leadership and are diffusing power in the international system. Ian Bremmer and Nouriel Roubini argue that the global financial crisis and the economic recession sent a much larger shock wave through the international system than anything that followed the collapse of the Soviet bloc.[23] Combined with other forces of globalization discussed in Chapter 1, these developments have further eroded the potency of military might and have enhanced economic power. Emerging market economies such as China, India, and Brazil are posing challenges to American dominance. Confident of their growing economic power, these countries are changing what they perceive to be an outmoded world order established by the United States and Western Europe. The diffusion of power is demonstrated by the transition of power from the G-7 (group of leading industrial countries) to the G-20, a group composed of the world's largest economies, including emerging market countries.

When faced with overwhelming power, represented by the giant Goliath, the Israelites employed a boy, David, with a slingshot to counteract that power. In Jonathan Swift's *Gulliver's Travels*, the Lilliputians are able to restrain the giant through cooperation. These stories illustrate the paradox of being a superpower. Instead of engaging a country that possesses overwhelming power with conventional weapons, the weak usually confront the strong in unorthodox ways. Suicide bombings by terrorist organizations challenge America's military and economic power. The United States is fighting its longest war against terrorist groups. This strategy of counteracting the dominant power of a hegemon is called asymmetrical warfare. It enables the weaker side to gain military advantages and level the playing field to some extent by using comparatively unsophisticated weapons and strategies. Joseph Nye argues that for all the fashionable predictions of China surpassing the United States, the greatest threat may come from nonstate

asymmetrical warfare ■ Strategy of counteracting the dominant power of a hegemon through unorthodox ways

Terrorist organizations are a threat to American dominance. After bin Laden's death, questions remained about al-Qaeda's future.

actors. In an information-based world, power diffusion may pose a bigger danger than power transition.[24]

Almost 98 percent of Americans view terrorist organizations as the most potent nonstate challengers to American dominance. Their ability to effectively utilize asymmetrical power has been facilitated by globalization. The United States has many interests around the world, which generate resentments that can escalate into violence. Finally, the openness of American society has allowed terrorist organizations to operate without being easily detected, even with the increased security measures implemented after the devastating terrorist attacks. Despite its superior military forces, America found itself bogged down in a war against insurgents in Iraq armed with roadside bombs and suicide bombers. The war against terrorism continues in Afghanistan and Pakistan.

Domestic Threats to American Hegemony

Empires decline not only because of challenges from rising powers, but also because of decisions made by their leaders and general attitudes and beliefs of ordinary citizens. In other words, empires are usually their own worst enemy. More important than what others do to them is often what they do to themselves that ultimately hastens their fall.

The collapse of the financial system created by the United States and the accompanying global economic recession eroded global confidence in America's leadership. America's access to easy credit and its failure to effectively regulate the financial system covered up many fundamental weaknesses. The manufacturing sector declined, and many of its high school graduates were unprepared to compete effectively in a global economy. In many ways, America's policies contributed to its relative decline. America became the world's biggest borrower, and its budget deficits continue to escalate. America seemed to lack fiscal and political discipline to rein in its debt. The national debt rose to $14 trillion in 2011. For the first time in its history, America's triple-A credit rating was downgraded to a double-A-plus rating by Standard and Poor's. This development reinforced global perceptions of America's relative decline and influenced China, which holds more than $1.3 trillion of U.S. debt, to advocate replacing the U.S. dollar with a new reserve currency. Niall Ferguson argues that most dominant countries fall due to fiscal crises.[25]

Public opinion polls consistently show that Americans have a definite lack of sustained interest in the rest of the world and in foreign relations. This reality influenced Samuel P. Huntington, an astute observer of American international and domestic affairs, to conclude that "however much foreign policy elites may ignore or deplore it, the United States lacks the domestic political base to create a unipolar world."[26]

Most Americans support a volunteer army, one composed of people who generally come from less-privileged economic backgrounds. The country as a whole has demonstrated a low tolerance for combat fatalities and long-term military involvement in dangerous regions. Americans remain primarily concerned with economic issues and the implications of economic globalization. They have constantly viewed economic rather than military power as the more important determinant of global dominance. However, their own financial problems, political stalemate and extreme partisanship, and the failure to reduce the budget deficit are undermining America's economic power.

Will the United States Remain the Dominant Power?

As American troops marched across Iraq and its planes and ships bombed Baghdad to effectuate what the Pentagon called "shock and awe," the rest of the world watched the most awesome military force the world has ever known unilaterally impose its will on another country. America clearly demonstrated that it is a hegemon with a preponderance of power. On the other hand, some scholars, such as Paul Kennedy, caution that overwhelming power often leads a country to engage in imperial overstretch or to expand its interests and obligations to such a great degree that it overburdens its resource base and is unable to defend all of its interests simultaneously.[27] America's difficulties in Iraq made this obvious. Another concern was America's emphasis on unilateralism. Stanley Hoffmann, a leading scholar of international relations, argued that there is nothing more dangerous for a hyperpower than the temptation of unilateralism. It may well believe that the constraints of international agreements and organizations are not necessary. But those constraints provide for better opportunities for leadership than does the arrogant demonstration of contempt for the behavior of other states.[28] The danger for the United States, it is argued, is that its unprecedented power is likely to influence it to become insensitive to other nations' fear and interests. Great powers often succumb to hubris. This hubris often leads the dominant nation to believe that it is a benevolent hegemon and that it is immunized from a backlash against its preponderance by the attractiveness of its ideology and culture. But because states are competitive and worry about the predominant country's capabilities, they are likely to coalesce against what they perceive to be a threat.[29]

Many scholars argue that discussions of America's decline are routine and wrong and that the country is likely to remain the dominant power for the foreseeable future. Samuel P. Huntington, for example, identified *five waves of declinism* that turned out to be wrong. The *first wave* occurred with the launch of *Sputnik* by the Soviets in 1957. The *second wave* was at the end of the 1960s, when the United States and the Soviet Union were perceived to be losing to rising economic powers, such as Japan and Western Europe. The *third wave* came with the oil embargo by the Organization of Petroleum Exporting Countries (OPEC) in 1973. The *fourth wave* was marked by America's defeat in Vietnam, the Watergate crisis that undermined public confidence in U.S. government and institutions, and the upsurge in Soviet-Cuban expansion in Angola, Afghanistan, Nicaragua, Ethiopia, and Mozambique. Finally, the *fifth wave* came in the late 1980s as a result of growing U.S. trade and budget deficits and Japan's economic might.[30] All of these waves subsided, leaving the United States as a dominant power.

Huntington and Joseph S. Nye contend that the United States will remain the dominant power. Huntington states that the ultimate test of a great power is its ability to renew itself, and that the United States meets this test to a far greater extent than past or present great powers. The *forces of renewal* are competition, mobility, and immigration. Furthermore, America's strength is multidimensional, meaning that it is based on military might, economic power, technological capabilities, cultural appeal, political leadership and influence in international institutions, an abundance of natural resources, and social cohesion and political stability at home.[31] Nye argues that the American problem is different from that of Britain, which faced challenges from a rising Germany and the United States itself. Instead, the United States will remain the dominant power but will have to cope with unprecedented problems of globalization that cannot be solved unilaterally. In Nye's view, the problem of American power in the twenty-first century is not one of decline, but what to do in light of the realization that even the largest country cannot achieve the outcomes it wants without the help of others.[32]

OPEC ■ Group of oil-exporting states that collaborate to elevate their export power

▶ CASE STUDY | Challenges Facing China

Discussions of China's rapid economic growth and its challenge to the United States for global leadership generally ignore not only the uncertainty of the future but also real and predictable problems confronting China. For example, natural disasters, as we will see in the case of Japan, can derail economic plans and have severe social and political consequences. China routinely suffers from earthquakes, destructive floods, and other natural disasters. As popular uprisings for democracy in the Middle East and North Africa demonstrate, generational change and the forces of globalization are undermining authoritarian

(continued)

governments. China has managed to retain Communist control during a period of unprecedented economic growth. Apart from the probability that China's high growth rates are unsustainable, growth also engenders conditions that empower individuals to seek more autonomy, freedom, and political participation. The challenge facing China is how to manage a transition to a more democratic society without creating domestic instability, which has been a serious problem in China's history.

China's power is largely one-dimensional. Its economic power is not combined with military and political power, especially when compared with the United States. Although China's Confucianism has appeal in parts of Asia, it is not a potent force globally. In general, China has a deficit of soft power, a key ingredient in the rise of great powers. Soft power is the ability to attract and to be admired by others. Although China attracts investments from around the world, unlike the United States, it is not a universal or global nation that is composed of immigrants from every corner of the earth. How does a Scandinavian, Nigerian, or Indian become Chinese? As we discussed earlier, countries that emerged as great powers were generally characterized by openness, an ability to attract immigrants and to integrate them into their social, economic, and political life. China's excessive pollution and large and generally poor population combine to discourage the migration of highly talented individuals from around the world. Nor does China's political and social system provide freedom essential for cultivating sustained creativity and innovation. China's failure to attract large numbers of immigrants is compounded by its demographic deterioration, caused partly by its one-child policy. China has a subreplacement fertility rate and will experience, like Western Europe and Japan, an explosive growth of older people.[33] Addressing the needs of an elderly population will exert great pressure on the country's resources and impede both economic growth and military power.

As we saw, rising powers usually confront reactions from other states. Chinese dependence on resources from around the world and global markets for its products increases its vulnerability to pressure from many different sources. Conflicts with China's neighbors, especially India and Japan, complicate China's rise to global leadership. Neighboring countries are likely to form alliances or to coordinate actions to counteract Chinese power if they perceive China as a threat. China will therefore have to allocate significant resources to resolving various conflicts and managing regional affairs. India, with its own global ambitions, will balance China's power. Numerous conflicts exist between the two countries. While India is democratic, China is authoritarian. There are also longstanding border disputes, disagreements about Tibet and Kashmir, conflicts over China's construction of huge dams in Tibet that could divert water from rivers flowing into India, and India's reluctance to allow its inefficient manufacturers to be exposed to Chinese competition. There is also tension between India and China resulting from China's close relations with Pakistan. Furthermore, the United States, as a Pacific power, retains strong military, economic, and political ties with countries in the region and is strengthening its relationship with India, in particular. China also faces economic competition from other low-cost manufacturing countries such as Indonesia and Vietnam. Rising standards of living and demands for higher wages will diminish China's competitive advantage. Furthermore, China's economic growth is closely tied to America's imports of Chinese products. Economic decline in the United States would lead to economic problems for China. The two countries are interdependent. In the near term, China faces a real estate bubble that could severely undermine its economic growth and have global implications.

China can resolve many of these challenges by accepting its global political responsibilities and working largely within the framework of established global institutions even as it seeks to modify them to reflect its growing power and that of emerging economic powers. By developing strong economic and political ties with its neighbors and maintaining a strong but not threatening military, China can reduce tensions and decrease chances of other countries forming alliances to balance against it. Power tends to breed hubris, and hubris often leads to unnecessary conflicts, as we will see in the case of the United States. If China can avoid the arrogance of power, its rise will be perceived as less of a threat. ▲

SUMMARY AND REVIEW

This chapter examined the rise and fall of great powers and the essential role of politics, economics, and culture in that process. Countries with strong economies and well-managed political systems are able to spread their culture globally and to exercise power over other states. A state, or in some cases a small group of states, that has extraordinary influence over the behavior of other states is said to have international primacy. States that enjoy international primacy are generally said to have diverse interests. When several great powers are in the international system, it is defined as being multipolar. During the Cold War, when the United States and the Soviet Union were superpowers, the system was bipolar. Today, the United States remains the dominant country in an increasingly multipolar world that is characterized by the diffusion of power.

States and groups of states become powerful and lose their power for many reasons. War is one major factor. Although investing in military power can help turn a state into a great power, it can also lead to its fall as a great nation. Many great powers decline because of hubris, or excessive pride, and imperial arrogance. These nations tend to overestimate their power and expand their military power so much that they ultimately erode their economic base. We discussed some challenges to the United States. Some of these challenges come from nations that are quickly advancing economically, such as China, India, and Brazil. We discussed the challenge to American power from nonstate actors, such as terrorist organizations, that try to undermine the strength of great nations. Finally, we examined how America's domestic problems, especially its growing budget deficits, threaten American power.

KEY TERMS

power transition theory   25
hegemons   25
multipolar   25
bipolar   25
unipolar   25
power   25
gross national product (GNP)   26
gross domestic product (GDP)   26
power conversion   26
structural leadership   26
institutional leadership   26
situational leadership   26
population pressures   27
uneven economic growth   27
hubris   27
Lippmann Gap   27

imperial overstretch   27
Concert of Europe   28
containment   28
binding   28
engagement   28
manifest destiny   29
Mexican-American War   29
Spanish-American War   30
Monroe Doctrine   30
League of Nations   30
Pearl Harbor   30
public goods   32
Treaty of Friendship and Cooperation   34
asymmetrical warfare   35
Organization of Petroleum Exporting
   Countries (OPEC)   38

DISCUSSION QUESTIONS

1. Economic power and military power are often discussed as the two most important factors that make up a great power. What are some other elements of power? How might they contribute to a nation's rise to superpower status?

2. What are the three types of leadership? Provide some examples of how the United States and past world powers have exercised these types of leadership.

3. What are some strategies for maintaining power and preventing rising powers from creating disorder in the international system? Provide some examples of countries that have used some of these strategies.

4. What are some current examples of challenges to American hegemony? What are the strongest challenges the United States faces to maintain its status as a great power? Explain.

5. Does China pose a major threat to the United States? How can U.S.–China relations be managed in light of increased competition?

SUGGESTED READINGS

Bardham, Pranab. *Awakening Giants, Feet of Clay*. Princeton, NJ: Princeton University Press, 2010. Examines the rise of China and India and the challenges they face, including social inequality, poverty, and demographic problems.

Burbank, Jane, and Frederick Cooper. *Empires in World History*. Princeton, NJ: Princeton University Press, 2010. Comparative study of global empires, from the third century B.C. to the Soviet and American empires.

Herd, Graeme P., ed. *Great Powers and Strategic Stability in the Twenty-First Century*. New York: Routledge, 2010. Discusses new security threats in a multipolar world as well as the strategies of rising powers.

Nye, Joseph S. *The Future of Power*. New York: Public Affairs, 2011. Debates the declining power of the United States and China's rise. Stresses the advantages of America's powerful military and soft power.

Page, Benjamin I., and Tao Xie. *Living With the Dragon*. New York: Columbia University Press, 2010. Americans have a moderate approach to China and have supported cooperation and engagement with it.

ENDNOTES

1. Samuel P. Huntington, "Why International Primacy Matters," *International Security* 17, No. 4 (Spring 1993), 68.

2. Ronald L. Tammen et al., *Power Transitions* (New York: Seven Bridges Press, 2000), 6.

3. Joseph S. Nye, "The Future of American Power," *Foreign Affairs* 89, No. 6 (November/December 2010), 3.

4. Joseph S. Nye, *Bound to Lead: The Changing Nature of American Power* (New York: Basic Books, 1990), 32.

5. John J. Mearsheimer, *The Tragedy of Great Power Politics* (New York: W. W. Norton, 2001), 61.

6. Nye, *Bound to Lead*, 27.

7. G. John Ikenberry, "The Future of International Leadership," *Political Science Quarterly* III (Fall 1996), 388.

8. Ikenberry, "The Future of International Leadership," 389.

9. Randall Schweller, "Managing the Rise of Great Powers," in *Engaging China*, eds. Alistair Johnston and Robert Ross (London: Routledge, 1999), 2.

10. Torbjorn L. Knutsen, *The Rise and Fall of World Orders* (Manchester, UK: Manchester University Press, 1999), 24.

11. Walter Lippmann, *U.S. Foreign Policy* (London: Hanish Hamilton, 1943), 5; and Paul Kennedy, *The Rise and Fall of Great Powers* (New York: Vintage Books, 1987), xvi.

12. G. John Ikenberry and Charles Kupchan, "The Legitimation of Hegemonic Power," in *World Leadership and Hegemony*, 49.

13. Schweller, "Managing the Rise of Great Powers," in *Engaging China*, 9.

14. Schweller, "Managing the Rise of Great Powers," in *Engaging China*, 14.

15. Knutsen, *The Rise and Fall of World Orders*, 175.

16. Ernest R. May, *Imperial Democracy: The Emergence of America as a Great Power* (Chicago: Imprint Publications, 1991), 7.

17. May, *Imperial Democracy*, 3.

18. Josef Joffe, "The Default Power: The False Prophecy of America's Decline," *Foreign Affairs* 88, No. 5 (September/October 2009), 24.

19. Andrew C. Revkin, "U.S. Making Weapons to Blast Underground Hide-Outs," *New York Times*, 3 December 2001, B4.

20. Roger C. Altman and Richard N. Haass, "American Profligacy and American Power," *Foreign Affairs* 89, No. 6 (November/December 2010), 32.

21. Robert D. Kaplan, "The Geography of Chinese Power," *Foreign Affairs* 89, No. 3 (May/June 2010), 23.

22. Charles Glaser, "Will China's Rise Lead to War?" *Foreign Affairs* 90, No. 2 (March/April 2011), 80.

23. Ian Bremmer and Nouriel Roubini, "A G-Zero World," *Foreign Affairs* 90, No. 2 (March/April 2011), 5.

24. Joseph S. Nye, *The Future of Power* (New York: Public Affairs, 2011), 2.

25. Niall Ferguson, "Complexity and Collapse," *Foreign Affairs* 89, No. 2 (March/April 2010), 30.

26. Huntington, "The Lonely Superpower," 40.

27. Kennedy, *The Rise and Fall of Great Powers*, 515.

28. Stanley Hoffmann, "Clash of Globalizations," *Foreign Affairs* 81, No. 4 (July/August 2002), 113.

29. Fareed Zakaria, "The Future of American Power," *Foreign Affairs* 87, No. 3 (May/June 2008), 19.

30. Samuel P. Huntington, "The U.S.-Decline or Renewal?" *Foreign Affairs* 67, No. 2 (Winter 1988/89), 94–95.

31. Huntington, "The U.S.-Decline or Renewal?" 90–91.

32. Joseph S. Nye, "The Future of American Power," *Foreign Affairs* 89, No. 6 (November/December 2010), 12.

33. Nicholas Eberstadt, "The Demographic Future," *Foreign Affairs* 89, No. 6 (November/December 2010), 58.

Human Rights

International human rights based organizations like the United Nations Commission on Human Rights have made the monitoring of human rights a global issue. The UN is headquartered in New York City.

INTRODUCTION

When Muammar Qaddafi used military force to suppress demonstrations in Libya for a transition to democracy, there was a general consensus that there was a global responsibility to protect civilians. Although cultural values differ significantly from one society to another, our common humanity has equipped us with many shared ideas about how human beings should treat each other. Aspects of globalization, especially communications and migration, reinforce perceptions of a common humanity. In general, there is global agreement that human beings, simply because we exist, are entitled to at least three types of rights. One is civil rights, which include personal liberties, such as freedom of speech, religion, and thought; the right to own property; and the right to equal treatment under the law. Second is political rights, including the right to vote, to voice political opinions, and to participate in the political process. Third is social rights, including the right to be secure from violence and other physical danger, the right to a decent standard of living, and the right to health care and education. Societies differ in terms of which rights they emphasize. *Four types of human rights claims* that dominate global politics are

1. Accusations that governments are abusing individuals;
2. Demands by ethnic, racial, and religious communities for autonomy or independence;
3. Claims in what is generally regarded as private life, including rights and obligations within families, and the demands for equality by minority groups with unconventional lifestyles; and
4. Demands by governments for protection against powerful governments and nonstate actors, as well as the right to economic development.[1]

We will examine historical and philosophical foundations undergirding the development of human rights. Economic and political sanctions are often used to achieve compliance with human rights commitments. In extreme cases, countries support humanitarian intervention to terminate violations of human rights. One of the most significant developments is the emphasis on women's human rights. In this chapter, we will discuss rape as a weapon of war. We will briefly examine the death penalty and the treatment of gays and lesbians. The chapter concludes with a case study on homosexuals and human rights.

civil rights ■ Personal liberties, such as freedom of speech, thought, and religion

political rights ■ Right to vote, voice political opinions, and participate in the political process

social rights ■ Right to health care, education, and other social benefits

GLOBALIZATION AND HUMAN RIGHTS

The modern state provided increased security, but often it also became a cold instrument for systematically abusing human rights. In fact, it was due to violence against Jews, Gypsies, gays and lesbians, communists, religious groups, and others in Nazi Germany, which culminated in the Holocaust, that human rights became so prominent in global affairs. The current wave of globalization has undoubtedly enhanced the observance of human rights. Telecommunications, trade, migration,

Holocaust ■ Mass murder of millions of Jews driven by ethnic and religious hate and discrimination

travel, the weakening of national boundaries, the decline of Westphalian sovereignty, and growing interdependence have strengthened a commitment to human
rights. Information is now relayed instantaneously, which helps to limit governments' ability to engage in secrecy and brutality. Because their interests are intertwined with those of leading global actors, countries must consider the costs and
benefits of decisions concerning their treatment of citizens.

The rise of the United States to global power and its competition with the Soviet
Union for the hearts and minds of people around the world marked a turning
point in the struggle for human rights. This period of globalization radically transformed the perception that domestic affairs could be automatically separated from
international politics. A deeper awareness of the indivisibility of humanity and of
our problems weakened the idea that governments are essentially free to treat their
citizens as they wish. America's self-definition as a redeemer nation and a positive
force made human rights a central global issue. Several other factors contributed
to the expansion of and commitment to the human rights agenda:

1. The *creation of global institutions* to protect human rights.
2. A growing acceptance of the interdependence and indivisibility of rights.
   Violations of rights in one country have implications for people in other
   countries.
3. An *emphasis on promoting democracy*. The idea that democracy is essential to
   peaceful international relations became a central part of U.S. foreign policy.
4. The view that *respect for human rights facilitated market-based economic
   development*.[2]
5. *The effectiveness of nonstate actors*.

Nongovernmental Organizations and Human Rights

Because many governments violate human rights, responsibility for protecting individual freedoms was taken up by numerous nonstate actors at the local, national,
and global levels. Human rights organizations directly challenged the assumption
that sovereignty allows governments to abuse internationally recognized human
rights. Partly due to frustrations with other governments' bureaucratic approaches
and often counterproductive measures to protect human rights, transnational
groups now take direct action to prevent violations of basic rights. Amnesty
International, one of the best-known human rights nongovernmental organizations (NGOs), was founded in London in 1961 by a group of writers and lawyers. It
publishes reports on human rights problems in countries worldwide. It also encourages its global membership to participate in letter-writing campaigns to seek
the release of prisoners of conscience; that is, individuals who are imprisoned because governments disapprove of their political, religious, social, or other beliefs.

Global Companies and Human Rights

Human rights activists are increasingly pressuring global companies to make
the promotion and observation of human rights a centerpiece of their corporate strategy. Google's operations in China and its willingness to cooperate with

Westphalian ■
Concept of state
sovereignty developed
over 350 years ago

**prisoners of
conscience** ■
Individuals
imprisoned because
of their political,
religious, or social
beliefs

the government raised questions about links between business and respect for human rights. Many students and activists around the world have made issues such as child labor and sweatshops integral components of human rights debates. Working conditions in India, Bangladesh, China, and in countries in Africa and Latin America are routinely condemned and efforts are made to improve them. Now we are seeing greater emphasis placed on corporate social responsibility, which includes safeguarding the fundamental rights and freedoms of individuals. Companies are expected to secure human rights in countries where governments routinely violate them. To some extent, the companies' new role reflects the growing power of nonstate actors vis-à-vis nation-states. It also demonstrates the power of NGOs in a global society. The most powerful companies with global recognition are also the most vulnerable to pressure from human rights NGOs and the global media. Although public awareness of human rights abuses does not automatically influence consumers to reject high-quality, brand-name products that are reasonably priced, many companies believe that supporting human rights is good for business. Increasingly, global companies are regarded as powerful instruments in the pursuit of human rights.[3]

How much companies observe and promote human rights depends to some extent on their strategies and what they produce. Corporations that pursue a market-building strategy are distinguished from those that adopt a cost-minimizing strategy. Market-building companies are less likely to abuse human rights than cost-minimizing firms, which are more short-term oriented and more vulnerable to the pressures of globalization to increase profits at the expense of employees' human rights. Market-building strategies involve making significant investments that are unlikely to produce immediate profits. Equally important, companies pursuing such strategies tend to have a greater commitment to the people and the country in which they operate.[4]

corporate social responsibility ■ Corporate initiatives aimed at achieving social justice

market-building strategy ■ Seeks profit by building up markets rather than assaulting worker rights

cost-minimizing strategy ■ Increases profits at the employees' expense

DEVELOPMENT OF HUMAN RIGHTS

Stoics ■ Ancient Greek and Roman philosophers

universal rights ■ Freedoms to which all humans are automatically entitled

Cicero ■ The leading Stoic and Rome's greatest lawyer and orator

Greek philosophers, known as Stoics, developed the idea that rights enjoyed by Greeks were universal rights, freedoms that humans everywhere were entitled to simply because humans exist. These rights emanated from a law that was higher and more permanent than civil law—a universal law that was equated with the laws of gods. These laws were natural laws. Greek philosophy was adopted by the Romans. Marcus Tullius Cicero, Lucius Annaeus Seneca, and Marcus Aurelius were some of the leading Roman Stoics. Cicero (106–43 B.C.), the most prominent lawyer and philosopher of the Roman Empire, wrote that "true law is right reason in agreement with nature; it is of universal application, unchanging and everlasting."[5]

Social Contract Theories and Human Rights

A major step toward widespread acceptance and practice of natural rights was the significant recognition by England's kings, barons, and others that citizens were entitled to exercise basic freedoms without interference from their leaders and that such leaders' powers were limited by law and a sense of justice and fairness. The signing of the Magna Carta in 1215 was followed by England's King Edward III's acceptance in 1354 of the concept of due process of law, which means that a person cannot be deprived of life, liberty, or property without a fair trial based on fair procedures and rules. Another important step toward consolidating human rights was the decision of King Charles I of England, in his Petition of Rights in 1628, to guarantee the right of habeas corpus; that is, the right of a person to be brought before a judge or a court to determine whether or not he or she should be imprisoned. Restrictions on governments emerged from various historical experiences, but more directly from social contract theories. *John Locke*, an English philosopher, argued in his *Second Treatise on Government* (1690) that the state of nature was governed by natural law. People were relatively secure and free and could acquire property. From Locke's perspective, the social contract between citizens and government protected these natural rights. Nowhere are Locke's ideas expressed more forcefully than in the American Declaration of Independence.

Another advocate of the social contract was the French philosopher *Jean-Jacques Rousseau*. However, Rousseau ended up supporting a social contract that subordinates individual freedoms to the tyranny of the majority. His philosophy justified the government's absolute power over citizens.[6] *Immanuel Kant* developed the idea that human rights are directly linked to an inviolable obligation that we have to ourselves and to others. Kant believed that these obligations are universal, binding on all of us no matter where we live, thereby underscoring the concept of the indivisibility of humanity and universal nature of human rights. The most profound of these obligations is the *categorical imperative*, that is, the absolute obligation that each of us should always treat humanity never simply as a means but always at the same time as an end.[7]

Utilitarianism, Libertarianism, and Marxism

Jeremy Bentham, James Mill, and John Stuart Mill were among those who developed the theory of utilitarianism, directly challenging the idea that human beings have natural rights. The utilitarians, led by Jeremy Bentham, believed that individuals determine what is good for them and what they want. Conversely, they avoid the things that cause them pain. In his *Principles of Morals and Legislation* (1789), Bentham used his training as an Oxford-educated lawyer to develop a scientific analysis of morals and legislation. Through the careful balancing of individual interests, individual rights arise and are protected.

But John Stuart Mill questioned major assumptions of utilitarianism. He stressed that the government, representing the majority, can brutally suppress the rights of individuals. This fear of the tyranny of the majority is what motivated Jefferson and others to insist on the inclusion of the Bill of Rights in the U.S. Constitution to protect individuals who disagree with the majority. Mill articulated his philosophy in *On Liberty* (1859). He argued that one could justify interfering with an individual's liberty only to prevent that person from harming others, an assumption that must be proven by government authorities.

Magna Carta ■ The first written legal protections for the British people

due process of law ■ Protection of individual life, liberty, and property through a fair trial system

habeas corpus ■ The right to be brought before a judge or court to determine guilt or innocence

Second Treatise on Government ■ By John Locke; addressed the state of nature and natural law

social contract ■ Government sovereignty over its people in exchange for protecting individual rights

utilitarianism ■ Theory contradicting the idea that humans have natural rights

Principles of Morals and Legislation ■ Bentham's scientific analysis of morals and legislation

Bill of Rights ■ Constitutional protections of individual political rights

On Liberty ■ Stated that an individual's civil liberties can be violated only to protect others' rights

Another challenge to prevailing perspectives on human rights came from so-cialist philosophers such as *Saint Simon* and *Karl Marx*. Marx believed that the history of society is a history of class struggle. Marx and Saint Simon argued that traditional human rights were largely irrelevant to the majority who lived in poverty. They advocated that governments should develop policies that give people economic and social rights.

Legal Positivism and Human Rights

Closely related to utilitarianism are the positivistic theories and conservatism. Some conservatives, such as Edmund Burke, strongly opposed natural rights theories. Strongly influenced by the Reign of Terror that followed the French Revolution, Burke believed that individuals derived whatever rights they have from tradition and concrete laws, not from abstract philosophical theories of natural laws.[8] What distinguished the legal positivists from the utilitarians was the extent to which the former insisted on the absolute supremacy of laws and courts in determining rights. After World War I, the legal positivists became more extremist, arguing that law was what courts upheld and that justice was the correct enforcement of the law. Yet those bound to honor specific laws had to have given their consent. Legal positivism was taken to its logical and devastatingly destructive conclusion in Germany under the Nazis. When Adolf Hitler came to power in Germany, he made the courts subservient to him and used them as a tool of legal positivism. Hitler enacted laws suppressing freedom of speech, as well as laws requiring children to spy on their parents and Germans to spy on each other. Individuals could be imprisoned and executed without public trials. Ultimately, laws were enacted that authorized the Jewish Holocaust.

Globalization of Human Rights: The Universal Declaration of Human Rights

Concerns about human rights occurred largely within the context of domestic politics. An overriding emphasis on state sovereignty, which included a preoccupation with independence and control over citizens' lives, prevented broader applications of human rights philosophies from emerging. But increasing globalization—especially European colonization of the Americas and the enslavement of Africans and others—engendered greater global attention to human rights issues that transcended national boundaries. The horrors of slavery shocked people in Europe and the Americas and led to an antislavery campaign in the nineteenth century. Leading countries generally supported abolishing the slave trade at the Congress of Vienna in 1815, seven years after the United States had ceased importing enslaved Africans as required by the U.S. Constitution. *The First Anti-Slavery Convention* was held in London in 1840 by the Anti-Slavery Society, the oldest global human rights NGO. Wars also helped to globalize human rights. Horrified by the death and suffering of soldiers at the battle of Solferino in Italy in 1859, *Jean Henry Dunant*, a Swiss citizen, decided to publicize what he saw and to "humanize" war. These efforts resulted in the creation of the International Committee of the Red Cross in 1863, followed by the approval of the First Geneva Convention in 1864. The convention was

legal positivists ■ Demand absolute court and legal authority over the individual

Adolf Hitler ■ Mastermind of the Nazi cause and the Holocaust

Anti-Slavery Society ■ The oldest global human rights NGO

designed to humanize war by making rules for the treatment of wounded and sick soldiers and sailors, prisoners of war, and medical personnel. World War I led to the creation of the League of Nations in 1919, which made protecting inhabitants of dependent territories and the trafficking in children and women international human rights issues.[9] The covenant of the League of Nations also made the protection and treatment of workers an international human rights concern.

Nazi Germany's brutal march across Europe and the rise of the United States as the leading global power under the leadership of President Franklin Delano Roosevelt combined to give the impetus to make human rights global. America's self-perception as a nation with a universal message facilitated this development. Addressing Congress in January 1941, President Roosevelt committed the United States to securing four freedoms for the world: freedom of speech and expression, freedom of religion, freedom from economic hardship, and freedom from fear. Achieving these freedoms became the centerpiece of the *Atlantic Declaration* made by President Roosevelt and Britain's Prime Minister Winston Churchill in August 1941. The allies met in Washington, D.C., under the auspices of the American Law Institute to draft a declaration or bill of international human rights.[10] These developments laid the foundation for including human rights in the charter of the United Nations (UN) when it was founded in 1945 in San Francisco. The UN Charter provided for the formation of the Human Rights Commission, with the major responsibility for drafting global human rights standards. The final result of these efforts was the adoption by the UN General Assembly of the Universal Declaration of Human Rights (UDHR) UDHR in 1948. *Eleanor Roosevelt* played a crucial role in this accomplishment. She was largely responsible for promoting the use of the term *human rights* instead of the traditional emphasis on the rights of man, which actually meant just that. It is also important to point out that the Convention on the Prevention and Punishment of the Crime of Genocide (the Genocide Convention), a direct response to the Holocaust, was adopted by the UN General Assembly the day before it adopted the UDHR. Although the world was united in its determination to promote human rights, differences between the United States and the Soviet Union later led to the adoption in 1966 of two separate international covenants: the International Covenant on Civil and Political Rights (ICCPR), which stressed negative rights and was favored by the United States, and the International Covenant on Economic, Social, and Cultural Rights (ICESCR), which focused on positive rights and was favored by the Soviet Union.

The UDHR helped to unleash global demands for national self-determination by stating that all peoples have this right. Defining "a people" would become more complex than imagined. Countries in Africa, Asia, and the Caribbean succeeded in getting the UN General Assembly to adopt the International Convention on the Elimination of All Forms of Racial Discrimination in 1965. The global human rights agenda expanded to include the Convention on the Elimination of All Forms of Discrimination Against Women (1981), the Convention on the Rights of the Child (1990), the Convention Concerning Indigenous and Tribal Peoples in Independent Countries (1991), the International Convention on the Protection of the Rights of All Migrant Workers and Members of Their Families (1991), the Convention on the Rights of Persons with Disabilities (2006), and a U.N. Resolution on Sexual Orientation (2010).

four freedoms ■ Freedoms espoused by Roosevelt that are necessary for a just society

UDHR ■ Universal rights entitled to all humankind

ICCPR ■ Stressed the protection of negative political and civil rights from government infringement

negative rights ■ Rights a government may not infringe upon

ICESCR ■ Stressed the protection and promotion of positive economic, cultural, and social rights that government should provide its people

PHILOSOPHICAL CONTROVERSIES OVER HUMAN RIGHTS

The question on justice or torture in Saudi Arabia raises a fundamental philosophical controversy over human rights, one that persists and grows as societies feel increasingly threatened by the realities of cultural globalization. Other such controversies involve (1) the relationship between individuals and the communities in which they live, (2) the relationship between rights and obligations, (3) the prioritizing of rights and responsibilities, and (4) the absolute or conditional quality of various human rights.

Universalism Versus Cultural Relativism

cultural relativism
■ Idea that culture determines the degree of human rights protections in each country

As we have seen, Greek and Roman Stoics articulated the view that people have natural rights no matter where they live. But even in societies that stress universal human rights, cultural factors often complicate these theories. The United States, for example, simultaneously embraced natural rights and slavery. In other words, countries modify their support of universal rights by practicing cultural relativism. Often, leaders and ordinary citizens do not recognize their own biases in this regard. Proponents of cultural relativism believe that rights enjoyed by individuals are determined by each country's specific cultural and historical experiences. Consequently, what is acceptable behavior in one country could be a violation of human rights in another. Amputating limbs in Saudi Arabia, for example, is viewed in that society as reasonable punishment. Americans reject that punishment as barbaric. On the other hand, America's support of the death penalty is widely regarded in Europe as barbaric. One version of cultural relativism that was popular when Japan was viewed as a rising superpower was Confucianism. Some argued that Asians were successful because their cultures embrace the Confucianism values of obedience to authority and intense allegiance to groups and stress collective identities over individual identities. Based on this perspective, the assumption was that universalism was essentially Western and largely incompatible with Asian values.

Confucianism ■
Stresses obedience to authority and the importance of collective identities

Individuals and Communities

Complicating discussions of human rights are varying perspectives on the relationship between the individual and the community to which she or he belongs. In societies strongly influenced by Buddhism, Hinduism, or Confucianism, individualism is discouraged and community solidarity is a virtue. The individual is inseparable from the community and enjoys certain benefits from belonging to the community. However, the danger of denying individual rights is that the least powerful in these societies are often brutally suppressed by elites.

Relationship Between Rights and Obligations

There is general recognition of a connection between rights and responsibilities or obligations. The basic argument is that rights are simply corresponding obligations. In other words, failing to act to prevent human rights violations is in itself a violation of human rights. This argument assumes that we are capable of doing something either to prevent such violations or to mitigate their severity. The idea that we are responsible for what happens to others goes back to the idea that we have a moral responsibility for both acts of omission and acts of commission.

Prioritizing Human Rights

As American and British troops entered Baghdad in April 2003, many Americans and Iraqis celebrated the destruction of Saddam Hussein's regime and the idea of restoring fundamental freedoms to the Iraqis. Above all, the Iraqis wanted security, food, and clean water. This situation demonstrates the philosophical controversy over prioritizing human rights. Freedom of religion, speech, assembly, and the press are often elevated above other concerns in the United States. But many other societies place a much higher priority on satisfying basic economic needs.

Absolutism Versus Consequentialism

Finally, there is the debate about whether we should be willing to compromise on upholding human rights under certain circumstances. Some human rights advocates believe that some rights are absolute; that is, they can never be violated. On the other hand, many of these same advocates would agree that some rights are sometimes limited because exercising them under specific circumstances could endanger the rights of others. The torture of terrorist suspects by the United States and the ongoing debate about their entitlement to basic human rights illustrate how easily human rights violations can be justified in the name of national security.

HUMAN RIGHTS REGIMES

Regimes, as defined in Chapter 1, are institutions, rules, and regulations governing particular types of behavior and interactions. *Human rights regimes* consist of global, regional, national, and local institutions and rules designed to protect human rights, as well as the activities of numerous nonstate human rights organizations and grassroots campaigns. The UN Commission on Human Rights (UNCHR) is charged with the responsibility of monitoring human rights globally and for informing the UN Security Council of human rights violations. Previously, we also noted that nations and NGOs, especially after World War I and World War II, succeeded in developing international laws concerning the treatment of national minorities and laborers. These are all components of the global human rights regimes. In this section we will examine regional human rights regimes, focusing on those in Europe. The main institutions dealing with human rights in Europe are the European Commission for Human Rights, the European Court of Justice, and the Organization for Security and Cooperation in Europe (OSCE). Latin America, Africa, and other regions have essentially adopted Europe's regime.

UNCHR ■
Commission responsible for monitoring human rights on a global level

Council of Europe ■ Created in 1949 to promote democracy and human rights

Meeting in The Hague in 1948, European representatives laid the foundations for establishing the Council of Europe in 1949 to promote democracy and protect human rights. Recent events in Europe propelled the states belonging to the council to sign the *European Convention for the Protection of Human Rights and Fundamental Freedoms* in 1950. This agreement focused on safeguarding civil and political rights. The European Social Charter, signed in 1961, dealt with economic and social rights. Continuing abuses of human rights in Europe, especially in countries under Soviet domination, influenced German Chancellor *Willy Brandt* to promote dialogue across ideological divisions. These efforts led to the adoption of the Helsinki Final Act in 1975 and the creation of the OSCE. The Helsinki Final Act provided for the dissemination of the agreement and information about it within countries that originated it. This allowed people in Eastern Europe and the Soviet Union to learn more about human rights initiatives and sparked debate within the Communist countries. Combined internal and external pressure influenced Soviet leader Mikhail Gorbachev to adopt policies conducive to the exercise of both civil and political rights and economic and social rights.

Helsinki Final Act ■ Created to implement civil and political rights throughout Europe and the Soviet Union

Latin Americans have adopted many features of the European human rights regime but have been less successful in implementing human rights protections. The two most important agreements that established the Inter-American Regime are the charter of the Organization of American States (OAS) and the American Human Rights Convention. Like Europeans, Latin Americans have a human rights commission (the Inter-American Commission on Human Rights) and a court (the Inter-American Court of Human Rights).

Inter-American Regime ■ Attempt to establish regional protections for human rights in Latin America

ENFORCING HUMAN RIGHTS GLOBALLY

Although much of the responsibility for enforcing human rights is placed on global institutions, governments, and various NGOs, we as individuals have the ultimate obligation for protecting human rights. Crimes against humanity are generally seen as crimes against all of us, a viewpoint supported by the widespread acceptance of the universal nature of human rights. Yet, as individuals, our effectiveness to combat major human rights violations, especially when they occur in distant countries and are carried out by governments, is limited. Consequently, government institutions and various organizations that represent individuals are regarded as bearing most of the responsibility for implementing human rights. The extent to which various global actors and individuals are morally obligated to take action depends on three factors: (1) the nature of the relationship with the rights being violated, (2) the degree of effectiveness, and (3) capacity. The nature of the *relationship* involves issues such as geographic, economic, cultural, or political ties and the depth and duration of those connections. Countries closest to where human rights abuses are taking place are generally expected to act to prevent them, although geographic proximity in an age of globalization is declining in importance. More stress is placed on the *degree of effectiveness* and *capacity*. These three factors are integral to the concept of a *fair allocation of responsibility*. Generally, there are two approaches to implementing human rights. One is the *soft systems of implementation*, which concentrate primarily on conducting inquiries, exposing human rights violations, empowering the victims, and finding ways to damage the violating state's reputation. The other is the *hard*, or *coercive*, *enforcement measures*, which include making interventions, setting up international tribunals to prosecute violators, and establishing a permanent international criminal court (ICC).

Sanctions

Sanctions are punishments or penalties imposed by one state, a group of states, or the global community on another state or group of states in order to gain compliance with widely accepted global standards of behavior. Because political, economic, and military-strategic considerations affect decisions to impose sanctions, there are usually inconsistencies in how sanctions are imposed. For example, allies often escape sanctions even though their behavior is similar to that of the states being sanctioned. In Darfur and Myanmar (Burma), economic interests of China, India, and other countries have undermined sanctions. The complexity of the factors involved in imposing sanctions results in much controversy about using them to force a country to comply with global rules for protecting and promoting human rights. Sanctions can be nonviolent or violent; most are nonviolent. Nonviolent sanctions include economic, diplomatic, political, and cultural measures. Economic sanctions, the most prevalent, often limit trade, reduce access to international investments and financing, and freeze or confiscate bank deposits of both countries and individuals. Diplomatic and political sanctions include actions that aim at embarrassing a government and its leaders and reducing its interactions with the global community. Cultural sanctions usually try to reduce or stop cultural exchanges, tourism, educational ties, and sporting activities with the target country. Often, sanctions not only fail to change the government's practices but also turn out to have devastating consequences for innocent civilians. For example, U.S. sanctions against Cuba, strengthened by the Bush administration, were widely perceived as being counterproductive as well as harmful to ordinary Cubans. Cuba's leader, Fidel Castro, relinquished power because of his poor health, not because of U.S. sanctions. Recognizing this reality, the United States lifted some of the sanctions. In 2011, President Barack Obama relaxed restrictions on travel by academic, religious, and cultural groups and permitted Americans to send money to Cuba to invest in private enterprise. America's actions were partly in response to economic reforms implemented by Raul Castro and the release of political prisoners.

Sanctions can be imposed unilaterally or multilaterally. Unilateral sanctions, imposed by one country, were used more often than multilateral sanctions and by several countries before the end of the Cold War. Since 1990, however, the use of multilateral sanctions has increased. Increased international cooperation has also encouraged using sanctions as an alternative to military force. At the same time, however, the spread of globalization, which engenders global cooperation, complicates efforts to impose sanctions that are ultimately successful. In an interdependent world, one country's loss due to sanctions can easily become another country's loss as well. In other words, sanctions aimed at an enemy often damage a friend.

sanctions ■
Punishments or penalties imposed on one or more states by another state, group of states, or the global community

economic sanctions
■ Designed to limit or freeze a state's trade, investments, or financing

diplomatic and political sanctions
■ Designed to isolate and embarrass a state on a political level

cultural sanctions
■ Seek to limit cultural exchanges, tourism, sports, and other interactions with a sanctioned state

unilateral sanctions
■ Sanctions imposed by only one country

multilateral sanctions ■
Sanctions imposed by more than one country

Although some sanctions have achieved their objectives, such as those applied against the apartheid regime in South Africa, the consensus is that they are usually ineffective. *Sanctions fail for several reasons.* One reason is that nationalism, present in all countries, spawns a rally-round-the-flag effect. Another is that globalization makes it extremely difficult to effectively isolate a state economically. Third, sanctions may enable repressive governments to use external threats to justify cracking down on domestic opponents and to avoid responsibility for deteriorating economic, health, and social conditions. Fourth, sanctions are costly to countries that impose them. Over time, domestic pressures build to support removing sanctions against the targeted country. Finally, sanctions reduce the availability of resources in the target state, thereby strengthening its power to allocate scarce resources strategically to maintain support for its policies.

Humanitarian Intervention: Responsibility to Protect

When Libyans protested for a transition to democracy, the government used military force to silence opposition. Led by France, the United Nations imposed a no-fly zone in Libya to protect civilians from both the air force and the army. In extreme cases, when human rights violations shock human conscience, humanitarian intervention is regarded as a collective global responsibility. Humanitarian intervention usually involves deploying military forces to prevent or stop a country or group from engaging in gross violations of human rights.[11] It also includes efforts to provide humanitarian relief, to evacuate individuals, and to separate and monitor forces involved in conflicts. Humanitarian interventions fall into two basic categories: consensual and imposed. Consensual interventions are agreed to by those in control of a country or region. There is little need for military force. Uniformed forces are involved primarily because they have essential skills and technical capabilities that facilitate rescue operations or the provision of humanitarian supplies. Imposed interventions are conducted in a far more hostile environment and often against the wishes of governments or armed groups. Significant military force is required to reduce hostilities, protect civilians, and protect individuals who are delivering humanitarian assistance.

Closely related to humanitarian intervention are peacekeeping and peacemaking operations. Peacekeeping, provided by Chapter 6 of the UN Charter, occurs within a consensual type of intervention. It involves largely impartial monitors and observers who are unarmed or lightly armed. They are generally required to monitor a separation of forces, verify and monitor troop withdrawals, provide some security, and supervise elections. Force is used as a last resort and only for self-defense. Peacemaking, on the other hand, involves military forces that are heavily armed, well trained, and prepared to fight. But peacemaking is a far more circumscribed activity compared with standard military operations. Peacemaking occurs in situations in which most of the forces involved are friendly. The basic objective of peacemaking is to reduce the fighting and to restore or create an environment that will enable peacekeeping forces to function effectively. Increasingly, humanitarian interventions involve a mixture of peacekeeping and peacemaking operations.

humanitarian intervention ■ The use of military force to protect human rights

consensual interventions ■ Interventions agreed upon by all states involved in the conflict

imposed interventions ■ Interventions conducted against the wishes of the occupied state/territory

peacekeeping ■ Intervention involving impartial monitors and lightly armed observers

peacemaking ■ Intervention by heavily armed military forces

Responding to Genocide

In 1948, the UN adopted the Genocide Convention, which defines genocide as the intent to destroy, in whole or in part, a national, ethnic, racial, or religious group. Whole populations have been displaced or destroyed as others expanded their control over areas, usually through military force. Such behavior was largely justified in terms of progress and civilization. Often, only a small minority was concerned with the crime of genocide. Convinced that human beings were divided into different races and that some races were inherently superior to others, Europeans expanded their rule to Asia, the Americas, and Africa. In the process, they destroyed many indigenous peoples. The Armenian genocide is widely viewed as the prototype of subsequent genocides in the twentieth century. In 1895, 1909, and 1915, Turkish troops massacred more than a million Armenians and deported others into the Syrian desert, where they died of starvation. The genocide committed by Nazi Germany marked a turning point in the human rights debate, as we have seen. The victorious allies united against such crimes and punished those most directly involved in carrying them out. However, genocide continued and is still going on. For example, between 1975 and 1979, the Khmer Rouge in Cambodia killed more than a million people. Another million people died in Rwanda's genocide. Genocide was part of the conflict in the former Yugoslavia. Sudan's actions in Darfur were declared to be genocide in 2004. Many countries refrain from declaring atrocities to be genocide partly because the Genocide Convention requires them to act to prevent and punish genocide.

A big step toward holding individuals and governments responsible for gross violations of human rights, including genocide, came at the end of World War I. Britain and France attempted to punish Germany for violating the neutrality of Belgium and Luxembourg by destroying their cities and creating large numbers of refugees and for using poison gas. The *Commission on the Responsibility of the Authors of War and the Enforcement of Penalties* was established at the Paris Peace Conference in 1919. Its main objective was to prosecute those accused of committing war crimes and crimes against humanity, including government leaders. France and Britain strongly supported prosecuting leaders, whereas the United States, Italy, and Japan opposed such trials, principally on the grounds that such actions would violate sovereignty.[12]

After World War II, however, the United States changed its position. It played the leading role in setting up the Nuremberg Tribunal to prosecute Nazi war crimes and the *Tokyo Tribunal* to prosecute crimes committed by Japan. Britain had also changed its position: Instead of trying the Nazis, Prime Minister Winston Churchill advocated shooting Nazi war criminals on sight. The United States, under Harry S. Truman's leadership, persuaded the allies to try the Nazis. The London Agreement—signed in 1945 by the United States, Britain, France, and the Soviet Union—provided for the creation of an international military tribunal for war criminals. This led to the establishment of the Nuremberg Tribunal, which focused on prosecuting high-level German officials. The tribunal held *individuals* responsible for (1) *crimes against peace*, which included planning, initiating, and launching a war of aggression; (2) war crimes, such as murder, abuse, and the destruction of private property and residential areas; and (3) crimes against humanity, including murder, enslavement, extermination, and deportation. The *Genocide Convention*, adopted by the UN Geneva Assembly in 1948, was a direct outgrowth of the Nuremberg Tribunal.[13]

genocide ■
Systematic mass murder of an ethnic, religious, or national group based on discriminatory preconceptions

Khmer Rouge ■
Communist government of Cambodia that slaughtered over a million people in its rural pacification programs

Nuremberg Tribunal ■ Created after World War II to punish Nazi aggression and genocide

London Agreement ■ Created an international war tribunal after World War II

war crimes ■
Include murder, the destruction of public property, and other abuses

crimes against humanity ■
Inhuman acts committed against civilians by states and individuals

Similar to Nazi Germany, Japan committed numerous atrocities, including the murder of prisoners, the extermination of civilians, sexual slavery, forced labor, and the use of humans in deadly medical experiments. Following America's defeat in the Philippines, Japan forced U.S. and Filipino troops to participate in the gruesome *Bataan Death March*, which resulted in the deaths of around ten thousand Filipino troops and six hundred American troops. Japan also committed crimes against Chinese civilians and soldiers. Even today, many Chinese continue to be suspicious of Japan. They talk about the indiscriminate bombings on Shanghai and other cities. But they are especially emotional when they recall the *Rape of Nanking*. Japanese soldiers, in October 1937, randomly raped, murdered, and executed Chinese civilians. Estimates of those killed range from forty-two thousand to one hundred thousand. On July 26, 1945, the United States, China, Britain, and the Soviet Union issued the Potsdam Declaration, stating their decision to prosecute Japanese war criminals. *U.S. General Douglas MacArthur*, the Supreme Commander for the Allied Powers in Japan, acting under the authority of the United States, established the *International Military Tribunal for the Far East* (Tokyo Tribunal) to try individuals for crimes against peace. Because the United States was primarily responsible for defeating Japan, Americans unilaterally created the Tokyo Tribunal.[14]

Potsdam Declaration
■ Announced the prosecution of Japanese war criminals after World War II

The Nuremberg and Tokyo Tribunals set the precedent for prosecuting war criminals in the former Yugoslavia and Rwanda. The disintegration of Yugoslavia in the 1990s and escalating conflicts among the Serbs, Croats, and Muslims culminated in widespread atrocities. Although all three ethnic groups committed war crimes and crimes against humanity, the dominant Serbs were clearly the most responsible for atrocities that included summary executions, torture, raping women as a weapon of war, mass internments, deportation and displacement of civilians, the inhumane treatment of prisoners, and the indiscriminate shelling of cities and villages. More than seven thousand unarmed Muslim men and boys were systematically executed near the Bosnian town of Srebrenica in July 1995. Roughly 740,000 ethnic Albanians were forcibly deported from Kosovo in 1999, and hundreds of Albanians disappeared or were murdered. The UN Security Council responded by establishing the *International Criminal Tribunal for the Former Yugoslavia* on May 25, 1993.[15] Based in The Hague, in the Netherlands, the tribunal indicted leading Serbians, including Serbian President Slobodan Milosevic, Radovan Karadzic, General Ratko Mladic, and Radislav Krstic for committing war crimes. Similarly, ethnic conflicts, primarily between Hutu extremists and Tutsis and moderate Hutus, in 1993 and 1994, stunned the world. Hutus systematically killed and raped. Almost one million people were slaughtered. Genocide in Rwanda led to the creation of the *International Tribunal for the Prosecution of Persons Responsible for Genocide in Rwanda (the Rwanda Tribunal)*. Ethnic conflicts and the accompanying atrocities have influenced the global community to establish the ICC as a permanent institution to prosecute those accused of war crimes and genocide.

Srebrenica ■ Bosnian town where over seven thousand unarmed Muslims were executed in 1995

Slobodan Milosevic
■ Former Serbian president prosecuted for war crimes

Hutu Extremists ■ Responsible for the genocide committed against over a million Rwandans in the early 1990s

ICC ■ Created to try to punish individuals responsible for crimes against humanity

The International Criminal Court

On April 11, 2002—more than fifty years after the victorious allies in World War II proposed the creation of a permanent international court to prosecute war criminals and others who engage in gross violations of human rights—the **ICC** was created. The International Court of Justice (ICJ), or World Court, based in The Hague, had been created in 1945 to adjudicate disputes between states. Individuals, however, came before tribunals established on an *ad hoc basis* to try specific crimes against humanity. Examples are the Nuremberg and Tokyo Tribunals and the tribunals for Yugoslavia and Rwanda.

The globalization of human rights laid the foundation of new thinking about bringing violators of human rights to justice, regardless of where they committed their crimes. The world, less preoccupied by ideological rivalries, turned its attention to issues ordinary people confront daily, including widespread atrocities. Small countries, unable to unilaterally deal with crimes against humanity, stressed the need to create a permanent ICC. At the request of Trinidad and Tobago and several other Caribbean and Latin American countries, the UN General Assembly asked the International Law Commission to return to the work it had started in 1948 to create an ICC.[16] Drawbacks of the country-by-country approach to prosecuting war crimes, genocide, and crimes against humanity had become increasingly obvious. The *two major drawbacks* were that (1) it was expensive and time consuming to create new tribunals and (2) securing the unanimous consent of the five permanent members of the UN Security Council (the United States, Britain, France, Russia, and China) was very difficult. More than 160 countries and numerous NGOs, many of which worked closely with smaller states, gathered in Rome in 1998 to create a tribunal with universal jurisdiction. The United States, which had initially signed the agreement under the Clinton administration, later renounced its involvement in creating the court under the Bush administration.[17]

Several leaders have been accused of violating human rights by the ICC. As we discuss in Chapter 14, Slobodan Milosevic of Yugoslavia was tried by the ICC and died in prison in The Hague. Charles Taylor of Liberia was convicted of crimes against humanity in 2011. An arrest warrant was issued for Omar al-Bashir of the Sudan for war crimes in Darfur, and Muammar Qaddafi was accused of violating human rights by deliberately using armed forces to kill civilians who protested for democracy. Three prominent Kenyans were on trial in 2011 for gross violations of human rights following a disputed election in 2007. Laurent Gbagbo, former president of Côte d'Ivoire, was also indicted by the ICC for human rights violations following a dispute about the 2010 election.

ICJ ■ World Court created to adjudicate disputes between states

WOMEN AND HUMAN RIGHTS

Images of Brazil, especially of sophisticated cities like Rio de Janeiro, portray women as enjoying equal rights and personal freedoms. But images can be deceptive. It took the Brazilian Congress twenty-six years to change the country's legal code to make women equal to men under the law. The new code, adopted in 2001, outlaws a provision that had allowed a husband to annul a marriage if he discovered that his wife was not a virgin when they were married. It also eliminates laws that allowed Brazilian fathers to have unrestricted legal rights to make decisions for their family.[18] Although women are clearly not a monolithic group and do not face the same restrictions across all societies, even where laws support hierarchical patriarchy, the global community embraces the view that most women face violations of their rights. Women's rights are widely regarded as a category of human rights that deserve special attention.

Human rights for women are directly and strongly influenced by how women perceive themselves and how others perceive them. Perceptions help to determine our role in society. Roles can be defined as expectations regarding the skills, rights, and responsibilities of individuals. Women's roles are closely connected to their lower status (compared with men) in virtually all societies. Status refers to one's position in the social, economic, and political hierarchy. The struggle for women's rights is as old as the struggle for human rights in general. Some people have always advocated equal treatment of men and women. International organizations composed primarily of women led the struggle for suffrage and various social policies. The 2011 Nobel Peace Prize was awarded to three women from Africa and the Arab world in recognition of their non-violent activism for women's rights: Liberian President Ellen Johnson Sirleaf, Liberian peace activist Leymah Gbowee, and Yemeni pro-democracy campaigner Tawakul Karman. The Nobel panel citation said, "We cannot achieve democracy and lasting peace in the world unless women obtain the same opportunities as men to influence developments at all levels of society." In earlier years, women were instrumental in getting protections for women written into the UN Charter and in the establishment of the UN Commission on the Status of Women. Increased emphasis was placed on women's rights as human rights in the 1970s. The UN Fund for Women was created by the UN General Assembly to support women in grassroots organizations. In 1981, the UN Convention on the Elimination of All Forms of Discrimination Against Women was adopted, thereby reaffirming the view that women's rights should receive special attention within broader discussions of human rights. The Women's Conference in Beijing in 1995 and the UN Forum of Women in New York in 2000, among others, underscore a growing global consensus on women's rights. The Entity for Gender Equality and Empowerment of Women, known as UN Women, was created in 2010 to advance women's rights. It is headed by the former president of Chile, Michelle Bachelet.

status ■ Refers to one's social, economic, or political position in society

Sexual Violence: Rape as a Weapon of War

Sexual violence against women has always been an integral part of most societies. Trafficking in women and children (i.e., buying and selling women as sex slaves) was outlawed at the global level by the *Convention for the Suppression of the Traffic in Persons and of the Exploitation of the Prostitution of Others* in 1949. Millions of women and children are victims of sexual violence within their own societies, and millions more are trafficked across national borders. Prior to the devastating earthquake in Haiti in 2010, it was estimated that 50 percent of Haitian women had been raped. After the earthquake, the rate increased to roughly 70 percent, due to lawlessness, homelessness, and conditions associated with incredible poverty.

Sexual violence against women is often built into the legal system as well as the social structure of many countries. Men routinely kill women to protect the family's honor or their own. In Jordan, Pakistan, Iraq, and other Islamic countries, honor killing, though illegal, is sustained by tradition and religion. Rape is often treated as a crime against the family, an approach that makes the woman who was raped guilty of dishonoring her family. Only in 1996 did Italy change its laws to emphasize that rape is a crime against the woman as opposed to being an offense against her family. Italy also recently abolished laws that enabled a rapist to avoid punishment by agreeing to marry the woman he had raped. Another example of how tradition, religion, and the law perpetuate sexual violence against women is the case of Zafran Bibi in Pakistan. While Zafran's husband was in prison, his brother raped her repeatedly. When she gave birth to a daughter, she was charged with adultery and sentenced to death by stoning. No charges were brought against her brother-in-law because, under Islamic laws in Pakistan, rape can be proved only with the testimony of four male witnesses. Domestic and global pressure persuaded General Pervez Musharraf, Pakistan's president, to force the court to overturn Zafran's death sentence.[19]

The emergence of rape during conflicts as a direct human rights issue reflects the growth of humanitarian international law as well as the willingness of women, especially the victims, to demand justice. For example, Koreans who were used as "comfort women" and subjected to sexual slavery by the Japanese military during World War II demanded justice from the Japanese government. Sexual enslavement is often used as an instrument of ethnic cleansing. Sexual violence is used to humiliate and destroy families and communities, to terrorize members of a particular ethnic group, and to force people to flee an area. Serb troops raped more than twenty thousand Muslim women in the former Yugoslavia as part of their ethnic-cleansing campaign. Rape of girls and women in the Democratic Republic of the Congo escalated as that country's ethnic warfare continued to rage. Rape as a weapon of war continues as violence remains widespread in the Congo. These atrocities helped to firmly establish global recognition of rape as a crime against humanity and as a war crime. Zoran Vukovic, Dragoljub Kunarac, and Radomir Kovac (Bosnian Serbs) were found guilty of such crimes by the Tribunal for Yugoslavia in The Hague in 2001. Genocidal rape is recognized as a crime against humanity by the ICC. The absence of functioning judicial systems makes prosecutions of rape rare. The American Bar Association works with rape victims to help them bring their cases to court in eastern Congo.[20]

ethnic cleansing
■ Violence based on race, ethnicity, sex, religion, or other social issues

ISLAM AND HUMAN RIGHTS

Negative stereotypes of Muslims and Islam are so prevalent and so profound in most Western societies that even isolated cases of human rights violations are perceived as reflections of a profound inability of Islamic countries to respect human rights. Such images are reinforced by extremists in Saudi Arabia, Afghanistan under the Taliban, Iran, and Northern Nigeria, for example. The general lack of a clear separation of religion and government and the dominance of Shari'a law as the foundation for legal codes in Islamic countries convey the impression of traditional societies that are fossilized, changing very little since the Prophet Muhammad (570–632 A.D.) founded the religion. But compared with Western societies, Islamic countries are far more repressive and disrespectful of fundamental rights and freedoms, as the popular uprisings in the Middle East and North Africa in

Islam is being challenged by forces within Muslim societies. Nobel Peace Prize winner Shirin Ebadi is an Iranian who promotes human rights in her country.

2010–2011 demonstrate. Saudi Arabia—Muhammad's birthplace and keeper of Islam's holiest places, Mecca and Medina, which are sacred to Muslims worldwide—is perhaps the most repressive Islamic society. But Islam's spread made it a global religion long before the emergence of Western Europe as a dominant power and the subsequent spread of Christianity. Consequently, Islam is diverse and complex, reflecting how very different cultures interpret and practice the religion. The decentralization of Islam undermines efforts to portray the Islamic world, especially regarding human rights, as monolithic. It is also useful to distinguish the policies of governments from the aspirations of ordinary citizens to enjoy basic freedoms.

Although Islamic cultures are composed of numerous beliefs and values that promote humanitarianism and respect for some forms of human rights, the religion emphasizes the priority of the Islamic community over the individual. Under the Koran, the ruler and the ruled are equal before God. However, unlike in Britain, for example, where limitations on the monarch were formalized into contracts, such as the Magna Carta, most Islamic countries did not develop formal institutions to restrain leaders and define their powers and responsibilities or to make them accountable to the people. As we discuss in Chapter 4, this lack of formal limits on power was prevalent throughout the world. Only a few countries were democratic. This enabled rulers to interpret the Koran in ways that served their own interests. The Western belief that each individual has natural rights stood in sharp contrast to the Islamic belief that the community mattered most and that God's law did not permit individuals to think for themselves. Justice, in Islam, is derived from obedience to God's commands as expressed in the Koran. In effect, challenging political authorities is tantamount to challenging the supremacy of religious thinking.[21] Even so, Islam is being challenged by forces within Muslim societies. In 2003, Shirin Ebadi won the Nobel Peace Prize for her efforts to promote human rights in Iran. Viewed as a threat by the Iranian government, her own rights continued to be routinely violated.

FIGHTING TERRORISM AND PROTECTING HUMAN RIGHTS

Believing that short-term restrictions on civil and political rights are essential to combat terrorism, many governments find themselves on a slippery slope that leads to more durable infringements on democratic freedoms. Britain, for example, responded in the early 1970s to Northern Ireland's Troubles, as the conflicts between the Protestants and Catholics are called, with increased arrests, essentially arbitrary detentions, increased surveillance capabilities, the creation of a special court to prosecute terrorist suspects, approval of inhumane treatment of prisoners, and excessive military force. Apart from having the unintended consequence of inflaming passions and escalating terrorism, British actions were scrutinized and severely criticized by the global community and within Britain itself. The European Court of Human Rights ruled against Britain in several cases, contending that it had violated the European Convention on Human Rights. Following the terrorist attacks in London in 2005, Britain adopted several policies that were perceived as threats to human rights.

Alan Dershowitz, a Harvard University law professor and a leading criminal defense lawyer, argues in favor of using nonlethal torture in extreme cases and of issuing torture warrants by judges.[22] Dershowitz posed the "ticking bomb" scenario. Imagine that you are a government official and you know that a bomb capable of killing thousands of people is about to be used by terrorists. You are almost certain that a suspect knows where the bomb is and believe that by torturing the suspect you can extract crucial information to save lives. Would you torture or support this suspect's torturing under these circumstances? Democratic societies routinely condemn other societies that torture people. No country, not even an authoritarian regime, openly admits to torturing its citizens. Some argue that legalization of torture in the United States would encourage its wider use and seriously erode democratic principles that are the country's foundations. Furthermore, the effectiveness of torturing individuals in the long- and short-term is highly debatable.

Alan Dershowitz ■ Argued for the use of nonlethal torture to gather information from terrorists

In the war against terrorism, the United States significantly altered its policy on human rights abroad. Prisoners taken during the war in Afghanistan were subject to "stress and duress" techniques, including sleep deprivation, physical abuse, hooding, waterboarding (simulated drowning), and being forced to hold awkward positions for long periods of time. Many prisoners held at the U.S. military base in Guantanamo Bay in Cuba were denied access to lawyers and their families. Some prisoners were transferred to countries that are not only strategically located but also known to violate human rights, including Pakistan and Uzbekistan. Widespread

Abu Ghraib ■
U.S.-run prison in
Iraq infamous for
abuse committed
against Iraqi war
detainees

abuse of prisoners held at Abu Ghraib in Iraq was vividly demonstrated by numerous photographs and videotapes that shocked the world in 2004 and undermined American credibility in promoting human rights, especially in the Islamic world. Some prisoners were killed, tortured, or suffered from inhumane treatment and degradation. U.S. Army dogs were used to abuse Iraqi prisoners.

THE DEATH PENALTY AND HUMAN RIGHTS

There is a growing consensus that the death penalty violates the most fundamental human right: the right to life. Several countries have outlawed the execution of teenagers. In Yemen, often criticized for violating human rights, the government abolished the death penalty for individuals under eighteen years. Only Saudi Arabia, Iran, Nigeria, and Pakistan allow teenagers to be executed. The United States executed teenagers until 2005, when the U.S. Supreme Court outlawed the practice. After briefly suspending executions in 2007 and early 2008, the U.S. Supreme Court reinstated executions by lethal injections in 2008. Japan, which typically executes five or six prisoners each year, has been criticized by Amnesty International and other groups for its secretive and sometimes sudden executions. Many prisoners are told of their execution only moments before they are hanged. Europeans are generally shocked by Americans' strong endorsement of the death penalty and will not extradite anyone to America if they face the death penalty. European societies abolished the death penalty in the latter half of the twentieth century, mostly in the early 1960s.

Gay rights marchers such as these in California have focused global attention on the human rights of homosexual individuals.

►CASE STUDY | Homosexuals and Human Rights

In December 2010, the United Nations passed a resolution to protect the human rights of homosexuals. Discrimination and violence against gays, lesbians, bisexuals, and transgendered people constitute a major global issue. America's debates on gays in the military and gay marriage and civil unions have helped focus global attention on the treatment of individuals based solely on their sexual orientation. The issue of human rights of homosexuals is fundamentally about the right of privacy and the right to be left alone. Think of all the groups of people, social relationships, and behaviors that were not approved by the majority of members of society but are now widely accepted. Social norms, attitudes, and traditions continue to be powerful impediments to implementing human rights for homosexuals. Human rights abuses are particularly severe in developing countries. General intolerance, low levels of education, and disregard for many democratic freedoms create an environment that is conducive for discrimination and violence. Roughly eighty countries criminalize consensual homosexual sex. Some countries, including Iran and Nigeria, impose the death sentence for men and up to a hundred lashes for women found guilty of homosexuality. In addition to legal corporal punishment, there are numerous cases of extrajudicial executions, kidnappings, rape, torture, and violence. Few governments in the developing world actively prosecute individuals for these violations.

Demographic factors are contributing to global tolerance of homosexuals and the active promotion of their human rights. Younger people, influenced by significant cultural change that characterized the 1960s and 1970s, are generally supportive of diversity, including sexual orientation. Their attitudes and behaviors are reinforced by cultural globalization, especially the Internet, television, movies, and magazines. Easy access to information enables individuals to make independent choices and to challenge conventional cultural values. College,

the workplace, sports, and the military, for example, bring people together from diverse backgrounds, which helps create awareness of different lifestyles and foster greater tolerance. Furthermore, many individuals interact with homosexuals as family members, colleagues, friends, and neighbors.

Economic globalization, as we will see in Chapter 7, engenders relentless competition for talented individuals, regardless of race, gender, nationality, or sexual orientation. Companies, like sports teams, that discriminate against individuals including homosexuals put themselves at a severe competitive disadvantage and make themselves vulnerable to global pressure and legal action. Furthermore, many leaders of global companies are part of the younger generation that generally rejects all forms of discrimination and values diversity and tolerance. Economic globalization also enables human rights organizations and gay rights groups to exert considerable pressure on governments that abuse human rights. Regional influences also help to determine respect for the human rights of homosexuals. In Europe, for example, the European Court of Human Rights found Poland guilty of discrimination against homosexuals. Mexico City (Mexico), Argentina, and Brazil have advanced gay and lesbian rights in Latin America.

America took a significant step toward protecting the rights of homosexuals when it repealed its policy of allowing homosexuals to serve in the military as long as they did not reveal their sexual orientation (also known as "Don't Ask, Don't Tell"). Most Americans disagreed with the policy and supported repealing it. In many ways, the struggle for human rights for homosexuals is reminiscent of the struggle to integrate the U.S. military. Experiences with successfully integrating the U.S. military after World War II played a pivotal role in the struggle to end segregation and discrimination in America. South Africa, which experienced pervasive human rights abuses under its system of rigid segregation and harsh discrimination known as apartheid, is the first

(*continued*)

country to ban discrimination in its constitution. It is the only country in Africa to allow gay marriage. The cases of the United States and South Africa demonstrate that countries that end discrimination, promote tolerance, and value diversity in relation to a particular group of people generally become more inclusive and respectful of human rights for the rest of their citizens. As we saw in Chapter 2, countries that are open, diverse, tolerant, and free are generally prosperous, innovative, and powerful. ◣

SUMMARY AND REVIEW

The promotion of universal human rights worldwide has become an increasingly contentious topic. This chapter examined how the progression and promotion of human rights have occurred within the broader political, economic, and cultural aspects of globalization. The concept of human rights has been significantly strengthened in recent history, especially with the growth of multilateral human rights NGOs, such as Amnesty International and Human Rights Watch, and international human rights–based institutions, such as the ICC and the UNCHR. Protecting human rights is no longer seen as an exclusively national issue, but one of global magnitude and scope. We examined the importance of and distinctions among civil, political, and social rights, as well as the distinction between positive and negative human rights. We also identified factors that have contributed to the expansion of human rights globally, including the globalization of human rights through the creation and strengthening of international institutions, the growing acceptance of interdependence among states, the international proliferation of democracy, the strengthening of human rights through economic development and corporate globalization, and the increasing effectiveness of nonstate actors dedicated to promoting human rights.

KEY TERMS

civil rights 44
political rights 44
social rights 44
Holocaust 44
Westphalian 45
prisoners of conscience 45
corporate social responsibility 46
market-building strategy 46
cost-minimizing strategy 46
Stoics 46
universal rights 46
Cicero 46
Magna Carta 47
due process of law 47
habeas corpus 47
Second Treatise on Government 47
social contract 47
utilitarianism 47

Principles of Morals and Legislation 47
Bill of Rights 47
On Liberty 47
legal positivists 48
Adolf Hitler 48
Anti-Slavery Society 48
four freedoms 49
Universal Declaration of Human Rights (UDHR) 49
International Covenant on Civil and Political Rights (ICCPR) 49
negative rights 49
International Covenant on Economic, Social, and Cultural Rights (ICESCR) 49
cultural relativism 50
Confucianism 50
UN Commission on Human Rights (UNCHR) 51

DISCUSSION QUESTIONS

1. Can you explain the differences between relativistic and universal human rights? How are they different in their scope and normative assumptions?
2. What are the differences between positive and negative human rights? How are positive and negative human rights related to the ICCPR and the ICESCR?
3. Are sanctions an effective weapon for promoting human rights? If so, how are they effective? If not, how do they hurt human rights?
4. What is ethnic cleansing? How was it used in Rwanda and Yugoslavia?
5. What is humanitarian intervention? Give examples.

SUGGESTED READINGS

Esposito, John L. *The Future of Islam.* New York: Oxford University Press, 2010. Addresses major questions posed by many Westerners about Islam and shows the close relationship between Islam, Judaism, and Christianity.

Feinstein, Lee, and Tod Lindberg. *Means to an End: U.S. Interest in the International Criminal Court.* Washington, DC: Brookings Institution Press, 2009. The United States should rethink its opposition to the International Criminal Court.

Haugen, Gary, and Victor Boutros. "And Justice for All: Enforcing Human Rights for the World's Poor," *Foreign Affairs* 89, No. 3 (May/June 2010): 51–62. The problem for the poor is that many human rights laws are not enforced, due partly to lawlessness and government corruption.

Mazower, Mark. *No Enchanted Palace: The End of Empire and the Ideological Origins of the United Nations.* Princeton, NJ: Princeton University Press, 2009. Argues that Victorian-era imperial internationalism rather than a pristine liberal vision of universal rights led to the creation of the United Nations.

Simmons, Beth A. *Mobilizing for Human Rights.* Cambridge, UK: Cambridge University Press, 2009. Beliefs that the sovereignty of states allowed them to abuse human rights have been replaced by a new international obligation to protect human rights.

ENDNOTES

1. Seyom Brown, *Human Rights in World Politics* (New York: Longman, 2000), 22.
2. Andrew Hurrell, "Power, Principles, and Prudence," in *Human Rights in Global Politics*, eds. Tim Dunne and Nicholas J. Wheeler (Cambridge, UK: Cambridge University Press, 1999), 279.
3. Stephanie Strom, "When Business Is Good," *New York Times*, 22 February 2011, B1.
4. Michael A. Santoro, *Profits and Principles: Global Capitalism and Human Rights in China* (Ithaca, NY: Cornell University Press, 2000), 29.
5. Marcus Tullius Cicero, *De Re Publica*, translated by Clinton Walker Keyes (Cambridge, MA: Harvard University Press, 1943), 385.
6. Micheline Ishay, *The History of Human Rights* (Berkeley: University of California Press, 2008).
7. Brown, *Human Rights*, 59.
8. Edmund Burke, *Reflections on the Revolution in France* (New York: Holt, Rinehart and Winston, 1959), 37.
9. Yves Beigbeder, *Judging War Criminals* (New York: St. Martin's Press, 1999), 18.
10. Asbjorn Eide, "The Historical Significance of the Universal Declaration," *International Social Science Journal* 50, No. 4 (December 1998), 478.
11. Gareth Evans, *Responsibility to Protect* (Washington, DC: Brookings Institution Press, 2008).
12. Beigbeder, *Judging War Criminals*, 28.
13. Beigbeder, *Judging War Criminals*, 34.
14. Beigbeder, *Judging War Criminals*, 55.
15. Theodor Meron, "Answering for War Crimes," *Foreign Affairs* 76, No. 1 (January/February 1997), 2.
16. David Wippman, "Can an International Criminal Court Prevent and Punish Genocide?" in *Protection Against Genocide*, ed. Neal Riemer (Westport, CT: Praeger, 2000), 89.
17. Lee Feinstein and Tod Lindberg, *Means to an End: U.S. Interest in the International Criminal Court* (Washington, DC: Brookings Institution Press, 2009).
18. Larry Rohter, "Brazil Passes Equal Rights for Its Women," *New York Times*, 19 August 2001, A9.
19. Seth Mydans, "Sentenced to Death, Rape Victim Is Freed by Pakistani Court," *New York Times*, 6 June 2002, A4.
20. "Violence Against Women," *Economist*, 15 January 2011, 63.
21. John L. Esposito, *The Future of Islam* (New York: Oxford University Press, 2010).
22. "Is Torture Ever Justified?" *Economist*, 11 January 2003, 9.

Promoting Democracy

Democracy is spreading at the global level and there have been democratic revolutions in the Middle East and

INTRODUCTION

Transitions to democracy in the Middle East and North Africa mark a pivotal development of the twenty-first century: one that will have significant global implications. Demographic changes, the rise of a new middle class, economic stagnation, government corruption and repression, and the spread of communications technologies contributed to spontaneous popular uprisings against entrenched political patriarchs. These democratic revolutions were clearly influenced by young people's awareness of life in other parts of the world. The Internet is an integral component of their lives. Social networks such as Facebook and Twitter undermined government control and enabled people to effectively organize mass protests.

Globalization has been, and remains, a potent force in the spread of democratic values and practices. The growth of the British Empire was accompanied by the spread of democracy to India, the English-speaking Caribbean, the United States, and Canada. America's rise as a superpower further consolidated the globalization of democracy, despite its embrace of some repressive regimes during the Cold War. But America's struggle against the Soviet Union ultimately helped to strengthen the emergence of democracy in Eastern Europe and in Russia itself. At the beginning of the twentieth century, there were few democracies, mostly in Western Europe and North America. There are now more than ninety democracies. Transitions to democracy have occurred around the world: in Africa, Asia, and Latin America. Globalization also contributes to weakening the power of centralized government and helps to empower citizens by fostering economic prosperity, the acquisition of private property, and the growth of the middle class.

This chapter examines factors that contribute to the growth and maintenance of democratic societies. We will analyze the roles of global civil society and the United States in facilitating and encouraging transitions to democracy, paying special attention to America's decision to impose democracy through military intervention and by occupying Iraq. Transitions to democracy in Latin America and Russia are also discussed. We will analyze how globalization is leading to greater global governance and spawning demands for more democracy at the global level. The chapter concludes with a case study of democratic transitions in the Middle East and North Africa.

democracy ■ Government that reflects the will of the people

direct self-government ■ Direct participation in the democratic process

indirect/ representative democracy ■ Democracy run through indirect means, such as elections and representatives

DEMOCRACY

A basic definition of democracy is rule by the people. Democracy in ancient Greece was a form of direct self-government, meaning that people voted directly on issues that affected them. Modern democratic societies practice indirect, or representative, democracy. Citizens elect representatives who vote for them and safeguard their interests.

Two questions that often arise are: Who will govern, and how will the interests of various groups and segments of the population be protected and advanced?

There are two dominant approaches to dealing with these questions. The first emphasizes that the majority of the people decide who will govern and who will benefit. Government by the people is synonymous with majority rule. This approach, practiced globally, is the majoritarian model of democracy. The second approach, also widely practiced, embraces the concept of majority rule but attempts to include as many of the people as possible in the decision-making process. The underlying objectives are to enlarge the size of the majority and to obtain widespread support for government policies. This approach is called the consensus model of democracy. The consensus model uses a system of proportional representation in which both majorities and minorities are represented because seats in elective bodies are determined by the proportion or percentage of votes received.[1] But neither the majoritarian nor the consensus model of democracy guarantees the functioning of liberal democracy, which is defined by limitations on the power of elected officials, freedom of speech, freedom of the press, the right to peacefully assemble, protection of private property, freedom of religion, protection of the rights of unpopular minorities, and respect for the rule of law.

Fully developed democracies are characterized by constitutional liberalism: that is, a commitment to protecting individuals' rights, freedoms, and dignity from abuse by the government, institutions, society as a whole, and other individuals. The basis for constitutional liberalism can be found in many societies, the most prominent being the Magna Carta of 1215, the English Bill of Rights of 1688, the American Declaration of Independence, and the American Constitution. The Helsinki Final Act of 1975—which focused on basic human rights such as freedom of speech, freedom of religion, and freedom of assembly—represents a continuation of the tradition of constitutional liberalism.

A constitution is defined as the fundamental framework or basic law of a country. A constitution assigns powers and responsibilities to government institutions, indicates how decision makers are to be selected, defines the scope of government authority, establishes the nature of the relationship between the people and their government, and has provisions for making political leaders accountable to the people. Central to democratic constitutions is the concept of the rule of law, which means that no person is above the law and that individuals are treated equally under the law.

Most democratic societies have either a presidential or a parliamentary form of democracy. The United States is the best example of the presidential democracy. The framers of the U.S. Constitution decided to have a clear separation of executive, legislative, and judicial powers and to provide for a system of checks and balances among these distinct branches of government. The parliamentary democracy is most strongly associated with Britain. There is no clear separation of powers in the parliamentary system. The prime minister—the chief executive—is an elected member of parliament who is chosen by the majority party in parliament for the leadership position.[2]

Political Participation and Democracy

Political participation entails communicating with elected officials and others in government—expressing viewpoints and demanding certain actions or public policies from the government. Vehicles for political participation include political

---

majoritarian model ■ The majority of the citizens decide who will govern

consensus model ■ Focuses on achieving widespread support for government policies

proportional representation ■ Political and electoral system under which both majorities and minorities are represented

liberal democracy ■ Defined by limitations on power of government and protections of civil liberties

constitutional liberalism ■ Government committed to ensuring individual rights and freedoms through constitutional protections

constitution ■ Framework of laws designed to designate specific powers and responsibilities to governmental institutions

rule of law ■ Mandatory adherence to state laws

presidential democracy ■ Democracy that elects a president to the executive level of government

parliamentary democracy ■ Governing system with no separation of powers

conventional participation ■
Traditional political activities, such as voting

unconventional participation ■
Engaging in less acceptable political activities, such as protesting

political parties ■
Competitive political groups that seek to win government positions and offices

loyal opposition ■
Antagonistic party in electoral politics that accepts the legitimacy of the ruling majority

interest group ■
Organization of individuals with common interests who attempt to influence public policy

civil society ■
Networks of social relations and structures that exist independently of the government

global civil society ■
Individuals and organizations that operate across national borders

parties, interest groups, and a free press. Political participation can be either conventional or unconventional. Conventional participation includes voting, running for office, assisting with political campaigns, writing to elected officials, writing letters to newspapers about particular issues, and joining an interest group to influence public policies. Unconventional participation includes protests, mass demonstrations, civil disobedience, and sometimes even acts of violence.

Political parties are coalitions of interests whose primary goal is to run the government by winning competitive elections. Political parties that are successful usually appeal to a wide range of interests. In some societies, minor parties form coalitions with each other or with a major party to exert greater influence on public policy and to gain more control over the government. The functioning of the loyal opposition is important in democratic societies. It means that the party out of power criticizes the ruling majority and suggests alternative programs and policies.

An interest group, or a pressure group, is composed of individuals who share common concerns and who believe that the most effective way to achieve their objectives is to organize and engage in political activities that exert pressure on government decision makers. Interest groups are an essential component of civil society. Civil society refers to the networks of social relations and institutions that exist and act independently of government institutions. Civil society is generally seen as encompassing the wide range of settings that bring individuals together to exchange ideas; discuss issues; and organize to achieve social, political, and economic objectives. Individuals, groups, and organizations that operate across national boundaries and are linked together by common interests comprise what is referred to as global civil society.

Women's Political Participation and Democracy

In the vast majority of political systems, women's participation in politics is influenced to a large extent by their societies' perceptions of women, their roles, their status, and levels of economic development in the various countries. Another major barrier to women's involvement in politics is the widespread perception among both men and women that politics is a male activity. Najma Chowdhury and Barbara J. Nelson refer to this tendency as the "maleness of politics." They argue that politics has always been closely connected to the traditional fatherly connotation of patriarchy and to fraternalism, which essentially exclude women from political activities and power.[3] *Three main arguments are articulated in favor of increased participation of women in the democratic process*: (1) equity and democratic justice, (2) representation of women's interests, and (3) developing and making the maximum use of available human resources.[4] The *equity and democratic justice* argument rests on the widely accepted view that gender equality and fully including women in political life are prerequisites for democracy. Failure to remove impediments to women's political participation undermines the legitimacy of democratic governments and erodes public confidence in the democratic process. The *representation-of-women's-interests* argument focuses on divergent interests between men and women and the need for women to protect and promote their

> **TABLE 4.1**

Women in National Parliaments (Lower or Single House)

Rank	Country	Election Year	No. of Seats (Total)	No. of Women	% of Women
1	Rwanda	2008	80	45	56.3
2	Sweden	2010	349	157	45.0
3	South Africa	2009	400	178	44.5
4	Cuba	2008	614	265	43.2
5	Iceland	2009	63	27	42.9
6	Finland	2007	200	80	40.0
7	Norway	2009	169	67	39.6
8	Belgium	2010	150	59	39.3
8	Netherlands	2010	150	59	39.3
9	Mozambique	2009	250	98	39.2
10	Angola	2008	220	85	38.6
10	Costa Rica	2010	57	22	38.6
11	Argentina	2009	257	99	38.5
12	Denmark	2007	179	68	38.0
13	Spain	2008	350	128	36.6
14	United Republic of Tanzania	2010	350	126	36.0
15	Andorra	2009	28	10	35.7
67	United States	2010	435	73	16.8

Source: "Women in Parliaments: World Classification," *Inter-Parliamentary Union,* March 31, 2011.

interests themselves by becoming directly involved in the political system. Finally, the *using-all-available-talent* argument stresses the pragmatism of allowing women to contribute to all aspects of development, including the growth of democratic institutions and processes.

Women's political participation is increasing in mature democracies as well as in countries that are transitioning to democracy, as illustrated in Table 4.1. This development is due primarily to three factors. *First*, globalization has facilitated the emergence of global networks that heighten women's political awareness and enable them to mobilize politically at local, national, and global levels. *Second*, removing barriers to women's political participation, making deliberate efforts to recruit women into politics, and modifying electoral systems have contributed to women's inclusion in political life. *Finally*, the proliferation of women in legislative and executive positions was facilitated by the termination of the Cold War. As traditional security issues receded and domestic challenges became a priority, women effectively articulated their ability to provide leadership.[5] There are many women who lead their countries. They include Angela Merkel of Germany, Dilma Rousseff of Brazil, Ellen Johnson Sirleaf of Liberia, and Helle Thorning-Schmidt of Denmark.

Women throughout the world are increasingly taking on leadership roles. When Dilma Rousseff was sworn in, she became Brazil's first female president.

Factors Conducive to Democracy

culture ■ A set of values, beliefs, and attitudes

Culture (i.e., a set of values, beliefs, and attitudes) is one of the most important prerequisites for the growth of democracy. Cultures that foster democracy are generally characterized by tolerance for divergent viewpoints and practices, compromise, and a willingness to accept the policies voted on by the majority of citizens. Cultural factors help to explain the existence of democratic governments in the English-speaking Caribbean as well as transitions to democracy in Botswana and Nigeria. Free and fair elections in Nigeria in 2011 marked a consolidation of democratic culture. The British brought many of their democratic institutions and values with them to their colonies in the Caribbean and implemented a process of decolonization aimed at deliberately preparing the new countries for democratic government. The Westminster model (i.e., the British model of government) had been practiced to a limited degree from as early as 1639, when the House of Assembly in Barbados was created, making it the third oldest legislative body in the Western Hemisphere, preceded only by Bermuda's legislature and Virginia's House of Burgesses. British rule helped to create a culture that emphasized the rule of law. Democratic competition was embraced, and attempts were made to use government as an instrument for promoting social welfare and economic equality.

Westminster model ■ British model of government dating back to as early as 1639

The *global or regional environment* is widely perceived as playing a crucial role in either facilitating or impeding the growth of democracy. As we will see, the ideological rivalry between the East and the West essentially diminished the opportunities for countries under Soviet domination to embrace democracy. On the other hand, Spain and Portugal became democratic partly because economic, political, and cultural forces in Western Europe undermined support for authoritarian rule in those countries. Changes in the global environment that occurred with the fall of the Soviet Union and the end of the Cold War led to democratic transitions in Eastern Europe and in Russia itself. Popular uprisings for democracy in the Middle East and North Africa are reminiscent of the wave of democratic transitions in Eastern Europe.

Another major factor that is conducive to democracy is economic development. As countries achieve greater economic prosperity, integration into global markets, exposure to democratic values, higher literacy rates and increased access to education, increased urbanization, and increased knowledge of other cultures through the global media and tourism, they tend to be more receptive to democracy. Globalization also creates economic insecurity that can motivate unemployed people to seek change. The global financial crisis and the economic recession diminished economic opportunities and played a role in uprisings in the Middle East and North Africa.

> **economic development** ■ Sometimes defined as greater economic growth and integration throughout the world

Finally, the emergence of a strong middle class is perceived as an important factor conducive to the growth of democracy and is closely related to economic development. Increased national wealth generally expands the middle class, which many people believe is essential to the acquisition and maintenance of democratic values. People who are middle class are better educated, have greater economic security, are generally less dependent on governments, tend to participate in politics to protect their interests and to hold government accountable, are unwilling to allow governments to violate their rights, and have greater confidence in their abilities to govern themselves.

> **middle class** ■ Class in capitalist society between the lower and upper classes

Promoting Democracy

The disintegration of the Soviet Union removed a significant obstacle to creating and strengthening democratic practices globally. Although the United States had formed alliances with undemocratic governments during the Cold War, it became the primary proponent of exporting democracy when that conflict ended. Many Western governments made the promotion of democracy a prerequisite for assistance. Representatives from more than half of the world's countries met in Warsaw, Poland, to exchange ideas on how to create a global community of democracies. They signed the Warsaw Declaration, which committed them to promoting democracy in countries lacking it and strengthening democracy in countries that were building it. This development and other actions clearly underscored a growing global consensus that promoting democracy is a global priority.[6]

> **Warsaw Declaration** ■ Global declaration made after the fall of the Soviet Union aiming at the proliferation of global democracy

Global Civil Society and the Promotion of Democracy

Global civil society transcends national boundaries. It consists of organizations and individuals who attempt to influence politics both within countries and globally. Economic, cultural, political, educational, technological, and other networks

CIVICUS ■
Organization of over
five hundred NGOs

Carter Center ■
Created to assist in
global conflict
resolution,
development, and
the promotion of
democracy

Varela Project ■
Cuban grassroots
campaign demanding
democratic reforms
in Cuba

combine to constitute global civil society. These nonstate voluntary associations blur distinctions between domestic and global political activities. Many cooperate with grassroots activists to effectuate democratic change. Increasingly, they are uniting to maximize their impact on governments. For example, CIVICUS consists of more than five hundred nongovernmental organizations (NGOs). The World Forum for Democracy, the National Endowment for Democracy (NED), and Transparency International also bring together many NGOs, a development reflecting the realities of globalization. Global civil society provides basic civic education, organizes and funds political parties and interest groups, assists with writing constitutions, observes and mediates elections, and lends credibility to the process of democratization among other activities. One of the most outspoken proponents of building global civil society and promoting democracy is former U.S. President Jimmy Carter.

Jimmy Carter made strengthening human rights and democracy a central component of America's foreign policy while he was president. He championed these causes with even greater passion, energy, and commitment after leaving office. He has monitored elections around the world and has served as an interlocutor in international crises involving the United States in, for example, Haiti and North Korea. He was also the first U.S. president since Calvin Coolidge (1928) to visit Cuba. In 1982, he founded the Carter Center, which is affiliated with Emory University in Atlanta, Georgia, to assist in conflict resolution and global development and to promote democracy globally. In 2002, Carter visited Cuba, and addressing the nation in Spanish on Cuba's only television network, he called on Fidel Castro and his government to implement democratic practices. Carter contacted leading Cuban dissidents, such as Oswaldo Payá and Elizardo Sánchez, who launched the Varela Project. That prodemocracy grassroots campaign collected more than eleven thousand signatures supporting demands for the Cuban National Assembly to hold a referendum on democratic reforms. The Varela Project was named in honor of Felix Varela, a Cuban-born priest who opposed slavery and spent three decades in New York as an advocate of the poor until his death in 1853. Castro's illness sparked renewed discussions about transitions to democracy in Cuba under new leadership. Castro's decision to relinquish power to his brother Raul Castro contributed to some economic and political reforms, including the release of political prisoners and encouraging private enterprises. Changes in U.S. policy toward Cuba, including easing restraints on travel to Cuba and allowing Cuban Americans to send more money to relatives in Cuba, offer hope for a transition to democracy.

Private foundations, as well as foundations connected to governments, are components of civil society involved in building democracy. Foundations not only control significant financial resources but also have experience working with other parts of civil society. Examples of such foundations are the NED, the Adenauer Foundation, the Ebert Foundation, the Ford Foundation, and the Seidel Stiftung Foundation. George Soros and his foundations played a prominent role in assisting democratization projects in Central Europe. Soros decided to provide resources quickly and to involve people at the local levels in the decision-making process.[7]

Minor political and economic reforms took place in Cuba after Fidel Castro, left, turned over leadership of the Communist-run country to his brother Raul. They are pictured at the Communist Party Congress in Havana, Cuba.

The Promotion of Democracy by the United States

Throughout its history, America has vacillated between splendid isolation, believing that it was a beacon on a hill providing light and direction to less fortunate societies, and military intervention to enforce its version of democracy in other countries. From its inception, the United States equated its perception of morality with universal ideals and often mobilized its vast resources to implement its socially constructed reality elsewhere. President Woodrow Wilson articulated America's involvement in World War I as a mission for democracy, as a struggle to secure the rights of individuals and for self-determination in small countries, and as a fight to make the world free. American attempts to promote democracy are inextricably linked to an entrenched ideology (i.e., set of beliefs that are often impervious to objective reality and verifiable facts). An ideological approach invariably oversimplifies reality by ignoring or downplaying obvious historical and contemporary contradictory developments.

The ideological polarization and military tensions that characterized the East–West struggle had many direct consequences for democratization. As Steven W. Hook observed, "The actual conduct of U.S. foreign policy reflected a consequential ethic that regarded anticommunism as a moral end in itself, one that superseded the means by which the outcome was achieved."[8] In the Cold War context, the United States believed that preventing the spread of communism justified both abandoning support for democratic principles and forming alliances with undemocratic governments in Africa, Asia, the Middle East, and Latin America.

Woodrow Wilson ■ Idealist U.S. president who articulated the U.S. role throughout the world as one of a leader in democracy and self-determination

ideology ■ A system of beliefs and values that influence one's activities and behavior

consequential ethic ■ Ethical system that prioritizes the end result of political actions

Despite its longstanding commitment to building democracy abroad, the United States continues to confront several obstacles, including the following:

1. *Inadequate Resources:* In most cases, the United States does not allocate enough financial assistance to build the political institutions, economic and social environment, and civil society essential for promoting democracy.
2. *Lack of Domestic Consensus:* Although in theory most Americans support promoting democracy in foreign countries, democratization in practice has generally failed to engender a lasting commitment, partly because of an overriding preoccupation with domestic concerns.
3. *Conflicting Policy Objectives:* Promoting democracy must often compete with other conflicting national interests.
4. *Limitations of the U.S. Democratic Model:* Each society has its own historical, social, and economic realities, which mitigate the usefulness of the American model of democracy.

Pressure on countries to adopt market economies, which included the privatization of state-owned economic activities, was widely regarded as an essential step toward democratization. However, the global financial crisis and economic recession have undermined the American model. The U.S. government enacted the **Support for Eastern European Democracy (SEED) Act** in 2001 to promote economic liberalization and privatization as well as democratic reforms. Foreign financial assistance—provided through the NED and the U.S. Agency for International Development (USAID)—was used to conduct free and fair elections, draft constitutions, establish independent judicial systems, train police forces, and reduce, if not eliminate, competition in government. Financial assistance was also used to build the forces of civil society.

SEED Act ■
Designed to promote economic liberalization, privatization, and democratic reforms worldwide

Imposing Democracy by Force in Iraq

America's decision to invade Iraq in March 2003 raised many questions about the efficacy of using military force to effectuate democratic change. Following a swift and successful American military campaign against Iraq, U.S. forces captured Baghdad on April 9, 2003. Saddam Hussein's tyrannical rule ended, and thousands of Iraqis greeted American troops, while other Iraqis looted government property and destroyed symbols of the old regime, especially the ubiquitous statues of Hussein. Optimism about regime change and spreading democracy not only in Iraq but also throughout the Middle East was bolstered by the easy U.S. military victory, significant Iraqi support for the invasion, and the fact that Iraq contains large oil reserves, is comparatively secular and Westernized, and has a well-educated population. Table 4.2 shows U.S. efforts to impose democracy.

President Bush appointed L. Paul Bremer III as the senior civilian administrator in Iraq. As head of the Coalition Provisional Authority, Bremer faced the daunting responsibility of stabilizing Iraq, rebuilding the country's economy and infrastructure, and imposing democracy. Iraq's ethnic and religious divisions complicated the task. It was a major challenge to create political and economic institutions and processes acceptable to the vast majority of Sunnis and Shiites, Arabs and Kurds, religious fundamentalists and secularists, and men and women.

L. Paul Bremer III ■
Senior U.S. civilian administrator in Iraq

Coalition Provisional Authority ■ Retained responsibility for stabilizing Iraq and helping the country transition from interim rule to upcoming elections

TABLE 4.2

U.S. Efforts to Impose Democracy

Years	Country	Multilateral or Unilateral	Democracy Achieved?
2003–Present	Iraq	Multilateral	?
2001–Present	Afghanistan	Multilateral	?
1994	Haiti	Multilateral	No
1989	Panama	Unilateral	Yes
1983	Grenada	Multilateral	Yes
1970–1973	Cambodia	Unilateral	No
1965–1973	South Vietnam	Unilateral	No
1965–1966	Dominican Republic	Unilateral	No
1945–1952	Japan	Multilateral	Yes
1944–1949	West Germany	Multilateral	Yes
1944–1947	Italy	Multilateral	Yes
1924–1925	Dominican Republic	Unilateral	No
1916–1924	Cuba	Unilateral	No
1917–1922	Haiti	Unilateral	No
1915–1919	Mexico	Unilateral	No
1914	Nicaragua	Unilateral	No
1909–1927	Nicaragua	Unilateral	No
1909	Cuba	Unilateral	No
1906–1909	Honduras	Unilateral	No

Despite widespread violence, elections for seats in a national assembly to draft Iraq's new constitution were held on January 30, 2005. In December 2005, elections were held for the 275 parliamentary seats and to form a government. These elections were viewed by the U.S. government as evidence of Iraq's transition to democracy and as the beginning of democratic change throughout the Middle East. Following elections in 2010, Iraq formed a coalition government that provided for a balance of power among Sunnis, Shiites, and Kurds.

TRANSITIONS TO DEMOCRACY

In 1795, the philosopher Immanuel Kant, in his book *Idea for a Universal History*, articulated the view that democratic government was destined to replace all other forms of government. The idea that progress was inevitable extended to beliefs about democracy. Despite history's cruel lessons, there was general optimism about a future characterized by justice, logic, and peace. But the auspicious beginnings of the twentieth century were destroyed by grave developments that threatened civilization and the survival of the human race. As Arthur Schlesinger, Jr., put it, "Democracy, striding confidently into the 1900s, found itself almost at once on the defensive. The Great War shattered old structures of security and unleashed angry revolutions against democracy. Bolshevism in Russia, fascism in Italy, Nazism in Germany, militarism in Japan all despised, denounced, and, wherever they could, destroyed individual rights and the processes of self-government."[9] The Great Depression further eroded confidence in democracy's ability to engender prosperity for the majority of citizens. This economic devastation was quickly followed by World War II, in which antidemocratic forces triumphantly trampled democratic societies and forced Britain, the United States, and their allies to make unprecedented sacrifices to protect lives and liberties globally. It is estimated that by 1941 only twelve democracies had survived worldwide.[10]

Democratization (i.e., a transition to democracy) is a process of changing from an authoritarian or totalitarian system of government to a democratic government that is widely regarded by the population and the global community as legitimate and permanent. A *democratic transition* involves the negotiation and acceptance of democratic rules and procedures; the building or restructuring of political, social, and economic institutions; and the channeling of political competition along democratic lines.[11] An essential component of this transition is deciding on a new constitution that reflects political, religious, cultural, and economic realities within the society and its regional environment.

liberalization ■
Traditionally equated with the implementation of Western concepts of liberal republicanism

Democratic transitions usually begin with liberalization. Liberalization includes implementing changes, such as imposing fewer restrictions on the freedom of the press and speech, recognizing the right of workers to unionize, moving away from arbitrarily arresting citizens, having greater respect for the rule of law, releasing political prisoners, and increasing tolerance for political opposition. *Democratization* includes liberalization but is a much broader concept. Democratization involves the right of citizens to compete in elections in order to gain control of the government and to determine the public policy agenda. But elections alone are not sufficient to bring about democratization. What is known as the electoralist fallacy (i.e., the view that free elections are a sufficient condition for democracy) is found in many societies transitioning to democracy. Even though nondemocratic leaders relinquish direct control of the government, they continue to exercise so much power that the democratically elected government is widely perceived as politically impotent.[12] Juan J. Linz and Alfred Stepan argue that a democratic transition is complete when there is a widespread agreement on how to elect a government; when the government has the authority to make decisions for the country; and when there is a legal separation of executive, legislature, and judicial powers.[13]

electoralist fallacy
■ The idea that elections are enough to foster democracy

There must be a general societal consensus that no alternative to democracy exists before the transition to democracy occurs.[14] Democracies must deliver tangible benefits to demonstrate their superiority over nondemocratic systems. They must improve economic opportunities, maintain order, and provide an enhanced quality of life for their citizens in order to obtain legitimacy or acceptance by the people. A full transition to democracy is accomplished when basic democratic rights and freedoms are an integral component of life and when the overwhelming majority of the citizens, despite problems in society, believe that democracy is better than its alternatives.

Many military regimes in Africa, Asia, and Latin America implemented managed transitions to democracy. These regimes try to control the process of change to protect their own interests, to ensure social stability, and to minimize concessions to those advocating political transformation. In managed transitions, the military often establishes a timetable for the restoration or creation of democratic rule and determines the process of democratic elections.[15] These managed transitions usually occur in response to widespread national unrest and severe economic crises.

Consolidating democracy is a long-term process that involves behavioral, attitudinal, and institutional transformations. Behaviorally, a democratic regime is consolidated when there is widespread popular acceptance of the idea that governments should not be changed by force. Attitudinally, a democratic regime is consolidated when a strong majority of the population believes that democratic institutions and procedures are most appropriate for their society. Institutionally, a democratic regime is consolidated when society as a whole, including the government, believes that certain laws, procedures, and institutions must be used to govern society.[16] Conditions must exist that are conducive for the development and proper functioning of civil society. Specific arrangements must be made for groups and individuals to compete fairly and openly for political power. Society must respect and uphold the rule of law, and an impartial and independent judiciary must be regarded as the ultimate authority. Finally, there must be an institutionalized economic society or a significant degree of market autonomy and the right of individuals to own property.[17]

Waves of democratization have occurred since the eighteenth century and continue today. Samuel P. Huntington defines *a wave of democratization* as a group of transitions from nondemocratic to democratic regimes that happen within a specific period of time and that outnumber transitions away from democracy.[18] *Three* distinct waves of democratization can be identified in modern history. The *first wave* began with the American and French Revolutions and included parts of the British Empire (e.g., Canada, Australia, and New Zealand) and several small European countries (e.g., Switzerland). The *second wave* grew out of the retreat of democracy and the rise of Nazism, Fascism, and totalitarianism in Europe and militarism in Japan. When these antidemocratic forces were defeated in World War II, democracy experienced a renewal or rebirth. Allied occupation of West Germany, Austria, Italy, and Japan led to the democratization of these former aggressive states. The *third wave* began with Portugal in 1974 and lasted until the late 1990s.[19] Because this wave was so expansive, we can subdivide it into *three distinct pathways to democracy* taken by various countries. The *first pathway* involved a movement away from military rule toward democracy in Greece, Spain, Portugal, Brazil, Argentina, and Chile. The *second pathway* toward democracy is characterized by a movement away from authoritarian regimes governed by a single dominant party. Examples are Taiwan, the Philippines, and South Africa. The *third pathway* toward democracy began in countries that had been dominated by Communism and a Communist oligarchy. Countries in Central and Eastern Europe and the former Soviet Union are the leading examples of this pathway.[20]

managed transitions ■
Attempt to create stable transitions of change throughout society

consolidating democracy ■
Long-term process that involves popular acceptance of democratic institutions and processes.

Latin America

Between 1978 and 1993, fifteen countries in Latin America transitioned to democracy. Several factors contributed to these developments. *First*, given the historical and cultural relationships between Latin America and Spain and Portugal, the end of the Francisco Franco regime in Spain and the Antonio de Oliveira Salazar regime in Portugal inspired democratic movements in Latin America. *Second*, economic difficulties, symbolized by the debt crisis, further eroded the legitimacy of nondemocratic governments, many of which justified their rule on the basis of the ability to develop the economy. *Third*, military conflicts in Nicaragua, El Salvador, Panama, and Argentina undermined dictatorships in those countries. The government in Argentina, for example, was weakened not only by economic problems but also by its defeat in the Falklands (Malvinas) by Britain. *Fourth*, the inability of governments to deal with the effects of natural disasters in countries such as Nicaragua and Bolivia contributed to their downfall. *Fifth*, some governments were pressured to democratize by sanctions, imposed primarily by the United States. *Sixth*, the demise of Communism in the Soviet Union and Eastern Europe further weakened the credibility of dictatorships globally. *Finally*, the United States changed its approach to Latin America, becoming more reluctant to support dictators who were allies. These changes reinforced pressures within various Latin American countries for democracy.[21]

Salvador Allende ■
Chilean Marxist who became president

Augusto Pinochet ■
General responsible for the military overthrow of Allende

Manuel Zelaya ■
President of Honduras elected in 2005 and ousted in June 2009 military coup

Roberto Micheletti ■
Interim president of Honduras sworn in after 2009 military coup that removed Manuel Zelaya

Chile, traditionally a stable democracy, is an example of a country in which democracy was replaced by authoritarian rule. In 1973, Salvador Allende, Chile's first democratically elected Marxist president, was overthrown and killed by General Augusto Pinochet, with the support of the United States. Pinochet and the military ruled Chile until the restoration of democracy in 1990. Domestic and international pressures, significant economic development under Pinochet, and the expansion of the middle class eventually influenced Pinochet to hold free and fair elections, which he lost. Although Pinochet continued to play an influential role in the government and the military, Chile had returned to its democratic roots. Despite progress toward democracy, many Latin American societies are confronted with numerous problems that weaken the democratic process. For example, violent protests against economic and political conditions in Ecuador forced President Lucio Gutierrez from office in 2005. Democracy in Honduras was undermined in 2009 when President Manuel Zelaya was ousted in a coup and replaced by Roberto Micheletti.

Russia

CPSU ■ Political party that exercised total economic, political, and cultural control over Soviet life

Emerging as a superpower after World War II, the Soviet Union embarked on an expansionist foreign policy and directly competed with the United States and its allies to promote Communism as the dominant ideology and way of life. Domestically, the Communist Party of the Soviet Union (CPSU) exercised complete control over the economy, politics, culture, and every aspect of Soviet life. Centrally planned economic activities excluded private enterprise and free markets. The government's control of the economy impeded the country's economic development and created many hardships for the population. Competition with the United States forced the Soviet Union to allocate a large proportion of its increasingly scarce resources to clients in the Third World and to military activities. Faced with a widening gap in living standards between themselves and the West, particularly the United States, Soviet citizens began to view global confrontation and the resources it required as undermining their own economic and social security. They began to turn their attention to domestic problems. As Marshall Brement observed, it was difficult to convince the Soviet public that events in distant places were more important than their own basic needs and interests. Only the most conservative ideologues within the leadership failed to grasp that the Soviet system was in crisis and that a radical shake-up was desperately needed.[22]

Mikhail Gorbachev, who was selected by the Communist Party in 1985 to lead the Soviet Union, inherited a stagnating economy and a deteriorating social and political system. Mounting Soviet casualties in Afghanistan, which the Soviets had invaded in 1979, further demonstrated the seriousness of the challenges confronting the Soviet Union. Gorbachev equated Soviet involvement in Afghanistan with America's failure in Vietnam and decided to stanch the "bleeding wound" by withdrawing Soviet forces from Afghanistan. These problems influenced Gorbachev to adopt radical economic reforms and political liberalization in an effort to strengthen the Soviet Union. His program of perestroika (i.e., restructuring of the Soviet economy) challenged the idea of a centrally planned economy and advocated implementing a more open economy that stressed greater local autonomy, economic incentives, and market forces. Another reform was the program of glasnost (i.e., openness), which challenged the Communist Party's assumption that it had a monopoly on truth. Instead, Gorbachev strongly supported more freedom of speech and freedom of the press, believing that truth emerges through the exchange of ideas, discussions, and debates. Finally, Gorbachev advocated a program of *demokratizatsiya* (i.e., democratization), a central component of which would be respect for the rule of law and the free and open election of government officials.

The Soviet Union disintegrated as the various republics declared their independence from Russia and Communism itself fell. Hardliners were replaced by reformers, the military and the KGB (secret police) were reformed, and many Communist Party activities were abolished. When supporters of the old regime attempted to overthrow Gorbachev in 1991, Russians demonstrated against them in Moscow, helping to guarantee the failure of the coup. Although Gorbachev resigned as president in December 1991 when the Soviet Union was officially disbanded, he had been awarded the Nobel Peace Prize in 1990 for both his domestic and foreign policy reforms.

Boris Yeltsin, the former Communist Party chief in Moscow, was elected to replace Gorbachev in Russia's first free presidential election. Opposition to change continued to frustrate efforts by Yeltsin to reform Russia. Yeltsin responded by disbanding the parliament, which was dominated by Communist conservatives who opposed change. His decision to schedule new elections and to create a constitutional assembly to draft a new constitution, to be approved by the voters, prompted an armed revolt against the government, which was suppressed by the army. In 1995, Russia held its first fully constitutional parliamentary elections since the 1917 Bolshevik Revolution. Yeltsin was reelected president in 1996.[23] Despite ongoing problems with transitioning to democracy, Vladimir Putin, a former KGB agent, was appointed by Yeltsin to be his prime minister and acting president in January 2000; he was elected president later that year. During his inauguration, Putin held a red, leather-bound copy of the Russian Constitution and took an oath to "respect and guard the human and civil rights" of Russia. This event marked the first democratic transfer of executive power in Russia's 1,100-year history.[24]

Mikhail Gorbachev ■
Leader who inherited the economic, political, and social problems during the final days of the declining Soviet Union

perestroika ■
Gorbachev's reforms of the Soviet economy

glasnost ■
Gorbachev's reforms to promote openness and social freedoms

demokratizatsiya ■
Program of democratization implemented by Gorbachev

Boris Yeltsin ■
Former Communist Party chief who was elected president of Russia

Despite significant steps toward democracy, Russia remains at a crossroads, often leaning more toward authoritarianism than democracy.[25] Putin used the threat of terrorism to justify his retreat from democracy. Although Dmitri A. Medvedev was elected as Russia's president in 2008, Putin, who became prime minister, retained significant power. That election did not advance democracy in Russia. Political choices are severely restrained. Elections in Russia are in many ways reminiscent of the Soviet era.[26]

Islam and Democracy in the Middle East

Muslims are obviously not a monolithic group, just as Christians and Jews are not monolithic. Muslims are conservative, radical, moderate, authoritarian, and democratic. Countries in which Islam is practiced have their own particular cultural practices and beliefs that differentiate them from each other and moderate religious influences on political life. Indonesia, the world's largest Muslim country, is not the same as Saudi Arabia.

Democratic revolutions in the Middle East and North Africa challenge misperceptions about the incompatibility of Islam and democracy. Just as there are democratic values in Christian thought, there are democratic values in Islamic thought. As Graham E. Fuller put it, "Democratic values are latent in Islamic thought if one wants to look for them."[27] The interpretation of the Christian holy book, the Bible, is often arbitrary and subject to debate. The Prophet Mohammad (570–632 A.D.), the founder of Islam, called for shura (i.e., consultation between the ruler and the ruled), which, as we discussed earlier, is the essence of democracy. The concept of limited government, a cornerstone of democracy, is central to Islam. Both the rulers and the ruled are, according to Islamic teachings on the state, subject to God's law. This means that not even the most powerful leaders are above the law. But unlike Christianity, which stresses that we should give to "Caesar what is Caesar's and to God what is God's," Islam makes no distinction between the secular and the sacred or between state and mosque. Despite difficulties inherent in using the Koran as the foundation of laws for Muslims, the authoritarian governments in the Middle East are less a product of strict adherence to Islamic teachings than they are creations of modernization and the universal human struggle for power.

Instead of viewing Islam as the primary obstacle to democratization, many citizens in the Middle East perceive U.S. policies that support authoritarian regimes as the most serious impediment to democracy.[28] As developments in 2011 clearly show, people in the Middle East routinely demonstrate against fundamentalist Islamic regimes and authoritarian governments and for democracy. In Iran, for example, students were instrumental in getting Mohammad Khatami, a moderate who advocated democratic changes, elected president. But powerful conservative clerics and their supporters prevented him from carrying out meaningful reforms. Many Iranian students have spearheaded protests against religious leaders. They want the same freedoms that they know exist in the West because of their access to television, the Internet, and other aspects of globalization. Iranians joined the wave of political dissent that spread across the Middle East. Supporters of Iran's Green movement led protests in Tehran.[29]

Ayatollah Khomeini ■ Leader of the Iranian Revolution and of the Iranian state

Mohammad ■ (570–632); founder of Islam

shura ■ Concept of consultation between the ruler and the ruled

Koran ■ Muslim holy book

Mohammad Khatami ■ Iranian president who has advocated moderate reforms

GLOBAL GOVERNANCE AND DEMOCRACY

Globalization is often viewed as depriving democratically elected governments of their ability to determine public policies or to regulate the consequences of global decisions on the people who elected them. The gap between democracy at the national and global levels is most apparent in the area of economic globalization. There is a widespread fear, especially within developed societies, that the global economy is undermining democracy by shifting power from elected national governments to faceless and often secretive global bureaucracies. In most cases citizens cannot use their votes to hold global institutions accountable, despite the fact that many global organizations were created and are controlled by nation-states. This loss of power, the relative inability of governments and citizens to influence decisions by global institutions, is generally referred to as a democratic deficit.

economic globalization ■ Predominantly known as the spread of market values, institutions, and trade across state lines

democratic deficit ■ Loss of citizen and government power in challenging the agendas of global institutions

International Regimes

Controversy surrounding the issue of a democratic deficit is a direct outgrowth of the proliferation of international regimes and global institutions as integral components of globalization. International regimes are basically institutions governing the behavior or actions of governmental as well as nongovernmental actors that are involved in specific activities. Regimes are characterized by complex interdependence and consist of rules, regulations, norms, and legal agreements that govern the behavior of those belonging to them. Because regimes reflect power in the international system, the dominant actors or groups of actors often shape their organization, its functioning, and its policies.

international regimes ■ International institutions that govern the behavior of governmental and nongovernmental actors

The proliferation and increasing complexity of international regimes combine to create a global governance system. Global governance is defined as "the formal institutions and organizations through which the rules governing world order are made and sustained as well as those organizations and pressure groups—from MNCs, transnational social movements to the plethora of nongovernmental organizations—which pursue goals and objectives that have a bearing on transnational rule and authority systems."[30] Global governance is based on cooperation as opposed to unilateralism. Coordination of actions occurs through governmental as well as NGOs.

global governance ■ The institutions and structures that combine to govern many aspects of state policies, especially concerning international relations

At the heart of global governance is the concept of global civil society, discussed earlier in this chapter. Global civil society is defined as a "decentralized network of autonomous social institutions that represent citizens and organized interests and engage in cooperative actions to achieve broad goals."[31] Just as the growth of civil society is essential to transitions to and consolidation of democracy within countries, global civil society plays a crucial role in promoting democracy at the global level. Global governance also reflects a growing awareness of the need to supply more global public goods as a consequence of increased globalization. *Global public goods* are characterized by nonrivalry in consumption and nonexcludability, as well as by the universal benefits they bestow on the majority of humanity. They include global financial stability, environmental protection, basic human security, and the nonproliferation of weapons of mass destruction.

Making Global Institutions More Democratic

Perceptions of a democratic deficit in global institutions and global governance have stimulated discussions about possible reforms to make the global system more accountable, transparent, and responsible to those affected by it.[32] The global financial crisis strengthened demands for change. The *first suggestion* for the democratization of global institutions is changing the formulation and implementation of rules and procedures. This requires rethinking how interests are represented at the global level. Citizens could pressure their own governments to send representatives to meetings of global institutions to safeguard their interests. A *second suggestion* is to make changes in the formal representation in global institutions, especially in relation to developing countries. The way seats and votes are allocated in many global organizations places developing countries at a disadvantage in terms of influence on decision making. The global financial crisis helped increase the power of China, India, Brazil, and other developing countries. A *third suggestion* is to expand representation in them to include citizens' representatives, in addition to government representatives and bureaucrats. This means including civil society actors. A *fourth suggestion* is to increase transparency in global organizations. A *final suggestion* is to enforce judicial-style accountability. This form of accountability is designed to ensure that organizations act within their powers. Specific actions or decisions are examined, and attention is drawn to violations of operating rules and procedures.

Zine el-Abidine Ben Ali ■ Longtime Tunisian leader ousted in democratic transition

Khaled Said ■ Young Internet user whose death helped spark demonstrations leading to democratic transition in Egypt

Hosni Mubarak ■ Longtime Egyptian ruler ousted in democratic transition

▶ CASE STUDY | Democratic Transitions in the Middle East and North Africa

Democratic transitions in the Middle East and North Africa are the most significant global developments of the twenty-first century. Just as the forces of globalization, especially communications technologies, contributed to undermining Communism in the Soviet Union and Eastern Europe, they played a crucial role in transforming the political landscape of the Arab world. New technologies and interaction with the rest of the world deprived autocratic rulers of a monopoly on information, which eroded their ability to control the people. Cell phones, the Internet, satellite television, Facebook, Twitter, YouTube, and other social media became essential political instruments for young people, the leaders and the vast majority of protestors for democracy. Global media created a global village in which the rest of the world could observe and participate in efforts to effectuate change. Globalization, which grew after the Cold War (a period of intense ideological conflict) weakened

ideology and strengthened pragmatism and concerns with human security.

Human security issues were at the heart of the popular uprisings. People from every social class demonstrated to end government corruption, which contributes to poverty (as we will see in Chapter 12). Soaring numbers of jobless youth demanded economic improvements as well as democratic freedoms and human rights. They wanted governments to adhere to the rule of law. Demonstrators demanded an end to oppression and the growing chasm between rich and poor. Concerns with poverty, unemployment, and humiliation influenced a wave of self-immolations across the Arab world that transformed popular grievances into demands for radical political change, beginning in Tunisia and spreading to Egypt and elsewhere. Self-immolation provided a potent and dramatic symbol to youth disillusioned with ideology and the failure of traditional organizations and

(continued)

political parties to achieve political change. In societies where youth comprise the vast majority of the population, aging autocrats and their political regimes became increasingly anachronistic and irrelevant. So widespread was popular resentment that the army and security forces eventually supported protestors in Egypt. However, in Libya, Syria, Bahrain, and other countries, the armed forces either remained loyal to the regimes or were divided, which prolonged violence and suffering, especially in Libya and Syria. It took months for Libya's military dictatorship to be ejected from the capital and most of the country so that a democratic government could begin to assume authority.

Transitions to democracy in Tunisia and Egypt occurred quickly partly because governments in those countries were caught off guard by the unprecedented overwhelming protests. Other governments, watching events in Tunisia and Egypt, decided to use military force to suppress protests. In the case of Bahrain, where the U.S. Navy's Fifth Fleet is based, Saudi Arabia and the United Arab Emirates (UAE) sent 2,000 troops under the banner of the Gulf Cooperation Council (composed of six Sunni monarchies) to crush the largely Shiite uprisings. Bahrain, which is predominantly Shiite, is ruled by the minority Sunnis. What are some underlying factors that influenced transitions to democracy in Tunisia and Egypt? Both countries are integrated into the Western World through historical experiences, geographic proximity, migration, tourism, access to global communications, and economic globalization. Despite oppression, both countries experienced a degree of freedom and openness to the outside world. Higher levels of education, greater equality for women, and the emergence of a large urban middle class helped. Gaps between the veneer of democracy and actual performance created widespread frustration and alienation, especially among young people, which fueled anger and demands for change. Finally, the political elite in both countries was not monolithic. Authoritarian regimes were challenged by opposition

groups. These were protests about food insecurity, and powerful citizens of both countries cultivated global support for democracy.

Tunisia, with a long history of political stability, connections to Europe, rising economic prosperity, an economy that is integrated into the global economy, high levels of education and home ownership, and a strong middle class, was governed by the corrupt and oppressive regime led by Zine el-Abidine Ben Ali for 23 years. The Tunisian government used censorship and little opportunity for people to express their grievances. Global communications technologies enabled Tunisians to challenge government control. Roughly 4 million people (out of a population of 10.5 million) are Internet users and had access to WikiLeaks' publication of government corruption in Tunisia. But what really galvanized mass demonstrations was the self-immolation of Muhammad Bouazizi, an unemployed college graduate who sold vegetables from a wheelbarrow to make a living for himself and his family. His unlicensed cart was confiscated by the police, and he was beaten and humiliated. His dramatic act sparked waves of unrelenting protests, aided by social networks, that culminated in the downfall of the regime.[33]

Popular uprisings spread across Egypt, where government corruption, police brutality, and blatant disregard for democracy were deeply entrenched. With more than 40 percent of the people living on less than $2 a day and income inequality escalating amid increased food insecurity, Egypt was primed for the eruption of spontaneous demonstrations that attracted millions of people. These protests were also triggered when a young Internet user, Khaled Said, was beaten to death by the police. A Facebook campaign was launched, calling on people to participate in a "day of rage." Roughly eighty thousand Egyptian Web surfers signed up and pledged to march in the streets and to gather in Tahrir Square in Central Cairo to demand political reforms and the end of Hosni Mubarak's regime, which ruled Egypt for thirty-one years. Mubarak's

(continued)

National Democratic Party (NDP) always claimed at least two thirds of the vote in elections and excluded opposition parties, especially the Muslim Brotherhood. Most Egyptians, alienated from the political process, never bothered to vote. Rulers became increasingly isolated from the people, especially the youth, who were less tolerant of the gap between promises and performance. Furthermore, believing in equality and meritocracy, young people resented Mubarak's grooming of his sons to continue his political dynasty. When the military refused to suppress the demonstrators, Mubarak had no option but to leave office. He and his two sons were arrested and held in detention for questioning regarding government corruption.

As we have seen, transitions to democracy take time. Beliefs, values, adherence to the rule of law, democratic institutions and processes, and a perception by the general population that there is no real alternative to democracy cannot be imposed. A first major step toward democracy in Egypt was the overwhelming public approval of amendments to the constitution that limit the president to two 4-year terms in office, provide for the independent supervision of elections, and revoked counterterrorism laws used by Mubarak to retain control. A major concern is the role of the Muslim Brotherhood in the transition to democracy. Although it embraces a range of attitudes and beliefs, many Egyptians worry about some conservative members who favor Shari'a law, veiling women, stoning to death for adultery, and amputation for theft. The fact that Egyptians are overwhelmingly secular and the youth are less traditional and more globalized will undoubtedly modify the influence of fundamentalist extremists. ◢

SUMMARY AND REVIEW

This chapter focused on the spread of democracy at the global level. It shows how politics, economics, and culture are inextricably linked to the promotion of democracy on one hand and are shaped by democracy on the other. Democracy is defined as government that reflects the will of the people. There is much diversity among the different forms of democracy throughout the world, and many divergent paths toward democratization exist. Competitive elections—where various political parties representing various political interests effectively and fairly compete—are vital in such a democratic system. Civil society and global civil society play an important role in the democratization process, as the individuals and groups involved exert pressure on autocratic regimes to initiate democratic reforms. This chapter reviewed the many global waves of democratization. The waves of democratization were split into (1) the American and French Revolutions, (2) World War II and the defeat of Nazism and Fascism, and (3) the explosion of democratization from the 1970s to the 1990s throughout Africa, Asia, Europe, the former Soviet Republics, and Latin America. We focused on democratic transitions in the Middle East and North Africa.

Although democracy has not been universally accepted by all leaders throughout all nation-states, the strengthening of global civil society—as well as the rising expectations of those long deprived of democracy—have been driving factors in the growth of democratic developments and accountability in government. Democracy has increasingly becoming globalized, as many throughout the world continue to fight for universal human rights and for the establishment and consolidation of democratic government. With the success of the various waves of democratization, countries worldwide have been able to demand democratic reforms from their governments.

KEY TERMS

democracy 68
direct self-government 68
indirect/representative democracy 68
majoritarian model 69
consensus model 69
proportional representation 69
liberal democracy 69
constitutional liberalism 69
constitution 69
rule of law 69
presidential democracy 69
parliamentary democracy 69
conventional participation 70
unconventional participation 70
political parties 70
loyal opposition 70
interest group 70
civil society 70
global civil society 70
culture 72
Westminster model 72
economic development 73
middle class 73
Warsaw Declaration 73
CIVICUS 74
Carter Center 74
Varela Project 74
Woodrow Wilson 75
ideology 75
consequential ethic 75
Support for Eastern European Democracy
  (SEED) Act 76

L. Paul Bremer III 76
Coalition Provisional Authority 76
liberalization 78
electoralist fallacy 78
managed transitions 79
consolidating democracy 79
Salvador Allende 80
Augusto Pinochet 80
Manuel Zelaya 80
Roberto Micheletti 80
Communist Party of the Soviet Union
  (CPSU) 80
Mikhail Gorbachev 81
perestroika 81
glasnost 81
demokratizatsiya 81
Boris Yeltsin 81
Ayatollah Khomeini 82
Mohammad 82
shura 82
Koran 82
Mohammad Khatami 82
economic globalization 83
democratic deficit 83
international regimes 83
global governance 83
Zine el-Abidine Ben Ali 84
Khaled Said 84
Hosni Mubarak 84

DISCUSSION QUESTIONS

1. How would you define democracy? What are some of the basic elements that are needed for democracy to flourish?
2. Discuss the role of civil society in promoting democracy.
3. Discuss ways in which the United States could better promote democracy throughout the world today.
4. Discuss ways in which global institutions have undermined democratic developments in individual nation-states.
5. Discuss democratic transition in the Middle East and North Africa.

SUGGESTED READINGS

Khanna, Parag. *How to Run the World.* New York: Random House, 2011. Examines growing competition for power among governments, international organizations, and nongovernmental organizations in a multipolar world.

Malloch-Brown, Mark. *The Unfinished Global Revolution.* New York: Penguin Press, 2011. Discusses positive and negative experiences with global governance and contends that states will have to increasingly cooperate to achieve their goals.

Nasr, Vali. *Forces of Fortune.* New York: Free Press, 2009. Free markets and the new middle class will defeat extremism and promote social liberalization.

Towns, Ann E. *Women and States.* Cambridge, UK: Cambridge University Press, 2010. Government reforms globally have brought women into political life. These include women's suffrage, the creation of government agencies to address women's issues, and gender quotas for national legislatures.

Treisman, Daniel. *The Return: Russia's Journey From Gorbachev to Medvedev.* New York: Free Press, 2011. Focuses on how economic decline and poor policies eroded democracy in Russia.

Youngs, Richard, ed. *The European Union and Democracy Promotion.* Baltimore: Johns Hopkins University Press, 2010. Evaluates European efforts to promote democracy and human rights. Case studies include Iraq and Ukraine.

ENDNOTES

1. Arend Lijphart, *Patterns of Democracy* (New Haven, CT: Yale University Press, 1999).
2. Lijphart, *Patterns of Democracy*, 105.
3. Najma Chowdhury and Barbara J. Nelson, "Redefining Politics: Patterns of Women's Political Engagement from a Global Perspective," in *Women and Politics Worldwide*, eds. Barbara J. Nelson and Najma Chowdhury (New Haven, CT: Yale University Press, 1994), 16.
4. Ruth Henig and Simon Henig, *Women and Political Power* (London: Routledge, 2001), 104.
5. Swanee Hunt, "Let Women Rule," *Foreign Affairs* 86, No. 3 (May/June 2007), 109–111.
6. Peter J. Schraeder, "Promoting an International Community of Democracies," in *Exporting Democracy*, ed. Peter J. Schraeder (Boulder, CO: Lynne Rienner, 2002), 1.
7. Kevin F.F. Quigley, *For Democracy's Sake: Foundations and Democracy Assistance in Central Europe* (Washington, DC: Woodrow Wilson Center Press, 1999),
8. Steven W. Hook, "Inconsistent U.S. Efforts to Promote Democracy Abroad," in *Exporting Democracy*, 111.
9. Arthur Schlesinger Jr., "Has Democracy a Future?" *Foreign Affairs* 76, No. 5 (September/October 1997), 3–4.
10. Schlesinger, "Has Democracy a Future?," 4.
11. Geoffrey Pridham et al., "The International Dimension of Democratization," in *Building Democracy*, eds. Geoffrey Pridham et al. (London: Leicester University Press, 1997), 2.
12. Juan J. Linz and Alfred Stepan, *Problems of Democratic Transitions and Consolidation* (Baltimore: Johns Hopkins University Press, 1996), 4.
13. Linz and Stepan, *Problems of Democratic Transitions*, 3.
14. George Sorenson, *Democracy and Democratization* (Boulder, CO: Westview Press, 1998), 39.

15. Michael Bratton and Nicolas van de Walle, *Democratic Experiments in Africa* (Cambridge, UK: Cambridge University Press, 1997), 239.
16. Linz and Stepan, *Problems of Democratic Transitions*, 6.
17. Linz and Stepan, *Problems of Democratic Transitions*, 7–11.
18. Samuel P. Huntington, *The Third Wave: Democratization in the Late Twentieth Century* (Norman: University of Oklahoma Press, 1993), 15.
19. Huntington, *The Third Wave*, 27.
20. James F. Hollifield and Calvin Jilson, "Introduction," in *Pathways to Democracy: The Political Economy of Democratic Transitions*, eds. James F. Hollifield and Calvin Jilson (New York: Routledge, 2000), 10.
21. Robert K. Shaeffer, *Power to the People: Democratization Around the World* (Boulder, CO: Westview Press, 1997), 124.
22. Marshall Brement, "Reaching Out to Moscow," *Foreign Policy*, No. 80 (Fall 1990), 58.
23. J. William Derleth, *The Transitions in Central and Eastern European Politics* (Upper Saddle River, NJ: Prentice Hall, 2000), 43.
24. Michael Wines, "Putin Is Made Russia's President," *New York Times*, 8 May 2000, A1; and Lilia Shevtsova, *Putin's Russia* (Washington, DC: Carnegie Endowment, 2005).
25. Daniel Treisman, *The Return* (New York: Free Press, 2011).
26. "Russia Revisits Its Past," *Economist*, 1 January 2011, 101.
27. Isobel Coleman, "Woman, Islam, and the New Iraq," *Foreign Affairs* 85, No. 1 (January/February 2006), 24.
28. Fuller, "The Future of Political Islam," 57.
29. "The Autumn of Patriarchs," *Economist*, 19 February 2011, 47.
30. 30 David Held et al., *Global Transformations* (Stanford, CA: Stanford University Press, 1999), 50.
31. Norman J. Vig, "Introduction," in *The Global Environment*, eds. Norman J. Vig and Regina S. Axelrod (Washington, DC: Congressional Quarterly Press, 1999), 5.
32. Mark Malloch-Brown, *The Unfinished Global Revolution* (New York: Penguin Press, 2011).
33. "Tunisia's Troubles," *Economist*, 8 January 2011, 48.

Global Terrorism

Nonstate adversaries, fundamentalist religious extremism, and weapons are three forces of global terrorism,

INTRODUCTION

Osama bin Laden, widely viewed as the embodiment of global terrorism, was killed by U.S. Special Forces on May 1, 2011, in Pakistan. Despite this significant development, the war on terrorism continues. Think about how the escalation of global terrorism affects our daily lives. This global problem is now virtually inseparable from personal concerns. Even traveling by plane from one city to another within the United States and Canada, which was once largely uneventful, has become much more complicated and stressful due to increased airport security. National and global institutions have also been profoundly affected by this problem. The U.S. Department of Homeland Security was created in 2003 as a direct response to the terrorist attacks in September 2001. It brought together twenty-two government agencies with 180,000 workers, making it the largest government reorganization in forty years. Domestic security has been strengthened, especially around bridges, water supplies, government offices, nuclear power plants, scientific laboratories, food supplies, and industrial factories.

This chapter emphasizes the growing importance of asymmetrical power in global affairs. When relatively weak groups use low-tech tools to inflict significant damage on very powerful countries that have the most advanced military technologies, they are using asymmetrical power.

While states are generally impeded by national boundaries, their nonstate adversaries routinely disregard national borders. This chapter discusses difficulties involved in defining terrorism; factors conducive to the rise of terrorism; and goals, strategies, and weapons of terrorist groups. After examining specific cases of terrorism, we will discuss various responses to terrorism and the dilemmas democracies face in attempting to eliminate or reduce this threat. This chapter concludes with a case study of terrorism in Pakistan.

asymmetrical power ■ Form of conflict in which weaker groups or forces can inflict significant damage against more powerful states or forces

DEFINING TERRORISM

Proudly proclaiming their commitment to liberty, equality, and fraternity, the architects of the French Revolution instituted a Reign of Terror (1793–1794) to preserve the radical changes. Headed by Maximilian Robespierre, the Committee of Public Safety embraced terrorism in its effort to rule France during a period that was regarded as a national emergency. The French zeal for the *Terror*, the period of widespread violence, public executions, and intimidation of civilians, was strongly rejected by Edmund Burke, the British conservative philosopher who regarded French terrorists as hellhounds. Although there is no universally accepted definition of terrorism, the standard view that one person's terrorist is another person's freedom fighter fails to distinguish among the various kinds and levels of terrorism and fails to acknowledge that freedom fighters' actions are not necessarily justified. What is clear is that terrorism is a contentious issue that becomes hopelessly muddled by political and military considerations.[1]

Reign of Terror ■ Terrorism committed by the French government during the French Revolution

Edmund Burke ■ British philosopher who strongly criticized the French Reign of Terror

All acts of terrorism are designed to create fear, to cause people to tremble. By using the most advanced technologies of global communication, terrorists seek to frighten people in distant places in order to exert pressure on governments. *Terrorism is essentially a form of psychological warfare*. Unlike most conventional wars, terrorism lasts for generations, as we will see in our discussions of the Irish Republican Army (IRA), the Basques in Spain, and the Palestinians. Terrorism is also *indiscriminate*. Most terrorist activities aim to create uncertainty and general fear by communicating that anyone can be a target. In many ways, *terrorism is closely associated with ideology*. This is clearly the case with al-Qaeda: It is less an organization than an ideology that inspires groups and people worldwide to engage in terrorist acts.

Distinguishing terrorism from guerrilla warfare and insurgency is often challenging. Guerrilla warfare, which means little war, is the use of selective violence against military targets. But when societies experience extensive violence, distinctions between guerrilla warfare and terrorism tend to blur. Following the 2001 attacks in the United States, many governments applied the label of terrorism to very old conflicts of their own that were previously regarded as insurgencies. For example, China annexed what is now Xinjiang in 1759. The inhabitants, known as Uighurs, practice Sufi Islam and speak a Turkic language. They resisted China's rule and launched their first uprising in 1865. The disintegration of the Soviet Union and the independence gained by some Muslim communities in Central Asia inspired the Uighurs to renew their struggle to establish a separate state. But China was quick to label the Uighurs as terrorists after the global developments in 2001. This raises the question: Who gets to define terrorism and why? Complicating definitions of terrorism is the general acceptance of war as a legitimate instrument of governments. Paul Wilkinson argues "terrorist campaigns inherently involve deliberate attacks on civilian targets and are therefore analogous to war crimes."[2] But who decides which military actions are war crimes?

guerrilla warfare ■ Use of selective violence against military targets by insurgency forces

Uighurs ■ Ethnic group that rebelled against China's annexation of Xinjiang in 1759

FACTORS CONDUCIVE TO TERRORISM

Examining the factors that make terrorism a useful tool to accomplish certain objectives is essential to any pragmatic effort to eliminate or diminish terrorist threats. Terrorism has many interrelated causes.

Poverty is widely perceived as the root of terrorism. Poverty is closely linked to economic and political isolation, feelings of hopelessness, violations of human rights, and the lack of democracy, which all provide a fertile breeding ground for terrorism. In Pakistan, students enroll in religious seminaries, called madrassas. Supported by Muslim charities worldwide—especially those in Saudi Arabia—they feed, shelter, clothe, and educate students from poverty-stricken families. In addition to receiving training in the Koran, these students are indoctrinated to hate the West, especially the United States. Many terrorists graduate from madrassas.[3] However, terrorists who attacked the United States, Spain, and Britain were not poor. Many of them came from the middle class.

Globalization is a major factor in global terrorism. In many ways, terrorism is a product of resistance to change brought about by cultural, economic, political,

madrassas ■ Religious seminaries supported by Muslim charities worldwide

military, and even environmental globalization. Individuals in distant places communicate instantaneously and are able to coordinate their activities on a global scale. Global transportation enables them to move easily from one country to another. Global cities provide an environment in which it is easy for people to be anonymous.

Legitimate grievances and the failure of governments to adequately address these problems often foment terrorism. In fact, most terrorist organizations trace their origins to political, religious, social, economic, and ethnic problems that were ignored, downplayed, or dismissed by those in power and by society in general. Why did the African National Congress (ANC) in South Africa, the Palestine Liberation Organization (PLO), and the IRA become terrorist organizations? Specific grievances motivated individuals to form these groups and to use terrorism to achieve their objectives. *Violence by governments* also causes terrorism. Governments routinely abuse their monopoly on legitimate violence regarding specific minority groups or majority groups that lack significant political, economic, and social power. The efficacy of official violence influences individuals and groups that want to change their circumstances to resort to violence.

Humiliation is another factor conducive to the use of terrorism. Terrorism, which was not a problem in Iraq before the U.S. invasion, became widespread. Many Iraqis felt humiliated by intrusive American searches, by being occupied, and by being mistreated. Thomas L. Friedman, an influential journalist with the *New York Times*, stated: "If I've learned one thing covering world affairs, it is this: The single most under-appreciated force in international relations is humiliation."[4]

The lack of democracy, and widespread and systematic violations of human rights, contributes to the rise of terrorism. The September 11 terrorist attacks in the United States drew attention to Saudi Arabia and Egypt, countries to which most of the terrorists belonged. Dissidents such as Osama bin Laden (from Saudi Arabia) and Mohammed Atta (the Egyptian-born leader of the terrorist attacks) were unable to express dissent at home, so they went to Afghanistan to organize al-Qaeda, a global terrorist network.

Foreign policies contribute to terrorism. Roman occupation of Israel generated strong resistance by the Jews, and some Jews adopted terrorism in a futile effort to end Roman oppression. European expansion and colonization laid the foundation for the emergence of national liberation movements that used terrorism to achieve independence. Many foreign policy and terrorism analysts view U.S. foreign policies in the Middle East—especially those involving the Palestinian-Israeli conflict, Saudi Arabia, and Egypt—as being conducive to terrorism. For example, Osama bin Laden strongly opposed the stationing of American troops in Saudi Arabia during the 1991 Gulf War. The U.S. policies are widely seen in the Middle East and elsewhere as contributing to the oppression of the Palestinians by Israel. Finally, *failed states provide an environment conducive to terrorism.* Failed states generally abuse human rights; are undemocratic; are intolerant of ethnic, political, and religious diversity; and have weak economies. State failure is often accompanied by an increase in bureaucratic corruption and cooperation among government officials and criminals. In essence, state authority and civil society are severely undermined, and many regions within a country are lawless. The most obvious example of how state failure breeds terrorism is al-Qaeda in Afghanistan.

Taliban ■ Former government of Afghanistan that repressed its people and supported al-Qaeda

Under the leadership of the Taliban (i.e., a group of extreme Islamic fundamentalists), Afghanistan provided bin Laden with an ideal environment in which terrorism could grow and from which terrorist activities could be organized.

GOALS, STRATEGIES, AND WEAPONS OF TERRORISM

The goals of terrorism include

1. *Social and Political Justice:* Terrorism has been used to achieve concrete political and social changes, including overthrowing repressive regimes.
2. *Self-determination:* Many terrorist organizations emerged as part of the struggle to gain national independence.
3. *Racial Superiority:* Many white supremacist groups attempt to preserve racial segregation and social, economic, and political power based on skin color.
4. *Foreign Policies:* Terrorism is often used to influence governments to take or refrain from taking certain actions.
5. *Publicity:* A central goal of most terrorist groups is to draw public attention to their cause.
6. *Demoralized Governments:* By making governments appear weak and incompetent, terrorists believe they can undermine their legitimacy and policies.

Terrorist organizations adopt several *strategies* to achieve their objectives. *Creating a climate of fear and insecurity*, partly to undermine people's confidence in their government, is an integral component of terrorists' strategies. But terrorism also depends on *cultivating popular support*. Terrorists are generally effective when they operate in an environment that enables them to hide, obtain resources (including weapons), gather information about government operations and plans, and communicate with each other. However, telecommunications and computer technologies have reduced the need for popular support as a component of strategy. Terrorists rely on virtual networks, a style of organization that is essentially leaderless and is facilitated by the Internet. American right-wing extremists developed this strategy to counteract the effectiveness of U.S. law enforcement agencies.[5]

virtual networks ■ A style of organization that is essentially leaderless and facilitated by the Internet

Some terrorist groups *reject the terrorist label* in order to gain greater legitimacy or acceptance in society. Governments, on the other hand, refuse to confer any kind of legitimacy on terrorist groups and reject defining terrorism as warfare. These terrorist groups are likely to select government targets, including embassies, military personnel and bases, and government officials. In Colombia, for example, terrorist groups launched a campaign of assassinations to get the attention of the government and its supporters. Judges, prosecutors, and elected officials were the main targets. This strategy attempts to undermine assumptions that government policies can ensure personal safety.[6] *Selective kidnappings* are also used by terrorists to achieve their goals. By taking government officials, soldiers, businesspeople, and prominent citizens hostage, the terrorists force the government to either take military action against them or bargain with them. Terrorists in Iraq adopted this strategy.

Weapons used by terrorists vary according to their goals, available technology, and resources at their disposal. Sarin gas, anthrax, and various poisons have been used in Japan and the United States. Motor vehicles packed with ammonium nitrate and fuel oil were used as bombs in Oklahoma City in 1995 and in Bali, Indonesia, in 2002. Suicide bombers are lethal weapons in many parts of the world, including Israel, Saudi Arabia, Pakistan, Afghanistan, and Iraq. The use of airliners fully loaded with fuel as missiles to destroy the World Trade Center and damage the Pentagon focused global attention on a new terrorist weapon. Terrorists also put bombs in the mail and on cargo planes. As terrorists use the Internet to spread their message and organize their activities, there is growing awareness of cyberspace warfare as a weapon in the terrorists' arsenal. Although few terrorists are capable of using weapons of mass destruction on a large scale, chemical and biological weapons in the possession of terrorists are a global concern.

FINANCING TERRORISM

Many terrorist cells are self-supporting, and many terrorists do not engage in financial activities that immediately draw attention. This makes it extremely difficult for governments to gather financial information. Furthermore, many terrorists use hawalas (i.e., an informal system of transferring money that is based primarily on trust and interpersonal relations). Developed in India before the arrival of Western banking, hawalas frustrate efforts to trace money because they leave no electronic and virtually no paper trail.[7]

Contributions from individuals and groups are a major source of money for terrorism. In the case of al-Qaeda, bin Laden used his considerable wealth to finance global terrorism. Many individuals make charitable contributions to organizations that are principally concerned with assisting the poor. However, some of this money is also used to support terrorism. *Governments finance terrorism*, both directly and inadvertently. The most obvious way is by sponsoring their activities. For many years, Libya's leader, Muammar Qaddafi, openly financed and trained terrorist groups in the Middle East and Africa.

Diamonds, oil, and other natural resources provide revenues for terrorism. Terrorists often prefer diamonds because they are easily transported, easily hidden, and easily converted into cash. Failed states in Africa often provide opportunities for rebel groups to cooperate with terrorist groups. One of the best examples is Sierra Leone in West Africa. Sierra Leone has some of the richest diamond fields in the world. It has also been plagued by political instability. The diamond trade helped to fund both Sierra Leone's civil wars and al-Qaeda. Senior members of Sierra Leone's Revolutionary United Front (RUF), a rebel group that challenged the government and engaged in horrific acts of violence and terrorism, took diamonds, often wrapped in rags, across the border into Liberia and exchanged them for cash from al-Qaeda and Hezbollah, a Shiite terrorist group in Lebanon. With the cooperation of corrupt customs and immigration officials, the diamonds, which were bought at below-market prices, were then taken to Europe by terrorist organizations and sold at much higher prices.[8] These diamonds are widely known as *conflict diamonds* because of their inextricable links with brutal civil wars and terrorism.

hawalas ■ Informal system of transferring money based primarily on trust and interpersonal relations

Muammar Qaddafi ■ Libyan leader accused of financing and training terrorist groups in the Middle East and Africa

RUF ■ Rebel group that challenged the government of Sierra Leone through acts of violence and terrorism

Hezbollah ■ Shiite terrorist group based in Lebanon

Abu Sayyaf ■
Terrorist group in the Philippines that regularly kidnaps people to finance its activities

Tamil Tigers ■
Group in Sri Lanka that smuggles contraband in the Indian Ocean region

Criminal activities are a major source of funding for terrorism. Terrorists are often involved in armed robbery, credit card fraud, identity theft, kidnapping, extortion, and other crimes. In the Philippines, for example, the terrorist group Abu Sayyaf routinely kidnaps people, including tourists, to finance its activities. The Tamil Tigers in Sri Lanka controlled and operated boats that smuggled contraband in the Indian Ocean region. Often, terrorist groups coerce civilians into paying protection money, sometimes called a revolutionary tax. The IRA is a group that used this method to finance terrorism. Other groups, such as the Taliban in Afghanistan, use money obtained from the sale of illegal drugs.

THE COSTS OF TERRORISM

Costs associated with terrorism are so widespread, complex, and intangible that they are virtually impossible to measure. Individuals, families, governments, companies, and nonstate actors worldwide bear the costs of terrorism to varying degrees. Time, money, and other resources are diverted from other problems. Migration, trade, travel, and interpersonal relations are affected. In September 2001, a very small group of individuals, nineteen of them, caused incalculable damage to the United States as well as the global community. Almost three thousand people from roughly fifty countries were killed. It is generally believed that the financial crisis and the global recession were caused in part by policies adopted by the Bush administration to fight global terrorism, including wars in Afghanistan and Iraq. Domestic terrorists, using anthrax, also damaged U.S. government offices, businesses, and individuals.

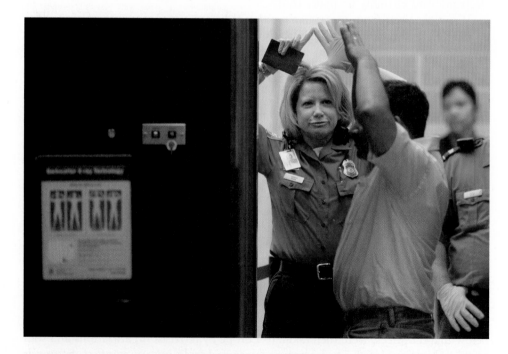

What does this photo convey about the costs of fighting terrorism? A Transportation Security Administration (TSA) official instructs a passenger at a full-body scan at Washington Dulles International Airport.

Costs to Individuals

Individuals usually suffer the most from terrorist acts in terms of loss of lives and social, psychological, and physical problems. Many citizens are made ill by fear and a sudden loss of personal freedom. They restrict their activities, limit their travel, and often distrust their neighbors, thereby weakening community bonds and support. For example, the 2001 attacks undermined trust between most non-Muslim Americans and Muslims in general, especially Arabs. Relations between non-Muslim Americans and Muslims remain problematic. President Barack Obama, as will be discussed in Chapter 14, made a concerted effort to improve relations with the Muslim world.

Economic Costs

Calculating the economic costs of terrorism and the responses to it is virtually impossible because they are so complex and far-reaching. For example, after the 2001 attacks, airlines suffered major financial losses and continue to feel the impact of terrorism. It is estimated that the global airline industry lost $18 billion in 2001 and $13 billion in 2002 following the attacks. Combined, these losses were more than the total profit of all the airlines since 1945.[9] High oil prices and continuing fears about terrorism continued to create severe financial problems, including bankruptcy for some airlines.

Costs to Governments

Governments generally increase resources to fight terrorism and to provide their citizens with a heightened sense of security. For example, as you prepare to board an airline, the costs become obvious. There are more security guards, bags are carefully checked, and individuals are often searched. While airlines pay some of these costs, the U.S. federal government is primarily responsible for airport security. The federal, state, and local governments in the United States also spend money to guard bridges, nuclear power plants, train stations, and so on. The most obvious costs are associated with military actions against terrorists. The invasion of Afghanistan to destroy al-Qaeda and the Taliban, as well as the invasion, occupation, and rebuilding of Iraq, has cost many lives and more than a trillion dollars.[10]

Foreign Policy Costs

Several times following the 2001 attacks, the United States closed its embassies in Saudi Arabia and elsewhere. These shutdowns meant that America was paying a price for not being able to conduct normal diplomatic relations. Furthermore, heightened security for embassies creates additional expenses.

Costs to Democracy

People who are afraid, as Thomas Hobbes observed, are willing to turn to all-powerful rulers who promise to provide security. But part of the price for that security is less freedom. In a climate of fear, governments often justify violating individuals' rights on the grounds of national security. Torturing terrorist suspects and denying them the fundamental right to habeas corpus continued to be debated in the United States.

KINDS OF TERRORISM

domestic terrorism ■ Occurs within borders of a state

nationalist terrorism ■ Occurs as a result of struggles for independence

religious terrorism ■ Occurs as a result of religious extremism

state terrorism ■ Government repression targeted against civilians

global terrorism ■ Partly a result of increased globalization

Although the types of terrorism tend to overlap, they vary in their implications and affect us in different ways. For example, the indiscriminate nature of global terrorism contrasts sharply with domestic terrorism aimed at specific groups or governments. In this section, we will discuss *five kinds of terrorism*:

1. *Domestic terrorism* occurs within the borders of a particular country and is associated with extremist groups.
2. *Nationalist terrorism* is closely associated with struggles for political autonomy and independence.
3. *Religious terrorism* grows out of extreme fundamentalist religious groups that believe that God is on their side and that their violence is divinely inspired and approved.
4. *State terrorism* is a cold, calculated, efficient, and extremely destructive form of terrorism, partly because of the overwhelming power at the disposal of governments.
5. *Global terrorism* is partly an outgrowth of the forces of globalization, which enable the different kinds of terrorism to spread worldwide.

Domestic terrorism has become a major global issue. These members of the National Socialist Movement, a right-wing military group in the United States, marched in California.

Domestic Terrorism

The emergence of terrorism as a major global issue has focused increased attention on domestic terrorism in the United States, Europe, and elsewhere. The murder of thirteen soldiers at Fort Hood by Major Nidal Malik Hasan, a Palestinian-American, in 2009 and numerous connections between homegrown terrorists and al-Qaeda have underscored America's vulnerability to internal threats from non-state actors. In June 2009 a doctor who performed abortions in Kansas was killed in a church by a gunman who opposed abortion. Later in June a white supremacist and neo-Nazi attacked the U.S. Holocaust Memorial Museum, killing a security guard. On April 19, 1995, Americans watched with incredulity as bloodied bodies were pulled from the federal building in Oklahoma City. Most Americans quickly blamed Middle Eastern terrorists for the Oklahoma City bombing, which killed 168 people. But the leader of this terrorist act was Timothy McVeigh, an American and a decorated Gulf War veteran. Domestic terrorism has existed in the United States and other countries for hundreds of years. Unlike most countries, where terrorist activities have been carried out primarily against governments, terrorism in America has been used mostly against racial, ethnic, or religious minorities. American terrorists are predominantly right-wing extremists who embrace white supremacist, anti-Jewish, antiforeign, and antigovernment philosophies based on a religious doctrine known as *Christian identity*. This doctrine essentially holds that white people are chosen by God, whereas Jews, Americans with African ancestry, Asians, and other racial minorities are "mud people." These terrorists generally believe that the U.S. government is dominated by Jews and is an occupying power and that the United States should not participate in the United Nations and other international organizations. Based on these beliefs, they have formed heavily armed militias, strongly oppose gun control, and refuse to pay taxes. Domestic terrorist groups include the National Alliance, the Ku Klux Klan, the Aryan Nation, Posse Comitatus, and the Confederate Hammerskins.

Domestic terrorism has long been a significant problem in several European countries. Throughout the 1970s and 1980s, the Red Brigades, an Italian terrorist group, launched a campaign of bombings and assassinations of government officials. Germany, France, and Greece have also been plagued by domestic terrorism. In Greece, for example, the Marxist-Leninist terrorist group Revolutionary Organization 17 November (or November 17) has been involved in terrorist activities since 1975. November 17 took its name from the date of a student protest in 1973 that was violently crushed by Greece's military government. Embracing strong anti-American and anti-imperialist views, November 17 is believed to have killed several American and British citizens. Many of the terrorist groups in Germany hold white supremacist, anti-Jewish, and antiforeigner views that are similar to those of their American counterparts. Bombings of trains in Spain and in Britain by Muslims, many of whom were born in these countries, underscored growing concerns about domestic terrorism. In July 2011, a Norwegian gunman dressed as a police officer killed sixty-nine Norwegians at a youth summer camp on an island, plus eight more in the bombing of a government building in Oslo.

Latin America has spawned many domestic terrorist organizations. Growing violence and terrorist activities by groups such as the *Montoneros* and the

Red Brigades ■ An Italian terrorist group that attacked government officials

November 17 ■ Marxist-Leninist group that committed terrorist acts in Greece

dirty war ■
Terrorist campaign by the Argentine military dictatorship directed against those critical of their government

Shining Path ■
Peruvian terrorist group

FARC ■ Colombian Marxist guerrilla group practicing terrorism against civilians and government officials

Ejercitos Revolucionares del Pueblo were met with extreme violence from right-wing groups and the Peronist regime. Argentina's military dictatorship launched what became known as the dirty war, in which thousands of people disappeared or were killed. Sendero Luminoso (Shining Path) in Peru and the Revolutionary Armed Forces of Colombia (FARC) are other examples of domestic terrorist groups in Latin America. Shining Path was formed by university students and professors who subscribed to the philosophy of *Mao Zedong* (*Mao Tse-Tung*). They sought to weaken the government's authority by inspiring Indians and others to rebel. Violence by Shining Path and the Peruvian government resulted in more than thirty thousand deaths.

Nationalist Terrorism

Many nationalist groups attempted to achieve nonviolent political change but were often brutally suppressed by governments. Often, nationalist terrorism is accompanied by peaceful, legitimate political activities designed to achieve autonomy, political freedom and equality, or independence. Nationalist groups are routinely labeled terrorists by the governments they oppose and labeled national liberation movements or freedom fighters by their supporters, including other governments. In this section, we will discuss nationalist terrorism in the Middle East (focusing on the Palestinian-Israeli conflict), Northern Ireland, and Spain.

The Middle East   The Palestinian-Israeli conflict stands out as the most prominent contemporary example of nationalist terrorism. This conflict has plunged the Middle East into four major wars and fuels ongoing violence in the region. Failure to resolve this conflict has global implications, largely because of the world's dependence on petroleum imports from the Middle East. Furthermore, global terrorists, such as al-Qaeda, use this conflict to justify their activities and to recruit members throughout the Islamic world. The spiritual and emotional components of this conflict, combined with the sufferings of both Jews and Palestinians, make any discussion of it highly controversial and often subjective. In many ways, the pain and humiliation of both Jews and Palestinians often prevent both sides from empathizing with each other and reaching mutually beneficial solutions to their problems. Instead, both sides have been locked in an increasingly deadly embrace from which neither side is capable of extricating itself. To a large extent, the Palestinian-Israeli conflict is an outgrowth of virulent anti-Jewish practices in Europe that culminated in the Holocaust.

Holocaust ■ Mass murder of millions of Jews driven by ethnic and religious hate and discrimination

Nationalist terrorism, one could argue, began when Jews attempted to end Roman occupation of Israel by killing Roman soldiers and officials. The modern period of nationalist terrorism has its origin in the British efforts to establish a national homeland for Jews in Palestine under the Balfour Declaration. Palestine was controlled by the Ottoman Turks. However, after the Ottoman Empire disintegrated following Turkey's defeat in World War I, Palestine became a British mandate under the League of Nations in 1922. Britain's responsibility was to prepare Palestinians for independence. The persecution of Jews in Europe, especially in Nazi Germany, complicated the situation in Palestine and set the stage for conflict. Led by Menachem Begin, who later became Israel's prime minister and a winner

Menachem Begin ■
Leader of the Jewish terrorist organization the Irgun, committed to Israeli independence

of the Nobel Peace Prize, some Jews formed a terrorist organization, known as the Irgun, to drive the British out of Palestine and to establish a Jewish state. The Irgun and other groups created a climate of fear in Palestine that ultimately undermined the public's confidence in Britain's ability to maintain order and to protect civilians. The most significant terrorist act against the British was the 1946 bombing of the *King David Hotel* in Jerusalem, the headquarters of British military forces in Palestine. Ninety-one persons were killed and forty-five others were injured.[11] This act was condemned by many Jews and Jewish organizations. The division of Palestine into a Jewish and a Palestinian state by the United Nations in 1947 ended Jewish terrorism but set the stage for Palestinian terrorism.

The creation of Israel was accompanied by a large Palestinian refugee problem, discussed in Chapter 10. Palestinian terrorists began to organize in the refugee camps and to form small groups of fedayeen (i.e., commandos). With military and financial assistance from Egypt's leader, Gamel Abdel Nasser, they began to conduct hit-and-run attacks inside Israel. Palestinian terrorism escalated following the defeat of Arab armies that had attempted to regain Palestinian land in the Six-Day War with Israel in June 1967. Instead of pushing Israel out, the conflict left Israel with the Sinai, the West Bank, Gaza, Jerusalem, and the Golan Heights. Palestinian terrorists, concluding that they could achieve their objectives only by attacking Israel and Jews, initiated a violent wave of bombings, hijacking airlines, and killing civilians. In 1968, the *Popular Front for the Liberation of Palestine*—one of the groups belonging to the umbrella Palestinian terrorist group the PLO, led by Yasser Arafat and his Fatah movement—hijacked an Israeli El Al commercial flight and held the passengers and crew hostage. Israel was forced to negotiate with the terrorists to secure their release.[12] One of the most serious terrorist attacks was launched by the Black September Organization (part of the PLO) in 1972 during which eleven Israeli athletes were seized and killed at the Olympic Games in Munich. This terrorist attack, together with the hijacking of airplanes, drew international attention to Palestinian nationalism and laid the foundation for increasing violence.

Despite numerous efforts to achieve a diplomatic settlement to the Palestinian-Israeli conflict, violence escalated. Israeli occupation of Palestinian areas and many counterterrorist activities contributed to the demise of many attempts to reach a peace agreement. Feeling abandoned by Arab states, Palestinians initiated a popular uprising, or intifada, in the late 1980s. During the second intifada, which began in September 2000, the Palestinian-Israeli conflict became even more violent as Palestinian terrorists from groups such as Hamas, Islamic Jihad, Fatah, and the Popular Front for the Liberation of Palestine decided to conduct devastating suicide bombings against innocent civilians and the government in Israel.[13] There were more than fifty suicide bombings in 2002, the height of this new wave of terrorism, which killed and wounded hundreds of Israelis. To prevent these attacks, Israel constructed a barrier or wall, much of which was built in disputed territory. From the Palestinian perspective, the barrier was essentially designed to seize their territory and make their lives even more difficult. In April 2004, Israel, under the leadership of Ariel Sharon, escalated its attacks on Palestinian terrorist leaders, killing Sheikh Ahmed Yasin, the founder of Hamas, and Abdel Aziz Rantisi, who replaced Yasin as the leader of Hamas, with rockets launched from helicopters. Kidnappings of Israeli soldiers by Hamas and Hezbollah in July 2006 led to

Irgun ■ Jewish terrorist group committed to driving the British out of Palestine

fedayeen ■ Small groups of Palestinian commandos

Gamel Abdel Nasser ■ Egyptian leader popular for his resistance to Israel

Six-Day War ■ 1967 war in which Israel seized the Sinai, the West Bank, Gaza, Jerusalem, and the Golan Heights

PLO ■ Once considered a terrorist organization, committed to fighting Israel and its occupation of the West Bank and Gaza

Black September Organization ■ Part of the PLO responsible for some of the most serious terrorist attacks

intifada ■ Collective Palestinian resistance to Israel's occupation of the West Bank and Gaza

Israel's invasion of Lebanon and the escalation of violence in the Palestinian territories. Conflict between Palestinians, especially those in Gaza, and Israelis continues.

Northern Ireland   Terrorism in Northern Ireland (also known as Ulster) was rooted in Ireland's resistance to English control, exploitation, and widespread violence that began in the twelfth century. Catholic Ireland, colonized by Protestants from Scotland and England, became engulfed in religious wars that characterized Europe for much of its recent history. Nationalist terrorism in Northern Ireland was essentially a struggle by Catholics to end Protestant political, economic, and social domination. Following numerous attempts to solve the "Irish problem," the Anglo-Irish Treaty was signed in 1921. It divided Ireland into the Republic of Ireland (an independent country) and Northern Ireland (which remained part of Britain). While the Republic of Ireland is predominantly Catholic, Northern Ireland has a Protestant majority. Catholics on both sides of this artificial border refused to accept the division of Ireland and maintained a strong sense of nationalism. Catholics in Northern Ireland, known as Republicans, remained committed to ending the British presence and reunifying the two parts of Ireland. The Protestants, known as Loyalists, or Unionists, were determined to retain Northern Ireland's ties with Britain and to perpetuate their economic and political power. Both Catholics and Protestants used terrorism to achieve their respective objectives.

Although terrorism in Northern Ireland was deeply rooted in Ireland's long struggle to resist British domination, the contemporary problems began in 1922 when the Unionist government implemented the Special Powers Act to suppress opposition to its control. The IRA, founded by Michael Collins and composed of rebel units that had launched the Easter Rebellion in 1916 against British rule, became the military wing. Sinn Fein, a political party that represented Catholics in Ireland, was widely regarded as the political wing of the terrorist movement. Opposed to the division of Ireland and committed to reunifying it, the IRA engaged in terrorism in both the Republic of Ireland and Northern Ireland and was outlawed by the governments of both places. Terrorist attacks against the British in Northern Ireland continued, escalating between 1956 and 1962.[14] However, many Catholics in Northern Ireland were strongly influenced by the nonviolent Civil Rights Movement in the United States under the leadership of *Dr. Martin Luther King*, a development that weakened the militant IRA. But the use of excessive violence against Catholic Civil Rights marchers and demonstrators in 1968 by the Royal Ulster Constabulary (RUC) and growing anti-Catholic hatred—inspired to a large degree by *Reverend Ian Paisley*, leader of the hard-line Protestant Democratic Unionists—rejuvenated the IRA and laid the foundation for terrorism that plagued Northern Ireland, London, and elsewhere in Britain. The IRA, widely perceived as ineffective in protecting Catholics, was challenged by the even more militant Provisional IRA (PIRA), which was formed in 1970. As is often the case in conflicts, the most extreme groups gain the most support. Catholics in Northern Ireland rallied around the PIRA.[15] Protestants formed their own terrorist groups.

Similar to the Palestinians and Israelis, Catholics and Protestants seemed hopelessly locked in a cycle of deadly violence. Both the Republic of Ireland and Britain are strong democracies. Britain's use of violence against the IRA was checked by democratic processes and strong support for peacefully resolving the

Loyalists/Unionists ■ Protestants committed to retaining Northern Ireland's ties with Britain

IRA ■ Rebel forces opposed to Britain's presence in Northern Ireland

Easter Rebellion ■ IRA rebellion against British rule

Sinn Fein ■ Catholic party in Ireland regarded as a terrorist threat to Britain

PIRA ■ Militant outgrowth of IRA

conflict. Close political, economic, and cultural links between Britain and Ireland also helped. Equally important was support among Irish-Americans for a negotiated settlement, despite the fact that the IRA received significant economic and military assistance from some of them. Another important factor was the growing unification of Europe and the declining nationalism that accompanied the process. The activities of the IRA were receiving less and less public support. Furthermore, European integration brought many economic opportunities, recognition, and responsibilities to Ireland, which influenced it to reduce its support for the IRA.

A major step toward ending sectarian violence was the 1985 Anglo-Irish Agreement, which gave Ireland increased responsibilities in Northern Ireland and provided greater security for the Unionists by requiring an electoral majority to change Northern Ireland's political status. The major breakthrough came with the signing of the Good Friday Agreement in 1998. U.S. President Bill Clinton, British Prime Minister Tony Blair, Irish Prime Minister Bertie Ahern, Gerry Adams (head of Sinn Fein), and David Trimble (head of the Ulster Unionists) cooperated to achieve this agreement. While Britain will control Northern Ireland as long as that is the wish of the majority, Ireland is more involved in the affairs of Northern Ireland. Ireland had to terminate its territorial claim on Northern Ireland in exchange for an institutionalized voice in its government.[16] Sinn Fein and the IRA were persuaded to support the Good Friday Agreement by President Clinton and by British promises to reduce its troop presence in Northern Ireland and to support reforms of the police force to enable more Catholics to join. The 2001 terrorist attacks in the United States reinforced the peace process in Northern Ireland as many Americans pressured the IRA to abandon terrorism and disarm. For the first time, Sinn Fein supported disarming the IRA. The Independent Monitoring Commission was established to disarm it. Although this international panel concluded in April 2004 that Northern Irish paramilitaries continued to carry out violent attacks and were engaged in various criminal activities, the destruction of weapons, ammunition, and explosives underscored progress toward disarmament and ending terrorism in Northern Ireland. In 2005, the IRA renounced the armed struggle and committed itself to peaceful change. By 2006 terrorism in Northern Ireland essentially had ceased. However, sporadic violence continues.[17]

Spain   In sharp contrast with nationalist terrorism in the Middle East and Northern Ireland, Basque separatists in Spain attracted relatively little attention beyond Europe. However, massive bombings of trains in Madrid in early 2004—in which ninety-one people died and seventeen hundred were wounded—focused the spotlight on Basque terrorism, despite the fact that terrorists linked to al-Qaeda were responsible for the bombings. The 2.5 million Basques, who are concentrated in mountainous northern Spain on the Bay of Biscay and across the border into Southern France, are one of the most ancient peoples in Europe. They speak a distinct language, Euskera, and have their own culture. Basques resisted Roman occupiers to maintain their independence. Spanish rulers, unable to exercise effective control over the Basque region and other parts of Spain, recognized the political, cultural, and economic autonomy of the Basques as early as the Middle Ages. This independence laid the foundation for the emergence of the Basque Homeland and Freedom (ETA). Figure 5.1 shows the Basque region of Spain.

Anglo-Irish Agreement ■ Gave Ireland increased responsibilities in Northern Ireland in exchange for security for the Unionists

Good Friday Agreement ■ Compromise that gave Britain control over Northern Ireland and the Irish a voice in government

ETA ■ Basque separatist movement operating in Spain

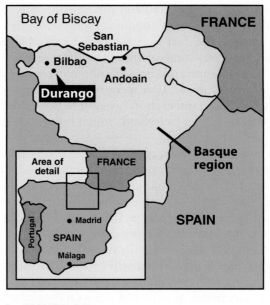

FIGURE 5.1
Basque Region of Spain

Determined to maintain their autonomy, the Basques participated in Spain's larger political and military struggle in the nineteenth century against the centralization of power in Madrid. Having joined the losing side in these conflicts, the Basques lost their autonomy and believed that their sense of identity was threatened. Between 1842 and 1868, the Basque provinces of Vizcaya and Guipuzcoa experienced rapid industrialization, urbanization, and significant population growth. While many Basques, especially the growing middle class and business leaders, strongly supported integrating the Basque region into Spain, resistance to these changes grew among the working class and others who wanted to preserve the status quo.[18] Prior to the Spanish Civil War (1936–1939), the government recognized the political and cultural autonomy of the Basque region. In return, Basques supported the government against insurgents led by Generalissimo **Francisco Franco**. Once again on the losing side in Spain's bloody struggle, the Basques were regarded as traitors by Franco, who centralized political power and abolished Basque autonomy. Any effort to maintain a separate Basque identity was severely repressed. Franco's authoritarianism, discussed in Chapter 4, fueled radicalization among the Basques. In 1959, a coalition of extremist youth groups separated from the more moderate Basque Nationalist Party to form ETA. Their principal objectives were achieving Basque independence from Spain and restoring Basque culture and language. ETA embraced a strategy of armed struggle against the Franco regime in 1962[19] but refrained from engaging in major acts of terrorism until 1968.

Following Franco's death in 1975 and Spain's transition to democracy, the Basques regained a significant degree of autonomy. They gained control over the police force, schools, and social welfare agencies. ETA continued to demand independence for the Basque region. But only about 30 percent of the Basques believed that independence was a viable option for them, compared with 60 percent who

Francisco Franco ■
Former dictator of Spain who repressed Basque separatists

claimed both Spanish and Basque identities and preferred to maintain the status quo.[20] In fact, ETA's political wing, Euskal Herritarrok, is relatively weak and has never received more than 18 percent of the Basques' votes. These realities influenced Euskal Herritarrok to work out an agreement in 1998 with more moderate Basque nationalist parties. Known as the Lizarra Agreement, it committed ETA to a cease-fire and the moderates to achieving independence through the democratic process.[21]

Intransigence and political maneuvering by the government under Prime Minister Jose Maria Aznar and ETA contributed to the demise of the cease-fire in December 1999. The government continued to maintain its hard-line policy toward ETA during the cease-fire, refusing to negotiate with it, ignoring its demands to bring ETA prisoners from the Canary Islands so that their relatives could visit them, and continuing to arrest and detain suspected ETA members. ETA became impatient with peace initiatives and escalated its terrorist activities. In a major departure from its practice of primarily targeting government officials, police officers, and members of the military, ETA became more indiscriminate in its use of violence, targeting anyone who opposed its demands for an independent Basque state.[22] Following the 2001 terrorist attacks on the United States, Aznar equated ETA with al-Qaeda and intensified Spain's fight against the Basque separatists. However, when Aznar quickly blamed the 2004 train bombings on ETA instead of al-Qaeda (the real terrorists), he lost the election that was held shortly thereafter, partly because the vast majority of Spaniards blamed his strong support for the U.S.-led invasion of Iraq for contributing to an escalation of terrorism in Europe. But the massive bombing in Madrid, Spain's consolidation of democracy and its integration into the European Union, and the sharp decline of terrorism in Northern Ireland weakened the public support for Basque terrorism and prompted the new government, led by Prime Minister Jose Luis Rodriguez Zapatero, to aggressively pursue Basque terrorists. The arrests of many of ETA's leaders significantly weakened the terrorist group. In 2006, ETA announced a permanent cease-fire. But in June 2007, ETA renounced the cease-fire and continued to engage in violent activities. In April 2009, French officials arrested Jurdan Martitegi Lizaso, the leader and military chief of ETA. Faced with declining support, ETA called a truce in 2010.[23]

Lizarra Agreement ■
Committed the ETA to a cease-fire in its struggle for independence

Religious Terrorism

Throughout history, religion has been used to justify committing acts of extreme cruelty and violence against human beings. Religious terrorism, especially that of al-Qaeda and other Islamic extremists, is widely perceived to be the most dangerous kind of terrorism, one that results in more destructive acts of indiscriminate violence. There are *four basic reasons for the extreme violence of religious terrorism*:

1. Violence is believed to be a sacramental act or divine duty in accordance with theology;
2. Religious terrorists view large-scale and indiscriminate violence as necessary for achieving their goals;
3. Religious terrorists do not feel constrained by public opinion or a need to gain popular support because they are engaged in a total war; and
4. Religious terrorists generally believe that modifying the system is insufficient; they seek fundamental changes in the existing order.[24]

Aum Supreme Truth ■ Japanese terrorist group fighting against the Japanese government

In the shadow of Mount Fuji, members of the Japanese terrorist group **Aum Supreme Truth** developed and practiced to implement their deadly attacks on innocent Japanese in 1995 under the watchful eyes of *Shiva*, the Hindu god of destruction and rebirth. If you have visited Tokyo, you know how crowded the trains are that converge on Kasumigaseki, the center of power in Japan. Imagine the death and injury an attack on the subway system would cause. This is precisely why Aum Supreme Truth selected it to launch a preemptive attack on the Japanese government to implement its mission of world domination. Armed with bags containing a chemical solution that was about 30 percent *sarin gas* (i.e., a colorless, odorless, and deadly gas invented by the Nazis), the terrorists boarded the trains, determined to inflict catastrophic damage. Twelve people were killed and more than 5500 were injured in the sarin gas attack.[25]

In the heart of America, terrorist groups also believe that they are on a mission from God to destroy the U.S. government, create a racially pure society for

Notes of Religious Terrorists Who Attacked America

The Last Night

1. Read al-Tauba (a book of the Koran) and what God has prepared for the believers and the everlasting life for the martyrs.

2. Spend the night praying for victory and to smooth our affairs and that we will not be uncovered.

3. Cleanse your heart and purify it from impurities and forget anything related to this world for the time of play is past and the time of truth has come, for we have wasted much of our lives, shouldn't we spend those remaining hours in offering repentance and obedience?

4. You should be content for there are only a few moments before the beginning of happy life and eternal paradise with all righteous and martyrs.

5. Bring yourself, your suitcase, your clothes, the knife, your equipment, your identification, your passport, and all your papers.

6. Tighten your clothes well around your bodies, for this is what the righteous ones did before the battle and make sure your shoes are not ill fitting, and that your socks do not hang out of your shoes.

7. When you board the plane and before you step in, read your prayer and repeat the same prayers we mentioned before, when you take your seat. Read this verse from the Koran: "When you meet a group, be steadfast and remember God, you will be triumphant."

8. Apply the rules of prisoners of war. Take them prisoner and kill them as God said. No Prophet can have prisoners of war. . . .

9. Open your chest welcoming death in the path of God and utter your prayer seconds before you go to your target. Let your last words be, "There is no God but God and Mohammad is His messenger." Then, God willing, you will be in heavens. ▲

Source: Excerpts from a document released by the Federal Bureau of Investigation (FBI) and reprinted in *New York Times*, 29 September 2001, B3.

whites only, and redeem the United States. The white supremacist Christian Identity movement and the Ku Klux Klan, among others, base their terrorist acts on Christianity. Their leaders often call themselves ministers. Muslim extremists also justify launching jihads (i.e., holy wars) on the basis of their religion. Many Islamic terrorists, including al-Qaeda, draw on medieval religious authorities to argue that killing innocents or even fellow Muslims is permitted if it serves the cause of jihad against the West.[26] Some Islamic terrorist organizations are closely tied to specific political and military developments in the Middle East. However, a common influence on the emergence of Islamic terrorism was the Iranian Islamic revolution, led by Ayatollah Khomeini, which overthrew the Shah in 1979.

jihad ■ Translated as "holy war" when described by Islamic terrorist groups

State Terrorism

Our definition of terrorism as the use of violence to coerce or intimidate and to generally create widespread fear among the population clearly covers many states, both historically and now. Governments have relied on torture, both physical and psychological, as their ultimate instrument of terror to control the population. Nazi Germany, Stalinist Russia, Iraq under Saddam Hussein, China, North Korea, Argentina, Chile, Guatemala, Uganda, and many other countries have used terrorism, especially torture, to repress the population and stifle dissent.

Three levels of internal state terrorism are

1. *Intimidation:* The state uses its overwhelming power to discourage opposition and dissent, usually through excessive force by the police and paramilitary organizations.
2. *Coerced Conversion:* This involves forcing the population to completely change its behavior, usually occurs after a revolution. The Soviet Union, China, and Iran are examples.
3. *Genocide:* This is the deliberate and systematic killing of an ethnic, religious, economic, intellectual, or any other group of people. Nazi Germany, Stalinist Russia, Cambodia under Pol Pot and his Khmer Rouge party, Uganda under Idi Amin, Bosnia, Sudan, and Rwanda are examples of internal state genocide.

States also use terrorism against other states or nationalist groups to secure foreign policy objectives. A distinction is often made between *state-sponsored terrorism* and *state-supported terrorism*. Both types of state terrorism are usually clandestine. In state-sponsored terrorism, states are more directly involved in the terrorist activities of the groups they support. States act through client groups and proxies. Sometimes they send terrorists to assassinate dissidents and opposition leaders who live abroad. In state-supported terrorism, states have less influence over the terrorist group.

Global Terrorism

Global terrorism encompasses activities by domestic, nationalist, religious, and state terrorists. It is characterized by its significant implications for a large number of major countries, nonstate actors, and individuals on several continents. Global terrorism is facilitated by various aspects of globalization. Terrorists take advantage of porous borders and their ability to blend into almost any major city in most parts of the world. Following al-Qaeda's 2001 attacks in the United States, it became increasingly obvious that global terrorists belonged to sleeper cells. Reminiscent of the Cold War, during which the Soviet Union relied heavily on sleeper agents to spy on the United States, global terrorists become part of a particular society, live what appear to be normal lives, and participate in terrorist activities against that society when instructed to do so. Sleeper terrorist cells have been found in the United States, Britain, Spain, Germany, Turkey, Belgium, Indonesia, Singapore, Malaysia, Italy, Pakistan, Morocco, the Philippines, and elsewhere. The Internet, inexpensive transportation, and the global media contribute to global cooperation among terrorists.

sleeper cells ■
Groups of terrorists who live what appear to be normal lives until instructed to commit terrorist attacks

Global terrorism is most often identified with Osama bin Laden and al-Qaeda. Al-Qaeda made a strong commitment to jihad as its principal objective. This struggle began in Afghanistan. Bin Laden and other holy warriors (or mujahedeen) were trained and supported by America's Central Intelligence Agency (CIA) to resist Soviet occupation of Afghanistan. However, this struggle evolved into a global jihad against the West, particularly the United States. By focusing on the United States as the country primarily responsible for creating problems for Muslims and as the common enemy of Muslims everywhere, leaders of al-Qaeda and other Islamic terrorist groups recruit and unite Islamic terrorists worldwide. Al-Qaeda evolved into an organization that is loosely hierarchical and very decentralized. Al-Qaeda, the organization, is based on an ideology articulated by Abdullah Azzam in 1987, which called for *Al-qaeda al-sulbah* (i.e., a vanguard of the strong). He envisioned Sunni Muslim radical activists who, through independent actions, would mobilize the *umma* (i.e., a global community of believers) to act against oppressors. The word *qaeda* is generally understood by Islamic militants as a precept or a method, as opposed to an organization. *Al-Qaedism* is essentially a world-view. The terrorist groups in Iraq, led by Abu al-Zarqawi, acted independently of al-Qaeda led by bin Laden.[27]

mujahedeen ■
Group of Islamic holy warriors fighting the Soviet occupation of Afghanistan

Global terrorism is directed primarily against the United States and its close allies. There are several *reasons why America is the target*:

1. The United States is the dominant global power. From the Roman Empire to the United States, leading countries have been targets.
2. America is widely regarded as the leader of globalization. Groups opposed to globalization target the United States.
3. Close ties between the United States and repressive governments—such as Saudi Arabia, Egypt, and Pakistan—motivate terrorists to attack it.
4. Establishing U.S. military bases on Muslim Holy Lands makes America a target of al-Qaeda.
5. Many American foreign policies are regarded by terrorists as hostile to Muslims.

RESPONDING TO TERRORISM

The complexity of terrorism requires employing a wide variety of instruments to combat it. In addition to military, traditional law enforcement, and intelligence responses, there is growing support for the view that increased attention must also be given to the underlying causes of terrorism. The importance of global cooperation as a component of any counterterrorism policy became increasingly obvious in the wake of al-Qaeda's attacks on the United States and other countries.

The most prevalent response to terrorism is the use of force, both domestically and internationally. Britain in Northern Ireland, Israel in the Palestinian territories, and the United States globally have relied on force, to varying degrees, to eliminate terrorism. Following the attacks on the United States, military action was taken in October 2001 against the Taliban regime and al-Qaeda in Afghanistan, a decision that was widely supported. President George W. Bush declared "war against terrorism" and stressed that America was engaged in a war of indefinite duration against a nonstate enemy that had no territory. As stated in the National Security Strategy of the United States, the priority of the United States was to disrupt and destroy terrorist organizations of global reach and attack their leadership; command, control, and communications; material support; and finances.[28] Global support of military action was underscored by the response of the North Atlantic Treaty Organization (NATO). A day following the attacks on the United States, NATO's secretary general, Lord Robertson, promised military assistance for America's campaign against terrorism. For the first time, NATO invoked the mutual defense clause in its treaty, which states that "any armed attack against allies in Europe or North America shall be considered an attack against them all."[29] America's invasion and occupation of Iraq in early 2003 was also designed, in part, to fight terrorism. Although there was no evidence linking the Iraqi leader Saddam Hussein to al-Qaeda, President Bush asserted that Hussein was involved in global terrorism.

Lord Robertson ■ NATO's secretary general who offered military assistance for America's fight against terrorism

An essential aspect of combating terrorism is gathering intelligence and using it. The purpose of acquiring information and analyzing it is to learn about impending threats and to develop strategies to counteract them. Many U.S. agencies are involved in gathering intelligence related to terrorism and other threats to national security. Governments worldwide also engage in similar activities. There are essentially *four ways to acquire intelligence*: (1) take aerial and satellite photographs and conduct general photo reconnaissance; (2) use a wide variety of listening devices to record conversations, intercept radio and other signals, and monitor computer activities; (3) use spies and informants; and (4) collaborate with intelligence agencies from other countries and nonstate organizations. The first two ways are referred to as *technical intelligence* methods and the last two are called *human intelligence* methods.

Terrorists and their supporters have access to technology and can counteract the effectiveness of technology. They may know satellite overflight schedules and how to use sophisticated encryption technologies. They also know not to use cell phones. In April 2002, terrorism investigators in Europe intercepted a cell phone call that lasted less than a minute, during which not a word was said. Suspecting that the call was a signal between terrorists, the investigators followed the trail first to one terror suspect, then to others, and eventually to terrorist cells on three continents. What linked them was a computer chip that carried prepaid minutes and allowed phones to be used globally. Authorities monitored the conversations, arrested several suspected al-Qaeda members, and prevented attacks on Saudi Arabia and Indonesia. But terrorists adjusted their strategies. They abandoned cell phones, preferring instead to use e-mail, Internet phone calls, and hand-delivered messages. Although technical intelligence is essential, the United States has relied too heavily on it and has allowed its human intelligence capabilities to deteriorate, partly by neglecting to learn foreign languages and about foreign cultures. Many terrorism experts believe that *human intelligence* is the most critical ingredient for rooting out terrorist groups because the essence of the terrorist threat is the capacity to conspire.

Simply acquiring information is insufficient to counteract terrorism. That information must be utilized, and ways of thinking about threats to national security must be critically examined. Richard A. Clarke, chief of counterterrorism in both the Clinton and Bush administrations, argued in his book, *Against All Enemies*, that the Bush administration essentially ignored the threat from al-Qaeda prior to the attacks on September 11, 2001. A major impediment to using intelligence effectively was inadequate communication between the FBI and the CIA. In an increasingly global society, distinctions between internal and external are becoming less relevant. In light of this reality, experts stressed the need to remove the barriers that divide domestic and foreign intelligence gathering.[30] Threats from global terrorism have influenced governments to strengthen their domestic security and to pay closer attention to how globalization and global terrorism intertwine. For example, water is the major link that countries have to the global economy. Almost all exports and imports are carried by ships. It is estimated that 95 percent of what comes into and goes out of America is by ships. Consequently, the global community, led by the United States, adopted a global code that requires the world's ships and ports to create counterterrorism systems, such as computers, communications gear, surveillance cameras, and security patrols. Ships that do not meet these standards or that have visited ports that do not meet these standards can be turned away from American waters.[31] Countering terrorism in this way could seriously undermine global trade. A major domestic step toward protecting the United States against terrorism was the creation of the *Department of Homeland Security*. Its functions include controlling immigration and U.S. borders, monitoring foreign students, enhancing airport security, inspecting foreign ports, examining cargo containers, and cooperating with state and local governments to prevent terrorist attacks.

Richard A. Clarke ■
Former chief antiterrorism adviser under the Clinton and Bush administrations

FIGHTING TERRORISM AND PROTECTING DEMOCRACY

During the U.S. invasion of Afghanistan in 2001, approximately 650 persons were arrested, transported to the U.S. naval base at Guantanamo Bay in Cuba, and imprisoned by the U.S. military without access to lawyers or visits from family members. In 2004, the U.S. Supreme Court ruled against President Bush and strongly supported an individual's right to due process of law. In April 2009, the U.S. Justice Department released classified memos describing harsh interrogation techniques, including torture, used by the CIA against terrorist suspects. Many of these techniques were used by Communist China. One prisoner was waterboarded 183 times. The United States, a leading advocate of individual rights, prosecuted some Japanese interrogators at the War Crimes trials in Tokyo after World War II for waterboarding and other techniques.[32] In January 2009, President Obama said

Guantanamo Bay ■
U.S. naval base where enemy prisoners of war are being held

America would close Guantanamo. However, in February 2011, he decided that Guantanamo trials would continue. Obama issued an executive order requiring a review of the status of prisoners and U.S. compliance with Geneva Conventions and international law banning torture and inhumane treatment.[33]

Immediately following the terrorist attacks in September 2001, the U.S. Congress enacted the USA Patriot Act to protect the country from terrorist attacks. This law gave the federal government the power to conduct wiretaps, monitor books borrowed from libraries, demand access to financial records, and employ a wide range of investigative tools against people suspected of terrorism. All of these cases raise fundamental questions about finding a balance between fighting terrorism and protecting democracy within the United States. With key provisions of the Patriot Act about to expire in May 2011, Congress passed a four-year extension of those post–September 11 powers. Those include laws giving federal investigators access to a suspect's materials and allowing them to conduct roving wiretaps of terrorist suspects as they change phones or locations, and laws enabling government officials to conduct surveillance on foreign terrorism suspects who do not appear to be connected to known terrorist groups.

USA Patriot Act ■
Controversial initiative passed by the Bush administration to fight terrorist threats

CASE STUDY | Terrorism in Pakistan

Although Osama bin Laden, widely viewed as the embodiment of global terrorism, was killed by U.S. Special Forces on May 1, 2011, the end of the war on terrorism is not in sight. Endemic terrorism in Pakistan, a country with nuclear weapons and an ongoing rivalry with India, which also has nuclear weapons, undermines America's struggle against both the Taliban and al-Qaeda in Afghanistan and Pakistan. Terrorism also complicates U.S. relations with India, a country that America perceives as an important economic and strategic partner to balance China's rising power and weaken its threat to America's global leadership. Furthermore, Pakistan is widely perceived as a failing state that poses significant security problems. Internal rivalries among government agencies responsible for fighting terrorism, political instability and government corruption, ethnic and regional fragmentation, and government incompetence complicate America's war on terrorism and make winning it highly unlikely. The rapid spread of Islamic fundamentalism, increasing religious intolerance, widespread poverty, and economic and social problems caused by devastating

floods provide an environment conducive to continuing violence by the Taliban, al-Qaeda, and other militant groups. The government's failure to provide timely assistance to flood victims not only helps terrorists recruit impoverished youth but also emboldens them by demonstrating Pakistan's fundamental weaknesses. Lack of trust between Pakistan and the United States, as manifested in the aftermath of the secret unilateral U.S. operation that killed bin Laden at his compound in Pakistan, erodes the effectiveness of efforts to combat terrorism. Mistrust is reinforced by Pakistan's duplicity and America's proclivity to act independently to find terrorists and its escalation of drone attacks on suspected terrorist targets. Many civilians have been killed, which engenders strong anti-American sentiments. Both ordinary Pakistanis and terrorist groups perceive America as a common enemy and the war on terrorism as an American war. Under these circumstances, the army has refrained from aggressively pursuing terrorists. Moreover, the army believes that protecting Pakistan's border with India is a more pressing priority than fighting the Taliban and al-Qaeda.

(continued)

CASE STUDY | continued

Pakistan's Taliban, which is not a monolithic group, embraces Saudi Arabia's version of Islam, known as Wahhabism. Wahhabism is extremely conservative, intolerant, hard-line, and rigid. Its traditions and practices were espoused by bin Laden, who was a Saudi Arabian and a Taliban supporter. Pakistan's internal politics and instability and the Soviet invasion of Afghanistan contributed to the use of Islamic fundamentalism and the Taliban in Pakistan. Political and military leaders advocated Islamic fundamentalism to strengthen their positions and enhance their claims to legitimate rule. Zia ul Haq, for example, a military dictator, introduced Shari'a law, favored by Islamic political parties, and promoted orthodox Muslims in the armed forces and bureaucracy.[34] As we will see in Chapter 14, conflict in Afghanistan contributed to the proliferation of small arms and an infusion of money into Pakistan. American and Saudi Arabian support of Afghan resistance to Soviet occupation eventually fostered the emergence of the Taliban and al-Qaeda. Saudi Arabia's hardline Wahhabism undermined Pakistan's more tolerant Sufi-based version of Islam, especially through Saudi funding of madrassas (Islamic schools) in Pakistan. In its conflict with India, Pakistan used its Inter-Services Intelligence agency (ISI) to provide support for the Taliban and other militants in both Indian-controlled Kashmir and Afghanistan. Ethnic divisions in Pakistan and the remoteness of many parts of the country helped al-Qaeda establish safe havens in Pakistan, with bin Laden as an example of that. As the army made progress against terrorists operating in these remote areas, the Taliban began targeting urban areas. The Taliban also cooperated with Pakistani fundamentalists who target both Christians and Muslims for violations of blasphemy laws. In early 2011, both Salman Taseer, the governor of Punjab, and Shahbaz Bhatti, a cabinet minister, were assassinated because of their support of religious tolerance and human rights. Their opposition to the blasphemy laws was widely perceived by many Pakistanis as part of a Western, primarily American, campaign against Islam.[35]

The complicated nature of politics in Pakistan, ongoing tensions with India, and America's broader foreign policy objectives to restrain China's rise make it extremely difficult to significantly weaken the Taliban and other terrorist groups. As more Pakistanis experience the costs of terrorism, it is likely that they will strengthen efforts to defeat the Taliban. Longer-term solutions include reducing poverty, improving education, promoting economic development, restoring religious and political tolerance, and diminishing tensions with India. ▶

Wahhabism ■
Conservative version
of Islam embraced
by the Taliban in
Pakistan

SUMMARY AND REVIEW

This chapter addressed the problem of global terrorism. Since the September 2001 attacks in the United States, the assumption that superior state military power ensures a high degree of national security has been seriously challenged. Specifically, we have seen a rise in what has become known as asymmetrical warfare, in which smaller, weaker groups—such as al-Qaeda—can inflict significant harm and damage against more powerful states, such as the United States. Increased globalization has created a global environment more conducive to international terrorism. Increased global migration, the growth of global cities, relatively inexpensive global and regional travel options, revolutions in communication technologies, and the explosion in global trade have all helped to create an environment in which global terrorism has gained prominence.

In this chapter, we discussed the difficulties involved in accurately defining terrorism. As acts of terrorism incite emotional responses, it becomes increasingly difficult to agree on an objective definition of terrorism. Terrorist acts are designed to achieve specific, concrete goals. Often terrorists commit acts of violence against civilians in order to create fear and confusion. Terrorist acts are usually intended to be indiscriminate, in order to arouse a more fearful response from a population that does not know which public targets may be attacked next. In effect, terrorists are waging a form of psychological warfare against civilian populations. Another goal of terrorist acts is to humiliate governments, as we see in the example of Iraqi terrorists opposed to the U.S. presence in Iraq who have decided to target humanitarian aid workers in Iraq. In addition to the goals of terrorists, we also addressed the reasons and motivations for committing terrorist acts. We also discussed various forms of terrorism, including domestic terrorism, nationalist terrorism, religious terrorism, state terrorism, and global terrorism. Following the forms of terrorism, we examined some of the methods of financing terrorism, as well as various responses to terrorist acts.

KEY TERMS

asymmetrical power   91
Reign of Terror   91
Edmund Burke   91
guerrilla warfare   92
Uighurs   92
madrassas   92
Taliban   94
virtual networks   94
hawalas   95
Muammar Qaddafi   95
Revolutionary United Front (RUF)   95
Hezbollah   95
Abu Sayyaf   96
Tamil Tigers   96
domestic terrorism   98
nationalist terrorism   98
religious terrorism   98
state terrorism   98
global terrorism   98
Red Brigades   99
November 17   99
dirty war   100
Shining Path   100
Revolutionary Armed Forces of Colombia
  (FARC)   100
Holocaust   100
Menachem Begin   100

Irgun   101
fedayeen   101
Gamel Abdel Nasser   101
Six-Day War   101
PLO   101
Black September Organization   101
intifada   101
Loyalists/Unionists   102
IRA   102
Easter Rebellion   102
Sinn Fein   102
Provisional IRA (PIRA)   102
Anglo-Irish Agreement   103
Good Friday Agreement   103
Basque Homeland and Freedom
  (ETA)   103
Francisco Franco   104
Lizarra Agreement   105
Aum Supreme Truth   106
jihad   107
sleeper cells   108
mujahedeen   108
Lord Robertson   109
Richard A. Clarke   110
Guantanamo Bay   110
USA Patriot Act   111
Wahhabism   112

DISCUSSION QUESTIONS

1. What is asymmetrical power? How does it relate to the war on terror? Give examples.
2. Do you believe one can objectively define terrorism, or will such attempts always result in subjective, relative definitions?
3. What are some of the goals of and reasons for terrorism discussed in this chapter?
4. Discuss the different kinds of terrorism. Give examples.
5. Discuss America's responses to terrorism. Evaluate the costs and effectiveness of those responses.

SUGGESTED READINGS

Bergen, Peter L. *The Longest War.* New York: Free Press, 2011. Discusses how strategic errors and America's harsh methods in Iraq contributed to prolonging the war against al-Qaeda.

English, Richard. *Terrorism: How to Respond.* New York: Oxford University Press, 2009. Governments must realize that the effectiveness of military responses to terrorism is limited and that an emphasis should be on gathering and using intelligence.

Farrall, Leah. "How al Qaeda Works," *Foreign Affairs 90*, No. 2 (March/April 2011): *128–139.* Despite the war against terrorism, al-Qaeda's power has increased. It has expanded its power by working with many groups and organizations.

Gross, Michael J. *Moral Dilemmas of Modern War.* Cambridge: Cambridge University Press, 2009. Analyzes how the role of civilians in conflicts challenges Western countries. They must decide if they will abandon prohibitions against torture.

Stern, Jessica. "Mind Over Martyr," *Foreign Affairs 89*, No. 1 (January/February 2010): *95–108.* Draws on experiences in Europe and the Middle East with terrorists and extremists and questions whether terrorists can be radicalized.

ENDNOTES

1. Martha Crenshaw, "Thoughts on Relating Terrorism to Historical Contexts," in *Terrorism in Context*, ed. Martha Crenshaw (University Park: Penn State University Press, 1995), 9–10.
2. Paul Wilkinson, *Terrorism Versus Democracy* (London: Frank Cass, 2000), 1.
3. Robert W. Hefner and Muhammad Zaman, *Schooling Islam* (Princeton, NJ: Princeton University Press, 2007).
4. Thomas L. Friedman, "The Humiliation Factor," *New York Times*, 9 November 2003, Sect. 4, 11.
5. Leah Farrall, "How al-Qaeda Works," *Foreign Affairs* 90, No. 2 (March/April 2011), 128.
6. Ingrid Betancourt, *Even Silence Has to End: My Six Years in the Colombian Jungle* (New York: Penguin Press, 2010).
7. Jeanne K. Giralda and Harold A. Trinkunas, eds., *Terrorism Financing and State Responses* (Stanford, CA: Stanford University Press, 2007).
8. Augustus Richard Norton, *Hezbollah* (Princeton, NJ: Princeton University Press, 2007).
9. "Airline Losses Hit $14 Billion Worldwide," *Chicago Tribune*, 7 January 2003, Sect. 3, 3.
10. Peter Bergen, *The Longest War: The Enduring Conflict Between America and al-Qaeda* (New York: Free Press, 2011).
11. Bruce Hoffman, *Inside Terrorism* (London: Victor Gollancz, 1998), 51.

12. Hoffman, *Inside Terrorism*, 68.
13. Gal Luft, "The Palestinian H-Bomb," *Foreign Affairs* 81, No. 4 (July/August 2002), 2.
14. Wilkinson, *Terrorism Versus Democracy*, 31.
15. Wilkinson, *Terrorism Versus Democracy*, 31.
16. Jonathan Stevenson, "Peace in Northern Ireland: Why Now?" *Foreign Policy* 112 (Fall 1998), 41–46.
17. "The Curse of the Conflict Junkies, *Economist*, 4 December 2010, 69.
18. Goldie Shabad and Francisco Ramo, "Political Violence in a Democratic State: Basque Terrorism in Spain," in *Terrorism in Context*, 411.
19. Shabad and Ramo, "Political Violence," in *Terrorism in Context*, 411.
20. Susanne Daley, "Fear Spreads as Spanish and Basque Blood Flows," *New York Times*, 11 August 2000, A3.
21. Ray Moseley, "Divides Run Deep and Long in Spain's Basque Conflict," *Chicago Tribune*, 10 September 2000, Sect. 1, 3.
22. Carlta Vitzthum, "Basque Separatists Escalate Terrorism," *Wall Street Journal*, 4 December 2000, A20.
23. "ETA's Ceasefire," *Economist*, 11 September 2010, 62.
24. Hoffman, *Inside Terrorism*, 94–95; and Tony Blair, "A Battle for Global Values," *Foreign Affairs* 86, No. 1 (January/February 2007), 79–80.
25. David E. Kaplan and Andrew Marshall, *The Cult at the End of the World* (New York: Crown Publishers, 1996), 1.
26. Robert Worth, "The Deep Intellectual Roots of Islamic Terror," *New York Times*, 13 October 2001, A13.
27. Leah Farrall, "How al-Qaeda Works," 128.
28. George W. Bush, "The National Security Strategy of the United States," *New York Times*, 20 September 2002, A10.
29. Suzanne Daley, "NATO Quickly Gives the U.S. All the Help That It Asked," *New York Times*, 5 October 2001, B6.
30. Mike McConnell, "Overhauling Intelligence," *Foreign Affairs* 86, No. 4 (July/August 2007), 49–50.
31. Tim Weiner, "U.S. Law Puts Honduran Port on Notice," *New York Times*, 24 March 2004, A6.
32. Kenneth Roth, "After Guantánomo," *Foreign Affairs* 87, No. 3 (May/June 2008), 9–11; and Mark Mazzetti and Scott Shane, "Memos Spell Out Brutal CIA Mode of Interrogation," *New York Times*, 17 April 2009, A1.
33. Scott Shane and Mark Landler, "Obama, in Reversal, Clears Way for Guantanamo Trials to Resume," *New York Times*, 8 March 2011, A19.
34. "Things Fall Apart," *Economist*, 5 March 2011, 43.
35. "Pakistan's Increasing Radicalization," *Economist*, 8 January 2011, 39.

Weapons Proliferation

INTRODUCTION

Inextricably linked to wars is the proliferation of weapons. Throughout history, human beings have used weapons deliberately designed to inflict maximum damage on their enemies. Ancient warriors regarded the catapult as the ultimate weapon of mass destruction. It was the sturdy springboard that hurled flaming missiles, diseased corpses, lethal arrows, and various projectiles over castle walls and into enemy territory.[1] The invention of gunpowder and the cannon marked another improvement in weapons of mass destruction. Biological weapons, and the terror they create, were also used during the American Revolutionary War by the British to prevent the colonies from gaining independence. Smallpox, which killed around 130,000 North Americans, was deliberately spread by British forces. General George Washington, aware that the British had infected Native Americans who threatened Fort Pitt, instructed the U.S. Postal Service to dip letters from Boston in vinegar to kill any germs. Smallpox devastated the Colonies because most people had not developed immunity to the disease. Furthermore, dislocations during the war facilitated the spread of smallpox. Armies going through towns, populations migrating to escape conflict, and demobilized soldiers became effective transmitters of the disease.[2] During the American Civil War, Dr. Luke Blackburn, a Southern sympathizer, arrived in Bermuda, which was being devastated by a yellow fever epidemic, claiming to be a specialist on the disease. Dr. Blackburn secretly collected victims' clothing, blankets, sheets, and poultices and put them into three trunks to be shipped to Canada and then to New York. His objective was to initiate a yellow fever epidemic in Northern cities. The plot was eventually discovered by spies loyal to the United States.[3] Diseases as weapons of mass destruction have a long history.

National defense has been the largely unquestioned dominant priority of governments throughout the world, and the development and deployment of weapons of mass destruction have been routinely justified on the grounds of national security. Competition among nations engenders arms races that directly contribute to the global proliferation of the most destructive weapons. As the frontiers of military technology advance, states attempt to maintain or enhance their relative position in the hierarchies of regional and global power.[4] However, as we pointed out in Chapter 2, the struggle for primacy among nations is complicated by the forces of globalization. Although weapons of mass destruction have long been a leading global issue, global terrorism has heightened concerns about the proliferation of nuclear, biological, and chemical weapons. However, this chapter shows that while such weapons are potentially catastrophic, small arms and light weapons are actually being used today as weapons of mass destruction. The chapter concludes with a case study of countries that abandoned nuclear weapons programs because of the belief that their security and other national interests would be enhanced without them.

smallpox ■ Disease that killed approximately 130,000 North Americans during the Revolutionary War; deliberately spread by British forces

THE PROLIFERATION OF WEAPONS

Competition for power among groups and nation-states essentially guaranteed advancements in military technology and the spread of new and more destructive weapons. A basic problem with efforts to reduce the proliferation of weapons is that individuals embrace the Hobbesian worldview, which places the constant struggle for power and dominance at the center of international relations. Many countries, especially the dominant powers, champion promoting nonproliferation regimes, but they generally remain committed to protecting their own national security interests primarily by developing even more deadly weapons and transferring more destructive weapons to their allies. Countries such as the United States, Russia, France, China, and Britain often resist global efforts to restrain their weapons sales. Nonproliferation efforts are undermined by the globalization of weapons production and trade. Modern nonproliferation efforts have generally concentrated on weapons of mass destruction, principally nuclear, chemical, and biological weapons.

Hobbesian worldview ■ Places the constant struggle for power and dominance at the center of international relations

Reasons for the Proliferation of Weapons

In this section we will briefly summarize the *strategic, economic, and political motivations for proliferation.* These include

1. *Superpower Rivalry During the Cold War:* Geopolitical considerations influenced the United States and the Soviet Union to transfer weapons to their respective allies. For example, both the North Atlantic Treaty Organization (NATO) and the Warsaw Pact justified the proliferation of weapons in terms of collective self-defense.

2. *Military Burden Sharing:* Reluctant to engage in direct military confrontation, both superpowers provided weapons, technical assistance, and arms production technologies to their allies so that they could defend themselves. An example of this was the Nixon Doctrine, which supported weapons transfers to Japan, South Korea, Taiwan, and other Asian countries.[5]

3. *Regional Balance of Power:* Arms sales are often defended on the grounds that such transfers contribute to regional stability and diminish the likelihood of war.

4. *Political, Military, and Economic Influence:* Given the dependence of the United States on petroleum supplies from the Middle East in general and Saudi Arabia in particular, arms transfers are instrumental not only in bolstering these countries' security but also in enabling the United States to gain and maintain access to these countries' political, military, and economic elites.

5. *Economies of Scale:* Many countries export weapons to obtain resources to finance the development and production of more advanced weapons.

6. *Self-Reliance:* Many countries develop their own weapons to preserve or enhance their independence.

7. *Economic Factors:* Much of the global weapons trade is motivated by financial considerations.

8. *Ethnic Conflicts:* Ethnic conflicts generate demand for weapons transfers.

9. *Authoritarian Regimes:* Governments that rule without the consent of the people generally rely on military force to exercise control.

military burden sharing ■ When superpowers provide weapons, technical assistance, and arms production technologies to their allies, they can defend themselves.

Nixon Doctrine ■ Approach announced by U.S. President Nixon in 1969 shifting more responsibility to allies to contribute to their own defense

10. *Global Criminal Activities:* Terrorism, drug trafficking, smuggling, money laundering, and other criminal activities stimulate demand for weapons.
11. *Cultural Values:* Beliefs in using force to resolve conflicts and the right of individuals to own weapons contribute to the proliferation of weapons.
12. *The Disintegration of the Soviet Union and the Fall of Communism.* Many countries in the Soviet bloc reduced their armed forces and have excess weapons, especially small arms.

The Proliferation of Small Arms

Although nuclear, chemical, and biological weapons pose catastrophic threats to global security, small arms and light weapons are now instrumental in mass destruction in many countries around the world. Roughly 300,000 to 500,000 people are killed every year by small arms and light weapons globally. Small arms and light weapons, many of them supplied by France, were used in the Rwandan genocide. Although the United States, Russia, and China are the dominant manufacturers and exporters of small arms and light weapons, it is estimated that one thousand companies in ninety-eight countries produce such weapons and that there are 380 million civilian owners of these weapons worldwide. In practical terms, distinguishing small arms from light weapons is not very useful. As we mentioned earlier, machetes and other crude weapons are used to kill people in conflict around the world. In 1997, the United Nations, realizing the futility of trying to formulate precise definitions of small arms and light weapons, simply described them collectively as weapons that can be carried by an individual or transported in light trucks. These weapons include handguns, assault rifles, machine guns, grenade launchers, mortars, and shoulder-fired missiles. Throughout the world, the Automat Kalashnikov (AK-47) is the favorite light weapon of governments, rebel groups, criminals, and terrorists. Designed by Mikhail Kalashnikov in the Soviet Union in 1947 for the Soviet military, the AK-47 has many advantages over the Israeli-made Uzi and the U.S.-made M-16. It is relatively inexpensive, widely available, has only nine moving parts, weighs roughly 10 pounds, has a range of more than 1,000 yards, and fires thirty rounds in just three seconds. The disintegration of the Soviet Union left many Eastern European countries with large stockpiles of AK-47s, which found their way onto the global market. These are the weapons most widely used by both terrorists and Afghan soldiers in Afghanistan.[6]

Confronted with escalating violence along the U.S.–Mexico border, U.S. Secretary of State Hillary Rodham Clinton stressed that America's inability to stop U.S. weapons from being smuggled into Mexico fueled the violence. President Barack Obama was reminded by Mexico's President Felipe Calderón that roughly 90 percent of the weapons seized in Mexico come from the United States. A U.S. ban on assault rifles expired in 2004, thereby enabling the virtually unrestricted sale of lethal weapons. The basic argument advanced by the U.S. National Rifle Association and opponents to laws regulating the sale and ownership of guns rests on America's belief that the Second Amendment to the U.S. Constitution guarantees individuals the right to keep and bear arms. In addition to roughly 78,000 gun dealers nationwide, individuals are also permitted to sell assault rifles. Many of the military-style rifles used in Mexico are sold by dealers in Texas, Arizona, and New Mexico.[7]

Although *land mines* and *cluster bombs* are often overlooked in discussions on weapons proliferation, they cause widespread suffering even after wars have ended. Thousands of innocent civilians are killed each year by these weapons. In fact, both weapons are deliberately deployed to inflict maximum physical damage and psychological terror. Millions of land mines have been laid in approximately sixty-two countries. Advances in technology have made land mines cheaper to produce but harder and more expensive to find and remove. Global opposition to land mines culminated in the 1997 Ottawa Treaty that banned land mines. However, major countries, including the United States, rejected banning these weapons. Although roughly 111 countries agreed to ban the use of cluster bombs, which are fired from aircraft and artillery and contain hundreds of bomblets that remain lethal long after the conflict, the United States, Israel, China, Russia, India, Brazil, Pakistan, and other military powers have not agreed to ban them. Cluster bombs were used by the United States and Britain during the invasion of Iraq, by Israel in its conflict with Lebanon, and by Libya against prodemocracy groups in 2011.[8]

There are several distinguishing characteristics that make small arms and light weapons attractive.[9] These include

1. *Low Cost:* These weapons are relatively inexpensive to produce because of economies+ of scale and their relatively low level of technological sophistication.
2. *Easy Availability:* As we mentioned earlier, there are one thousand companies in ninety-eight countries producing them.
3. *Lethality:* These deadly weapons provide sufficient firepower to enable their users to effectively engage military forces and law enforcement agents.
4. *Simplicity and Durability:* They often require little training to be used effectively, are easy to maintain, and are very reliable under difficult environmental conditions.
5. *Portability and Concealability:* As you have seen many times, terrorists, rebel groups, criminals, and others are able to hide these weapons until they decide to use them.
6. *Dual Usage:* Small arms and light weapons in many countries are available to both military and police forces and ordinary civilians.

Small arms and light weapons are transferred in four basic ways: (1) governments transferring weapons to other governments, (2) government-sanctioned commercial sales, (3) covert deliveries by governments or private firms with the assistance of governments, and (4) illicit sales.[10]

conventional weapons ■ Regular weapons used in military conflict, including heavy artillery, missiles, tanks, aircraft, ships, submarines, and armored vehicles

Discussions of the nonproliferation of weapons also generally ignore transfers of conventional weapons, such as heavy artillery, missiles, tanks, aircraft, ships, submarines, and armored vehicles. Conventional weapons are widely regarded as acceptable for use in conflicts and are responsible for mass destruction in many countries. Given the lethality of both conventional weapons and small arms and light weapons and their routine use in conflicts, separating them from potentially catastrophic nuclear, chemical, and biological weapons is largely a matter of semantics.

THE PROLIFERATION OF NUCLEAR WEAPONS

As the brutal war raged across the Pacific between the United States and Japan, scientists at the Los Alamos laboratory in New Mexico were developing the first atomic bomb. By July 16, 1945, the bomb was successfully tested near Alamogordo, New Mexico. The destructive power of this weapon, clearly recognized by its creators, became a reality when the American B-29 bomber, the Enola Gay, piloted by Colonel Paul Tibbets, dropped the first atomic bomb, nicknamed Little Boy, on Hiroshima, Japan, at 8:16 A.M. on August 6, 1945. A blinding flash of white light was followed by a huge fireball of several million degrees centigrade that vaporized people and buildings. Radioactive "black rain" and fires left roughly 130,000 people dead or injured and 70,000 buildings (out of a total of 76,000) destroyed or severely damaged. Three days later, a much more powerful atomic bomb, nicknamed Fat Man, was dropped on Nagasaki, Japan, killing or injuring around 100,000 people.[11] The nuclear age revolutionized warfare. These weapons of mass destruction could literally destroy our planet. America's nuclear monopoly was challenged by the Soviet Union, which developed its own atomic weapon in 1949. Britain became a nuclear power in 1952, followed by France in 1960 and China in 1964.

The nuclear age was accompanied by the emerging Cold War, a reality that underscored the dangers of nuclear proliferation. The Soviet Union began building long-range bombers that could reach the United States. Concerned about the bomber gap between the two superpowers, America escalated its own military build-up. It successfully tested a new and more powerful weapon, the hydrogen bomb (also known as a thermonuclear bomb), only to be followed by the Soviet Union nine months later (in 1953). Taking advantage of captured German technology on rocketry and German scientists, the Soviets began mass production of medium-range ballistic missiles in 1955. In 1957, the Soviet Union shocked the world in general and the United States in particular with the launching of Sputnik, the world's first artificial satellite. Using the same rocket engines that shot Sputnik into orbit, the Soviets fired an intercontinental missile over a range of 5,000 miles,[12] clearly demonstrating the Soviet Union's ability to strike the United States with nuclear weapons. The United States, determined to close the missile gap and to prevent the Soviet Union from gaining nuclear superiority, developed a wide range of nuclear weapons. This nuclear arms race created what Britain's Prime Minister Winston Churchill called a mutual balance of terror. Neither the United States nor the Soviet Union could launch nuclear weapons against the other without suffering catastrophic consequences itself. The awesome destructiveness of nuclear weapons actually deterred countries from using them. The concept of mutual assured destruction (MAD) emanated from the reality that a nuclear exchange between the superpowers would be suicidal.[13]

In addition to providing security through deterrence, nuclear weapons are also perceived as enhancing a country's global status, strengthening its sovereignty, and enabling it to intimidate other countries. A major concern about nuclear proliferation is that the larger the group of countries possessing them, the more likely it is that some countries will deliberately or accidentally start a nuclear war. A hallmark of the Cold War was the restraint exercised by the

Hiroshima ■ Japanese city on which the United States dropped the world's first atomic bomb, killing 130,000 people and causing unprecedented destruction.

bomber gap ■ During the Cold War, the Soviet Union began building long-range bombers that could reach the United States; the United States did not yet have this capability.

Sputnik ■ The world's first artificial satellite created by the Soviet Union

mutual balance of terror ■ Situation during the Cold War nuclear arms race in which neither the United States nor the Soviet Union could launch nuclear weapons against the other without suffering catastrophic consequences itself

MAD ■ The reality that a nuclear exchange between the superpowers would be suicidal

superpowers. They emphasized deterrence and the development of a system of command and control. The major exception to this was the Cuban missile crisis in October 1962. When the United States discovered that the Soviet Union had nuclear missiles in Cuba, President John F. Kennedy implemented a naval block-ade of Cuba and demanded that the Soviet Union withdraw its missiles. The cri-sis ended October 28 when the Soviet Union, under the leadership of Premier Nikita S. Krushchev, agreed to withdraw the missiles immediately in exchange for ending the blockade, a U.S. pledge to not invade Cuba, and the removal of U.S. missiles from Turkey. By contrast, nuclear powers such as India and Pakistan have not implemented institutional safeguards to prevent accidental nuclear war. Furthermore, unlike the United States and the Soviet Union, which were allies in two world wars, India and Pakistan have engaged in military conflicts since their creation in 1947. In the following section, we will briefly discuss examples of nuclear proliferation.

China and Japan

America's use of nuclear weapons against Japan and the subsequent nuclear arms race between the United States and the Soviet Union influenced China to develop its own nuclear weapons to deter nuclear attacks and to inflict unacceptable dam-age on the enemy. China's policy of minimum deterrence called for potential retal-iatory strikes against large value targets, such as major cities. Unlike global powers, such as the United States and the Soviet Union, China perceived itself more as a regional power that had to develop sufficient nuclear power to be taken seriously by the major countries. Most of its nuclear weapons are short and medium range, which are suitable for use in Eurasia. However, China has developed a smaller number of intercontinental nuclear weapons that are capable of hitting targets in the United States. It accepted international restraints on its nuclear weapons activ-ity in 1996 by signing the Comprehensive Test Ban Treaty, which limits the right of countries to conduct nuclear weapons tests.

Several factors have contributed to China's decision to become a more robust nuclear power. As we saw in our discussion of the rise and fall of great pow-ers in Chapter 2, economic success often fuels military growth and changes how countries perceive their position in the global system relative to that of dominant powers. China's rapid economic growth is undoubtedly influencing it to acquire greater military power. From the perspective of power transition theory, discussed in Chapter 2, China is likely to challenge the United States for global leadership. Another factor contributing to China's modernization of its nuclear weapons is the nuclear capability of both the United States and Russia. China would like to have an effective nuclear deterrence against both countries, especially in light of America's efforts to build a missile defense system that would lessen its own vul-nerability to nuclear attacks while leaving other countries vulnerable to nuclear attacks. An important component of China's concerns is the United States' strong support for Taiwan. These concerns were diminished following the election of a more pro-China government in Taiwan in 2008. Furthermore, China's reassess-ment of its nuclear capabilities is influenced by the emergence of India and Paki-stan, neighboring countries, as nuclear powers.[14]

Although Japan, the only country against which nuclear bombs were used, does not have nuclear weapons, nuclear proliferation in Asia, among other factors, has heightened concerns about Japan's rise as a nuclear power. Influenced by the bombing of Hiroshima and Nagasaki and forced demilitarization by the United States as the occupying power, Japan adopted a policy of pacifism, which rejected owning, producing, or allowing nuclear weapons to be placed on its territory. In fact, the Japanese Constitution, written by the United States during the occupation (1945–1952), prohibits Japan from having an army and from using military force to resolve disputes. However, Japan's emergence as a global economic and technological power has enabled it to acquire the ability to produce nuclear weapons. Japan, which relies heavily on nuclear energy, has enough plutonium and uranium to construct thousands of nuclear weapons. Japan's space program enables it to rapidly convert its rockets into missile launchers. North Korea's decision to test a ballistic missile that flew over Japan in 1998, China's rising military power, the nuclearization of India and Pakistan, and growing doubts among Japanese leaders about America's commitment to Japan's security have all contributed to increased public support in Japan for developing nuclear weapons.[15] However, nuclear radiation from the nuclear power plant that was damaged in the 2011 earthquake and tsunami reminded many Japanese of Hiroshima and Nagasaki and reinforced their ambivalence about building nuclear weapons.

policy of pacifism
■ Japan's decision to not own, produce, or allow nuclear weapons on its territory

India and Pakistan

Although India's disputes with Pakistan played a pivotal role in its development of nuclear weapons, to understand the emergence of the second nuclear age in Asia we need to briefly examine India's perception of its position in contemporary global society. As we discussed in Chapter 1, an earlier period of globalization that was marked by European expansion into Asia, the Americas, and Africa heralded what many developing countries, including India, perceived as an unequal distribution of power. The acquisition of nuclear weapons by Asian countries represents a direct challenge to the world order constructed by Europeans. It is widely believed that both India and China, with combined populations representing a third of humanity and rapidly growing economies, are rising powers that view military strength as an essential component of global power. Based on their historical as well as contemporary experience, these countries have concluded that military might enables Europeans and Americans to shape the global economic, cultural, and political system. When the Portuguese, led by Vasco da Gama, arrived in India in 1498, Indians began their long experience of colonization by Europeans who had superior military technology. India's status as a nuclear power marks what has been called a post–Vasco da Gama era.[16]

Vasco da Gama ■
Portuguese explorer who arrived in India in 1498

Fueled by nationalism and a determination to reject the virtual nuclear weapons monopoly enjoyed by the five permanent members of the UN Security Council, India believes nuclear nonproliferation is not in its national interest. From India's perspective, the nuclear Non-Proliferation Treaty (NPT), the Comprehensive Test Ban Treaty, and other similar agreements are not really about nuclear disarmament. Instead, they are designed to ratify the nuclear status quo.[17] Shortly after gaining independence in 1947, India's first Prime Minister, Jawaharlal Nehru,

Jawaharlal Nehru
■ India's first prime minister; advocated ending all nuclear testing

advocated ending all nuclear testing. In 1962, China and India briefly fought each other over a disputed border. As we mentioned earlier, China became a nuclear power in 1964, a development that influenced India to focus on becoming a nuclear power. Although India declared its continued commitment to nuclear disarmament, it refused to sign the nuclear NPT. By 1974, the world learned that India had conducted its first nuclear test.

Pakistan, a country formed in opposition to India, was clearly worried by its rival's nuclear capabilities and was determined to counteract India's power by developing nuclear weapons. As we will discuss in Chapter 11, global migration contributes to the globalization of scientific knowledge. In an effort to develop their own enriched uranium for their nuclear power industry and lessen their dependence on the United States, several European countries—Britain, Germany, and the Netherlands—concluded the Treaty of Almelo in 1970. This agreement led to the establishment of the Uranium Enrichment Company (Urenco) in 1971 in the Netherlands. Dr. Abdul Qadeer Khan, a Pakistani scientist, was employed as a metallurgist by Physics Dynamic Research Laboratory, a subcontractor working with Urenco. Khan had access to top-secret information. Following India's nuclear test, Khan stole the blueprints of the world's best centrifuges, hollow metal tubes that spin very fast to enrich natural uranium into bomb fuel, and returned to Pakistan to develop a nuclear bomb.[18] Known as the "father" of Pakistan's bomb, Khan admitted helping Iran, North Korea, and Libya obtain centrifuge parts, thereby contributing to nuclear proliferation. Pakistan's nuclear weapons program was aided by China and essentially condoned by the United States. In 1998, the world faced the dawn of the second nuclear age as India, followed shortly by Pakistan, detonated nuclear bombs in underground tests. Both countries remain committed to building more sophisticated nuclear weapons. By June 2004, India and Pakistan retreated from their belligerent positions, which had brought them to the brink of war in January 2002, and held talks on ways to diminish the possibility of an outbreak of a nuclear war between them. Significant steps have been taken to reduce tensions, including cricket matches, bilateral talks, and encouraging transportation links between parts of Kashmir controlled by the two countries. However, growing political unrest in Pakistan raises global concerns about the security of Pakistan's nuclear weapons and the dangers posed by terrorists' access to them and to nuclear material. Furthermore, increased nuclear cooperation between the United States and India, on one hand, and a growing nuclear cooperation between China and Pakistan, on the other hand, cannot be assuring.

The Middle East

The proliferation of nuclear weapons as well as efforts to obtain nuclear weapons in the Middle East cannot be separated from the Arab-Israeli conflict. Israel, under the leadership of Prime Minister David Ben-Gurion in 1952, built its nuclear arsenal preemptively but also sought to counter the conventional military power of the neighboring Arab states that threatened to destroy it.[19] In other words, nuclear weapons are viewed by Israel as a deterrent. Although Israel is widely recognized as a significant nuclear power, with roughly two hundred nuclear weapons, it has not ratified the nuclear NPT, which allows the International Atomic

Treaty of Almelo ■ International agreement that led to the establishment of the Urenco in 1971 in the Netherlands

NPT ■ International treaty allowing the IAEA of the United Nations to monitor global nuclear weapons activities

Energy Agency (IAEA) of the United Nations to monitor nuclear weapons activities. Israel, India, and Pakistan have not committed themselves to pursuing negotiations to end the nuclear arms race or to move toward nuclear disarmament because of their refusal to ratify the NPT. Unlike India and Pakistan, which are declared nuclear powers, Israel, under its policy of nuclear ambiguity, does not confirm or deny its nuclear capacity. Israel confirmed this position during a visit to that country in June 2004 by Mohamed ElBaradei, the director of the IAEA, as part of a larger effort to move toward a nuclear-free Middle East. However, Mordechai Vanunu, an Israeli nuclear technician who worked on Israel's nuclear weapons, revealed the extent of Israel's nuclear arsenal in 1986 when he provided photographs and details of Israel's reactor near the town of Dimona to the *Sunday Times of London*. Lured by a female agent of the Mossad, Israel's spy agency, to travel from London to meet her in Italy, Vanunu was kidnapped by the Mossad, transported to Israel, and held in solitary confinement for most of the eighteen years he was imprisoned. Following his release from prison in April 2004, Israeli officials continued to be fearful that Vanunu would disclose new details of Israel's nuclear program and draw attention to it. In April 2008, Ben-Ami Kadish, an American, admitted that he had leaked between fifty and a hundred secret U.S. government documents on nuclear arms, missiles, and fighter jets to the Israeli government during the early 1980s. Israel is a nuclear power.[20]

policy of nuclear ambiguity ■ Israel's decision to not confirm or deny that it has nuclear weapons

Mossad ■ Israeli spy agency

As we have seen so far, nuclear proliferation is often fueled by fear of countries that already have nuclear weapons or have the technological capability to produce them. Jonathan Schell pointed out that "every nuclear arsenal is linked to every other nuclear arsenal in the world by powerful ties of terror and response."[21] Iraq, Iran, and Libya have attempted to acquire nuclear weapons, partly due to the security dynamics of the Middle East, just as India developed nuclear weapons out of concerns about China's military power. Iranian officials, for example, justify their efforts to secure nuclear weapons on the grounds that Israel, India, and Pakistan have the nuclear bomb. Iran, while allowing the IAEA to conduct limited inspections of its nuclear facilities, in accordance with the NPT, remains committed to pursuing nuclear technology for peaceful purposes. However, Iran's ability to produce its own enriched uranium was generally perceived as enabling it to become a nuclear power.[22] Furthermore, Russia's involvement in building nuclear facilities in Iran and Iran's ability to purchase weapons designs, technical knowledge, and sophisticated technology on the global market strengthened its capacity to produce nuclear weapons.

North Korea

Widely known as the Hermit Kingdom because of its largely self-imposed isolation from the global community, North Korea emphasizes building a strong military to protect its interests. As we mentioned earlier, North Korea test-fired a ballistic missile over Japan in 1998, clearly demonstrating its ability to launch a military strike against that country. Furthermore, North Korea remains a Communist state and continues to concentrate its military power along the demilitarized zone (DMZ) that divides the Korean peninsula. Despite North Korea's admission that it is a nuclear power, the United States refrained from attacking it. In light of America's decision

Hermit Kingdom ■ Label given to North Korea due to its largely self-imposed isolation from the global community

Kim Jong Il ■ Current leader of North Korea

to invade and occupy Iraq, North Korea's leader Kim Jong Il stressed his country's nuclear capability to deter the United States from taking military action against it. North Korea, with close ties to China, has long been regarded as having nuclear ambitions. It has also played a significant role in weapons proliferation by providing ballistic missile technology and missiles to Iraq, Iran, Pakistan, Libya, Syria, and Yemen. North Korea has also received nuclear technology from Pakistan.

North Korea's determination to produce nuclear weapons created a crisis with the United States in 1993–1994. American officials considered the option of bombing North Korea's nuclear facilities but decided that the consequences of doing so would be catastrophic for both North Korea and South Korea. Instead of taking military action, the United States negotiated an agreement with North Korea that required North Korea to cease operating its plutonium reprocessing plant. In exchange, the United States and its allies agreed to put two light-water reactors in North Korea and to provide enough heavy fuel oil to compensate for lost energy from its nuclear production power plants while these reactors were being constructed.[23] In January 2003, North Korea restarted its nuclear power plants, terminated inspections by the IAEA, and asked the inspectors to leave the country. North Korea's production of plutonium for nuclear bombs and its rejection of the nuclear NPT occurred at the height of America's global efforts to prevent the proliferation of weapons of mass destruction. Partly due to pressure from China, Japan, Russia, and South Korea, the United States decided to negotiate with North Korea to resolve the conflict over nuclear weapons. In exchange for dismantling its plutonium and uranium weapons programs, permitting international inspectors to examine suspected nuclear sites, and dismantling and shipping its nuclear technology out of the country, the United States, China, Japan, Russia, and South Korea would supply North Korea with heavy fuel oil, retrain the scientists involved in nuclear weapons programs, and lift economic sanctions, and the United States would agree not to invade the country.[24] North Korea agreed to dismantle its nuclear program and to comply with the NPT. In exchange, the United States and the other countries agreed to provide energy assistance to and promote economic cooperation with North Korea. The United States also agreed to refrain from attacking North Korea and to normalize relations. Despite these efforts, negotiations ended, and North Korea continues to build nuclear weapons and to test long-range missiles.

Nuclear Posture Review ■ Bush administration document that advocated a revitalized nuclear weapons complex capable of designing, developing, manufacturing, and certifying new nuclear warheads in response to emerging global threats

AMERICA'S NUCLEAR RESPONSE TO NUCLEAR PROLIFERATION

As the war against terrorism intensified and as countries such as India, Pakistan, North Korea, Iran, Iraq, and Libya demonstrated an interest in strengthening their nuclear capabilities or acquiring nuclear weapons, the United States increased its efforts to prevent the proliferation of weapons of mass destruction. Simultaneously, however, the Bush administration sent Congress its Nuclear Posture Review, in which it advocated a revitalized nuclear weapons complex capable of designing, developing, manufacturing, and certifying new nuclear warheads in response to emerging global threats. In sharp contrast to the traditional reluctance to advocate actually using nuclear weapons, the United States embraced the unprecedented view that nuclear warheads could be used preemptively against potential or actual adversaries. Specifically, the Pentagon regarded the development of the Robust Nuclear Earth Penetrator, a nuclear weapon capable of hitting reinforced concrete bunkers as deep as 40 feet underground, as an effective deterrent against the development of weapons of mass destruction by countries as well as terrorist groups. Such a response to nuclear weapons proliferation is widely perceived as fundamentally undermining global efforts to prevent other countries from acquiring nuclear weapons to deter an attack by America. Furthermore, critics of America's nuclear response believe that using any type of nuclear weapon "will breach the firewall between conventional and nuclear war and pose a new threat to world security."[25]

While the United States pressures countries regarded as having hostile military intentions not to develop nuclear weapons, it has pursued an essentially selective policy, ignoring allies such as Israel, Pakistan, and India that possess nuclear weapons. Furthermore, the United States' current nuclear posture remains basically as it was during the Cold War. The United States seems oblivious to the fact that its unwillingness to significantly reduce the size of its own nuclear arsenal in light of the new strategic environment engendered by the end of military competition with the Soviet Union creates insecurity among vulnerable states.[26] Robert S. McNamara, a former U.S. Secretary of Defense, argued that keeping such large numbers of weapons and maintaining them on hair-trigger alert are potent signs that the United States was not seriously working toward the elimination of its arsenal and raised troubling questions as to why any other state should restrain its nuclear ambitions.[27] This perception was challenged by President Barack Obama's agreement with President Dmitri A. Medvedev in July 2009 to reduce U.S. and Russian nuclear arsenals by at least one quarter. The New Strategic Arms Reduction Treaty, New START, between the United States and Russia in 2010 cut strategic nuclear warheads (for both countries) from 2,200 to 1,500 and the number of deployed missiles and bombers to 700 each.

Robust Nuclear Earth Penetrator ■ Nuclear weapon capable of hitting reinforced concrete underground bunkers; used as an effective deterrent against the development of weapons of mass destruction by countries as well as terrorist groups

New START ■ The United States and Russia agreed to cut strategic nuclear warheads, deployed missiles, and bombers

CHEMICAL AND BIOLOGICAL WEAPONS

Although chemical and biological weapons are often referred to as though they are indistinguishable, in this section we will discuss them separately. Chemical weapons are extremely toxic and can be dispersed as a gas, vapor, liquid, or aerosol or absorbed onto a fine talcum-like powder to create "dusty" agents.[28] Chemical weapons are generally classified based on their effects. Categories include

chemical weapons ■ Weapons that are dispersed as a gas, vapor, liquid, or aerosol or are absorbed; generally classified based on their effects

1. *Checking agents*, which destroy lung tissue, such as chlorine phosgene;
2. *Blood agents*, which interfere with cellular respiration and include toxins such as hydrogen cyanide;
3. *Blister agents*, such as mustard gas, which cause severe burns to the skin and lungs; and
4. *Nerve agents*, such as sarin gas, that disrupt nerve impulse transmission and cause death by respiratory paralysis.[29]

Chemical weapons cause damage within minutes or hours. Some chemical agents, such as sarin gas, disperse relatively fast, whereas others, such as sulfur, mustard, and VX nerve agent, continue to be highly toxic for days or weeks.

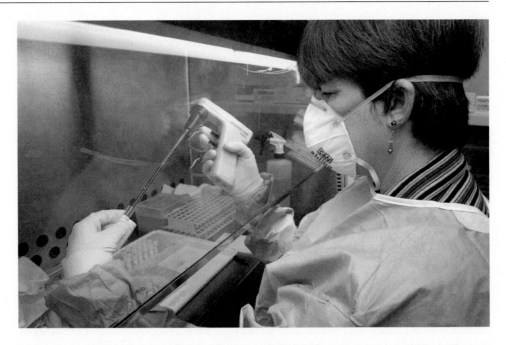

Viruses from research labs could be used by terrorists. SARS specimens are used here at the Special Pathogens Branch of the Center for Disease Control.

Contrary to general assumptions about the ease with which chemical weapons can be used by terrorist organizations and countries, most chemical agents are extremely difficult and dangerous to work with and relatively hard to weaponize. Nevertheless, chemical weapons have been used, and several countries have them or are attempting to acquire them.

Although countries have attempted to use chemicals in conflicts throughout history, chemical weapons were introduced into modern warfare on a massive scale by Germany during World War I. The Germans used chlorine gas against the allies in 1915 and mustard gas later on. But both sides soon realized that the consequences of these chemical weapons were extremely difficult to control. Wind speeds and wind direction determined the dispersal of chemicals on the battlefields, rendering it virtually impossible to predict which side would suffer greater casualties from their usage. Experiences with chemical weapons during World War I restrained Europeans from using them in World War II, despite large stockpiles that were developed by both sides. In Asia, however, Japan employed chemical weapons against China. As part of the arms race between the superpowers, chemical weapons were produced on a massive scale by the Soviet Union, the United States, and other countries. Contemporary debates about weapons of mass destruction often obscure the role of the superpowers in accelerating the proliferation of nuclear, biological, and chemical weapons. The United States used **Agent Orange**, an extremely toxic chemical spray, to defoliate forests in Vietnam in its war against the Vietcong forces. As we will discuss in Chapter 12, the United States routinely uses chemicals in Colombia and elsewhere in South America to destroy coca crops as part of its war on drugs. Usage of these chemicals that poison the environment and threaten public health is strongly opposed by many groups and members of the European Union.

Agent Orange ■
Extremely toxic chemical spray; used to defoliate forests in Vietnam in its war against the Vietcong forces

Far more controversial is America's role in enabling Iraq to acquire chemical weapons. During the Iraq–Iran war (1980–1988), the United States and pro-American countries such as Saudi Arabia, Kuwait, and Jordan viewed Iraq as a bulwark against the spread of radical and militant Shiite fundamentalism from Iran. Consequently, the administrations of Presidents Ronald Reagan and George H. W. Bush authorized the sale of toxic chemicals to Iraq that were weaponized to strengthen Iraq's defenses against "human wave" attacks by suicidal Iranian troops. It was widely known that Iraq, under Saddam Hussein, routinely used chemical weapons against the Iranians, the Kurds, and others.[30] In the context of instability in the Middle East, the United States perceived Iraq as a valuable ally and ignored Hussein's chemical warfare until Iraq invaded Kuwait in 1990.

As we mentioned earlier in this chapter, using biological weapons in conflicts has deep historical roots. Biological weapons are composed of living microorganisms and toxins that are capable of causing fatal diseases such as smallpox, plague, and hemorrhagic fever. Anthrax spores delivered to U.S. government offices through the U.S. postal service shortly after the terrorist attack in 2001 underscored the threat posed by biological weapons. In response to threats posed by anthrax, the U.S. government passed legislation in 2004, known as Project Bioshield, to provide funding for American drug companies to enable them to develop a vaccine against anthrax. Although biological agents such as anthrax cannot be transmitted from an infected person to others, smallpox, as we discussed earlier, is highly contagious and could be easily spread around the world, thereby creating a pandemic. Although biological weapons agents can be developed by a country or nonstate organization that produces vaccines, antibiotics, feed supplements, and fermented beverages, there are only two significant cases in which they were used in the twentieth century. These are the German efforts during World War I to infect livestock and contaminate animal feed to be exported from neutral countries to Allied forces and Japan's deployment of biological weapons against China during World War II.[31] The globalization of biotechnology and endemic military conflicts combine to influence countries to acquire biological weapons. Russia, North Korea, Iran, Egypt, Israel, and Syria are among the countries suspected of having such weapons. Until the 1991 Persian Gulf War, companies in the United States and France were instrumental in enabling Iraq to develop tons of biological weapons. Specifically, the American Type Culture of Manassas, Virginia, and the Pasteur Institute in Paris provided germ samples to Iraq.[32]

biological weapons
■ Weapons composed of living microorganisms and toxins capable of causing fatal diseases

Project Bioshield
■ U.S. legislation provided funding for American drug companies to develop a vaccine against anthrax

NONPROLIFERATION REGIMES

For more than fifty years, the global community has cooperated to construct a nonproliferation regime, which is defined as an interlocking network of treaties, agreements, and organizations designed to prevent the spread or use of weapons of mass destruction.[33] Although building the nonproliferation regime is clearly a global effort, the United States, as a dominant power after World War II, provided indispensable leadership. However, inconsistent and outright contradictory American foreign policies often undermine attempts to strengthen the nonproliferation regime. For example, the United States has largely ignored nuclear ambitions of allies such as Israel and Pakistan. Furthermore, American embrace of unilateralism has weakened its commitment to supporting international arms control agreements, even as it places a greater emphasis on developing new weapons and a missile defense system. Nevertheless, counterproliferation remains a cornerstone of U.S. foreign policy. During the Clinton administration, the U.S. Department of Defense stressed what it called the "8 D's" of the nonproliferation regime: dissuasion, disarmament, diplomacy, denial, defusing, deterrence, defenses, and destruction.[34]

Dissuasion is an attempt to convince countries to refrain from acquiring unconventional weapons in exchange for security guarantees.

Disarmament involves agreements to prevent proliferation, such as the NPT.

Diplomacy is instrumental in convincing countries to terminate their weapons programs. Diplomacy has been successful in many cases, including Belarus, Ukraine, Brazil, Argentina, South Africa, and Libya.

Denial deals with enforcing stricter international controls on exports of sensitive technologies and materials.

Defusing concentrates on preventing hair-trigger alert postures and securing weapons.

Deterrence is based on the threat of retaliation.

Defenses range from providing chemical suits, inhalation masks, and vaccines for the population to missile defense.

Destruction of weapons facilities and weapons is a preemptive act.

Nuclear Nonproliferation

Realizing the destructiveness of the bombs dropped on Japan in World War II and aware of the military and strategic stalemate engendered by the proliferation of nuclear weapons, the United States and the Soviet Union, the dominant nuclear powers, collaborated with Britain, France, and China (the other nuclear powers) to develop a nuclear nonproliferation regime. An underlying assumption of this regime was that risks of nuclear war would be diminished by limiting the acquisition of nuclear weapons to this small group of countries that already possessed them. However, given the competitive nature of nations, this nuclear monopoly would be challenged. As George Perkovich observed, to persuade the rest of the world to relinquish its prerogative to acquire nuclear weapons, the nuclear weapons possessors had to do the following:

1. Promise to abandon their nuclear weapons eventually.
2. Pledge not to use their weapons to threaten countries that did not possess nuclear weapons.
3. Help countries that renounced nuclear weapons and accepted international monitoring to acquire and use nuclear technology for civilian and peaceful purposes.
4. Enhance global security by ensuring nonnuclear states that their neighbors would be prevented from becoming nuclear powers.[35]

These objectives are clearly reflected in the nonproliferation agreements signed by American presidents. For example, President Dwight D. Eisenhower proposed creating the IAEA to promote the peaceful uses of atomic energy. President John F. Kennedy signed the Limited Test Ban Treaty to terminate nuclear tests in the atmosphere, in outer space, and under water. President Lyndon B. Johnson negotiated the nuclear NPT, designed to limit the transfer of nuclear weapons, nuclear technology, and nuclear materials to other countries, and Presidents Richard M. Nixon, Jimmy Carter, and Ronald Reagan concluded various agreements to reduce the number of nuclear weapons possessed by the superpowers. As we have seen, despite progress on nonproliferation between the United States and Russia, countries such as India, Pakistan, Israel, and North Korea became nuclear powers. Furthermore, in a significant departure from the traditional approach that embraced the eventual elimination of nuclear weapons, U.S. President George W. Bush concentrated on preventing enemy nations from acquiring nuclear weapons while ignoring nuclear ambitions of friendly nations. In December 2001, Bush announced that America would withdraw from the Antiballistic Missile Treaty, which prohibits the development, testing, or deployment of antiballistic missile systems capable of defending entire territories from intercontinental ballistic missile (ICBM) attacks in order to enable the United States to build a missile defense system. Table 6.1 shows significant nuclear weapons agreements. Bush advocated developing and preemptively using small nuclear weapons, known as bunker busters. A nuclear arms agreement signed by President Bush and Russia's President Vladimir Putin in May 2002 essentially provided the United States and Russia flexibility to retain as many nuclear weapons as they want. The only significant restraint on them was that they had to reduce their nuclear warheads to between 1,700 and 2,200 by the end of 2012. At that point the treaty would have expired, enabling both sides to increase their nuclear weapons. In April 2010, President Barack Obama and President Dmitry Medvedev signed a New Strategic Arms Limitation Treaty to reduce American and Russian strategic and nuclear arsenals by one third. The new treaty was ratified by the U.S. Senate in December 2010.[36]

Antiballistic Missile Treaty ■ International treaty prohibiting the development, testing, or deployment of antiballistic missile systems

Curbing Chemical and Biological Weapons

An important component of the nonproliferation regime in relation to chemical weapons was the 1925 Geneva Protocol, which prohibited the use of biological and chemical weapons in war. Due partly to the leadership of President Nixon, the United States eventually ratified the Geneva Protocol in 1975 (during the Ford administration). In 1933, the Chemical Weapons Convention (CWC), which prohibits the development, acquisition, transfer, stockpiling, or use of chemical weapons, was signed and ratified by more than 125 countries, including Russia and the United States. The CWC also mandated the internationally monitored destruction of all chemical stockpiles by 2007. Apart from the fact that several countries refused to sign the agreement and continued to produce chemical weapons, most

1925 Geneva Protocol ■ International treaty that prohibited the use of biological and chemical weapons in war

TABLE 6.1	
Major Nuclear Weapons Agreements	
Date Signed	**Agreement**
August 1963	**Limited Test Ban Treaty.** Prohibits nuclear explosions in the atmosphere, in outer space, and under water.
July 1968	**Nuclear Non-Proliferation Treaty.** Prohibits countries from transferring nuclear weapons or helping other countries acquire them.
May 1972	**Strategic Arms Limitation Treaty (SALT1).** Limited strategic nuclear missile launchers and missile firing submarines.
July 1974	**Threshold Test Ban Treaty.** Limited U.S. and Soviet Union underground nuclear weapons tests.
December 1987	**Intermediate-Range Nuclear Forces Treaty.** Dismantled all Soviet and American medium- and short-range land-based missiles.
July 1991	**Strategic Arms Reduction Treaty (STARTI).** Reduces the number of U.S. and Soviet long-range nuclear warheads from 11,000 to 6,000.
January 1993	**Strategic Arms Reduction Treaty (STARTII).** Requires U.S. and Russia to reduce nuclear warheads and bombs to 3,500 by 2007.
September 1996	**Comprehensive Test Ban Treaty.** Prohibits all nuclear weapons test explosions. (Not ratified by the U.S. Senate.)
May 2002	**U.S.-Russian Nuclear Arms Treaty.** Commits each country to reduce nuclear warheads to between 1,700 and 2,200 by the end of 2012.
December 2010	**New Strategic Arms Reduction Treaty (New START).** Cuts strategic nuclear warheads (for both countries) from 2,200 to 1,500, and the number of deployed missiles and bombers to 700 each.

Sources: U.S. State Department, U.S. Congressional Research Services, and *New York Times*.

of Russia's massive arsenal of chemical weapons remain in storage, partly because Russia lacks adequate resources to destroy them.

The international regime concerning the nonproliferation of biological weapons began with the 1925 Geneva Protocol. Although the Protocol abolished the use of biological weapons in warfare, it enabled many countries to make reservations, attachments to treaties that allow states to be excluded from the legal effects of certain provisions of the agreement.[37] The Protocol also made compliance with the ban on biological weapons conditional on reciprocity. President Nixon laid the foundation for strengthening the nonproliferation regime when he announced in 1969 that the United States would unilaterally and unconditionally renounce biological weapons and subsequently ordered the destruction of U.S. weapons stockpiles. Nixon negotiated the Biological Weapons Convention (BWC), an agreement prohibiting the development, manufacture, and stockpiling of biological weapons.[38] The treaty was signed in 1972.

BWC ■ 1972 agreement negotiated by President Nixon prohibiting the development, manufacture, and stockpiling of biological weapons

The 2010 New START between the United States and Russia was an important step in nuclear nonproliferation by reducing the countries' strategic nuclear arsenals by one-third. Signed by President Barack Obama and Russian President Dmitry Medvedev at the Prague castle, it is a successor to the previous START treaty, which expired.

CASE STUDY | Countries That Abandoned Nuclear Weapons Programs

Given the reality of mutually assured destruction (MAD) during the Cold War, when there was intense military rivalry between the United States and the Soviet Union, both superpowers refrained from using nuclear weapons and supported nuclear nonproliferation. As more countries acquire nuclear weapons, there is a greater probability that these weapons will influence neighboring states to also acquire nuclear weapons for security and other reasons. Under these circumstances, the likelihood of nuclear war increases, thereby destroying these countries' security as well as global security. This problem forced many countries to rethink the logic of proliferation.

Seventeen countries decided to abandon efforts to acquire or retain nuclear weapons. Argentina, Brazil, Australia, Canada, Egypt, Iraq, Italy, Libya, Romania, South Korea, Sweden, Taiwan, and

Yugoslavia ended their research and development programs, stopping before they produced nuclear weapons. Belarus, Kazakhstan, and Ukraine acquired nuclear weapons as part of the Soviet Union. South Africa actually had six nuclear weapons but dismantled them when the country ended apartheid and transitioned to democracy.

The end of the Cold War and the disintegration of the Soviet Union in 1991 enabled presidents George H.W. Bush and Bill Clinton to negotiate with Russia and the various countries of the former Soviet Union to dismantle more than four thousand strategic nuclear weapons. Under the Nunn-Lugar-Domenici Cooperative Threat Reduction Program, named after senators Sam Nunn, Richard Lugar, and Pete Domenici, the United States provided financial and technical assistance to these new states to help them denuclearize.

(continued)

CASE STUDY | continued

Brazil began its nuclear weapons programs when it was ruled by military dictators in the 1970s. A major motivation for acquiring nuclear weapons was its historical antagonism with Argentina, which also had a nuclear weapons program. As the dominant country in South America, Brazil also saw having nuclear weapons as a way to be recognized as a global leader and to enhance its international status. Brazil, like other countries that attempted to acquire nuclear weapons, was threatened with U.S. sanctions. Furthermore, there was growing emphasis on improving Brazil's economy. As Brazil transitioned to democracy and improved relations with Argentina, both countries decided that their security and international ambitions could be best secured without nuclear weapons. They signed the Treaty of Tlatelolco, committing them to peaceful nuclear programs and creating a binational verification program.[39]

The case of South Africa illustrated how global developments, ending apartheid, and transitioning to democracy radically altered perceptions about national security and the utility of nuclear weapons.

In an effort to perpetuate a system of rigid racial separation, discrimination, and white rule (known as apartheid), South Africa engaged in clandestine relations with other countries to acquire nuclear weapons. The Cold War and Soviet-Cuban expansion in Africa in support of countries and groups opposed to the apartheid regime convinced the white minority that their security would be enhanced with nuclear weapons. Due to unrelenting mass demonstrations, global pressures, the attention paid to South Africa by the global media, the end of the Cold War, and new progressive leaders such as F.W. de Klerk, South Africa ended apartheid through negotiations between the African National Congress (ANC) and the white minority regime. Nelson Mandela (who had been imprisoned for twenty-seven years for opposing apartheid) was released, and democratic elections that brought about majority rule were held. Mandela became South Africa's president in 1994. Prior to the transfer of power, the apartheid regime dismantled six nuclear weapons, partly because it did not want the new black majority government to have them. South Africa's integration in the global economy and the dependence of the white minority on black labor enabled the anti-apartheid groups around the world to use economic sanctions effectively. Although racial segregation was central to apartheid, the reality was that blacks and whites interacted daily. Nuclear weapons could not be used against blacks without destroying whites. Given the unconventional nature of the armed struggle against apartheid, nuclear weapons were essentially useless. Faced with a changed global, regional, and domestic environment, South Africa concluded that it was more secure without nuclear weapons. ◣

SUMMARY AND REVIEW

This chapter addressed the dangers of the proliferation of conventional weapons and weapons of mass destruction. It focused on recent developments in the proliferation of conventional weapons and weapons of mass destruction. First, we looked at the dangers involved in the proliferation of specific conventional weapons. We identified many reasons for the proliferation of conventional weapons, such as superpower rivalry during the Cold War; government concern with political, military, and economic influence over other states; the growth of ethnic and national conflicts throughout the world; and the growth in authoritarian, repressive regimes. Next, we elaborated on the development of various unconventional weapons, including biological, chemical, and nuclear weapons. In this debate over nuclear weapons, we identified emerging nuclear powers, such as Israel, North Korea, and Iran. We also identified many of the efforts made to control the spread and development of all forms of unconventional weapons (biological, chemical, and nuclear), including the Limited Test Ban Treaty, the nuclear NPT, the Antiballistic Missile Treaty, the Geneva Protocol, and the Biological and Chemical Weapons Conventions. A major factor influencing other countries, such as Iran and Korea, to acquire nuclear weapons is America's reluctance to reduce its own nuclear weapons. Furthermore, many analysts believe that the United States pursues a selective policy on nuclear proliferation, ignoring its friends with nuclear weapons and punishing its enemies who are attempting to acquire weapons. A major concern is the availability of nuclear weapons materials in parts of the former Soviet Union.

KEY TERMS

smallpox   117
Hobbesian worldview   118
military burden sharing   118
Nixon Doctrine   118
conventional weapons   120
Hiroshima   121
bomber gap   121
Sputnik   121
mutual balance of terror   121
mutual assured destruction (MAD)   121
Cuban missile crisis   122
minimum deterrence   122
Comprehensive Test Ban Treaty   122
power transition theory   122
policy of pacifism   123
Vasco da Gama   123
Jawaharlal Nehru   123

Treaty of Almelo   124
NPT   124
policy of nuclear ambiguity   125
Mossad   125
Hermit Kingdom   125
Kim Jong II   126
Nuclear Posture Review   126
Robust Nuclear Earth Penetrator   127
New START   127
chemical weapons   127
Agent Orange   128
biological weapons   129
Project Bioshield   129
Antiballistic Missile Treaty   131
1925 Geneva Protocol   132
Biological Weapons Convention (BWC)   134

DISCUSSION QUESTIONS

1. In light of America's declining power and the need to cooperate with other nations, how should it deal with Iran and North Korea?
2. Do you think the world would be a safer place without nuclear weapons?
3. Discuss the dangers of small arms proliferation. Give examples.
4. Discuss the logic behind developing national missile defense systems. Do you think such efforts will help increase or decrease the level of nuclear proliferation? Why or why not?
5. Discuss global efforts to control chemical and biological weapons.

SUGGESTED READINGS

Albright, David. *Peddling Peril.* New York: Free Press, 2010. Discusses how the Pakistan scientist A.Q. Khan acquired information from his job in the Netherlands to enable Pakistan to build nuclear weapons.

Ganguly, Sumit, and S. Paul Kapur. *India, Pakistan, and the Bomb.* New York: Columbia University Press, 2010. Debates whether the acquisition of nuclear weapons by India and Pakistan has helped prevent the escalation of conflicts between them.

Koblentz, Gregory. *Living Weapons.* Ithaca, NY: Cornell University Press, 2009. Examines the dangers of biological weapons and points out how many of those weapons resulted from efforts to find cures for diseases.

Rublee, Maria Rost. *Nonproliferation Norms: Why States Choose Nuclear Restraint.* Athens: University of Georgia Press, 2009. Explains why some countries that were moving toward acquiring nuclear weapons abandoned their projects.

Wright, Robin, ed. *The Iran Primer.* Washington, DC: Institute of Peace Press, 2010. Wide-ranging discussion of Iran's relations with its neighbors, the United States, China, Russia, and the European Union. It also discusses Iran's institutions and politics.

ENDNOTES

1. John Noble Wilford, "How Catapults Married Science, Politics, and War," *New York Times*, 24 February 2004, D3.
2. Tina Rosenberg, "When Smallpox Struck During the Revolutionary War," *New York Times*, 23 December 2001, D8.
3. Gina Kolata, "New York Was Bioterrorism Target, in 1864," *New York Times*, 13 November 2001, D7.
4. David Held et al., *Global Transformations* (Stanford, CA: Stanford University Press, 1999), 103.
5. William W. Keller and Jane E. Nolan, "The Arms Trade: Business as Usual," *Foreign Policy* 109 (Winter 1997/1998), 114.
6. C.J. Chivers, "Small Arms, Big Problems," *Foreign Affairs* 90, No. 1 (January/February 2011), 114.
7. James C. McKinley, "U.S. Stymied as Guns Flow to Mexican Cartels," *New York Times*, 15 April 2009, A1.
8. John F. Burns, "Britain Joins a Draft Treaty to Ban Cluster Munitions," *New York Times*, 29 May 2008, A13.
9. Jeffrey Boutwell and Michael T. Klare, "Introduction," in *Light Weapons and Civil Conflict*, eds. Jeffrey Boutwell and Michael T. Klare (Lanham, MD: Rowman and Littlefield, 1999), 2.
10. Michael T. Klare, "International Trade in Light Weapons," in *Light Weapons and Civil Conflict*, 21.
11. Peter R. Beckman et al., *The Nuclear Predicament* (Upper Saddle River, NJ: Prentice Hall, 2000), 2.
12. Paul Kennedy, *The Rise and Fall of the Great Powers* (New York: Random House, 1987), 388.
13. Graham Allison, "How to Stop Nuclear Terror," *Foreign Affairs* 83, No. 1 (January/February 2004), 66.
14. Evan S. Medeiros, Reluctant Restraint: *The Evolution of China's Nonproliferation Policies and Practices* (Stanford, CA: Stanford University Press, 2007).
15. Howard W. French, "Taboo Against Nuclear Arms Is Being Challenged in Japan," *New York Times*, 9 June 2002, A1.
16. Paul Bracken, "The Second Nuclear Age," *Foreign Affairs* 79, No. 1 (January/February 2000), 149.
17. Jaswant Singh, "Against Nuclear Apartheid," *Foreign Affairs* 77, No. 5 (September/October 1998), 41.

18. S. Paul Kapur, *Dangerous Deterrent: Nuclear Weapons Proliferation and Conflict in South Asia* (Stanford, CA: Stanford University Press, 2007).

19. Jonathan Schell, "The Folly of Arms Control," *Foreign Affairs* 79, No. 5 (September/October 2000), 33.

20. Avner Cohen and Marvin Miller, "Bringing Israel's Bomb Out of the Basement," *Foreign Affairs* 89, No. 5 (September/October 2010), 30.

21. Schell, "The Folly of Arms Control," 33.

22. Vali Nasr and Ray Takeyh, "The Costs of Containing Iran," *Foreign Affairs* 87, No. 1 (January/February 2008), 85; and Eric S. Edelman et al., "The Dangers of a Nuclear Iran," *Foreign Affairs* 90, No. 1 (January/February 2011), 66–67.

23. "Closing Pandora's Box," *The Economist*, 4 January 2003, 30.

24. Josef Joffe and James W. David, "Less Than Zero," *Foreign Affairs* 90, No. 1 (January/February 2011), 9.

25. Wolfgang K. H. Panofsky, "Nuclear Insecurity," *Foreign Affairs* 86, No. 5 (September/October 2007), 109–110.

26. John Deutch, "A Nuclear Posture for Today," *Foreign Affairs* 84, No. 1 (January/February 2005), 56.

27. Robert S. McNamara, "Apocalypse Soon," *Foreign Policy* 148 (May/June 2005), 31; and Mark Silver, "U.S., India Embrace Nuclear Deal," *Chicago Tribute*, 3 March 2006, Sect. 1, 1.

28. Jonathan B. Tucker, "Introduction," in *Toxic Terror: Assessing Terrorist Use of Chemical and Biological Weapons*, ed. Jonathan B. Tucker (Cambridge, MA: MIT Press, 2000), 3.

29. Tucker, "Introduction," in *Toxic Terror*, 3.

30. Michael Dobbs, "When an Ally Becomes the Enemy," *Washington Post National Weekly Edition*, 6–12 January 2003, 9.

31. David P. Fidler, *International Law and Infectious Diseases* (Oxford: Clarendon Press, 1999), 225.

32. Philip Shenon, "Iraq Links Germs for Weapons to U.S. and France," *New York Times*, 16 March 2003, A16.

33. Joseph Cirincione, "Historical Overview and Introduction," in *Repairing the Regime*, ed. Joseph Cirincione (New York: Routledge, 2000), 3.

34. Ashton B. Carter, "How to Counter WMD," *Foreign Affairs* 83, No. 5 (September/October 2004), 73.

35. George Perkovich, "Bush's Nuclear Revolution," *Foreign Affairs* 82, No. 2 (March/April 2003), 3.

36. Bruce Blair et al., "Smaller and Safer," *Foreign Affairs* 89, No. 5 (September/October 2010), 10.

37. Louis Henkin et al., *International Law* (St. Paul, MN: West Publishing Co., 1980), 605.

38. Cirincione, "Historical Overview," 7.

39. Graham Allison, "Nuclear Disorder," *Foreign Affairs* 89, No. 1 (January/February 2010), 82; and Julia E. Sweig, "A New Global Power: Brazil's Far-Flung Agenda," *Foreign Affairs* 89, No. 6 (November/December 2010), 178.

The Global Financial Crisis

The global financial crisis had widespread effects. Out of work like many, marketing executive Chuck Bridges

INTRODUCTION

Financial crises and accompanying economic recessions have occurred throughout history. Periodic crises appear to be part of financial systems of dominant or global powers. The United States is the epicenter of the current financial crisis. Enjoying a unipolar moment following the collapse of the Soviet Union and the failure of Communism, the United States was confident that economic liberalization and the proliferation of computer and communications technologies would contribute to ever-increasing global economic growth and prosperity. Globalization contributed to the extraordinary accumulation of wealth by a relatively few individuals and created greater inequality. In an effort to reduce inequality in the United States, the government implemented policies that engendered the financial crisis.

As we discussed in Chapter 1, finance is usually the leading force in the growth of globalization. The rise of great powers is inextricably linked to access to investments and their ability to function as leading financial centers, as we saw in Chapter 2. Their decline is also closely linked to financial problems. Finance enables entrepreneurs to start various enterprises and to become competitors of established companies. It is also essential to innovation and scientific discoveries. Finance also facilitates risk sharing and provides insurance for risk takers. Countries that have large financial sectors tend to grow faster, their inhabitants are generally richer, and there are more opportunities. Financial globalization contributed to the unprecedented growth and prosperity around the world. China and India became significant economic powers, and the industrialized countries grew even richer.[1] Closely integrated into the financial system are banks and investment firms. When the financial system is in crisis, banks reduce lending, companies often face bankruptcy, and unemployment rises. Ultimately, as we saw in the financial crisis of 2008–2009, many banks fail.

The financial crisis triggered a global economic recession that resulted in more than $4.1 trillion in losses, unemployment rates that climbed to more than 10 percent in the United States and higher elsewhere, and increased poverty. Stock markets around the world crashed. American investors lost roughly 40 percent of the value of their savings. Housing prices plummeted from their record highs in 2006. Consumers reduced their spending, manufacturing declined, global trade diminished, and countries adopted protectionist measures, many turning their attention inward to focus on problems caused by the financial crisis. Given the central importance of finance to virtually all aspects of globalization, issues such as trade, the environment, crime, disease, inequality, migration, ethnic conflicts, human rights, and promoting democracy are affected. Furthermore, the financial crisis weakened some countries more than others, thereby engendering significant shifts of power among countries, especially between the United States and China. The European Union struggled over how much to shore up or bail out banks and nations using the euro currency. The financial, economic, social, and political fallout continue. Citizens took to the streets in a protest movement against financial

finance ■ The major catalyst in the growth of globalization and national power inequality that began in New York City as "Occupy Wall Street" and spread around the world. This chapter examines the causes of the financial crisis, its impact, and responses to it. It concludes with a case study of the decline of the Celtic Tiger (Ireland).

CAUSES OF THE GLOBAL FINANCIAL CRISIS

The causes of financial crises are as complex as many of the crises themselves and the human beings responsible for them. There have been at least sixty recorded crises since the early seventeenth century. Human beings seem to have always been obsessed with money, and greed drives them to obtain increasing amounts of it. And humans generally spend more than they have, thereby creating huge debts that undermine the stability of the financial system. As early as 33 A.D., Emperor Tiberius of Rome had to inject public funds into the financial system to prevent it from collapsing.[2] Euphoria and excessive optimism, which often accompany financial bubbles, are usually followed by fear and panic when crisis arrives. Generally, people claim to not know how the crisis happened or that they could not see it coming. The Asian Financial Crisis in 1997 was a precursor to the financial crisis of 2008–2009. It started in Indonesia and spread to Malaysia, South Korea, other parts of Asia, and the rest of the world. Once-prosperous economies were now in deep recession, with stock markets crashing and capital flowing out of the various countries at unprecedented rates. The Asian crisis was largely caused by "hasty and imprudent financial liberalization, almost always under foreign pressure, allowing free international flows of short-term capital without adequate attention to the potentially potent downside of such globalization."[3]

Asian Financial Crisis ■ Started in Indonesia, caused stock markets to crash, and reversed economic growth

But the Asian crisis was part of larger global developments, many of which were driven by the United States. The end of the Cold War left America standing as the world's sole superpower with unprecedented power and unlimited options, or so it seemed. Affected by hubris, and made overly confident by the exponential growth of computer and telecommunications technologies, the United States believed, in the words of Thomas Paine, that it could build a brand-new world characterized by unlimited success. However, terrorist attacks on September 11, 2001, fundamentally altered America's sense of security and plunged the country into a recession.

An integral component of the struggle against terrorism was the restoration of domestic and global confidence in America's economic system in general and its financial system in particular. President George W. Bush launched a war against terrorism. To accomplish this, the U.S. defense budget was rapidly increased, a department of Homeland Security was created, and two wars, one in Afghanistan and the other in Iraq, were launched. Furthermore, part of the new security strategy was a comprehensive globalization agenda, in which American companies operating in foreign countries would be free from restraints imposed by those countries.[4] This meant increasing government debt and encouraging consumers to spend even more to strengthen both the economy and national security. With easy access to capital created by economic globalization, consumers and the U.S.

government relied on other people's money. In addition to concentrating on fighting a perpetual war against nonstate actors, an atmosphere was created in which questioning was discouraged and taking excessive financial risks and getting rich quickly were lauded. From John C. Bogle's perspective, at the root of the problem was a societal change. America valued form over substance, prestige over virtue, money over achievement, charisma over character, and the ephemeral over the enduring.[5] While it is almost impossible to disentangle the causes of the global financial crisis, we will concentrate on those that are most often discussed. They include (1) deregulation of financial markets; (2) sophisticated financial innovations linked to rapid changes in computer technologies; (3) excessive executive compensation; (4) low interest rates; (5) subprime loans, especially for mortgages; and (6) speculation in general, with an emphasis on speculation in housing.

Deregulation of Financial Markets

Just as the current financial crisis has engendered demands for reforms, the Great Depression of the 1930s led to the implementation of financial regulations to stabilize the economy and to give American savers confidence in banks. Banks were widely perceived as boring but safe. Although interest rates were low, inflation was also low. Furthermore, deposits were protected by the Federal Deposit Insurance Corporation (FDIC). An outgrowth of the Great Depression, rising inflation, which also occurred following rapid and dramatic increases in oil prices in 1973–1974, contributed to the erosion of confidence in regulations designed during the Great Depression. Rising inflation in the United States prompted foreigners to lose confidence in the U.S. dollar as the leading currency and to seek security by purchasing gold. In response, President Richard Nixon unlinked the dollar from gold and adopted a regimen of floating interest rates. This created greater volatility in the financial system as well as increased opportunities to earn higher interest rates.[6]

> **FDIC** ■ Insures individual bank deposits for up to $250,000

Significant societal changes and developments in technology combined to serve as a catalyst to propel deregulation. Although large banks and financial institutions initiated efforts to eliminate or modify regulations that restrained them, individuals were also more assertive in gaining control over their savings pension funds and investments in the stock market. Between 1974 and 1980, many regulations were removed. For example, in 1980, commercial banks and savings and loans institutions were permitted to determine their own interest rates on deposits and loans, thereby spurring greater competition. Many smaller banks were acquired by larger, more distant banks. The local bank was fast becoming an outdated institution.[7]

> **deregulation** ■ Removed many government restrictions on financial institutions in the United States and other countries

Just as financial globalization drives economic globalization, the rapid growth of trade was now facilitating global financial liberalization. Globalization in general enabled American banks to argue that they were disadvantaged in competition with British, German, Japanese, and other foreign banks that were free of restrictions faced by American banks. Moreover, American banks adopted a global outlook that freed them from limiting their operations to the United States. Many were moving their activities offshore to places such as the Cayman Islands, Bermuda, and the Bahamas. President Ronald Reagan, elected on a platform of limiting the role of government, pressured other countries to open their financial

> **global financial liberalization** ■ Opening banks around the world to competition

systems to American firms. Financial deregulation in the United States was now inseparable from the globalization of trade and financial services. However, impeding global competition in banking was the Glass-Steagall Act of 1933, which prohibited commercial banks from underwriting or marketing securities.[8] The rapid growth of capital flows across national borders and the increasing power of investment bankers eventually led to the demise of the Glass-Steagall Act in 1999.

The phenomenal proliferation of sophisticated computer technologies and an almost unquestioning faith in the wisdom of markets contributed to escalating demands for and acceptance of less regulation. In essence, federal agencies designed to regulate banking became less effective. There was a general loss of control at all levels, which led to exponential risk taking at many companies, largely hidden from public scrutiny. Violations of financial regulations went largely unpunished.[9] Simon Johnson argues that from the confluence of campaign finance, personal connections, and ideology flowed a river of deregulatory policies. These included:

1. Insistence on free movement of capital across borders
2. The repeal of Depression-era regulations separating commercial and investment banking
3. Decreased regulatory enforcement by the Securities and Exchange Commission
4. Allowing banks to measure their own riskiness
5. Failure to update regulations to keep up with the tremendous pace of financial innovations[10]

Financial Innovations

As the global financial crisis unfolded, it was obvious that many of those in the banking and investment communities did not fully comprehend how the financial system they created functioned, or the scope and severity of the crisis. The financial wizards, the best and the brightest from leading business schools, could not really explain what was happening on Wall Street and in global financial markets. Ironically, financial innovations, designed by brilliant computer experts to manage risk and make capital less expensive and more available, ultimately led to the global financial crisis. Financial innovations, with instantaneous global impacts due to technologies that made electronic transactions faster and less expensive, raced ahead of regulations. Complex financial products created in one financial center involved assets in another and were sold to investors in a third financial market. As we saw in Chapter 1, governments are increasingly challenged to operate effectively in a globalized world. Whereas governments are restrained by issues of sovereignty, global financial firms enjoy relatively greater flexibility. Furthermore, many different agencies in the United States have regulatory authority, a situation that creates confusion and ineffectiveness.[11] Among the numerous financial innovations that led to the global financial crisis were securitization and hedge funds.

Prior to the widespread use of securitization, banks, many of them local, provided loans to customers they often knew, and the banks were responsible for the risks involved in making loans. This meant that bankers gave loans only to individuals and companies they believed could repay the loans. With securitization, risks inherent in granting loans were passed from the bank giving the loans to others who had no direct interest in the customers' ability to repay the loans. Subprime mortgages, student loans, car loans, and credit card debts were securitized. Securitization is a sophisticated process of financial engineering that allows global investment to be spread out and separated into multiple income streams to reduce risk.[12] It involves bundling loans into securities and selling them to investors. In 2009, an estimated $8.7 trillion of assets globally were funded by securitization.[13] This innovation made vast sums of money available to borrowers. For example, securitization increased the amount of money available to individuals purchasing homes. This led to unprecedented growth in house prices. It also resulted in high default rates and the housing crisis. As we will discuss, applicants for mortgages were not carefully examined and were encouraged to obtain subprime loans.

securitization ■ Financial engineering designed to reduce risk

Another financial innovation was credit derivatives, which were bets on the creditworthiness of a particular company, like insurance on a loan. There were two types of credit derivatives: credit default swaps and collateralized debt obligations.[14] Credit default swaps were widely used, especially by insurance companies such as the American International Group (AIG). Life insurance companies invested in credit default swaps as assets. Parties involved in a credit default swap agreed that one would pay the other if a particular borrower, a third party, could not repay its loans. Credit default swaps were used to transfer credit risks away from banks. A major problem with credit default swaps was the lack of transparency. They were also unregulated. Ultimately, credit default swaps created confusion and encouraged excessive risk taking. It was difficult to determine where the risk ended up. Designed to pass on risks, loans were packaged as securities. Collateralized debt obligations were linked to mortgage companies, which passed on the risk. Mortgages, instead of being held by banks and mortgage companies, were sold to investors shortly after the loans closed, and investors packaged them as securities.

derivatives ■ Bets on the creditworthiness of a particular company, like insurance on a loan

credit default swaps ■ Financial innovation used to transfer credit risks away from banks

collateralized debt obligations ■ Linked to mortgage companies

Similar to securitization, hedge funds grew rapidly, accounting for more than $1.3 trillion in assets globally before the financial crisis of 2008–2009. The name hedge funds implies investment funds with a particular sort of hedging strategy. Created by the Investment Company Act of 1940, hedge funds allowed wealthy investors to avoid many financial regulations, and hedge funds were early participants in financial globalization.[15] Essentially, hedge fund managers created portfolios reflecting an assessment of the performance of diverse global markets. As long as the number of participants was relatively small, hedge funds avoided great systemic risks. This changed with revolutions in computer technology that allowed split-second timing on huge volumes of trades. An integral component of the hedge fund strategy is a technique known as arbitrage. This involves simultaneously buying at a lower price in one market and selling at a higher price in another market to make a profit on the spread between the two prices.[16]

hedge funds ■ Enabled wealthy investors to avoid some financial regulations in global financial markets

arbitrage ■ Simultaneously buying at a lower price in one market and selling at a higher price in another market to make a profit

Executive Compensation

Excessive executive compensation is widely perceived as playing a pivotal role in creating the global financial crisis. Wall Street became a magnet for the brightest

Americans who wanted to make a large amount of money very quickly. Most companies rewarded short-term performance without much regard for market fundamentals and long-term earnings. Executives were given stock options, which they could manipulate to earn more money. The more an executive could drive up his or her company's stock price or its earnings per share, the more money he or she would get. Frank Partnoy argues that a mercenary culture developed among corporate executives. They merged with or acquired higher-growth companies and, in many cases, committed accounting fraud.[17] This fraud led to the bankruptcy of companies such as Enron, Global Crossing, and WorldCom. Many executives received long prison sentences.

Low Interest Rates

Alan Greenspan ■ Chairman of the U.S. Federal Reserve who kept interest rates low

A fundamental cause of the global financial crisis was the easy availability of too much money globally. An oversupply of money created unprecedented levels of liquidity and historically low interest rates. As we mentioned earlier, the terrorist attacks on the United States on September 11, 2001, triggered a national embrace of increased government spending as well as consumer spending. To accomplish this, the U.S. Federal Reserve, led by Alan Greenspan, lowered interest rates to around 1 percent in late 2001. The European Central Bank and the Bank of Japan also reduced interest rates to record lows. The U.S. government encouraged Americans to purchase homes and to refinance or borrow against the value of homes they owned. As consumers and the government lived beyond their means, they were able to borrow from developing countries that were accumulating huge reserves from the phenomenal growth of global trade. Much of the surplus of money in the global system also came from declining investment in the Asian economies following the 1997 financial crisis. Rising oil prices in the Middle East, Russia, and elsewhere enabled many countries to earn more money than they could spend rationally. By the end of 2008, central banks in emerging economies held $5 trillion in reserves.[18]

sovereign wealth funds ■ Created by countries to save and recycle surplus revenues

The money supply increased rapidly in China, India, Russia, and the Persian Gulf states. Whereas it was generally assumed that global monetary policies were set by central banks in the United States, Europe, and Japan, the reality was that three fifths of the world's money supply growth flowed from emerging economies.[19] Based on their experiences with financial problems, many developing countries decided to save for a rainy day, as it were. They believed that high oil prices or trade surpluses would not last forever. Many of these countries created sovereign wealth funds to recycle their financial surpluses.

Subprime Loans

subprime loans ■ High-risk credit given to individuals who fail to meet rigorous standards

Another major cause of the financial crisis was the availability of subprime loans, which were directly an outgrowth of easy credit. Subprime loans generally refer to credit given to individuals who fail to meet rigorous standards usually expected by lending institutions. These individuals could not really afford their loans because of inadequate income and poor credit histories. In most cases, borrowers were not required to have a down payment. With excess liquidity globally, interest rates remained low. People with weak financial histories are generally more vulnerable to being charged higher interest rates. For example, poor people pay exorbitant rates for payday loans. A basic reality of finance is that yields on loans are inversely proportional to credit quality: the stronger the borrower, the lower the yield, and vice versa.[20] Driving the demand for subprime loans was the development of a culture of entitlement and a false egalitarianism that appealed to people's egos. Home ownership was pushed by the U.S. government as an inalienable right, despite borrowers' inability to repay loans. Fannie Mae (Federal National Mortgage Association) and Freddie Mac (Federal Home Loan Mortgage Corporation), both U.S. government corporations, made more money available to lenders and borrowers by purchasing loans from the lenders and selling them to investors in the secondary markets. Huge amounts of money gravitated to subprime mortgages in the United States and Europe and, ultimately, to weak borrowers globally. Given the complex interdependence that characterizes financial globalization, problems emanating from subprime loans in the United States rapidly spread around the world. Governments were largely unaware of the risks associated with new forms of financing and were unable to prevent the global financial crisis.[21]

Fannie Mae and Freddie Mac ■ U.S. government corporations involved in real estate

As the unprecedented sums of money flowed into commercial and residential real estate, housing prices escalated. For thirty years before the housing boom, the average American house appreciated at an average of 1.4 percent a year. This low return of prime loans discouraged homeowners from viewing their houses as cash machines. Home equity lines of credit were not available until recently. Things changed dramatically after 2000. Appreciation rates climbed to 7.6 percent between 2000 and 2006, reaching 11 percent before the market crashed between 2006 and 2007. Real estate prices in California, Arizona, Nevada, Florida, and other areas grew even faster.

There was a wide variety of subprime mortgages. These included adjustable-rate mortgages, balloon mortgages, piggyback loans, and interest-only loans. An adjustable-rate mortgage is a long-term loan that does not have a fixed interest rate. The interest can be changed, with low rates at the beginning and high rates at the end. It is also possible, but highly unlikely, that rates could decline. Adjustable-rate mortgages were attractive to homebuyers who moved frequently. They were less expensive, or so it seemed, than fixed-rate mortgages, which offered more protection. A variation of the adjustable-rate mortgage is a balloon mortgage. Under this arrangement, lower payments are made on a loan for five to ten years, with a final installment, or balloon payment, that is significantly larger than earlier payments. Most borrowers could not afford to pay the balloon payment. The piggyback loan allows the homeowner to take out a second mortgage that is piggybacked onto the first mortgage. This is a high-risk loan because it clearly indicates that the borrower cannot afford the down payment to purchase real estate.[22] In an environment that encourages consumption over savings, easy credit fueled the housing crisis. Interest-only loans required borrowers to pay the interest on a loan without reducing the principal balance. This enabled weak borrowers to obtain larger loans.

adjustable-rate mortgage ■ A long-term loan that has varying interest rates

Speculation

A combination of low interest rates, unprecedented liquidity, and a belief that the Internet and various computer technologies virtually guaranteed unending and ever-increasing prosperity facilitated the growth of speculative financial forces. Excessive risk taking replaced caution, which was often equated with a lack of optimism. Speculation, a deeply ingrained human characteristic, fosters the development of a herd mentality. As prices continued to rise, even the most cautious individuals get caught up in speculation. Ultimately, a speculative bubble is created. *Speculative bubbles generally go through four stages:*

speculation ■ Involves excessive risk taking, excessive optimism, and the development of a herd mentality

1. A new technology or invention changes people's expectations and those who are well informed try to profit from it.
2. Prices or profits continue to rise, which draws more people into the market.
3. The boom passes into euphoria and rational decision making is suspended.
4. The bust is almost inevitable. Prices and profits fall, companies and individuals go bankrupt, and the economy plunges into a recession.[23]

Taxpayer Relief Act of 1997 ■ Exempted profits from taxes gained from selling one's home

Many homeowners became speculators. In addition to low-interest loans and financial innovations in the housing market, political pressures to reduce taxes, including real estate taxes, contributed to the housing boom. Congress passed the Taxpayer Relief Act of 1997, which, among other things, exempted profits realized from the sale of a home if the home was owned and used as a principal residence for two of the last five years before it was sold. This new provision enabled homeowners to exclude up to $500,000 for couples and $250,000 for singles from capital gains tax. In many cases, removal of the capital gains tax encouraged home buyers to engage in a form of speculation known as flipping. The buyer would own the house for a short period with the sole intention of selling it very quickly for a higher price, thereby gaining a significant profit without much effort and by using very little of his or her own money as an investment. When the stock market crashed in 2000, real estate became more attractive to investors. Furthermore, the shock of the terrorist attacks on September 11, 2001, influenced more Americans to seek security in their homes. Consequently, they concentrated their investments in real estate. Because of the huge amounts of money that went into real estate globally and the preponderance of subprime loans and excessive risk taken in home mortgages, the housing crisis was at the epicenter of the global financial crisis.

THE IMPACT OF THE GLOBAL FINANCIAL CRISIS

As we mentioned earlier, the global financial crisis affected virtually all areas, including the process of globalization. Housing prices crashed; foreclosures became commonplace; unemployment reached 10 percent in the United States and higher levels in Europe and elsewhere; manufacturing declined sharply, especially in the automotive industry; students were faced with higher costs as colleges suffered financial losses; finding jobs after college became more challenging; and a global recession created widespread hardships. On the other hand, many developing countries that took a prudent approach to finance and saved money were not as badly damaged. In fact, countries that did not fully embrace financial liberalization were less affected than those that gave in to American pressure to fully engage in financial globalization. We also saw a global power shift, with the United States losing ground to China, India, Brazil, and other developing countries.

Housing was at the epicenter of the financial crisis. Falling house prices directly affect government revenues, including spending for education.

Foreclosures

Plunging real estate prices affected virtually all areas of the economy. People could no longer afford to purchase homes, which meant that homebuilders were forced to abandon construction projects. Think of all the products that are used in building and furnishing a home; all of the industries that produced these products generally experienced declining sales. Because houses became primary sources of wealth or perceptions of wealth, falling real estate prices made homeowners feel less economically secure. In a vicious circle, the economic recession, fueled by declining real estate markets, further eroded demand for real estate. But, mortgages must be repaid or the consequences can be severe. Despite decreasing home values, homeowners must continue to pay real estate taxes and spend money on maintenance. Many homes were bought at prices much higher than their actual worth just two or three years later. Rising levels of unemployment also pushed homeowners with strong credit into foreclosure. One in forty-five U.S. households, or 3 million, received a foreclosure filing, and banks repossessed 1 million homes in 2010. Housing prices continued to fall in 2011, the construction of new houses declined the most in twenty-seven years, and building permits dropped to their lowest level on record.[24]

The mortgage crisis inevitably spread to financial institutions, causing reputable Wall Street firms such as Lehman Brothers to collapse overnight. Because of Lehman's pivotal role in finance, its demise in September 2008 is generally perceived as the most tangible evidence of the financial crisis on Wall Street. Iceland, which had a very successful banking system, saw its economy and currency collapse along with the banking system. Ireland, widely regarded as the Celtic Tiger for its rapid economic growth, experienced a deep recession. American consumers, the backbone of the United States and, to some extent, the global economy, had exhausted their resources and had a savings rate that was close to zero.

Decline in Manufacturing and Trade

Manufacturing, already in decline, fell dramatically. This especially was the case in the automotive industry, with General Motors and Chrysler declaring bankruptcy after closing many factories and dealerships, despite unprecedented financial support from the U.S. government. Industrial production was down by 12 percent in Europe, 11 percent in the United States, and 43 percent in Taiwan. Tightening credit and consumer fear ultimately created a downward spiral that significantly diminished global trade. Germany saw its exports drop by 20 percent. China's exports fell by more than 25 percent, and U.S. exports fell by almost 24 percent in 2008.[25] Both economies rebounded, with China surpassing Japan to become the world's second-largest economy and Germany experiencing the highest economic growth rate in Europe.

Global Power Shift

BRIC countries ■
Brazil, Russia, India, and China; emerging global powers

Yaga Venugobal Reddy ■ Governor of the Reserve Bank of India; credited with helping India avoid the financial crisis

Another major impact of the global financial crisis is a global power shift. Although most countries were negatively affected by the financial crisis and global recession, some emerged stronger than others. Brazil, Russia, India, and China, also known as the BRIC countries, enhanced their power vis-à-vis the United States, Western Europe, and Japan. Within the EU, Germany emerged with the strongest financial and economic system and greater political and economic power. In sharp contrast to the policies adopted by the U.S. Federal Reserve under Chairman Alan Greenspan, the Reserve Bank of India, led by Yaga Venugobal Reddy, rejected many financial innovations and limited the participation of foreign investors in India's financial system. Instead of believing that markets are self-regulating, as many Americans do, the Indian government favored regulations and was quick to recognize financial bubbles. Reddy restricted bank lending to real estate developers, increased the amount of money banks had to set aside as reserves, and blocked the use of some derivatives. This conservative approach enabled India to largely avoid the global financial crisis.[26] Given America's role in pressuring the world to adopt a financial system that failed, BRIC countries perceive the financial crisis as a serious economic and political setback for the United States and free-market capitalism. All of these countries, sensing America's vulnerabilities, are becoming more politically and financially assertive. From their perspective, America is declining. It has escalating budget deficits, it is extremely dependent on foreign creditors such as China, and the dollar's status as the main global reserve currency has eroded. As we saw in Chapter 2, America's economic power following World War II enabled it to shape global financial institutions such as the International Monetary Fund (IMF) and the World Bank. However, the BRIC countries are now challenging America's leadership.[27] Economic power has shifted from the G-7 to the G-20, the group composed of countries with the largest economies, many of

---

> **TABLE 7.1**
>
> **Growth of Foreign Banks in the United States**
>
> | Leading Banks (1999) | Share of Market (%) | Leading Banks (2009) | Share of Market (%) |
> |---|---|---|---|
> | 1. Citi (U.S.) | 13.9 | J.P. Morgan (U.S.) | 14.8 |
> | 2. Merrill Lynch (U.S.) | 13.7 | Citi (U.S.) | 14.7 |
> | 3. Goldman Sachs (U.S.) | 10.4 | Bank of America Merrill Lynch (U.S.) | 12.9 |
> | 4. Morgan Stanley (U.S.) | 10.4 | Morgan Stanley (U.S.) | 10.4 |
> | 5. Lehman Brothers (U.S.) | 8.2 | Goldman Sachs (U.S.) | 8.8 |
> | 6. Chase Manhattan (U.S.) | 7.3 | Barclays Capital (British) | 7.1 |
> | 7. Credit Suisse First Boston (Swiss) | 6.0 | HSBC (British) | 4.5 |
> | 8. J.P. Morgan (U.S.) | 6.2 | Deutsche Bank (German) | 4.2 |
> | 9. Donaldson Lufkin Jenrette (U.S.) | 4.9 | Credit Suisse (Swiss) | 4.1 |
> | 10. Bear Stearns (U.S.) | 4.6 | RBS (Scotland) | 3.7 |
>
> *Source:* Graham Bowley, "Stalking a Weaker Wall Street," *New York Times*, 17 June 2009, B1.

them in the developing world. In 2011, when a new leader was being chosen for the IMF, countries with emerging economies called for the end of the tradition of European leadership of the IMF. Another indication of a power shift is the growing role of foreign banks in America's financial system, as indicated in Table 7.1.

GLOBAL RESPONSES TO THE FINANCIAL CRISIS
America's Response

Responses to the global financial crisis varied from country to country, with the strongest actions occurring in the United States. Being largely responsible for the crisis, the United States was not only the most severely affected but also the most shell shocked and anxious to find solutions. In a sharp reversal of its strong commitment to economic and financial liberalization and free-market capitalism, the United States has led efforts to nationalize its financial and some aspects of its manufacturing sectors to an unprecedented degree. There was general consensus among Republicans and Democrats that a massive financial and economic stimulus package, engineered primarily by Secretary of the Treasury Henry Paulson, was essential not just to rescue America's financial institutions but also to reassure Americans that their savings and investments were secure. A $787 billion stimulus package was passed by Congress. Because the financial crisis was reminiscent of the Great Depression, with its high levels of unemployment and massive withdrawals from banks, the U.S. government responded to avoid repeating the mistakes of the 1930s. Despite various protections

Henry Paulson ■
U.S. Secretary of the Treasury who initiated the stimulus package to rescue banks on Wall Street

stimulus package ■
Money allocated by governments to financial institutions and selected industries to prevent their collapse and reinvigorate economic growth

implemented to insure the safety of deposits, such as the FDIC, Americans withdrew $150 billion from money market funds over a two-day period in September 2008, compared with average weekly outflows of roughly $5 billion. The huge amount of money poured into credit markets and banks was designed to restore confidence in financial institutions and to expand credit. Concerned about high unemployment rates and stagnant economic growth, the U.S. Federal Reserve enacted a type of monetary stimulus known as quantitative easing (QE). It bought $600 billion in long-term Treasury bonds to push down long-term interest rates.[28] That depreciated the value of the dollar, thereby making American exports less expensive and raising the cost of imports. That, in turn, fueled debates about currency wars. America also responded by electing Republicans in 2010 to replace Democrats who controlled the House of Representatives. A greater emphasis was placed on reducing budget deficits at both the national and state levels. Many public service employees lost their jobs, and public sector unions were severely weakened.

quantitative easing ■
A type of monetary stimulus used by the U.S. Federal Reserve. Long-term Treasury bonds are purchased to decrease interest rates.

European Responses

Although other countries also implemented stimulus packages, their concerns differed to a significant degree from those of the United States. Germany, for

Fallout from the financial crisis and economic recession is seen in Portugal, at a workers' protest against the government's new budget policies for trimming the country's budget deficit. Portugal asked the European Union for financial assistance to help solve its crisis.

example, resisted American pressure to adopt a more comprehensive, coordinated global stimulus package, partly because many Germans believe that the crisis was primarily an outgrowth of American financial policies and would have to be solved domestically. Germans worry about the possibility of hyperinflation, which the country experienced in the 1920s. Germans are also more frugal than Americans and are reluctant to impose huge deficits on future generations, especially in light of Germany's shrinking population. Europeans in general took a less-frantic approach to the financial crisis because in normal times their governments had created numerous safety nets. European governments provide national health insurance and generous pensions, and they have implemented programs to reduce unemployment and lost wages. Because they save a greater percentage of their income, at reduced levels, they have avoided losing their homes on such a massive scale as is the case in the United States. However, faced with mounting debts and a worsening financial crisis, many governments implemented austerity programs that cut government budget deficits and raised the minimum retirement age. These changes caused protests in France, Greece, Portugal, Britain, and elsewhere. Leaders of the "euro zone" countries, in which the single European currency is used, struggled to create an overall policy to deal with the region's growing debt crisis. Students in Britain protested the government's decision to increase college tuition and fees. Similar to the United States, the government that was in power in Britain during the financial crisis (Labor), lost its majority to a coalition of Conservatives and Liberal Democrats.

safety nets ■
The health insurance, pensions, and other programs that European governments provide citizens and that lessen losses in economic hard times

China's Response

China's response involved taking measures to strengthen its power vis-à-vis the United States. Unlike the United States, China regulates its financial institutions, has more than $2 trillion in reserves, and continues to have economic growth rates in excess of 7 percent, and the Chinese save more than 40 percent of their income. Despite rising unemployment and declining exports, China emerged from the financial crisis in a strong position and is taking advantage of new opportunities created by the crisis. China is using its $600 billion economic stimulus package to improve its infrastructure, to help its companies to become more competitive domestically and globally, and to enhance research and development. It is also gaining greater access to resources and augmenting its relations in Latin America, Africa, the Middle East, and elsewhere, even as the United States is preoccupied with its financial and economic crises as well as with fighting wars in Iraq and Afghanistan. China is also acquiring European and American companies in the automotive, textile, food, energy, machinery, electronics, and environmental protection sectors. One of the most visible acquisitions is the Hummer from General Motors.

Financial Regulations

In light of the general consensus among experts that deregulation and the lax enforcement of regulations in the financial sector contributed significantly to the global financial crisis, an immediate response to the crash was to try to

Ben S. Bernanke ■
Chairman of the U.S.
Federal Reserve

Bank for
International
Settlements ■
Based in Basel,
Switzerland; created
to regulate banking
and harmonize
banking standards

strengthen and update regulations. The chairman of the U.S. Federal Reserve, Ben S. Bernanke, was particularly aware of the need for new regulations. As a professor at Princeton University, Bernanke focused his research on the Great Depression. The American government was now determined to avoid mistakes made during that financial and economic crisis. Efforts to enact international banking regulations began with the creation of the Bank for International Settlements, based in Basel, Switzerland. In 1988, the banking community signed the Basel Capital Accord, which attempted to harmonize banking standards, especially those requiring banks to set aside capital to cover the level of risk they faced. However, due to the dominant influence of bankers, the Bank for International Settlements was not very focused on regulations.[29] Since 1999, there has been a greater effort to develop a stronger regulatory framework, known as Basel 2. The accord gave credit-rating agencies an explicit role in determining how much capital is enough to cover certain risks. In 2010, an agreement known as *Basel 3* created new international rules for banks. They raised the amount capital lenders are required to have as a cushion against unexpected financial losses to 7 percent of their capital.[30] But, the failures of financial institutions in the United States, Europe, and elsewhere demonstrate that individual countries' unwillingness or inability to supervise their financial sectors was at the heart of the problem. Consequently, domestic regulatory reforms are likely to be more effective than global regulations. Financial innovations such as derivatives and executive compensation are the primary targets for greater supervision. However, the complex nature of the global financial system and strong reservations in the United States about the government's role in the economy will most likely diminish the effectiveness of regulations.

▶ CASE STUDY | Ireland: The Decline of the Celtic Tiger

Ireland, the second-richest country in Europe before the global financial and economic crisis, now has one of Europe's weakest economies. What makes the Irish case different and of special interest is that after such a long history of hardship and poverty, Ireland was radically transformed into a highly successful country, becoming the Celtic Tiger in the 1990s, only to see prosperity decline precipitously by 2007. Massive public debt, due largely to the banking crisis, forced Ireland to turn to the European Union and the IMF for financial assistance. Unemployment rose to 14 percent and consumer spending and incomes fell. Ghost estates proliferated, homelessness increased, and younger Irish emigrated to the United States, Canada, Australia, and elsewhere to find employment.[31]

Ireland endured severe economic problems in the 1980s. Emigration, an integral part of the Irish experience for more than 150 years, rose sharply, draining the country of many talented individuals. High tax rates discouraged foreign investment, and high inflation and high interest rates made it difficult for the economy to recover. Ireland's entry into the EU and its adoption of the euro marked a major step toward Ireland's integration in the global economy. Ireland gained access to low interest rates, and the Anglo Irish Bank and other financial institutions borrowed heavily in the euro interbank market to finance property loans. Ireland's rapid economic growth was aided by policies implemented by the government led by Charles Haughey. Those included cuts in public spending to reduce the budget deficit, a three-year freeze on wages, and lowering inflation and interest rates. Ireland attracted many companies, especially high-tech industries like Intel,

(continued)

that wanted to gain entry in the EU before the removal of trade barriers among member countries in 1992. Ireland in many ways resembled South Korea, Taiwan, and other Asian Tigers. It offered a relatively low-wage workforce, highly educated individuals, low tax rates, and concessions to companies that invested. It also had the advantage of being an English-speaking country with a global diaspora. Ireland's economic prosperity was closely linked to America's. Many in the Irish diaspora, especially in the United States, returned to Ireland during the boom in the 1990s, bringing with them skills and capital. Ireland also became a magnet for immigrants from Eastern Europe and elsewhere, many of whom worked in the booming construction industry and in the service sector. Between 1993 and 2000, average GDP growth rates were around 10 percent, similar to rates in China and other Asian countries. Ireland became a Celtic Tiger during this period. But a financial bubble was also developing. Wages and prices rose faster than those in Ireland's trading partners, which diminished Ireland's competitiveness. Imports became less expensive and government deficits grew, as was the case in the United States. At the same time, the cost of living escalated. Ireland had become Europe's second-richest country overnight.

Ireland, like the United States, turned to investing in real estate following the dot-com bust. The general belief among many Irish was that real estate was a safe investment that would continue to appreciate. Low interest rates, the lack of stringent government regulations, and government corruption fueled a construction boom. Small down payments enabled financially vulnerable individuals to purchase homes. Buyers routinely secured loans worth more than 90 percent of the home's value, which pushed them into negative equity when property values declined. Speculation was common. People wanting to make money quickly invested in second homes and commercial property. The number of people employed in construction reached 272,000 in 2007, accounting for one eighth of the workforce. When employment in areas related to housing is considered, such as real estate agencies, mortgage brokers, and banks, the housing sector employed a fifth of Ireland's population. Housing problems were the main cause of the decline of the Celtic Tiger. Ireland experienced a precipitous drop in housing prices.[32]

In an effort to solve its economic problems, Ireland borrowed money, primarily to bail out banks. Germany, the leading EU economy and the biggest creditor, opposed lowering interest rates on Ireland's debt, favoring instead fiscal discipline. But austerity programs and high unemployment rates lessen the likelihood that consumers will be able to reinvigorate the economy. Ireland faces many difficult choices. The financial and budgetary crises will take time to be resolved. By keeping corporate taxes low, Ireland is likely to attract foreign investment as the global economy improves. Ireland's young and talented workforce will continue to be a major asset that will assist in the country's economic recovery. ▸

SUMMARY AND REVIEW

The global financial crisis of 2008–2009 ushered in the most severe global recession since the Great Depression of the 1930s. Given the central role played by finances in globalization, the crisis has serious implications for virtually all global issues and for globalization itself. Although this chapter argued that financial crises seem to be an integral component of capitalism, human beings are ultimately responsible for creating them. Revolutions in computer and telecommunications technologies fostered the development of complex financial engineering that radically altered the global financial system. An emphasis on government deregulation, the growth of a culture that encouraged quick profits and excessive executive compensation, and the availability of low interest rates played significant roles in creating the financial crisis. But a crisis presents both dangers and opportunities. While the United States has suffered severe setbacks, China has gained, thereby shifting global power. The financial crisis has significantly reduced global trade and caused unprecedented home foreclosures and high levels of unemployment. The global response has centered around regulating some of the financial innovations, paying greater attention to risk management, and monitoring executive compensation. Overall, the financial crisis has diminished support for financial liberalization and strengthened the role of governments around the world in economic affairs.

KEY TERMS

finance   139
Asian Financial Crisis   140
Federal Deposit Insurance Corporation
   (FDIC)   141
deregulation   141
global financial liberalization   141
Glass-Steagall Act of 1933   142
financial innovations   142
securitization   143
derivatives   143
credit default swaps   143
collateralized debt obligations   143
hedge funds   143
arbitrage   143
Alan Greenspan   144

sovereign wealth funds   144
subprime loans   144
Fannie Mae and Freddie Mac   145
adjustable-rate mortgage   145
speculation   146
Taxpayer Relief Act of 1997   146
BRIC countries   148
Yaga Venugobal Reddy   148
Henry Paulson   149
stimulus package   149
quantitative easing   150
safety nets   151
Ben S. Bernanke   152
Bank for International Settlements   152

DISCUSSION QUESTIONS

1. Discuss how deregulation of financial markets and low interest rates contributed to creating the financial crisis.
2. Discuss the implications of the stimulus package for the United States. In light of the benefits derived from Europe's safety net, discuss the pros and cons of America's adoption of European policies, such as universal health care and job protection.
3. Discuss the role of subprime loans in real estate in the financial crisis and their broader social and economic implications.
4. In your view, has the financial crisis weakened the United States globally and strengthened China? Discuss.
5. Evaluate the global responses to the financial crisis. Give examples.

SUGGESTED READINGS

Altman, Roger C. "The Great Crash, 2008," *Foreign Affairs* 88, No. 1 (January/February 2009): 2–14. Gives historical perspective to the 2008 crash.

Davis, Howard, and David Green. *Banking on the Future.* Princeton, NJ: Princeton University Press, 2010. Reviews the financial crisis and suggests specific reforms, such as giving central banks greater responsibility for the stability of the financial system.

Lynch, David J. *When the Luck of the Irish Ran Out.* New York: Palgrave Macmillan, 2010. Analysis of how direct investment and real estate speculation contributed to Ireland's rapid economic growth and how they crashed during the global/financial crisis.

Paulson, Henry M. *On the Brink*. New York: Business Plus, 2010. An account by the U.S. Secretary of the Treasury on efforts to manage the financial crisis and prevent it from becoming an economic catastrophe.

Reinhart, Carmen M., and Kenneth S. Rogoff. *This Time Is Different*. Princeton, NJ: Princeton University Press, 2009. Examines financial crises over eight centuries and concludes that banking crises become more common as countries develop.

ENDNOTES

1. "The Financial Crisis," *Economist*, 17 January 2009, 81.
2. Liaquat Ahamed, *Lords of Finance* (New York: Penguin Press, 2009), 14.
3. Jadish Bhagwati, *In Defense of Globalization* (New York: Oxford University Press, 2004), 199.
4. Antonia Juhasz, *The Bush Agenda* (New York: Regan Books, 2006), 47.
5. John C. Bogle, *The Battle for the Soul of Capitalism* (New Haven, CT: Yale University Press, 2005), 3.
6. Robert Kuttner, *The Squandering of America* (New York: Alfred A. Knopf, 2007), 68.
7. Robert B. Reich, *Supercapitalism* (New York: Alfred A. Knopf, 2007), 96.
8. Kuttner, *The Squandering of America*, 250.
9. Frank Partnoy, *Infectious Greed* (New York: Times Books, 2003), 3.
10. Simon Johnson, "The Quiet Coup," *The Atlantic*, May 2009, 52.
11. "The Rules of the Game," *Economist*, 15 September 2007, 16.
12. David M. Smick, *The World Is Curved* (New York: Portfolio, 2008), 44.
13. "Too Big to Swallow," *Economist*, 16 May 2009, 11.
14. Partnoy, *Infectious Greed*, 374.
15. Kuttner, *The Squandering of America*, 106.
16. Virginia B. Morris and Kenneth A. Morris, *Dictionary of Financial Terms* (New York: Lightbulb Press, 2008), 12.
17. Partnoy, *Infectious Greed*, 157.
18. "A Monetary Malaise," *Economist*, 11 October 2008, 22.
19. "Central Banks in the Rich World No Longer Determine Global Monetary Conditions," *Economist*, 11 August 2007, 70.
20. (20) Roger C. Altman, "The Great Crash, 2008," *Foreign Affairs* 88, No. 1 (January/February 2009), 4.
21. Altman, "The Great Crash, 2008," 4.
22. Blanche Evans, *Bubbles, Booms, and Busts* (New York: McGraw-Hill, 2007), 19.
23. John Cassidy, *dot.con: The Greatest Story Ever Sold* (New York: HarperCollins, 2002), 5; and Charles P. Kindleberger and Robert Aliber, *Manias, Panics, and Crashes: A History of Financial Crises* (New York: Wiley, 2005), 29.
24. "Housing Starts Decline," *New York Times*, 17 March 2011, B5.
25. "Will Germany Now Take Center Stage?" *Economist*, 23 October 2010, 27.
26. Vikas Bajaj, "In India, Central Banker Played It Safe," *New York Times*, 26 June 2009, B4; and "Germany's Economy," *Economist*, 5 February 2011, 17.
27. Clifford J. Levy, "Seeking Greater Financial Clout, Emerging Powers Prepare to Meet in Russia," *New York Times*, 16 June 2009, A5.
28. Altman, "The Great Crash, 2008," 5; and Raghuram Rajan, "Currencies Aren't the Problem," *Foreign Affairs* 90, No. 2 (March/April 2011), 104.
29. Kuttner, *The Squandering of America*, 251.
30. "Business: Basel 3," *Economist*, 18 September 2010, 10.
31. "Ireland's Crash," *Economist*, 19 February 2011, 25.
32. "A Special Report on Property," *Economist*, 5 March 2011, 7.

Global Trade

Global companies improve lives and promote equality. "Infoscions," employees of Infosys, India's largest software company, walk at the company's headquarters outside Bangalore, Karnataka, India.

INTRODUCTION

The origins of global trade are as old as human society. Lacking complete self-sufficiency, human beings traded goods and services within their communities and gradually expanded trade with people in distant areas. Global trade clearly shows the political, economic, and cultural aspects of globalization. Global trade is so integral to our daily lives that we are generally oblivious to how it links us to the rest of the world. Some of our most important agricultural crops are not native to North America. In fact, it is difficult to think of a country that has not been affected by the transfer of food crops from some distant area.

The story of *sugarcane* vividly illustrates this point, as Figure 8.1 shows. More than eight thousand years ago, inhabitants of New Guinea, located north of Australia, discovered that grass, similar to bamboo, not only was sweet but could be easily cultivated by planting segments of it. This was the beginning of the global sugar trade, a development that would profoundly affect most of the world. Human craving for sweet foods facilitated the spread of sugarcane from New Guinea across Southeast Asia to India, which began producing crystal sugar around 500 B.C. Traders soon took sugarcane from India to China and Persia (now Iran). The spread of Islam from Saudi Arabia to Egypt, across North Africa, and into the Mediterranean and Spain was accompanied by the spread of sugar cultivation.

Spanish and Portuguese colonization of the Americas marked a turning point in the cultivation, production, and consumption of sugar. Widely regarded by Europeans as a luxury product, sugarcane was soon cultivated on a massive scale throughout the Caribbean and Latin America. Requiring intensive labor, sugarcane cultivation fueled the trans-Atlantic slave trade and numerous conflicts among European countries for control of the sugar-producing Caribbean islands. For example, France gave its territory in Canada to Britain partly in exchange for the two sugar-growing islands of Martinique and Guadeloupe under the Treaty of Paris of 1763, which ended the Seven Years' War between the two European powers. By the 1830s, sugar cultivation spread to Hawaii, thereby completing its journey around the world and becoming a significant part of our diet. Our lives are increasingly affected by the webs of global interdependence that are integral parts of global trade. What's more, the ability of countries to control their economic activities is steadily being eroded by economic globalization.

Many scholars have concluded that global trade and other aspects of globalization are transforming the functions of states. They see a shift in power away from countries to global companies and point to taxing power, an essential component of national sovereignty, to illustrate their point. Even more important is the weakening of traditional bonds between citizens and governments. One scholar, Kenichi Ohmae, contends that "the nation-state has become an unnatural, even dysfunctional, unit for organizing human activity and managing economic endeavor in a borderless world."[1]

Treaty of Paris of 1763 ■ Ended the Seven Years' War between France and Britain

This chapter examines the growth of free trade, concerns about trade deficits and surpluses among countries, and how budget deficits and the relative value of currencies affect global trade. We will discuss various trade disputes and how those disputes are resolved by emerging global institutions. Finally, we will discuss the impact of trade on the environment and the global spread of diseases and their implications for global trade and trade blocs. The chapter concludes with a case study of growing power of emerging markets, with special reference to Brazil.

THE GLOBALIZATION OF FREE TRADE

Silk Road ■ Trade route linking China with the West

mercantilist model ■ Trade model stressing the role of government in trade and emphasizing the importance of balance-of-payment surpluses

autarky ■ Ideology promoting economic national self-sufficiency and an end to economic interaction with other countries

comparative advantage ■ Theory that each country specializes in producing specific products in order to better trade with other states

competitive advantage ■ Shift toward the production of goods and services based on cost considerations, arbitrary specialization, and government and corporate policies

As early as the third century B.C., various nomadic groups and Chinese merchants established a trading route known as the Silk Road. Linking China with the West, the Silk Road served as a commercial and cultural bridge between the two regions. The spread of Islam from Saudi Arabia to North Africa and the Middle East and across Asia and reaching as far as Indonesia (the most populous Muslim country) was accompanied by trade. But trade in Europe, Asia, and elsewhere was often restricted by protectionist measures imposed by governments. Many governments adopted the mercantilist model of trade. It stressed the role of government in trade and emphasized the importance of balance-of-payment surpluses in trade with other countries. At the extreme is autarky, which promotes economic national self-sufficiency.

Removing impediments to the free flow of goods and services among countries is the foundation of *free trade* or *trade liberalization*. The consensus among advocates of free trade is that it reduces prices, raises the standard of living for more people, makes a wider variety of products available, and contributes to improvements in the quality of goods and services. Adam Smith, David Ricardo, and other economists believed that by removing barriers to the free movement of goods among countries, as well as within them, countries would be encouraged to specialize in producing certain goods, thereby contributing to the optimum utilization of resources such as land, labor, capital, and entrepreneurial ability. If countries focused on what they do best and freely trade their goods with each other, all of them would benefit. David Ricardo (1772–1823), a British economist, best articulated this concept, known as comparative advantage. Ricardo explained, for example, how it was more economically advantageous for Britain to produce cloth and for Portugal to produce wine, as long as they engaged in free trade.

The theory of comparative advantage has been undermined by the current wave of economic globalization. The growth of transnational or multinational corporations (MNCs) complicates global trading. The production of goods and services is strongly influenced by costs, arbitrary specialization, and government and corporate policies. These developments mark a shift from the conventional theory of comparative advantage to what is known as competitive advantage.[2] Despite global acceptance of the concept of free trade, governments continue to engage in protectionism. For example, the European Union (EU) and the United States each support their own commercial aircraft industries so that those industries can

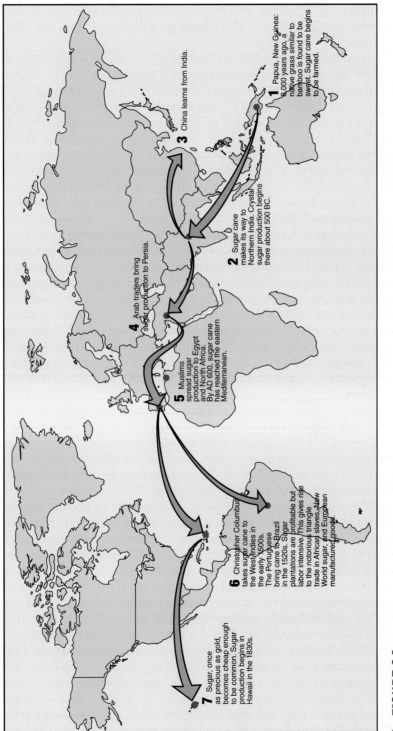

FIGURE 8.1

The Global Spread of Sugar

Sources: Kenneth Kiple and Kriemhild Ornelas, eds., *The Cambridge World History of Food* (Cambridge: Cambridge University Press, 2000); and *Christian Science Monitor*, 5 August 2003, 18.

1 Papua, New Guinea: 8,000 years ago, a native grass similar to bamboo is found to be sweet. Sugar cane begins to be farmed.

2 Sugar cane makes its way to Northern India. Crystal sugar production begins there about 500 BC.

3 China learns from India.

4 Arab traders bring sugar production to Persia.

5 Muslims spread sugar production to Egypt and North Africa. By AD 600, sugar cane has reached the eastern Mediterranean.

6 Christopher Columbus takes sugar cane to the West Indies in the early 1500s. The Portuguese bring cane to Brazil in the 1520s. Sugar plantations are profitable but labor intensive. This gives rise to the notorious triangle trade in African slaves, New World sugar, and European manufactured goods.

7 Sugar, once as precious as gold, becomes cheap enough to be common. Sugar production begins in Hawaii in the 1830s.

159

compete more effectively in a market dominated by a few companies. The idea of assisting such industries, which represents a departure from free trade, is known as the strategic trade theory.[3]

strategic trade theory ■ Supports government subsidies of private industry

Movement toward free trade occurs because of a consensus that free trade is more beneficial to more countries and individuals than its alternatives. This is demonstrated by Britain's repeal of its Corn Laws and the United States' retreat from protectionism. In 1815, the British Parliament passed the Corn Laws to protect the wealthy producers of grain from foreign competition, thereby ensuring that the landed upper classes would receive high prices for their crops. Simultaneously, Britain promoted exports of its manufactured products to Europe, the United States, and its colonies. However, it became increasingly apparent that Britain could not produce sufficient food to feed its population and that the United States and European countries were adopting their own protectionist policies to safeguard their infant industries from British manufactured products. The Irish potato blight and the accompanying famine highlighted the dangerous and deadly consequences of Britain's policy of keeping food prices artificially high to protect upper-class interests. Outraged by widespread starvation, Britain's trade liberals, inspired by Ricardo's theory of comparative advantage, formed the *Anti-Corn Law League* to influence Britain to repeal the Corn Laws and to unilaterally adopt free-trade policies, regardless of whether other countries reciprocated. To a large extent, Britain's global leadership enabled it to induce other countries to adopt free-trade practices by setting the example. Britain's repeal of the Corn Laws and the *Navigation Acts* in 1846, which restricted the transport of goods to British ships, brought about the first period of relatively free trade among Western countries.

Corn Laws ■ Passed in Britain to protect wealthy producers of grain from foreign competition

Trade protectionism did not retreat completely, however. By the end of the nineteenth century, many countries engaged in trade protectionism. The outbreak of World War I radically altered the global economic system and led to increased international economic instability. Widespread international economic problems that came with the onset of the *Great Depression* in 1929 influenced many countries to pursue autarky and protectionism. The enactment of the Smoot-Hawley Tariff Act in the United States in 1930, designed to protect American industries and trade, ultimately influenced other countries to increase their own tariffs. This development worsened global economic conditions. Attempting to diminish the negative economic consequences, the United States moved away from its protectionist policies by enacting the Reciprocal Trade Agreement Act of 1934, which authorized the president to negotiate substantial tariff reductions on a reciprocal and *bilateral* (i.e., between two countries) basis with other countries.[4] The rapid decline in global trade between World War I and World War II strongly influenced the United States and Western Europe to embrace freer trade.

Smoot-Hawley Tariff Act ■ Designed to protect American industries and trade from foreign competition

Reciprocal Trade Agreement Act ■ Authorized the president to negotiate tariff reductions on a bilateral basis

At the *Bretton Woods Conference* in New Hampshire in 1944, the United States and its allies created (1) the International Monetary Fund (IMF) to manage exchange rates and payment imbalances among nations and (2) the International Bank for Reconstruction and Development (World Bank) to supplement private capital for international investment, with an emphasis on the reconstruction of Western Europe. American and European concerns about the negative consequences of protectionism and their strong desire to promote free trade led to the

IMF ■ Created to manage exchange rates and payment imbalances among nations

World Bank ■ Created to supplement private capital for international investment, originally with the intent of reconstructing Europe

establishment of the General Agreement on Tariffs and Trade (GATT) in 1947 to serve as a negotiating forum for the reduction of tariffs and other barriers to trade. The original goal was to establish the International Trade Organization (ITO). However, American dissatisfaction with restrictions the ITO placed primarily on the United States led the U.S. Senate to reject it. GATT was then established as a second-choice organization that did not require the same degree of Senate support as did the treaty establishing the ITO. GATT was not a treaty.

> **GATT** ■ Created in 1947 to promote free trade and to reduce tariffs and other trade barriers

There were several *premises*, or assumptions, of *GATT*. These stated that

1. Multilateral negotiations (involving many countries) are preferable to bilateral negotiations (between two nations) on trade issues.
2. Private economic actors are preferable to governments for conducting and managing international trade.
3. Free trade ultimately benefits the global society.
4. Governments distort the operation of the free market and should minimize their involvement.

Between 1947 and 1992, various meetings of GATT (known as rounds) resulted in significant reductions in tariffs and freer trade. However, GATT covered manufactured products but excluded trade in agriculture and services. The Uruguay Round (meetings of GATT held in Uruguay from 1986 to 1992) added services and agriculture to the global trade framework and replaced GATT with the World Trade Organization (WTO) in 1993.

> **Uruguay Round** ■ Meetings that replaced the GATT with the WTO

Although the premises of GATT continue to be the foundations of global trade liberalization, the *WTO differs significantly from GATT*. To a much greater extent than GATT, the WTO directly challenges fundamental aspects of national sovereignty by diminishing both the national barriers to global trade and governments' economic activities. For example, when China joined the WTO in 2001, it was required to make its domestic market more accessible to foreign competition and to privatize its state-owned industries. On the other hand, China benefited from provisions of the Most-Favored Nation Clause, which was a key component of GATT. This clause reduces trade discrimination among members. WTO rules apply to activities generally regarded as domestic policies and beyond the reach of international regulations. Compared with GATT, the WTO is much more powerful in terms of governing global commerce and is empowered to settle trade disputes among countries. Agreements establishing the WTO extended GATT rules to cover agriculture, consumer services (restaurants, hotels, travel agencies, and so on), producer services (investment, banking, insurance, intellectual property rights, or the control people have over their artistic, creative, scientific, industrial, and educational inventions, and data processing), textiles, clothing, telecommunications, labor standards, and the environment. They also call for greater transparency in writing product standards and testing procedures and in soliciting bids on government contracts.[5] WTO regulations also reduced or eliminated many import quotas and subsidies. For example, the *Multifiber Agreement*, an international arrangement concluded in 1974, used import quotas to regulate the more than $350 billion world trade in garments to benefit many developing countries and to protect domestic industries. Because such arrangements violate WTO rules, the Multifiber Agreement was allowed to expire in 2004.

> **Most-Favored Nation Clause** ■ Prohibits trade discrimination among WTO members

> **intellectual property rights** ■ Control that people and corporations have over their artistic, creative, scientific, industrial, and educational inventions

Doha Agreement ■
Relaxed patent
protection for
brand-name
drugs by allowing
poor countries to
manufacture generic
medicines

The 142 member countries of the WTO met in Doha, Qatar, in 2001 to further reduce barriers to trade. The Doha Agreement, which reflected the growing power of developing countries regarding trade issues, relaxed patent protection for brand-name drugs by giving poor countries the right to make inexpensive generic medicines patented by global pharmaceutical corporations. Brazil, India, and many other developing countries, especially those ravaged by AIDS, viewed this concession as an important victory.[6] However, resistance to certain aspects of trade globalization in the developing world led to the collapse of two subsequent WTO meetings. At the heart of the controversy was the extent to which domestic industries should be protected from foreign competition. The global economic recession, which sharply reduced global trade, put these issues on the back burner and focused attention on currency problems and the need for major changes.

Exchange Rates, Budget Deficits, and Trade

exchange rate ■
How much of one
country's money
can be bought with
a specified amount
of another country's
money

The exchange rate for a currency is how much of one country's money can be bought with a specified amount of another country's money.[7] The business sections of major newspapers show that the values of currencies fluctuate constantly as a result of trading in foreign exchange markets, just as the values of stocks fluctuate on stock markets. The strength or weakness of currencies is determined by supply and demand, as is the case with commodities. Supply and demand can often be influenced by deliberate actions of governments and their central banks to buy or sell currencies, thereby affecting the price of currencies.

The relative values of currencies directly affect global trade and domestic economies. A weak dollar (weak relative to other currencies) increases prices for imports in the United States. But a weak dollar also makes American exports less expensive in foreign markets, which stimulates economic productivity in the United States. More jobs are created and trade deficits with other countries decline. It allows American manufacturers to more effectively compete with less expensive imported manufactured products. But not all countries allow their currencies to fluctuate, which complicates the positive effects of a weak American dollar. China, for example, is likely to continue to have a trade surplus with the United States as long as its currency, which is pegged to the U.S. dollar, remains cheap compared with the dollar. Countries can also buy more dollars to increase the dollar's value relative to their own currencies, thereby protecting their exports to both the United States and Europe. A weak U.S. dollar can have substantial negative implications for America. Because the United States is so dependent on imported products—such as electronics, clothing, cars, and petroleum—a weaker dollar ultimately leads to higher consumer prices. Furthermore, huge U.S. budget deficits are funded by a *net inflow of capital* from abroad, meaning that the United States gets more money from other countries than it sends to them. Emerging market economy countries, mainly China, hold two thirds of global foreign exchange reserves, which are roughly $8.4 trillion. Because they are reluctant to allow their currencies to rise against the dollar, they essentially shadow the dollar in an arrangement that is called Bretton Woods 2. A weak dollar increases demands from China, for example, to replace the dollar as the leading global reserve currency. But China has accumulated so many dollars that it resists allowing the Yuan to fall against the dollar. China limits credit growth to prevent domestic inflation.[8]

Bretton Woods 2 ■
An arrangement under
which countries
prevent their
currencies from rising
against the dollar.

Barriers to Free Trade

Even though most countries embrace *trade liberalization* (i.e., the movement toward unrestrained free trade), many governments engage in protectionist practices that impede the global free flow of goods and services. Many contemporary opponents to free trade essentially embrace *neomercantilism* (i.e., a new and more modern version of mercantilism). They argue that protectionism is essential to protect national security. Similarly, many developing countries argue that their need to achieve economic development, which includes economic diversification, justifies implementing protectionist policies. Finally, many antiglobalization activists view free trade as a threat to both the environment and respect for human rights. However, increasing violence against the Roma in Hungary and elsewhere underscores that rising unemployment and economic hardships that resulted from a decline in global trade can intensify human rights violations.[9]

The United States has maintained a trade embargo against Cuba to end the Castro regime and promote democracy that has effectively impeded free trade between the two countries. Furthermore, the United States attempted to pressure other countries, such as Canada and members of the EU, to refrain from engaging in commercial relations with Cuba. These efforts have largely failed. Another barrier to free trade is the formation of natural resource cartels, such as the *Organization of Petroleum Exporting Countries (OPEC)*, which deliberately limit supplies to increase prices or impose sanctions on importers to influence their political decisions or to punish them for particular actions.

Do Trade Deficits Matter?

Huge American trade deficits, especially with China, have linked the loss of manufacturing jobs to trade deficits in the minds of many Americans. The persistent rise in the U.S. trade deficit has arisen as a potent social and political issue. The trade deficit is the difference between the value of goods and services that a country buys from overseas and the value of goods and services it sells to other countries. The global economic recession led to significant declines in both exports and imports. Apart from the loss of manufacturing and service jobs in the United States, trade deficits have other significant consequences. Higher levels of unemployment mean less revenue for the government and higher government expenditures on social services and other benefits for the unemployed. Trade deficits are closely related to budget deficits, although many other factors contribute to the large U.S. budget deficit. To pay for its trade and budget deficits, the United States borrows money from foreign investors, such as China and Japan, and global financial institutions. This reliance on foreign capital to pay for debt makes America vulnerable to pressure from abroad.[10] Having a trade deficit in the United States means that other countries have a trade surplus; that is, the value of the goods and services they export is greater than the value of goods and services they import. From a neomercantilist viewpoint, trade deficits and surpluses directly affect a country's economic and military power. Countries with a trade surplus produce more engineers and scientists, attract more talent, and accumulate more financial resources to continue having high levels of productivity and innovation. This means that they acquire greater manufacturing capacity, higher levels of employment, and improvements in the development of intellectual property.

trade deficit ■ Difference between the value of goods and services that a country buys overseas and the value of goods and services it sells to other countries

trade surplus ■ Occurs when the value of exported goods and services is larger than the value of imported goods and services

Contrary to the view that trade surpluses are positive and trade deficits are negative, some scholars, such as Joseph Quinlan and Marc Chandler, argue that this thinking is outdated and does not reflect contemporary global trade realities.[11] A fixation on imports and exports ignores how global companies operate. Many American companies pioneered the practice of establishing foreign affiliates and subsidiaries through which they sell goods and services instead of exporting them from the United States. Most global companies follow the rule of "make where you sell" because of growing competition for global markets. While most Americans think of trade in national terms, American companies focus less on national ties and more on global market considerations.

GLOBAL COMPANIES AND GLOBAL FACTORIES

MNCs are closely associated with what some scholars call *Fordism* (i.e., the manufacturing system that stressed mass production of standardized products, and the centralization and vertical integration of production processes). Initially, these companies' factories were located in a major industrial city in Europe or the United States. Between World War II and the early 1970s, many of these companies expanded their operations into industrialized countries but remained characterized by large-scale fixed investments and large structures. They were relatively immobile and vulnerable to sudden interruptions of production due to material shortages or strikes by workers. *Post-Fordism* refers to the period after the mid-1970s when companies became more decentralized in virtually all aspects of production. Corporations became more transnational, or more global, in both their outlook and their operations.

Revolutions in communications and computer technologies and transportation radically altered the way companies organize and conduct business. Communication within corporations occurs almost effortlessly, regardless of where various operations of the corporation are located. Financial globalization also contributes to the growth of global companies because it enables them to gain access to investment capital from around the world. Increasingly, most of America's corporations derive most of their revenues from abroad. Despite the recession in the United States, companies such as Caterpillar, Coca Cola, and McDonald's made money because of their foreign operations. In 2011, Wal-Mart's profits declined in the United States but grew globally.

Global companies establish global factories that produce a wide range of goods. Most likely the labels on our clothes indicate that they were made in Mexico, China, Malaysia, Bangladesh, Singapore, Indonesia, or Fiji. Gillette, an American Company in Massachusetts, has razor handles made in China and cartridges manufactured in Germany. Most consumers are not overly concerned about where these products are made. Distance is less of a factor in determining where factories are located. The fact that transportation by water is so much less expensive than by land encourages global trade and gives certain countries a definite advantage. However, the earthquake and tsunami that devastated Japan in 2011 directly affected global trade. Many companies were unable to ship products to or from Japan because of the destruction. The practice of *just-in-time production* (which avoids maintaining an inventory and gets materials only when they are needed) was severely undermined.[12]

GLOBAL TRADE AND LOW WAGES

The relentless search for lower production costs in politically stable countries has led to what is known as a *race to the bottom*. The constant loss of manufacturing jobs in the United States, Japan, and Europe as companies move production to countries with low wages and competent workers has motivated coalitions of labor union members, consumers, and environmentalists to try to slow this race to the bottom. However, from the perspective of many developing countries, these efforts are thinly disguised protectionist measures aimed at safeguarding jobs in the developed countries. This is a common theme in the outsourcing debate.

China has an almost inexhaustible supply of skilled workers who are willing to work for low wages. In many ways, China is rapidly becoming a factory to the world. Japanese apparel companies, such as Fast Retailing, have built factories in China to avoid paying high wages in Japan. Japanese electronic companies—such as Toshiba Corporation, Sony, Matsushita Electric Industrial Company, and Canon—have operations in China. Like many American workers, Japanese workers accuse these companies of exporting jobs to China. Countries such as Vietnam and Indonesia are competing with China in the area of manufacturing. Furthermore, growth in China has led to demands by workers for higher wages and better working conditions.

GLOBAL COMPANIES PROMOTE EQUALITY

As we saw in Chapter 2, global companies build global teams that are composed of some of the most talented individuals in the world. This means that American students must compete with Indian or German students for employment. Because companies compete for market, they must also cultivate consumers for their products. Furthermore, they are vulnerable to pressure from shareholders, governments, and nongovernmental organizations to behave in certain ways. Consequently, they develop business and management practices that are virtually uniform globally. The realities faced by global companies influence them to promote equality. Also, many leaders of global companies come from societies where equality is widely practiced.

In India, where the caste system remains embedded in the culture in many parts of the country and is an impediment to equality, global companies directly challenge it by providing special training and employment opportunities for the *dalits*, also known as untouchables. At its California-style campus in Bangalore, the corporation Infosys hires *dalits*, many of whom take on a corporate identity as Infocions. This directly challenges their identity derived from the caste system. In South Korea, where talented and highly educated women rarely become senior managers, foreign global companies recruit and promote Korean women. In 2010, Goldman Sachs had more women than men in its office in Seoul.[13] As the rapid economic growth of emerging market countries encourages global companies to expand business operations there, opportunities for the poor increase, and women in particular benefit from the companies' commitment to equality. Gender disparity is greatest in the developing world. The growth in the number of female senior managers, board members, and executives in Western companies helps put equality for women on the global corporate agenda.[14]

LABOR UNIONS AND GLOBAL TRADE

In this section, we will discuss some of the reasons for the relative decline of the power of unions, as well as strategies unions use to enhance their bargaining power as trade becomes increasingly globalized. *Several factors contribute to labor unions' decline.* These include

1. *Public Perceptions of Unions:* Prior to the 1980s, unions throughout the industrialized world exerted great pressure on industries to obtain better wages and benefits. Often, they became forces of conservatism, resisting much-needed changes. Consequently, they were perceived by many citizens as being responsible for the economic problems that resulted from this rigidity.
2. *Political Change:* During the 1980s, many European countries, the United States, and Canada elected leaders who were strongly committed to free trade, including the operation of free-labor markets. Combined with a wave of privatization and the declining role of government in the economy, the embrace of economic neoliberalism undermined unions' power.
3. *The Shift from Manufacturing to a Knowledge-Based Economy:* Most unions are in the manufacturing and public sectors. The rise of information technology and a knowledge-based economy radically shifted power away from manufacturing to industries that rely on highly educated employees.
4. *The Globalization of Individualism:* A growing sense of individual autonomy and the weakening of loyalties to organizations and institutions worldwide helped to undermine the power of unions, which depend on group solidarity.
5. *Global Competition for Employment:* Workers in developing countries realize that their low wages give them an advantage in their competition with workers in rich countries.
6. *The Global Financial Crisis and Economic Recession:* The crisis, which led to high unemployment in Europe and the United States, weakened unions.

Facing these formidable obstacles, labor unions have attempted to demonstrate that globalization is detrimental to too many people and beneficial to too few. Labor leaders view globalization as a leading cause of both domestic and global inequality and environmental degradation. Consequently, they have formed alliances with environmentalists, consumer advocates, students, and human rights groups to counteract global trade's negative impact on them. Another strategy widely used by labor unions is to organize workers in developing countries to establish acceptable labor conditions. However, competition among countries for employment diminishes the success of this strategy. Linking labor standards to global trade agreements would, in the view of poor countries, effectively undermine their competitive advantage.

GLOBAL TRADE DISPUTES

Controversy is an inevitable part of life. Global trade is no exception. Each country tries to influence other countries to abide by free-trade rules while simultaneously trying to find ways to avoid following free-trade rules that undermine their own economic interests. Although Europeans and Americans steadfastly provide subsidies for their farmers, they routinely accuse each other of engaging in unfair trade because of those subsidies. Trade disputes are often complicated by divergent interests within countries. Inexpensive imports from China benefit many Americans who are raising families on tight budgets but deprive others of their jobs and thus their ability to provide for themselves and their families. Trade disputes are intertwined with domestic politics and with cultural preferences in virtually all countries. For example, disputes between Europeans and Americans about genetically modified foods are political, economic, and cultural. European political leaders are constrained by the reluctance of European consumers to eat such foods, whereas American political leaders are pressured to secure export markets by industries producing genetically modified food and are supported by most Americans who are more receptive to scientific advances and less concerned about consuming genetically modified food.

Tariffs

It is generally believed that many tariffs stifle trade. For example, Ghana sells cocoa beans to Europe without having to pay customs tariffs. However, when Ghana processes cocoa beans to make chocolate and other products, which are far more profitable and beneficial to that country's economy than exporting beans is, its exports of processed cocoa are subject to a 50 percent tariff. Despite their emphasis on both global free trade and economic development, the United States, Europe, and Japan impose very high tariffs on basic exports—such as sugar, textiles, and fruits and vegetables—in which developing countries enjoy a comparative advantage because of their low labor costs. Brazil, for example, raised concerns about U.S. tariffs on Brazilian ethanol during President Obama's visit to that country in 2011. Brazil, the world's largest exporter of frozen orange juice, mainly to the United States and Western Europe, accused the United States of imposing unfair tariffs. The WTO ruled that the United States was illegally taxing Brazil's orange juice.[15]

tariffs ■ Taxes imposed on exports and imports that increase their cost

Quotas

A trans-Atlantic banana war raged between Europe and the United States for eight years following Europe's decision to erect barriers against imports of bananas grown by Chiquita and Dole (American companies) in Latin America in an effort to protect banana imports from its former colonies in the Caribbean and Africa. Beginning in 1993, when Europe formed a single agricultural market, banana quotas were imposed. The United States challenged Europe's preferential system in the WTO. The WTO concluded that the European banana quota violated trade rules and authorized the United States to impose retaliatory sanctions on $191 million worth of EU exports. The United States targeted high-end European imports such as Louis Vuitton plastic handbags, Palais Royale bed linens, and pecorino cheese. It imposed 100 percent tariffs on them to make them so costly that consumers would not purchase them. However, Americans continued to purchase Louis Vuitton handbags, which normally sold for around $400 before the tariffs, at twice their usual price after the tariffs went into effect. Exhausted by this relatively insignificant trade dispute that was negatively affecting far more important aspects of their relationship, Europeans and Americans decided to compromise. The Europeans agreed to a transition period of modified

quotas ■ Specified limits on products to create a barrier to importing them

quotas and tariffs that lasted until 2006. The United States, which had originally demanded an immediate end to all quotas, agreed to remove its punitive tariffs.[16] The banana war finally ended in 2009 when Europe removed banana quotas.

Now that China has emerged as the country with which America has the largest trade deficit, Chinese exports are becoming a source of dispute between the two countries. In 2003, the United States imposed import quotas on selected Chinese textiles and clothing, largely in response to pressure from elected officials, businesses, and workers in North Carolina. While China claimed that such quotas violate free trade, the United States invoked a *safeguard clause*, which allows countries facing a sharp increase in textile or apparel imports, combined with job losses, to limit such imports.[17] However, industrialized countries agreed to eliminate all quotas and tariffs on textile and apparel imports from developing countries by 2005. China's apparel exports to Europe, the United States, and other countries increased dramatically in 2005.

Subsidies

subsidies ■ Government payments to industries that keep their prices artificially low

The WTO ruled in 2011 that the U.S. federal and state governments had provided illegal subsidies to Boeing so it would gain an advantage over its European rival, Airbus. But the WTO also found that the European Union had illegally subsidized Airbus. Although government subsidies to various industries create trade disputes among nations, nothing evokes more controversy and conflict than agricultural subsidies in Europe, the United Sates, Japan, and other rich countries. Even as these rich countries prohibit governments in the developing world from subsidizing farming—an occupation that provides a livelihood for roughly two thirds of the population in poor countries—they continue to subsidize their own farmers and to give them an unfair advantage in the global market. Agricultural subsidies in developed countries originated largely to assist farmers and to provide more food security. In Europe and the United States, these subsidies contribute to overproduction and waste. In both Europe and the United Sates, huge amounts of grain, butter, cheese, wine, and other agricultural products are in storage. This overproduction problem is solved partly by encouraging Americans and Europeans to consume more food and by dumping agricultural products in developing countries' markets, selling them for below-cost prices. The EU provides subsidies to agriculture under the common agricultural policy (CAP). The original objectives of CAP included (1) improving agricultural productivity, (2) improving living standards for those engaged in agriculture, (3) stabilizing markets, (4) guaranteeing regular food supplies, and (5) providing food at reasonable prices to consumers.[18] However, agriculture has changed significantly since CAP was established in 1968. Only about 5 percent of Europeans are engaged in agriculture, and agricultural science has contributed to dramatic increases in productivity.

CAP ■ Supports agricultural subsidies to EU member countries

Influenced by the devastating impact of the Great Depression on farmers, the United States enacted *agricultural legislation in 1933* as part of the New Deal in order to stabilize farm prices and to save family farming. At that time roughly 21 percent of the American population engaged in farming, compared with less than 2 percent today. Improved seeds, better farm machinery, and general advances in agricultural science and technology have raised the productivity of an acre planted in corn from

34 bushels then to more than 137 bushels now. Despite revolutionary developments in farming and the success of American farmers, the U.S. government continues to subsidize agriculture. The larger the farm, the greater the amount in subsidies it will receive. This system influences farmers to expand their acreage and to overproduce. As is the case in Europe, American agricultural subsidies are maintained through what is known as the iron triangle: that is, the political relationship among members of congressional committees who are affected by farm issues, interest groups, and government agencies whose existence is closely linked to farming interests.

iron triangle ■
Relationship among politicians, interest groups, and government agencies linked to farming interests

Genetically Modified Food

As global trade facilitates transferring food from one country to another and as consumers become more aware of health risks associated with food, trade disputes based on real and perceived health problems are proliferating. Unlike the other trade disputes we have discussed so far, food disputes are more about cultural (or more precisely, culinary) differences than they are about protecting jobs and financial gains. We are aware of the growing emphasis on consuming organic foods, ranging from milk to eggs. In general, Europeans tend to be more concerned than Americans are about consuming genetically modified foods, partly because they are more skeptical of science.

An example of a dispute relating to food safety is Europe's decision to ban imports of American beef produced from cattle that had been fed growth hormones.

Is genetically modified (GM) food a solution to the growing food crisis? What are the costs and benefits of GM food? A Greenpeace activist holds up a cob of black corn during a demonstration in Mexico City aimed at keeping GM crops such as corn from being planted in Mexico.

These hormones, used to accelerate beef production, are generally accepted by American consumers. However, Europeans, especially the extremely food-conscious French and Italians, prefer beef that has not been fed hormones. These cultural differences became the source for a trade dispute between Europe and the United States. Under global trade agreements, countries are allowed to ban imports of foods if there is scientific evidence to support concerns about safety. Americans argued that scientific evidence showed that beef hormones did not endanger human health. The WTO agreed with the United States and authorized the imposition of punitive tariffs of $117 million a year against European exports. Despite high tariffs on Danish ham, Italian tomatoes, and other European products, Europe refused to lift the ban, citing its own scientific findings that showed that high doses of hormones cause cancer.[19]

Although human beings have engaged in genetic modifications for centuries, experiments conducted by *Gregor Mendel* with pea plants in his monastery garden in 1866 represented a breakthrough in this area and set the stage for more advanced genetic research. While advances in agricultural science have been embraced globally, the ability to transfer isolated genes into the DNA of another organism is widely viewed as a threat. The idea that a trait for cold resistance can be transferred from a fish to a plant has encountered resistance from environmentalists, consumers, and farmers in Europe and elsewhere. From the other perspective, genetically modified crops, developed by *Monsanto,* solve many problems that plague farmers, such as pest control, soil preservation, and weed control. Most American farmers embraced genetically modified crops.

There was no sense of urgency in Europe to consume genetically modified crops. Environmental groups, such as Greenpeace, launched a global campaign against them, stressing not only the dangers they posed to consumers but also the dangers they posed to the natural environment. This campaign and others reinforced Europeans' concerns about eating genetically modified foods. Public pressure influenced the European Parliament to enact a food-labeling law requiring merchants to clearly indicate if packaged foods contain any amount of genetically modified ingredients. Major food-importing countries, such as Japan and South Korea, also resisted consuming genetically modified crops. The United States, on the other hand, viewed Europe as using the genetically modified food issue to exclude American exports. Attitudes toward genetically modified crops are changing due to rapidly increasing food prices and growing food shortages around the world.[20]

GLOBAL TRADE AND THE ENVIRONMENT

Many environmentalists, trade analysts, and antiglobalization activists believe that relentless competition in global trade inevitably leads to a disregard for environmental standards. Global trade advocates, on the other hand, tend to believe that economic globalization is instrumental in improving and safeguarding the global environment.[21] Environmental protection is sometimes used as a barrier to free trade. A coalition of environmental, labor, and consumer groups mounted strong opposition to changing the U.S. policy of excluding Mexican trucks from operating in the United States. Their basic argument was that Mexican trucks were unable to comply with the higher American environmental standards and that they posed a serious threat to public health. Given the interest of labor groups in limiting competition from Mexican trucks, these environmental concerns could not be entirely separated from tangible economic interests. Growing competition from shrimp producers in developing countries was also a factor in the U.S. decision to use environmental laws—requiring shrimp nets to have turtle extruder devices to protect endangered turtles that are often caught in fishing nets—against shrimp exporters. The WTO ruled against the United States, viewing the application of the environmental laws as an illegal barrier to free trade.

Global trade creates many environmental problems. The sharp increase in the number of global factories has contributed to higher levels of pollution. The maquiladoras along the U.S.-Mexican border have increased pollution. *China's phenomenal economic growth is closely linked to widespread pollution.* It is apparent to anyone visiting China that economic progress has contributed to the country's environmental problems. The air and water in many of China's major cities rank among the dirtiest and most dangerous in the world. China is the world's largest consumer of coal as well as the world's fastest-growing importer of petroleum. As an expanding middle class demands more energy for appliances, cars, and air conditioners, pollution will increase.

Diseases and Global Trade

The speed of international travel and the expansion of free trade make diseases in almost any part of the world an immediate threat to other places. Many products purchased at the grocery store are imported. Economic globalization and global migration help to create global cities that are characterized by great ethnic diversity. Demographic changes have been accompanied by the proliferation of agricultural products available in grocery stores. At the same time, however, the relentless march toward reducing governments' involvement in the economy has resulted in a smaller number of food inspectors. Furthermore, the globalization of many aspects of the food industry means that there is much mixing of products from different countries, which facilitates the spread of food-related diseases. An outbreak of foot-and-mouth disease in Britain in early 2001 illustrates the impact of diseases on global trade. The United States and Canada quickly banned imports of animals and animal products from the EU. Similarly, an outbreak of bovine spongiform encephalopathy (BSE), commonly known as mad cow disease, in Britain in the same year demonstrates how global trade spreads diseases. The problem was soon discovered in countries that imported British cattle, beef, and animal feed. Because animal feed is globally traded like any other commodity, and mixed in with other feed, it is difficult to identify the source of many food-related diseases. In late December 2003, mad cow disease was discovered on a farm in Washington State. The impact on global markets was immediate. Japan, South Korea, Venezuela, and many other countries banned imports of beef and beef by-products from the United States. On the other hand, Brazil, which has the most beef cattle in the world and is the main competitor of the United States, viewed America's problems as presenting an opportunity for its own beef industry to increase exports. Contaminated pet food from China brought the problem of unsafe products to America's attention. Furthermore, widespread use of lead paint on children's toys made in China forced the United States to take action to inspect imported goods to a much greater extent.

REGIONAL TRADE BLOCS

There are several *reasons for the formation of regional trade blocs*, which vary from one trade group to another. These reasons include

1. *Economic Development:* Many countries pool their resources and create larger markets by integrating their economies.
2. *Managing Trade Regionally:* Many countries regarded global trade institutions as too bureaucratic and slow in responding to both trade opportunities and trade problems.
3. *Economic Competition:* Countries can become far more economically prosperous and enhance their ability to compete in the global market by forming trade blocs.
4. *Political and Strategic Considerations:* Many countries form trade blocs for political and security reasons. The EU, for example, originated because of concerns about Germany's aggression in both World Wars.

Trade organizations range from free-trade areas to economic unions. We will briefly discuss the *main types of regional trade groups*, going from the most basic to the most complex. Free-trade areas are characterized by the removal of trade barriers among members. However, each country in the free-trade area maintains its own trade policies toward other countries, which often include significant trade barriers. *Customs unions* are free-trade areas that have a common external commercial and trade policy. Imports to the customs union are treated the same regardless of where they enter. This requires more cooperation and centralization of administrative tasks than in free-trade areas. The Southern African Customs Union—formed in 1910 and composed of South Africa, Botswana, Lesotho, Swaziland, and Namibia—is the world's oldest customs union. *Common markets* embrace the characteristics of free-trade areas and customs unions. They go further by providing for the free movement of people and capital, more harmonization of taxation and domestic policies, and more extensive administration. Finally, *economic unions*, which encompass all the features of common markets, represent the highest form of political and economic integration of sovereign countries. Besides the harmonization of government spending and taxation (*fiscal policy*), they have a central bank, a common currency, and numerous political institutions to achieve greater cohesion in foreign as well as internal affairs. The most powerful and recognized trade bloc is the EU.

free-trade areas ■ Characterized by the removal of trade barriers among members

Southern African Customs Union ■ World's oldest customs union, formed in 1910

The European Union

As you travel through Europe, you see that the euro is the common currency (with the notable exceptions of Sweden, Denmark, and Britain) and that passports are not required to cross national boundaries. In fact, common administrative regulations, the free movement of people across national boundaries, and the creation of numerous political, economic, and legal institutions are creating a stronger European identity. Stretching from Ireland and Britain in the west to Poland in the east and from Finland in the north to Cyprus in the south, the EU is the most advanced trade bloc in the world. Beginning with the European Coal and Steel Community (a treaty signed in 1951 that came into effect in 1952), European integration evolved into the European Economic Community (EEC) or Common Market in 1957 with the signing of the Treaty of Rome. Two steps toward transforming the EEC into the EU in 1993 under the Maastricht Treaty of 1991 were, first, the establishment of the *European Monetary System (EMS)* in 1979 to stabilize monetary affairs in Western Europe and to safeguard against fluctuations in the value of the U.S. dollar, and, second, the signing of the Single European Act in 1986, which set the objective of building a unified European trade system by 1992. As we discussed in Chapter 2, European integration focused primarily on political objectives, despite the emphasis on trade. In an effort to create a union that would resemble the United States, European leaders created a constitution. The constitution provides for EU citizenship for nationals of member states, stresses the supremacy of EU law over those of member states, and designates certain areas (e.g., trade and foreign policy) over which the EU will have full authority and other areas (e.g., justice, transportation, and economic and social policy) over which authority is to be shared between the EU and the countries that belong to it. In an attempt to counter the power of the EU,

Maastricht Treaty ◼ Established the European Monetary System to stabilize monetary affairs in Western Europe

Single European Act ◼ Set the objective of building a unified European trading system

What are the costs and benefits of NAFTA to the United States? Workers at Volkswagen's (VW) Mexico plant, Germany's only VW factory in North America, went on strike after pay negotiations collapsed.

the United States, Canada, and Mexico formed the North American Free Trade Agreement (NAFTA).

The North American Free Trade Agreement

NAFTA (The North American Free Trade Agreement) ■ Formed by the United States, Canada, and Mexico to promote free trade among them

Unlike the EU, which was formed primarily in response to the consequences of war, NAFTA (The North American Free Trade Agreement), is predominantly concerned with economic issues. Signed on November 18, 1993, NAFTA entered into force on January 1, 1994. It brought together three different economies, with the United States the dominant power, Canada in the middle, and Mexico on the bottom. These divergent levels of economic development motivated the United States, Canada, and Mexico to form the agreement. Mexico, burdened with debt, regarded a trade agreement with the United States as essential to achieving economic development. The United States desired to maintain stability in Mexico and saw abundant and inexpensive Mexican labor as beneficial to U.S. companies that were anxious to gain a competitive advantage over the Japanese and Europeans. Canada viewed economic integration in North America as a way of countering U.S. dominance of the Americas.

The level of integration among the United States, Canada, and Mexico differs significantly from that achieved by the EU. NAFTA, unlike the EU, does not provide for the free movement of people across borders. NAFTA countries pursue their own independent trade, foreign, domestic, and defense policies. Compared with the Europeans, who have given up some aspects of national sovereignty in exchange for European political and economic unification, NAFTA members jealously guard their sovereignty. Consequently, there are few institutions in NAFTA that are comparable to those in the EU (e.g., the European Court of Justice, the Council of Ministers, the European Parliament, and the European Commission) that would diminish the autonomy of the United States, Canada, and Mexico. However, NAFTA has a significant supranational institution, the *Free Trade Commission*, which consists of cabinet-level officials or their designated representatives and is responsible for formulating policies dealing with trade.[22]

The Association of Southeast Asian Nations

ASEAN ■ Formed in 1967, purpose changed from security to trade interests of non-leading-power nations.

China's rapid economic growth has helped to focus increased attention on the Association of Southeast Asian Nations (ASEAN). Although we generally perceive Asia primarily in terms of its pivotal role in global trade and think of organizations such as ASEAN as trade blocs like the EU, ASEAN's origins were more strongly influenced by political and strategic considerations than by trade competition. The establishment of ASEAN in 1967 resulted primarily from the political and military concerns of Indonesia, Thailand, the Philippines, Malaysia, and Singapore. Southeast Asia had become ground zero in the Cold War. The United States, perceiving nationalist movements in Vietnam as part of the Soviet Union's strategy to expand Communism throughout Asia, inexorably militarized the conflict in Vietnam. But while America's policies in Vietnam are now regarded as having been seriously flawed, the threat of Communism was real to ASEAN. Only a united front against Communism could effectively counteract this threat.

Despite their obvious preoccupation with defeating Communism, ASEAN members emphasized that their organization's purpose was to promote economic, cultural, and technological cooperation. As the Vietnam conflict receded, ASEAN membership expanded to include Brunei, Vietnam, Cambodia, Laos, and Burma. In 2003, China and India joined ASEAN's *Treaty of Amity and Cooperation*, a nonaggression agreement designed to promote regional stability. They also agreed to collaborate in the fight against regional terrorism. But the focus has clearly shifted from traditional security issues to trade. ASEAN members believe that only through economic cooperation can they attract foreign investment and effectively compete with China.

The South American Common Market

Latin Americans have made numerous attempts to integrate their economies to achieve economic development and to balance the economic and political power of the United States in the region. The formation of the South American Common Market (Mercosur) in 1991 represents a culmination of these efforts. Economic problems plaguing Latin America and economic, political, and border disputes impeded integration efforts. Furthermore, authoritarianism and military dictatorships throughout the region created such antagonism, competition, and distrust among the countries, especially Brazil and Argentina, that economic cooperation was virtually impossible. Not until these countries had resolved their economic and border disputes and had abandoned dictatorship and started to democratize were they able to begin integrating their economies.

Brazil and Argentina, the dominant countries in the region, were cognizant of growing economic regionalization and competition for investments and markets among trade blocs. They initiated the development of closer economic and political ties by signing the Program for Integration and Economic Cooperation (PIEC) in 1986. Given the economic competition between them, they decided to negotiate integrating specific sectors such as capital goods, food, iron and steel, and the automotive industry. This allowed them to diminish business losses in both countries and to consolidate industrial processes. This effort to open trade between Brazil and Argentina was consolidated by the signing of the *Treaty of Integration, Cooperation, and Development* in 1988. In 1991, Brazil, Argentina, Paraguay, and Uruguay signed the *Treaty of Asunción*, creating Mercosur. Bolivia, Peru, Chile, and Venezuela later joined the trade group as associate members. Barriers to trade among the members were removed; common external tariffs (against nonmembers) were adopted; and a commitment was made to coordinate trade, agricultural, industrial, fiscal, and monetary policies. In addition, they agreed to work toward harmonizing their domestic legislation to facilitate economic integration.

Mercosur ■ Trade group created to integrate Latin American economies and foster stronger trading ties with the United States

PIEC ■ Agreement to develop closer economic and political ties between Brazil and Argentina

CASE STUDY | The Growing Power of Emerging Markets: Brazil

The rapid growth of emerging market countries marks a fundamental shift in global economics, politics, and culture. As developed countries confront challenges arising from aging populations and struggle to recover from devastating consequences of the global financial and economic crisis, countries such as China, Brazil, and India are attracting investments from around the world and experiencing rising domestic demand due to expanding middle-class consumers. Large young populations in developing countries reinforce economic growth by providing relatively inexpensive labor. The outstanding performance of emerging economies has shifted power from the exclusive G-7, composed of leading industrial countries, to the G-20, which includes both developed and developing countries with the largest economies. Emerging economies are also changing the distribution of power in global institutions. For example, the International Monetary Fund (IMF), long dominated by Western Europe and the United States, gave two additional seats to developing countries in the wake of the global financial and economic crisis. The IMF also reformed its lending policies to allow countries that successfully manage their economies to gain access to more financial resources during a financial crisis.

An important indicator of the shift of power to emerging-market countries is the proliferation of global companies based in China, India, and Brazil, and the acquisition of some leading European and American multinationals by developing countries. This development reinforces economic globalization by changing the traditional relationship between developed and developing countries. Global companies are no longer just European, American, or Japanese. For example, Budweiser is owned by a Belgian-Brazilian conglomerate. Lenovo, a Chinese computer company, bought IBM's personal computer business, including the ThinkPad laptop. Tata, based in India, acquired Jaguar and Land Rover from Ford. Global companies from emerging-market countries include Infosys, Ranbaxy, Reliance, and Arcelor Mittal from India, Haier from China, Cemex from Mexico, and Embraer from Brazil.[23]

President Barack Obama went to Brazil in 2011. This was the first time an American president had gone to Brazil to talk with a new Brazilian president. Brazilian presidents come to the United States. This development marks a change in America's global power and recognition of Brazil as an emerging economic power. Brazil is growing by roughly 7.5 percent a year and offers many opportunities for companies based in America, especially in the petroleum industry. By 2011, Brazil was the world's seventh-largest economy, with a GDP of $2.089 trillion. Brazil has abundant natural resources, including vast expanses of fertile agricultural land and large water supplies from the Amazon River. Both China and India import significant quantities of food and raw materials from Brazil. Brazil is on track to replace the United States as the world's leading food exporter. Brazil is the world's largest exporter of coffee, sugar, orange juice, ethanol, beef, and chicken, and the second-largest exporter of soybeans. Brazil also benefits from sound financial management, democracy, political cohesion, growing economic equality, a significant reduction in poverty, geographic proximity to the United States, and peaceful relations and cooperation with neighboring countries. Furthermore, Brazil, like the United States, is a country of immigrants. It attracts migrants from around the world and integrates them into all areas of Brazilian life. Brazil's rapid growth is attracting highly educated Europeans, especially Portuguese and Spanish, who see greater economic opportunities in Latin America. As India and China become increasingly difficult places to conduct business, several global companies are investing more money in Brazil. Brazil's diverse economy, strong democratic institutions, and its ability to renew itself through immigration will enable it to continue to experience sustainable economic growth. ▴

SUMMARY AND REVIEW

This chapter focused on the growth of and challenges to global trade and free trade as a way of increasing each country's economic prosperity. It showed how trade is intricately linked to politics, economics, and culture. In an era of global trade and interdependence, we are seeing the power to formulate trade policies shift away from countries and national sovereignty toward MNCs. Accompanying this shift is another: a shift toward increased privatization of national industries and services and a smaller role for the state in providing social services and social welfare programs. Lower prices provided by companies such as Wal-Mart, however, have been accompanied by an increase in corporate reliance on sweatshops that demand employees work long hours for relatively low pay. Such a "race to the bottom," where corporations disregard labor protections and rights in pursuit of the cheapest bottom line, has been a main factor in the backlash against corporate globalization and free trade.

In this chapter, we also looked at the history of the globalization of free trade. As global trade became more important, we saw the development of various trade models distinguishing between the benefits of comparative and competitive advantage. In recent years, we have seen a trend toward increased liberalization in the transition toward free trade and global capitalism. In this transition, we witnessed the conflict between protectionist policies and state socialism and increasingly popular notions of free trade and corporate globalization. With the emergence of the Bretton Woods System after World War II, we saw a strengthening of free trade as promoted by organizations such as the World Bank, the IMF, GATT, and most recently, the WTO. Under the WTO, we have seen the growing importance of reducing trade barriers and protecting intellectual property rights as valuable components of global capitalism.

KEY TERMS

Treaty of Paris of 1763   157
Silk Road   158
mercantilist model   158
autarky   158
comparative advantage   158
competitive advantage   158
strategic trade theory   160
Corn Laws   160
Smoot-Hawley Tariff Act   160
Reciprocal Trade Agreement Act   160
International Monetary Fund (IMF)   160
International Bank for Reconstruction and
   Development (World Bank)   160
General Agreement on Tariffs and Trade
   (GATT)   161
Uruguay Round   161
Most-Favored Nation Clause   161
intellectual property rights   161
Doha Agreement   162
exchange rate   162

Bretton Woods 2   162
trade deficit   163
trade surplus   163
tariffs   167
quotas   167
subsidies   168
common agricultural policy (CAP)   168
iron triangle   169
free-trade areas   172
Southern African Customs Union   172
Maastricht Treaty   173
Single European Act   173
NAFTA (The North American Free Trade
   Agreement)   174
Association of Southeast Asian Nations
   (ASEAN)   174
South American Common Market
   (Mercosur)   175
Program for Integration and Economic
   Cooperation (PIEC)   175

DISCUSSION QUESTIONS

1. What exactly is the mercantilist model? Give examples.
2. Do you think that globalization contributes to improving living standards around the world? Give examples.
3. What are the premises and principles of GATT addressed in this chapter? Discuss the major trade disputes. Give examples.
4. What are intellectual property rights? Do intellectual property rights potentially violate principles of free trade? Please explain.
5. What factors discussed in this chapter have helped environmental issues become a concern in global trade?

SUGGESTED READINGS

Ahamed, Liaquat. "Currency Wars, Then and Now," *Foreign Affairs* 90, No. 2 (March/April 2011): 92–103. Currency devaluations and protectionism threaten to undermine confidence in an open global economy.

Erlichman, Howard. *Conquest, Tribute, and Trade*. New York: Prometheus Books, 2010. Looks at how competition among European countries for sources of money led to the globalization of disease and the cultivation of new plants.

Johns, Adrian. *Piracy*. Chicago: University of Chicago Press, 2010. Examines the origins and evolution of the theft of intellectual property.

Rodrik, Dani. *The Globalization Paradox*. New York: Norton, 2011. Challenges proponents of globalization. Argues that globalization can have unintended negative consequences.

Roett, Riordan. *The New Brazil*. Washington, DC: Brookings Institution Press, 2010. Covers Brazil's history, economic success, and the challenges it faces as it emerges as a regional power with global influence.

ENDNOTES

1. Kenichi Ohmae, "The Rise of the Region State," *Foreign Affairs* 72, No. 2 (Spring 1993), 78.
2. Robert Gilpin, *The Challenge of Global Capitalism* (Princeton, NJ: Princeton University Press, 2000), 95.
3. Gilpin, *The Challenge*, 96.
4. Thomas D. Lairson and David Skidmore, *International Political Economy* (Forth Worth, TX: Holt, Rinehart, and Winston, 1993), 57.
5. Peter Morici, "Export Our Way to Prosperity," *Foreign Policy* 101 (Winter 1995–1996), 12.
6. Celia W. Dugger, "A Catch-22 on Drugs for the World's Poor," *New York Times*, 16 November 2001, W1.
7. Lairson and Skidmore, *International Political Economy*, 24.
8. Liaquat Ahamed, "Currency Wars, Then and Now," *Foreign Affairs* 90, No. 2 (March/April 2011), 97.
9. Nicholas Kulish, "As Economic Turmoil Mounts, So Do Deadly Attacks on Hungary's Gypsies," *New York Times*, 27 April 2009, A1.
10. Mark Landler, "IMF Puts Bank Losses from Global Financial Crisis at $4.1 Trillion," *New York Times*, 13 May 2009, B1.

11. Joseph Quinlan and Marc Chandler, "The U.S. Trade Deficit: A Dangerous Obsession," *Foreign Affairs* 80, No. 3 (May/June 2001), 87–97.
12. David Jolly, "Long Pause for Japanese Industry Raises Concerns About Supply Chain," *New York Times*, 17 March 2011, B1.
13. "Profiting From Sexism," *Economist*, 23 October 2010, 77.
14. Isobel Coleman, "The Global Glass Ceiling," *Foreign Affairs* 89, No. 3 (May/June 2010), 15.
15. "U.S. Taxes Brazilian Juice Illegally, WTO Says," *Miami Herald*, 28 March 2011, 3B.
16. Anthony DePalma, "U.S. and Europeans Agree on Deal to End Banana Trade War," *New York Times*, 12 April 2001, C1.
17. Keith Bradsner, "China Protests U.S. Limit on Textiles," *New York Times*, 20 November 2003, A1.
18. John S. Marsh and Pamela J. Swanney, "The Common Agricultural Policy," in *Institutions and Policies of the European Community*, ed. Juliet Lodge (New York: St. Martin's Press, 1983), 57.
19. Edmund L. Andrews, "Europe Refuses to Drop Ban on Hormone-Fed U.S. Beef," *New York Times*, 25 May 2000, C4.
20. "The Future of Food," *Economist*, 26 February 2011, 12.
21. Gary Hufbauer et al., *Global Warming and the World Trading System* (Washington, DC: Peterson Institute for International Economics, 2009).
22. Lloyd Gruber, *Ruling the World: Power Politics and the Rise of Supranational Institutions* (Princeton, NJ: Princeton University Press, 2000), 96.
23. "The Other Elephant," *Economist*, 6 November 2010, 8.

Global Inequality and Poverty

One photo captures a sharp contrast between rich and poor in the developing world. The high-rise buildings in

INTRODUCTION

Roughly half a percent of the world's adult population (about 24 million people) controls $69 trillion in assets, more than a third of the global total. Forty-one percent of them live in the United States, ten percent in Japan, and three percent in China.[1] The global financial crisis and economic recession have rekindled debates about inequality and its consequences. Discussions about wealth and poverty and how to achieve greater equality are as old as human society. They demonstrate a perennial concern about the implications of inequality for the security and well-being of communities. Given the persistence of inequality among individuals, groups, and nations over centuries, this debate is interminable. Struggles to achieve equality are also endless. Issues pertaining to global inequality and poverty permeate almost every significant global problem, from trade to the environment, from terrorism and criminal activities to democratization and human rights, and from ethnic conflicts to the proliferation of weapons of mass destruction. As we have seen, popular uprisings in the Middle East and North Africa were strongly influenced by widespread inequality and poverty. Consequently, as our discussion shows, inequality and poverty are closely connected to politics, economics, and culture.

A central question addressed in this chapter is whether inequality matters. Human societies are inherently unequal due to variations of abilities, opportunities, geographic location, luck, personal characteristics, and so on. But why is it important to address issues of inequality, something that societies have struggled with historically? Globalization is widely perceived as the major cause of global inequality. Yet, as we have noted, unequal distributions of wealth existed independent of the current wave of globalization and are present in societies little affected by it. This chapter analyzes the globalization and inequality debate, and the current state of global inequality. In addition to focusing on inequality between rich and poor countries and inequality within both developed and developing societies, we will examine the issue of gender inequality. It discusses the enduring issues of global poverty, hunger, and malnutrition and efforts to close the gap between rich and poor and reduce the negative effects of inequality and poverty. The chapter concludes with a case study of food security and rising food prices.

DOES INEQUALITY MATTER?

The existence of inequality is not automatically a major problem, especially when the economy is growing and there are many opportunities for upward mobility. As long as the standard of living is improving for those on the bottom of the economic ladder, concerns about inequality tend to diminish. The last two decades of the twentieth century and the first decade of this century were characterized by a widening gap between rich and poor and the proliferation of millionaires and billionaires. While economic disparities remained a serious problem in developing countries, the forces of globalization created conditions that helped widen the gap between rich and poor in industrialized societies. When the economy deteriorates, the gap between rich and poor tends to be narrower but concerns about inequality are heightened. During the global economic recession, the wealthy lost money, but the poor lost their jobs, houses, and health insurance. In the United States, the poverty rate climbed to 13.2 percent in 2008, 14.3 percent in 2009, and 15.1 percent in 2010, its highest level since 1993. Widespread demonstrations in the United States against excessive executive compensation, especially those in companies that received financial assistance from the government, underscores the dangers of economic inequality. Ironically, policies implemented by the U.S. government to reduce inequality by making easy credit available for housing, in particular, helped cause the global financial crisis. But the financial and economic crisis increased inequality and heightened awareness of the concentration of wealth held by the top one percent of Americans. That awareness led to "We are the 99 percent," a battle cry of the "Occupy Wall Street" protests against financial inequality that began in New York City and spread around the world. The perception that economic inequality is essentially transitory when opportunities for economic advancement are widely available mitigates negative effects of actual inequality.

However, persistent inequality and enduring poverty challenge beliefs in the equality of opportunity and the possibility of upward mobility. Eventually, the legitimacy of the economic system and political and social institutions are challenged. The legitimacy of the global economic system is likely to be strengthened if a larger number of countries and individuals are benefiting from it. Extreme inequality perpetuates poverty and the concentration of economic and political power and reduces economic efficiency. It strengthens inequality-perpetuating institutions in *three ways*:

1. Inequality discourages the political participation of poor people, which, in turn, diminishes their access to education, health care, and other services that contribute to economic growth and development.
2. Inequality often prevents the building and proper functioning of impartial institutions and observance of the rule of law.
3. Inequality enables the wealthy to refuse to compromise politically or economically, which further weakens poor societies in a global society that requires relatively fast responses to economic developments.[2]

These consequences of inequality combine to ensure that poor societies will remain poor and unequal, trapping most of their inhabitants in a destructive cycle of poverty. Growing inequality among as well as within nations has direct and indirect implications for globalization. Inequality could undermine globalization by influencing countries to adopt protectionist policies and disengage, to the extent possible, from the global economy. But the ramifications extend beyond economic issues to problems such as terrorism, the environment, and the spread of infectious diseases.

As Chapter 4 shows, the democratization process and the effective functioning of consolidated democracy depend largely on a significant degree of economic and social equality. The legitimacy of any democratic system is contingent upon the voters' belief that they have a vested interest in its preservation. Their allegiance to the democracy is influenced partly by the benefits they derive from the economic system. Widespread protests in Thailand in 2010 against the government underscore this point. The unequal distribution of wealth is often mitigated by government redistributive policies. Extreme inequality sometimes results in the voters pressuring governments to enact trade protection legislation to safeguard their employment and livelihoods. In this case, voters exercising their democratic rights could inadvertently undermine the economic system that supports democracy.

Global and domestic inequalities often directly affect many areas. The 2001 terrorist attacks in the United States were widely linked to poverty within developing nations, especially Afghanistan. Huge inequalities often fuel resentment, which finds expression in global crime and a general disregard for the rules and norms of global society. Those who are extremely poor are often excluded from participation in decisions that negatively impact their lives. They become vulnerable to being influenced by radical minorities who are committed to violent change. Poverty contributes to global and regional problems by fueling ethnic and regional conflicts, creating large numbers of refugees, and inhibiting access to resources, such as petroleum. Finally, global and domestic inequality is perceived as stimulating the global drug trade. For example, poor farmers in Bolivia regard the cultivation of coca as essential to their survival. More than three-quarters of the heroin sold in Europe is refined from opium grown in Afghanistan by poor farmers. The costs of fighting the war against drugs in poor countries, such as Colombia and Afghanistan, are extremely high.

THE GLOBALIZATION AND INEQUALITY DEBATE

The impact of globalization on income distribution and living standards is a controversial topic. Preoccupation with globalization to the exclusion of other factors often muddles the debate about globalization and inequality. Would less globalization produce more equality, and would more equality among and within nations result in an improved quality of life for the poor? There are two dominant, but sometimes overlapping, viewpoints on this issue. The globalists argue that globalization has increased economic growth and decreased global inequality and poverty. The antiglobalists generally perceive globalization as a negative and destructive force that is responsible for the increasing global inequality and poverty and the declining levels of human welfare.[3]

Globalists Make Their Case

From the globalists' perspective, the basic cause of inequality and poverty is the relatively low level of globalization in some countries. In other words, the poorest societies are the least integrated into the global economy. Openness to foreign trade, investments, and technology—combined with reforms such as the privatization of the domestic economy—will ultimately accelerate economic growth. The Organization for Economic Cooperation and Development (OECD) calculated that countries that are relatively open to trade grew about twice as fast as those that are relatively closed to trade.[4] China's rapid economic growth is an obvious example. On the other hand, North Korea, Myanmar (formerly Burma), and Kenya are on the margins of globalization and remain impoverished.

OECD ■
Organization focusing on global economic development

Globalists also argue that globalization has contributed to the decline of inequality. Furthermore, poverty can be reduced even as inequality increases. David Dollar and Aart Kraay found that "a long-term global trend toward greater inequality prevailed for at least 200 years; it peaked around 1975. But since then, it has stabilized and possibly even reversed."[5] The accelerated economic growth of China and India, the world's two most populous countries, which is seen as directly linked to globalization, is given as the principal reason for the change. Much of the inequality that persists within countries is due less to globalization and more to policies dealing with education, taxation, and social problems. Moreover, more inequality in China, for example, has been accompanied by a spectacular reduction in poverty.[6]

Globalists emphasize that the number of people moving out of poverty has increased. More than 800 million people have abandoned the ranks of absolute poverty since 1990. The number of people living on less than one U.S. dollar a day remains high—around 1.2 billion. But given rapid population growth rates in the poorest countries, the decline in global poverty is impressive. The world's poor are seen as getting to be less poor in both absolute and relative terms.[7] The more globalized poor nations become, the better off their populations are in both absolute and relative terms. Globalization has generally helped the poor by contributing to reductions in the cost of numerous consumer products. Less money has higher purchasing power in a globalized economy. Finally, by facilitating migration, establishing small businesses that rely on the Internet, and improving access to jobs in telecommunications and computer technologies in countries such as India and China, globalization improves the quality of life for the poor.

Antiglobalists Make Their Case

Antiglobalists believe that globalization is widening the gap between the haves and the have-nots. Concerned with making global capitalism more equitable, they view globalization as primarily benefiting the rich while making life more difficult for the poor. Antiglobalists argue that globalization is a *zero-sum* game, meaning that the rich are winning at the expense of the poor. Antiglobalists also argue that globalization benefits rich countries, such as the United States. China is one of the few developing countries that is generally regarded as profiting from free trade and open markets. The United States, the locomotive of globalization, benefits the most from open markets worldwide. George Soros—a leading financier, philanthropist, and critic of globalization, though not an antiglobalist—believes that globalization drains surplus capital from periphery or developing countries to the United States, thereby allowing Americans to spend more than they save and import more than they export.[8] Similarly, Jack Beatty contends that the foundation of inequality resulting from globalization is that rich countries do not play by the rules that they made to govern the global economic system. Basically, the United States and other Western countries require developing countries to open their markets without reciprocating commensurably. To support this argument, Beatty points out that although global rules on trade discourage governments from subsidizing industries, rich countries continue to provide subsidies to agriculture.[9]

George Soros ■
Leading financier, philanthropist, and critic of corporate globalization

Critics also argue that globalization is like an "economic temptress," promising riches but not delivering. Global communications have heightened awareness of the vast disparities between rich and poor within the same society and especially between rich and poor countries. Simultaneously, global communications spawn aspirations of escaping poverty and enjoying the good life. Unfortunately, globalization is unable to make these dreams real. Countries integrated into the global economic system are the most severely affected by downturns in the economy. For example, Southeast Asia, which depends on exports of steel, textiles, and electronic components, suffers significantly in global economic crises and is unable to generate enough jobs and sufficient wages for a population with aspirations nurtured by television programs that depict prosperity. Although conceding that globalization is not entirely responsible for global poverty, antiglobalists generally view globalization as a tide that lifts a few boats while leaving the majority mired to the bottom. Even when global companies create jobs within societies, the race to the bottom in labor standards and wages inevitably results in the poor in developing countries being unable to escape poverty while, at the same time, reducing the wages for workers in rich countries or depriving them of employment.

Antiglobalists contend that globalization compounds existing inequalities and creates more inequality. By giving priority to privatization, globalization weakens governments' commitment to the public sector. Vito Tanzi states that "even as the forces of globalization boost the demand for strong social safety nets to protect the poor, these forces also erode the ability of governments to finance and implement large-scale social welfare policies."[10] The emphasis on integrating poor nations into the global economy diverts resources from more urgent development needs, such as education, public health, industrial capacity, and social cohesion. Many trade agreements impose tight prerequisites on developing countries in exchange for crumbs of enhanced market access. The African Growth and Opportunity Act is an example. It provides increased access to the U.S. market only if African apparel manufacturers use fabric and yarns produced in the United States, instead of using their own or supplies from less expensive sources. In other words, the antiglobalists perceive globalization as perpetuating inequality by impeding development. Furthermore, they argue, countries such as South Korea and Taiwan, frequently held up as models for the benefits of globalization by the globalists, developed under radically different conditions. These countries were not required to pay the costs that are now an integral component of integration into global markets. During the 1960s and 1970s, when they were rapidly growing, Taiwan and South Korea did not face contemporary globalization's pressures to privatize their economies and open their borders to capital flows. The demands of globalization undermine efforts essential for a comprehensive development agenda.

African Growth and Opportunity Act ■ Trade agreement to strengthen apparel trade between the U.S. and African states

GLOBAL INEQUALITY

Discussions of global inequality remind us of many of the reasons some societies created powerful and prosperous civilizations while others did not. Western Europe emerged as the most prosperous region of the world. Areas that are now the United States, Canada, Australia, and New Zealand were conquered and settled by Europeans, many of whom embodied the characteristics that contributed to Europe's rise to global prominence and economic prosperity. The advantages Europeans enjoyed have been consolidated. This, in turn, contributes to global inequality today. Several factors combined to produce Europe's economic success and profound global economic inequality. A major factor is *freedom of expression*. Societies that encouraged people to have their own ideas, to be innovative, and to interact with each other eventually surpassed societies that were totalitarian or authoritarian. The latter generally stifled innovation because of their preoccupation with traditions, conformity, and respect for authority. Initiative was often equated with heresy. Another factor encompasses *social values*. Chief among these is an emphasis on economic opportunity and social equality. In his *Wealth and Poverty of Nations*, David S. Landes stresses that China's restrictions on women hampered its growth, whereas women in Europe, who were less confined to the home and were free to find employment in certain occupations, were instrumental in that region's industrial development and expansion.[11] A third factor is the functioning of a free market and institutionalized property rights. Chinese authorities became antagonistic toward free enterprise and eventually regulated it out of existence. Muslim countries failed to develop institutions that would have enabled businesses to expand. Islamic partnership law and inheritance law worked against the growth of large corporations. In Europe, a partner in a business could designate heirs, thereby providing continuity in the business after the partner's death. Islamic law did not provide mechanisms for partnerships to be easily reconstituted following a partner's death. Similarly, Islamic law prescribed in rigid detail both immediate and extended family members who had to inherit property. Europe, on the other hand, allowed property to be inherited by one person, thereby minimizing the chances that a business would disintegrate and be prevented from getting larger. Virginia Postrel points out that "the fragmentation produced by inheritance law, combined with the structures of partnership law, kept Middle Eastern enterprises small. That, in turn, limited the pressure to evolve new economic forms."[12] However, increasing wealth from petroleum has significantly strengthened many companies in the Persian Gulf area, especially those involved in finance.

A final factor undergirding Europe's economic success and setting the foundation for global inequality is the *separation of the secular from the religious*. Whereas Islam became inseparable from the state, the origins of Christianity and its spread to Rome forced it to compromise with secular authority, a compromise encapsulated in the warning that Christians should give to Caesar what belongs to him and give God what is God's. However, Muslim societies prospered when religion was less restrictive. Muslims, commanded by the Koran to seek knowledge, became leading scientists, physicians, artists, mathematicians, philosophers, architects, and builders. For more than five hundred years, Arabic was the language of scholars and scientists. The Muslims transmitted Chinese scientific inventions, Greek and Persian texts, and their own impressive scientific discoveries and inventions to Europe. From the tenth to the thirteenth century, Europeans translated Arabic works into Hebrew and Latin, thereby giving impetus to a rebirth of learning that ultimately transformed Western civilization.

free market and institutionalized property rights ■ Rights to private property protected under the market system

TABLE 9.1

Income Inequality Among Countries GDP per capita ($) 2008

Rich Countries	
Luxembourg	109,903
United States	**46,350**
Ireland	60,460
Norway	94,759
Iceland	52,479
Switzerland	64,327
Austria	49,599
Denmark	62,118
Netherlands	52,963
Canada	45,070
Belgium	47,085
Australia	47,370
Japan	38,455
Poor Countries	
China	3,267
Egypt	1,991
India	1,017
Pakistan	991
Haiti	729
Bangladesh	497
Nigeria	1,370
Zambia	1,134
Ethiopia	317
Sierra Leone	352
High-Income Countries	40,748
Middle-Income Countries	2,200
Low-Income Countries	781
World	9,120

Source: United Nations Development Programme, *Human Development Report 2010* (Basingstoke, Hampshire, UK, and New York: Palgrave Macmillan, 2010).

Inequality Between Developed and Developing Countries

Despite rising living standards throughout most of the world in the last century, the gap between rich and poor countries has steadily widened. Tables 9.1 and 9.2 show some of those disparities in greater detail. Historic trends suggest that most of the richest countries will maintain their lead over most of the poorest countries. The gap between the richest country and the poorest country was 3 to 1 in 1820,

TABLE 9.2

Health Inequalities

Country	Physicians (per 10,000 People) 2000–2009	Life Expectancy at Birth (Years) 2006	Life Expectancy at Birth (Years) 2010	Under Age 5 Mortality Rate (per 1,000 Live Births) 2008
High Human Development				
Norway	39	79.9	81.0	4
Canada	19	80.4	81.0	6
United States	**27**	**78.0**	**79.6**	**8**
Japan	21	82.4	83.2	4
France	37	80.4	81.6	4
United Kingdom	21	79.2	79.8	6
Italy	37	80.4	81.4	4
Israel	36	80.5	81.2	5
Mexico	29	75.8	76.7	17
Russian Federation	43	65.2	67.2	13
Saudi Arabia	16	72.4	73.3	21
Brazil	17	72.0	72.9	22
Medium Human Development				
Thailand	3	70.0	69.3	14
Philippines	12	71.3	72.3	32
India	6	64.1	64.4	69
Pakistan	8	64.9	67.2	89
Low Human Development				
Sudan	3	57.8	58.9	109
Sierra Leone	<0.5	42.1	48.2	194
Zambia	1	41.2	47.3	148
Nigeria	4	46.6	48.4	186
Chad	<0.5	50.4	49.2	209

Source: United Nations Development Programme, *Human Development Report 2010* (Basingstoke, Hampshire, UK, and New York: Palgrave Macmillan, 2010); and United Nations Development Programme, *Human Development Report 2007/2008* (New York: Oxford University Press, 2007).

11 to 1 in 1913, 35 to 1 in 1950, 44 to 1 in 1973, and 72 to 1 in 1992. By the end of the twentieth century, the richest 20 percent of the world's population had eighty-six times as much income as the poorest 20 percent. At the beginning of the twenty-first century, the average income in the richest twenty countries was thirty-seven times that in the poorest twenty countries.[13] As Table 9.1 indicates, income disparities between developed and developing countries are very wide. Economic development, while dramatically improving the standard of living in most countries, has not significantly closed the gap because of differential growth rates between rich and poor countries. Rich countries have experienced higher economic

growth rates than poor countries. Furthermore, per capita income actually declined in more than one hundred of the world's poorest countries, many of them in Africa. Even developing countries that have enjoyed unprecedented economic growth, such as China and India, have failed to close the gap between themselves and rich countries. It is estimated that it would take China and India a hundred years of constant growth rates higher than those now experienced by industrialized countries just to reach current American income levels. However, given the extraordinarily high standard of living in the United States, both China and India would be relatively prosperous if they achieved half the income level of Americans. Furthermore, globalization is profoundly altering many old assumptions. Because the income gap between rich and poor countries has widened historically, it does not necessarily follow that this will always be the case. Singapore and Kuwait, two high-income countries, illustrate that poor countries can become prosperous by implementing astute political, social, and economic policies (in the case of Singapore) or by having valuable natural resources (in the case of Kuwait). Economic disparities between the developed and the developing world have focused on the global digital divide. But access to the Internet and improved telecommunications are not automatic panaceas for solving the problems of developing societies.

global digital divide ■ Contrast between those who have and those who don't have access to the Internet and other forms of digital communication

Causes of Inequality Between Rich and Poor Countries

In this section, we will briefly discuss some causes of the widening gap between rich and poor countries. It is important to remember that *several factors combine to contribute to inequality*: (1) geography, (2) colonialism and its legacies, (3) the structure of the global economy, (4) population growth, (5) government policies, (6) political instability, and (7) natural disasters.

Geography   Countries that are poor, some argue, have certain geographic characteristics that contribute to their economic problems. For example, they are in tropical regions or face high transportation costs in accessing global markets because of their location. Apart from the prevalence of tropical diseases, which have been controlled to a large extent by modern medicines and practices, countries in the Southern Hemisphere also tend to suffer from being landlocked. Countries with extensive coastlines and good harbors tend to be better off economically than landlocked countries that lack the physical infrastructure (i.e., a system of roads and railroads) essential for gaining access to navigable rivers and the sea. Landlocked countries or countries located far from global markets are disadvantaged by high transportation costs.

infrastructure ■ Essential systems, such as education, roads, and hospitals, needed by nation-states in order to provide necessary public services

Colonialism   Many argue that European colonization of Africa, Asia, and Latin America laid the foundation for economic disparities between rich and poor nations. Inequality breeds inequality. Just as wealth tends to perpetuate wealth, poverty tends to perpetuate poverty. Countries that grew rich two hundred years ago, partly because of their colonization of the developing world, are generally still rich today. European groups that migrated to Australia, Canada, the United States, South Africa, New Zealand, and throughout Latin America continue to enjoy significant advantages over indigenous populations. However, it is also argued that colonization is not the main reason for ongoing global inequality. Some states, such as Singapore, South Korea, and Taiwan, that were colonized are now relatively rich.

Structure of the Global Economy   Colonialism and historical experiences, as well as contemporary economic practices, are widely perceived as creating an unfair global economy that keeps poor countries poor and rich countries rich. The Scottish economist Adam Smith, who wrote *An Inquiry into the Nature and Causes of the Wealth of Nations*, believed that governments should not interfere with the functioning of markets and that business persons would be led by an invisible hand to do the best for society. However, many leaders of poor countries argue that governments and multinational corporations in rich countries cooperate to maintain an unfair global economy. They generally subscribe to the dependency theory, which holds that poor countries' reliance on exports of primary commodities, many of which were started during colonization for the benefit of Europeans, puts them at a severe economic disadvantage. The prices obtained from their exports decline relative to the prices of manufactured imports from industrialized countries.

Population Growth   Rapid population growth in most developing countries plays a central role in perpetuating the economic chasm between rich and poor countries. Population growth decreased in the industrialized countries as the economic gap was widening. Since 1950, the population in rich countries grew by about 50 percent. In sharp contrast, the population in poor countries grew by 250 percent. Large families perpetuate poverty in most cases.

Government Policies   Discussing causes of poverty in the Arab world, Alan Schwartz observed that many of these countries are poor because of the policies they pursue. For example, Saudi Arabia tolerates monopolies that help to sustain an elite clan that all too often opposes technological, economic, and social change. Many Arab countries use import duties to discourage trade and impede the flow of investment by disregarding the rule of law. Furthermore, many of these governments emphasize religion instead of science and technology and therefore do not adequately develop human capital. Perhaps the most serious policy failure is the lack of adequate investment in women's education and opposition to allowing women to have equal employment opportunities. When Korea was divided in 1948, South Korea adopted capitalist policies that fostered economic success, whereas North Korea isolated itself from the global community and adopted a Communist system of government. Today, South Korea is prosperous and North Korea routinely faces starvation. The People's Republic of China, India, Malaysia, and Singapore, for example, implemented policies that have a positive impact on their economies. Latin America, on the other hand, allocates resources disproportionately to the wealthy. Although several countries, especially Brazil, have made progress toward enlarging the middle class, many of the poor there remain trapped in the cycle of poverty.

Political Instability   Angola, a country twice the size of Texas, has abundant supplies of petroleum, diamonds, fish, and fresh water. However, life expectancy there is forty-five years, infant mortality is among the highest in the world, and

Adam Smith ■
Scottish economist and historic proponent of the capitalist system

dependency theory ■
Concept that poor countries' overreliance on exports puts them at an economic disadvantage

Angolans are extremely poor. For twenty-seven years, the country was devastated by ethnic conflicts. Political instability directly contributes to economic disparities between developed and developing countries. Conflict not only discourages foreign investment; it also influences the best educated, most talented, and most financially successful citizens to flee or to invest their money outside the country.

Natural Disasters   At the beginning of this section, we discussed how geographic location directly affects the wealth and poverty of countries. Drought, earthquakes, volcanic eruptions, hurricanes, and other natural disasters are closely linked to geography. The earthquake and tsunami in Japan in 2011, the tsunamis in Asia in 2004 and 2006, hurricanes Katrina and Rita in the United States in 2005, earthquakes in China in 2008, and flooding in Pakistan in 2010 are the most obvious examples. These natural disasters routinely destroy important economic sectors, increase severe infrastructure problems, force the relocation of a large number of people, and lead to greater impoverishment.

INEQUALITY WITHIN RICH COUNTRIES

History and literature are replete with examples of the difficulties endured by the poverty-stricken citizens of Britain and the United States and how the lives of the poor sharply contrasted with those of the wealthy. Theories of socialism and Communism, articulated by Karl Marx, who was living in Britain, underscore the durability of inequality within rich countries. Great economic disparities have existed in the United States throughout its history, with the *Gilded Age* of the nineteenth century, the *Roaring Twenties*, and the *Roaring Nineties* bringing unprecedented levels of both prosperity and economic inequality. The stock market crash of 1929, the Great Depression of the 1930s, the implementation of the New Deal programs designed to help the poor, and the outbreak of World War II combined to redistribute wealth in the United States. The concentration of income declined dramatically, and the middle class grew rapidly. Income distribution remained relatively equal until the 1970s. In virtually all industrial countries, income inequality grew between the 1970s and the early twenty-first century. Globalization, new technologies, the financial crisis and economic recession, and other factors contributed to this development.

Karl Marx ■ German thinker who pioneered the theories of socialism and Communism

New Deal ■ Social welfare system created in the 1930s to help the poor and restore trust in capitalism and government

The United States

The United States has the greatest degree of income inequality among industrialized countries. The richest country on earth also has pockets of poverty that are similar to many parts of the developing world. In 2010, 15.1 percent of Americans—46.2 million people—lived below the poverty line, which was defined as an annual income below $22,314 for a family of four. The poorest 10 percent of Americans receive 1.8 percent of the total income, whereas the richest 10 percent gets almost a third. The average for rich countries is 2.9 percent of the total income going to the poorest 10 percent of the population. Economic statistics support the general perception of unprecedented inequality in the United States, with most of the income concentrated at the very top of society. The top 20 percent of households earned 56 percent of

poverty line ■ The income level under which people cannot adequately sustain themselves; a measure of need

the nation's income and controlled 83 percent of the nation's wealth, which includes stocks, bonds, real estate, businesses, savings, insurance, and other assets.

Between 1980 and 2006, the top 1 percent of Americans earned ten times more than the rest at the start of the period and twenty times more than the rest at the end. For the top 0.1 percent, the gain rose from twenty times the earnings of the lower 90 percent to almost eighty times by 2006.[14] The tax cuts passed in 2001 and 2003 were widely regarded as creating an even wider gap between the rich and poor in the United States. While most Americans received modest increases between 1979 and 2000, averaging 10 percent, compensation for the nation's top one hundred chief executive officers (CEOs) climbed from $1.3 million, or thirty-nine times the pay of an average worker, to $37.5 million, or more than one thousand times the pay of ordinary workers. For example, Lee R. Raymond, chairman and chief executive of Exxon, got $144,573 for each day he led the company between 1993 and 2005. Various corporate scandals and the financial crisis influenced U.S. leaders to more closely examine these disparities. Although the median pay for chief executives fell in 2008, many of them received more than three hundred times the pay of the average American worker. In 2010, the median pay for top executives at two hundred major companies was $9.6 million. While poverty grew and wages declined for most Americans, salaries and bonuses for executives, those who brought about the financial crisis, saw their incomes rise by roughly 5 percent. Think of the salaries of major athletes compared with what the average American makes. The devastation caused by Hurricane Katrina in August 2005 and the economic recession underscored the gap between rich and poor in the United States. Between 2008 and 2011, the number of homeless families had increased by roughly 30 percent. More than 1.6 million people used an emergency shelter and the number of homeless children grew.[15]

Perhaps one of the most overlooked aspects of inequality is the growing income gap between urban areas and rural America. As one drives through the numerous small towns in Illinois, Iowa, North Dakota, Alabama, and elsewhere, these income disparities become obvious. Homes, businesses, barns, and grain elevators have been abandoned and are decaying, creating what are referred to as rural ghettos. Two New York academics, Frank and Debra Popper, have suggested that, given the relentless decay of rural towns, the federal government should accelerate the depopulation of the entire Great Plains region and turn it into a vast "Buffalo Commons," a refuge for large mammals, hikers, and a reviving Native American population. As we saw in Chapter 7, the global financial and economic crises forced factories to close and people to abandon their homes. Cities dependent on the automobile industry were devastated. Detroit, for example, lost roughly half its population and is in the process of downsizing. Arizona, California, Nevada, and Florida suffered from widespread foreclosures. It is in those states that poverty and homelessness grew the most.[16]

rural ghettos ■ Poverty-stricken rural areas

Buffalo Commons ■ Proposed refuge for wildlife and Native American populations

Other Industrialized Countries

Germany, Britain, Japan, Ireland, and Canada are also experiencing high levels of income inequality. Like the United States, Germany is a very unequal society. The widening gap between the rich and poor is a major concern. There are more rich

Many Americans concentrated their investments in housing, and the financial crisis left some of them homeless. A "tent city" in California demonstrates that reality.

people and more poor people. Over the past ten years, the monthly income for persons in the poorest income bracket declined from $912 to $864. Those in upper income brackets saw their incomes rise from $3,216 to $3,618 a month. Britain's rural areas have higher poverty rates than urban areas, and schools, railroad stations, and post offices are closing, just as they are in rural parts of the United States. The gap between the prosperous Southeast and the poorer North has steadily expanded. Londoners enjoy a higher share of the country's income than people living in the northern part of England, Wales, and Scotland. Japan's long economic recession has heightened the problem of inequality. Unlike the United States, which is more tolerant of huge economic gaps among different groups, Japan emphasizes the oneness of its society. Although about 90 percent of Japan's citizens regard themselves as middle class, the economic recession that began in the early 1990s has weakened the middle class and sharpened distinctions between rich and poor.

Rapid economic growth in Ireland, fueled largely by an influx of investments in technology and the country's increased globalization, had contributed to significant income inequality. However, the global financial crisis severely eroded Ireland's economy, thereby diminishing income inequality. Canada, generally regarded as a very egalitarian society, ranks 22nd of 31 rich countries in the area of child poverty. Ten percent of Canadians are poor, including 600,000 children. Around 300,000 Canadians are homeless.

Globalization is generally seen as a major cause of the rapid rise in inequality. Integral to globalization is the proliferation of new telecommunications and computer technologies. Individuals with technical skills have outperformed those who have few or no technical skills. The globalization of trade also contributed to

globalization ■ The worldwide spread of ideas, values, markets, technology, and other developments

shifting employment patterns, with low-wage workers in industrial countries losing out to workers in the developing world. Closely related to globalization and technology is *education*. The knowledge-based economies of rich countries give educated individuals an advantage over those who are less educated, less skilled, and less entrepreneurial. The interdependence of economies enables educated people to be more mobile and marketable. The new global elites are mainly entrepreneurs. Many of them are inventors in the area of communications technologies. The disparity in income between those with a high school education on the one hand and those with a college education on the other became obvious between 1979 and the early 1990s. In 1979, the average American male college graduate earned 49 percent more than a male high school graduate. By 1993, the gap had grown to 89 percent. The forces of globalization continue to widen this gap. Individuals with doctorates and professional graduate degrees experience significant income growth. The *weakening of labor unions* as we discussed in Chapter 8 also contributes to rising inequality.

INEQUALITY WITHIN POOR COUNTRIES

Carlos Slim of Mexico is the world's richest man. It is estimated that he has $74 billion, compared with Bill Gates' $56 billion and Warren Buffet's $50 billion. Almost 60 percent of Mexicans make $15 or less a day. Although leaders of the developing world consistently stress the inequality between rich and poor countries, very little emphasis is put on the gulf that separates rich and poor in developing countries. One persistent characteristic of the developing world is the lack of a large enough middle class to bridge the extremes of wealth and poverty. In most poor countries, there are basically two distinct worlds: one inhabited by the middle and upper classes that comprise a small percentage of the population and the other by the poor majority. Traveling in the developing world, one observes high walls around the homes of the wealthy people to protect them from the poor. One also notices that the lifestyles of the rich are virtually identical to those of rich individuals in the developed countries.

Despite significant progress toward diminishing inequality, Latin America has some of the world's most unequal societies. Although Mexico has the world's richest person, almost 60 percent of Mexico's people are mired in poverty. Despite significant progress made under the North America Free Trade Agreement (NAFTA), inequality in Mexico is extreme. Roughly 10 percent of the population controls half the country's wealth. Inequality in Brazil remains a significant problem. Globalization and Brazil's rapid economic growth have contributed to an increase in the wealthy, including a growing number of billionaires. Roughly 31 percent of the population remains below the poverty line, and 43 million people live on less than $2 a day. On the other hand, Brazil is making a concerted effort to reduce poverty and diminish inequality through programs such as Bolsa Familia, or Family Fund. Under Bolsa Familia, which is a model for other countries, more than 11 million families receive financial assistance and are encouraged to send their children to school and given them medical care. Extreme poverty has declined by more than 50 percent since 2003.[17]

NAFTA ■ Trade agreement signed by Canada, the United States, and Mexico aiming at economic integration under the capitalist system

Bolsa Familia ■ Brazil's model poverty reduction program

In some developing societies, inequality is institutionalized. During the period when South Africa was ruled by apartheid laws—which rigidly segregated blacks, whites, Asians, and mixed-race people and distributed resources according to a racial hierarchy—whites enjoyed a privileged position and blacks faced widespread and persistent discrimination. The economic chasm between whites and blacks still exists. However, since apartheid was abolished in 1991, an economic gap within the black group has grown as more opportunities have opened up for blacks. The government's Black Empowerment Initiative, which uses lucrative government contracts as leverage to encourage the expansion of black-owned businesses, has created black millionaires in a relatively short period of time, further widening inequality among blacks.

India's caste system is the most obvious and pervasive example of structured inequality. The caste system is a rigid hierarchical system of social classes in *Hinduism*, which determines the status, rights, privileges, occupations, and social interactions of each person from birth. One inherits one's caste or social standing in the community. Each child is born into one of four main castes: Brahmans, Ksatriyas, Vaisyas, and Sudras. Even though the caste system has been outlawed and is constantly challenged, it is widely adhered to in Indian society. Brahmans (the priests and scholars) stand at the top, the Ksatriyas (the military, lawmakers, and rulers) are second, the Vaisyas (merchants, landowners, industrialists, and artisans) are third, and the Sudras (laborers and farm workers) are at the bottom of the caste system. The lowest group in India is the untouchables, who are literally regarded as outcasts. This means that they do not belong to a caste or class. In contrast to most developing countries, inequality has increased in India. There are more than 400 million poor Indians. More than 43 percent of India's children under five years are malnourished, or roughly one third of the world's total. More than 35 percent of Indians are illiterate, and more than 20 million children do not attend school.[18]

The same set of factors that have contributed to the widening gap between rich and poor in the developed world are also present in developing countries. China is an example of this phenomenon. Economic benefits of China's rapid growth are most concentrated in urban coastal areas. Small towns, rural areas, and the interior experience much slower growth rates and are poorer than coastal industrial centers. About 84 percent of foreign investment is in the eastern coastal cities, 9 percent in the central region, and 4.6 percent in the western part of China. Similarly, 57 percent of the country's income is generated on the east coast, compared with 17 percent in the west. Finding ways to diminish economic disparities became a major priority of the Chinese government. By 2011, China had 3 percent of the world's richest people.[19]

Gender Inequality

Women worldwide experience various degrees of inequality. In all countries, the poorest of the poor are women, the majority of those at the bottom of society. Perceptions of women and the reality of inequality are mutually reinforcing, creating a vicious cycle of inequality. Clearly, women are not a monolithic group. Some enjoy great wealth, power, and high positions in society. More women, especially in the industrialized countries, are gaining equality with men of similar educational

apartheid laws ■ Laws that legally and forcibly separate people of different ethnic and racial backgrounds

Black Empowerment Initiative ■ South African government effort to encourage the expansion of black-owned businesses

caste system ■ Religiously driven ideology and social system that promote hierarchy and inequality

Brahmans ■ Priests and scholars at the top of the caste system

Ksatriyas ■ The second-highest group in the caste system includes those in the military, lawmakers, and rulers

Vaisyas ■ The third-highest group in the caste system includes merchants, landowners, industrialists, and artisans

Sudras ■ Laborers and farm workers at the bottom of the caste system

untouchables ■ Outcasts excluded from the caste system

achievement. Based on our previous discussion about the economic advantages college-educated people enjoy over those who do not attend college, women are beginning to surpass men in terms of income. Observing gender composition of college classes, it is obvious that women outnumber men by a significant margin. The economic recession created higher unemployment rates for men than for women, thereby giving women a relative economic advantage. Leadership roles in society twenty years from now are likely to be dominated by women.

gender ideology ■
Beliefs, values, perceptions, and ideas about the roles of men and women and power relations between them

The beliefs, values, perceptions, and ideas about the roles of men and women and power relations between them are referred to as gender ideology. Gender ideology is based on the assumption that women are naturally suited for particular jobs. In Afghanistan, for example, cultural beliefs and practices make family planning very difficult, and many women have ten or more children. Women's role as child bearers reinforces their unequal status, trapping them and their children, especially girls, in a cycle of poverty. As popular uprisings spread across the Arab world, many women in Saudi Arabia are using social media to organize women and to encourage them to challenge deeply rooted traditional practices that deprive women of basic rights. The 2011 Nobel Peace Prize was awarded to three activist women from Africa and the Arab world in recognition of their "non-violent struggle" for women's safety and equal rights. The Nobel Prize recipients were Liberian President Ellen Johnson Sirleaf, Liberian peace activist Leymah Gbowee, and Yemeni pro-democracy campaigner Tawakul Karman. In many parts of the world, women are perceived as being naturally suited for factory jobs that are part of globalization. In Mexico, China, Thailand, and elsewhere, women are concentrated in low-wage employment. But as we discussed in Chapter 8, global companies are helping women get better jobs.

Countries that are the least globalized tend to have higher levels of inequality. For example, the gender gap in education is concentrated largely in the developing world, particularly in Africa, which is the least globalized continent. Women in the United States, by contrast, are experiencing increased equality with men. For decades following World War II, income inequality remained relatively unchanged. Women received about three fifths of what men received for similar work. However, as we mentioned previously, the gap is closing as more women attend college and abandon lower-paying professions (such as teaching) for more lucrative employment in business, engineering, and the sciences. Generational change and the enactment of civil rights legislation in the 1960s facilitated women's access to employment outside the home and equalized pay for men and women to a greater degree than previously. Nevertheless, women's pay still lags behind men's in almost every sector of the economy. In 2006, the gap narrowed, with women making 81 percent of what men were paid. This disparity remains. Globalization, particularly the Internet, created new ways of conducting business as well as new opportunities for women, who are increasingly able to integrate family responsibilities and business endeavors. Trends toward gender equality are being consolidated in every field.

GLOBAL POVERTY

Poverty, the most obvious indicator of global and domestic inequality, is an enduring reality for more than two thirds of the world's population. Although poverty in developing countries is readily apparent, poverty is a growing reality in the richest countries, including the United States. Poverty persists despite improvements in living standards. But improvements—such as increases in per capita income, declining infant mortality rates, increased access to clean water, and decreases in illiteracy—are often counteracted by rapid population growth rates in the developing world. Nonetheless, the percentage of people living in extreme poverty, defined as living on less than $1 a day, has declined. Economic growth in China and India contributed to this decrease in extreme poverty. In 2000, the UN adopted the Millennium Declaration, which aimed at reducing extreme poverty by half and child mortality by two thirds by 2015. A quarter of the children in the developing world are malnourished, one out of six people in the world do not have clean drinking water, and roughly half live in unsanitary conditions. Meeting the Millennium goals by 2015 is impossible. The struggle to further reduce poverty must take into consideration some powerful realities. These include

extreme poverty ■ The very poorest of the poor, or those living on less than $1 a day

1. *Weak political support for foreign assistance* in most rich countries, including the United States;
2. *Uncertainty of commitment* from the World Bank, the International Monetary Fund (IMF), the WTO, and other multilateral agencies; and
3. *Ongoing armed conflicts* that impede efforts to help the poor in many parts of the developing world.

These realities are compounded by the diminished role of governments worldwide in efforts to alleviate poverty.

Defining poverty is to some extent subjective. There are basically two aspects to poverty: absolute poverty (i.e., the absolute number of poor people below the defined poverty line) and relative poverty (which reflects the distribution of income in society). For example, in relative terms, many Americans are poor. However, a much smaller number of Americans are poor in absolute terms. Although poverty is not always easily defined, an important aspect of poverty is a subjective feeling of being poor either absolutely or relative to others. The concept of the poverty line is not always a reliable indicator of poverty. The poverty line in the United States was developed in 1963–1964 by the Social Security Administration on the basis of a 1955 household food consumption survey by the U.S. Department of Agriculture. The poverty line is adjusted each year to reflect changes in the Consumer Price Index (CPI). The CPI measures changes over time in the cost of purchasing the "market basket" of goods and services used by a typical family. But the poverty line does not adequately reflect higher costs for transportation, child care, health care, and other costs associated with employment. Unlike the 1960s, when many mothers stayed home, both parents now work, thereby incurring expenses that were not taken into consideration when the poverty line was developed. Furthermore, the poverty level measurement assumes that costs are the same across the United States, with the exception of Alaska and Hawaii, where the poverty level is higher. Global measurements of poverty are in reality estimates, despite the certainty conveyed by statistics.

absolute poverty ■ The absolute number of poor people below the defined poverty line

relative poverty ■ Level of poverty based on the society in question

CPI ■ Released by the U.S. Department of Labor to measure the price of consumer goods and services as well as the rate of inflation

Regardless of where poor people live, there are at least *six dimensions of poverty*:

1. *Hunger.* Poverty throughout the world is about inadequate food supplies.
2. *Psychological Dimensions.* Poverty is usually characterized by a sense of powerlessness, dependency, humiliation, and shame.

3. *Inadequate Infrastructure.* Poor people generally lack access to roads, electricity, clean water, and transportation.
4. *Low Levels of Literacy.* Educational opportunities are often unavailable.
5. *Health Problems.* Poor people everywhere generally suffer from illness, which further impoverishes them.
6. *Inadequate Income.* Poor people stress managing physical, human, social, and environmental assets to cope with their vulnerability. Incomes receive less emphasis.

Table 9.3 shows the percentage of the population in selected countries living on $1.25 or less a day. Hunger and malnutrition are at the foundation of global inequality. Malnutrition causes impaired vision, an inability to concentrate and to learn, greater vulnerability to disease and poor health, and a shorter life expectancy. Hunger and malnutrition plague roughly one billion people globally. The worst drought in sixty years, combined with widespread violence and state failure in Somalia, caused unprecedented famine that affected more than 10 million East Africans, primarily Somalis. Despite India's economic growth, malnutrition, especially among children, remains extremely high. Both population growth and rising food prices are contributing to increases in hunger and malnutrition. Furthermore, the production of biofuels reduces food supplies.

malnutrition ■ Poor nutrition resulting from an insufficient or unbalanced diet

TABLE 9.3	
Percentage of Population Living Below Income Poverty Line in Medium- and Low-Human Development Countries (Expressed in Purchasing Power Comparable to That of U.S. Dollars in the United States)	
Country	**Population Below $1.25 a Day (2000–2008) (%)**
Sri Lanka	14.0
Paraguay	6.5
China	15.9
Indonesia	29.4
Egypt	<2.0
India	41.6
Ghana	30.0
Kenya	19.7
Pakistan	22.6
Nigeria	64.4
Zambia	64.3
Central African Rep.	62.4
Ethiopia	39.0
Sierra Leone	53.4

Source: United Nations Development Programme, *Human Development Report 2010* (Basingstoke, Hampshire, UK, and New York: Palgrave Macmillan, 2010).

CLOSING THE GAP

As we saw in Chapter 8, global companies help promote equality by providing job opportunities that contribute to diminishing poverty and reducing inequality. By providing training opportunities for women in particular, global companies help the poorest of the poor improve their lives. Globalization not only makes national borders less significant; it also links the fates of rich and poor nations in an unprecedented web of interdependence. This section offers some suggestions for diminishing inequality.

Education and Family Planning Education and family planning are essential for diminishing inequality. Societies that make education available to as many people as possible, such as the United States, are also the most prosperous societies. Because education affects ways of thinking, perceptions, and creativity, it is at the foundation of any effort to alleviate poverty. Education, especially for women, has a direct impact on the number of children women have, their level of education, and their quality of life. Countries that make education and family planning priorities usually have healthier, more productive, and more economically and technologically competitive populations.

Democracy May Help India, the world's largest democracy, is also one of the world's poorest and most unequal societies. Nevertheless, democratic societies offer poor people an opportunity to improve their lives through their voting power. Democratic governments may be pressured to reduce economic inequalities by interest groups and political parties. Brazil is an example of how a transition to democracy helped reduce poverty and inequality.

Government Policies and Free Trade Could Make a Difference Decisions made by governments have profound implications for inequality within and among nations. Brazil launched an antipoverty program, Bolsa Familia, or Family Fund, that is a model for many countries. Poor families receive financial assistance and are encouraged to send their children to school and give them medical care. By increasing economic growth, the program also decreases inequality. China's government has tried to diminish regional inequalities by investing more money in economically depressed areas. Brazil decided to address inequality by "democratizing" land titles and expanding poor people's access to credit. Granting formal property rights to millions of slum dwellers is viewed as a way of creating greater economic opportunities for the poor. Korea, Brazil, and India have implemented various forms of affirmative action programs to diminish regional, racial, or caste inequalities.

Reduce Corruption The poorest countries in the world are invariably the most corrupt countries. Corruption drains scarce resources away from vital public services and infrastructural projects, rewards incompetence and stifles innovation and change, and discourages foreign investment. At a more fundamental level, corruption infuses society with cynicism, which is detrimental to efforts to achieve economic development and greater equality. Much of the illegally obtained money is invested abroad, instead of being invested at home.

gender budgeting ■
Analysis of national budgets to determine how spending priorities affect women

Pay Attention to Women   Societies that reward women for their participation in economic, political, and social life benefit from the talents of more than half of their population. Because women play a crucial role in raising, educating, and encouraging children to achieve, their treatment directly influences economic development and equality issues. The UN, the World Bank, and other international organizations recognize that women must be included in the decision-making process. Governments are paying attention to gender budgeting, which is essentially an analysis of national budgets to determine how spending priorities affect women. Gender-responsive budgets were developed to hold public officials accountable for promoting gender equity.

Green Revolution ■
Dramatic increase in agricultural production involving hybrids, fast-growing plants, and the use of fertilizer and insecticides

Improve Agriculture in Poor Countries   Poverty and inequality are reinforced by the inability of the poor to produce sufficient food. The poorest countries routinely suffer from food shortages and malnutrition. Many of the world's poorest people live in societies where land is concentrated in the hands of a relatively small number of powerful families. Land redistribution in places such as Brazil and Venezuela is regarded as a major step toward reducing hunger and creating greater equality of opportunity. The Green Revolution—which dramatically increased agricultural production through the development of high-yielding hybrids and faster-growing plants and the application of large amounts of fertilizers and insecticides—enabled countries such as Mexico and India to produce more food and reduce starvation. Brazil's success in agriculture shows that scientific research and advanced agricultural practices help increase productivity. The Bill and Melinda Gates Foundation and the Rockefeller Foundation are helping increase agricultural productivity in Africa.

Think Small   Many college students are involved in volunteer efforts, and some think that joining the Peace Corps can help improve living conditions in an African or Latin American village. Similarly, poor people in Brazil have decided to help people even poorer than themselves by volunteering. Volunteers work in soup kitchens, homeless shelters, legal-aid clinics, and antiviolence organizations. Another example of how thinking small can help to close the gap between rich and poor is microlending, or the granting of small loans to help the smallest entrepreneurs, who do not have access to conventional financial services, expand their businesses and climb out of poverty. Started in Bangladesh by Muhammad Yunus, founder of the Grameen Bank, microcredit is now a global phenomenon. However, microfinance institutions have been blamed for extending credit to individuals who cannot repay the loans, many of whom commit suicide.[20] Though Yunus won the Nobel Peace Prize in 2006, by 2011 he had come under attack from the Bangladeshi government and he left the bank he founded.

microlending ■
Practice of granting small loans to help those who do not have access to conventional financial loan services

Muhammad Yunus ■
Founder of the Grameen Bank microlending institution

Remittances and Foreign Aid Help   During the 1980s, the prevailing view in industrialized countries was that economic globalization offered greater benefits to poor countries than official development assistance did. Consequently, foreign aid declined sharply. The financial crisis and global recession have influenced most governments to reduce aid. Many rich countries have implemented austerity programs to help cut their budget deficits. However, NGOs, especially private

New middle-class consumers around the world are eating more meat. Consequently, more grain is needed to produce beef, pork, and chicken, which adds to problems of hunger and malnutrition. In this photo, Chinese customers shop for meat at a supermarket in Binzhou City, China.

foundations, continue to provide foreign aid. Although the global recession diminished job opportunities, migrants continue to assist their homelands through remittances. In fact, remittances provide more money for poor countries than they receive from foreign aid.[21]

CASE STUDY | Food Insecurity and Rising Food Prices

Food security is a leading global priority. Roughly one billion people are hungry. Rising food prices have already pushed an additional 44 million people into extreme poverty, with millions more in imminent danger of falling into extreme poverty due to food prices and severe malnutrition rising in the poorest countries. Food insecurity is the greatest threat to the world's poor. As we discussed earlier, hunger and malnutrition negatively affect people's health, ability to earn a living, and their chances of climbing out of poverty. Children are the most vulnerable. Malnutrition levels rose by more than 25 percent in Pakistan, due largely to food shortages caused by devastating floods. Food

(continued)

insecurity in the developing world is heightened by rapid urbanization and overcrowded slums and by the fact that the poor generally spend as much as 80 percent of their income on food, much of which is imported. Higher food prices have helped strengthen terrorist groups in Pakistan, triggered food riots in more than thirty countries, and threaten to weaken global economic growth and prolong the global recession.

Global concerns about severe food shortages and Malthusian nightmares about massive starvation were alleviated by the Green Revolution, pioneered to a large extent by Norman Borlaug and the Rockefeller and Ford foundations. The Green Revolution concentrated on producing more food from the same amount of land by improved plant breeding, greater use of fertilizers, and irrigation. But the world has reached the point where crop yields are growing more slowly than the population. Furthermore, the success of the Green Revolution led to complacency in agricultural research. At the same time, excessive use of fertilizers is polluting water resources around the world, creating toxic blooms of algae and dead zones such as the one in the northern Gulf of Mexico.

There are numerous causes of the global food crisis. Those include drought in Russia, China, and Argentina; floods in Canada, Brazil, Pakistan, and Australia; export bans by countries wanting to protect domestic food supplies; stagnant agricultural productivity; high fuel prices that raise the cost of production, transportation, and processing; a relatively weak dollar that facilitates building up stockpiles of food; and widespread waste of food due to inadequate storage facilities, poor transportation, insufficient refrigeration, and throwing away food, especially in the United States and other rich countries. Two of the most important causes of the global food crisis are the rapid economic growth of Asia and manufacturing biofuels from food crops, especially from corn in the United States.

Cultural globalization has changed consumer tastes and lifestyles. Diets of mostly carbohydrates are being replaced by protein. This means that more grain is used to produce beef, poultry, and pork, which increases demand for grain globally. Economic globalization is fueling rapid growth in residential and industrial construction. Infrastructural projects require significant amounts of land. As the developing world builds more roads for automobiles, farmland is being lost. That is especially the case in China, which is trying to deal with the shortage of productive agricultural land by acquiring land in Indonesia and Africa.

Faced with rising petroleum prices and demands by environmentalists for clean energy, governments around the world have concentrated on producing biofuels. The United States, for example, has policies that aim at reducing dependence on foreign oil through increased production of ethanol. Although Brazil, which uses sugar cane to produce ethanol, would like to sell biofuel to the United States at prices lower than what it costs in America, the U.S. government has implemented tariffs and provides subsidies to protect its inefficient and environmentally unsound domestic ethanol industry. Coal and oil are used to power distilleries that produce ethanol from corn. Because the energy market is more profitable than the market for food, there is great demand for grain for biofuels. Ethanol, which accounts for around 8 percent of America's fuel for vehicles, consumes almost 40 percent of America's huge corn crop.[22]

To improve global food security and reduce hunger, governments could implement cash transfer programs such as Bolsa Familia in Brazil and Oportunidades in Mexico, to enable families to purchase food. Eliminating tariffs and subsidies in rich countries would help farmers in poor countries increase food production for domestic consumption and export. Deemphasizing the production of biofuels from corn and focusing

(continued)

more on other renewal sources of energy would lessen demand for grain for ethanol and lower food prices. Sugar cane, sorghum, switchgrass, and miscanthus (an ornamental grass) could be used to produce biofuels. Improved storage, transportation, and refrigeration would help prevent food waste. Agricultural research, especially in the tropics, offers hope for meeting the growing demand for food as the population increases. The Guinea belt in Africa, an expansive area that stretches from West Africa to Mozambique in the east, is a new agricultural frontier.[23] Several countries in Latin America, including Brazil and Argentina, also have excellent uncultivated land. As we discussed in Chapter 8, Europeans generally reject genetically modified (GM) foods. However, GM crops are embraced by the developing world and are an essential part of the solution of the global food crisis. GM crops can also provide essential micronutrients such as minerals and vitamins to improve nutrition and health. Finally, it helps to think small. Home gardeners can make a difference by becoming more self-sufficient. ◣

SUMMARY AND REVIEW

This chapter examined global and domestic inequality in an attempt to identify some of the causes of poverty. It discussed the linkages between inequality and politics, economics, and culture. It showed that global concerns about inequality are durable. We addressed colonialism, gender inequality, malnutrition, global poverty, and globalization in order to identify their roles in exacerbating or reducing global and domestic inequality. We focused on the inequality gap between rich and poor countries, as well as the inequality gaps within both developed and developing societies. We also addressed a central question in the debate over inequality: Does inequality matter? Since human societies are inherently unequal due to variations in individual abilities, opportunities, and geographic locations, it seems that inequality will always be a feature in society. As a result, we focused less on the existence of social inequality within countries and more on the importance of the degree of opportunity for upward mobility available to each individual within given societies. We examined a number of concepts and developments, such as extreme poverty, malnutrition, and relative and absolute poverty. We elaborated on the views of globalists and antiglobalists, who take contending views on the importance and effects of globalization. We identified factors that contribute to global inequality, including geography, colonialism, global economic structures, population growth, government policies, political instability, and natural disasters. Next, we examined conditions contributing to inequality at the national level. Women are disproportionately represented among the poorest of the poor throughout all countries today. As we discussed, various reasons help explain such a trend, including prevalence of religious ideology and patriarchal morals and values; traditional repression of women; and lower levels of education, pay, and job opportunities for women. Finally, we looked at possible solutions for reducing global and national poverty and inequality.

KEY TERMS

Organization for Economic Cooperation
  and Development (OECD)   183
George Soros   184
African Growth and Opportunity Act   185
free market and institutionalized property
  rights   186
global digital divide   189
infrastructure   189
Adam Smith   190
dependency theory   190
Karl Marx   191
New Deal   191
poverty line   191
rural ghettos   192
Buffalo Commons   192
globalization   193
North American Free Trade Agreement
  (NAFTA)   194
Bolsa Familia   194

apartheid laws   195
Black Empowerment Initiative   195
caste system   195
Brahmans   195
Ksatriyas   195
Vaisyas   195
Sudras   195
untouchables   195
gender ideology   196
extreme poverty   197
absolute poverty   197
relative poverty   197
Consumer Price Index (CPI)   197
malnutrition   198
gender budgeting   200
Green Revolution   200
microlending   200
Muhammad Yunus   200

DISCUSSION QUESTIONS

1. What role do government redistributive programs have in either increasing or decreasing inequality? Can you think of specific examples of such programs implemented in the United States?
2. Do you think globalization increases or reduces global and domestic inequality?
3. What effect does domestic or global inequality have on promoting or hindering democratization? Is there an inverse relationship between increasing inequality and lower prospects for democratization?
4. What are some of the main factors contributing to increasing global and domestic inequality discussed in this chapter?
5. Discuss the global food crisis, including its causes and possible solutions. What can you do to help improve food security?

SUGGESTED READINGS

Hacker, Jacob S., and Paul Pierson. *Winner-Take-All Politics.* New York: Simon and Schuster, 2010. Growing inequality in the United States is largely the result of government policies that have directed wealth toward the rich.

Hubbard, Glenn, and William Duggan. *The Aid Trap: Hard Truths About Ending Poverty.* New York: Columbia Business School Publishing, 2009. The most effective way to reduce global poverty is to foster business growth in the private sector.

López-Calva, Luis F., and Nora Lustig, eds. *Declining Inequality in Latin America.* Washington, DC: Brookings Institution Press, 2010. Reduced inequality is due partly to the massive expansion of elementary education and government programs that transfer cash to the poor.

Paarlberg, Robert. *Food Politics.* New York: Oxford University Press, 2010. Examines basic issues in agriculture, such as food safety, subsidies, and food prices.

Thurow, Roger. "The Fertile Continent: Africa, Agriculture's Final Frontier," *Foreign Affairs* 89, No. 6 (November/December 2010): 102–110. Africa was essentially excluded from the Green Revolution. With investments in improved seed, fertilizers, and irrigation technologies, Africa could feed itself and the rest of the world.

ENDNOTES

1. "Taking Stock of the World's Plutocrats," *Economist*, 22 January 2011, 4.
2. World Bank, *World Development Report 2003* (New York: Oxford University Press, 2003), 89.
3. Jacob S. Hacker and Paul Pierson, *Winner-Take-All Politics* (New York: Simon and Schuster, 2010).
4. John Micklethwait and Adrian Wooldridge, "The Globalization Backlash," *Foreign Policy* 126 (September/October 2001), 22.
5. David Dollar and Aart Kraay, "Spreading the Wealth," *Foreign Affairs* 81, No. 1 (January/February 2002), 120.
6. Dollar and Kraay, "Spreading the Wealth," 121.
7. Robert Wright, "Will Globalization Make You Happy?" *Foreign Policy* 120 (September/October 2000), 58.
8. Joseph Kahn, "Losing Faith: Globalization Proves Disappointing," *New York Times*, 21 March 2002, 24.
9. Jack Beatty, "Do as We Say, Not as We Do," *The Atlantic Monthly*, February 2002, 24.
10. Vito Tanzi, "Globalization Without a Net," *Foreign Policy* 125 (July/August 2001), 78.
11. David S. Landes, *The Wealth and Poverty of Nations* (New York: W. W. Norton, 1998), 56.
12. Virginia Postrel, "Economic Scene: The Decline of the Muslim Middle East," *New York Times*, 8 November 2001, C2; and Nicholas D. Kristof, "Is Islam the Problem?" *New York Times*, 6 March 2011, A11.
13. UN Development Program, *Human Development Report 1999* (New York: Oxford University Press, 1999), 38; and World Bank, *World Development Report 2003*, 2.
14. "Inequality," *Economist*, 22 January 2011, 71; and Robert Lieberman, "Why the Rich are Are Getting Richer," *Foreign Affairs* 90, No. 1 (January/February 2011), 154.
15. "Tackling Homelessness," *Economist*, 26 June 2010, 36.
16. "Recession and Homelessness," *Economist*, 29 January 2011, 27.
17. "Brazil's Growing Middle Class," *Economist*, 14 November 2009, 16.
18. "The Rights Approach," *Economist*, 20 March 2010, 50.
19. "More Millionaires Than Australians," *Economist*, 22 January 2011, 4.
20. "Under Water," *Economist*, 11 December 2010, 56.
21. Glenn Hubbard and William Duggan, *The Aid Trap* (New York: Columbia Business School Publishing, 2009).
22. "Plagued by Politics," *Economist*, 26 February 2011, 6.
23. Roger Thurow, "The Fertile Continent," *Foreign Affairs* 89, No. 6 (November/December 2010), 103.

CHAPTER
10

Environmental Issues

For indigenous peoples like the Inuit, economic gains from climate change and tapping natural resources like gas and oil will be accompanied by the loss of some parts of their culture. This Inuit hunter and his dogsled

INTRODUCTION

Widespread destruction caused by the earthquake and tsunami in Japan in 2011 reinforced concerns about the environment. Environmental issues remind us that the Earth is a single biosphere and that problems in one country are other countries' problems as well. Imagine that you are a resident of Boston in 1676 and that your cows are grazing the commons, which is land used by the entire community. Overgrazing would eventually destroy the commons and the cattle. But overgrazing is a problem that cannot be solved by restraining only a few members of the community. It is only through the cooperation of all members that overgrazing can be avoided. On a larger scale, environmental problems underscore the reality of global interdependence. Where these problems originate is less important than their global impact. A Soviet nuclear power plant in Chernobyl that exploded in 1986 illustrates this point. The power plant explosion released extensive radioactive material that spread to Europe, killing thirty people, damaging crops and animals, and polluting the environment for thousands of miles from the explosion. When the Fukushima Daiichi nuclear power plant was damaged by the earthquake and tsunami in 2011, small amounts of radiation reached Washington, California, Oregon, and Colorado.

Increasingly, scholars, politicians, leaders of international organizations and nongovernmental organizations (NGOs), and ordinary citizens worldwide are linking environmental security to human security (i.e., the challenges ordinary people face every day) and to traditional concerns about national security. The environmental security approach to international relations emphasizes that the ecological crisis we face is also a threat to national security. Environmental degradation is perceived to be as serious a threat to human societies as the traditional military threat. For the Carteret Islands, Tuvalu, Kiribati, Palau, the Maldives, and Bangladesh, climate change is a direct and growing threat to their survival.[1]

Throughout history, environmental factors have had serious implications for all aspects of human existence, including the rise and fall of great civilizations, the spread of infectious diseases, war and peace, economic prosperity and hunger, migration and resettlement, population growth, and global inequality. The destruction of Mayan civilization on the Yucatan peninsula in southern Mexico in the tenth century shows how climate change and population pressures can dramatically alter human societies. This chapter discusses how environmental problems became central concerns of the global community. It concludes with a case study of the earthquake and tsunami in Japan.

commons ■ Land designated for use by the entire community

Chernobyl ■ Soviet nuclear power plant that suffered a meltdown in 1986

environmental security ■ A concept placing protection of the environment on equal ground with national security

THE GLOBALIZATION OF ENVIRONMENTAL PROBLEMS

Ancient civilizations confronted some of the environmental challenges that are familiar to modern societies. For example, almost 3,700 years ago, Sumerian cities in the southern part of Mesopotamia (now modern Iraq) prospered

Mesopotamia ■ An ancient civilization between the Tigris and Euphrates rivers, now known as Iraq

because high levels of agricultural productivity supported permanent human resettlements. But these agricultural surpluses that helped develop the cradle of civilization came at a cost: extensive irrigation, which ultimately resulted in fields that were saline and waterlogged. Environmental decay forced people to abandon the Sumerian cities. Air pollution from burning coal in medieval England was so bad that by 1661 the naturalist John Evelyn compared London with the "Court of Vulcan or the Suburbs of Hell."[2] Despite obvious environmental problems, the environmental movements did not germinate until 1865, when a private group called the Commons, Footpaths, and Spaces Preservation Society was founded in Britain. By the late 1890s and the turn of the century, groups in the United States that were committed to wilderness preservation and resource conservation emerged, strongly supported by President Theodore Roosevelt.

John Evelyn ■ Naturalist who criticized London for its high levels of pollution

Contemporary ecological challenges differ significantly from those of earlier periods in *four main ways*:

1. Contemporary environmental problems are predominantly global in their cumulative consequences.
2. Whereas our current environmental problems represent biodegenerative products of humanity—such as air and water pollution, deforestation, overfishing, and soil erosion—our ancestors faced environmental constraints that were primarily related to the biophysical parameters of nature, such as access to water, soil fertility, and temperature.
3. Natural forces created environmental problems for our ancestors. Today, however, some populations are more vulnerable to environmental crises principally because of human activities and government policies.
4. Ancient societies had more time and space to deal with environmental threats than we do today.[3]

Globalizing environmental issues is always a gradual, controversial, and complex process. In the past, most attempts to diminish environmental damage were primarily at the local and national levels. Before World War II, concerns about endangered wildlife and growing threats of ocean oil pollution led to bilateral and limited international environmental agreements. The globalization of environmental issues reflects the growth of global interdependence after World War II and the emergence of the United States as a superpower. The global environmental movement emerged principally in Western Europe, the United States, and Canada. A catalyst for growing concerns about how we are destroying our environment, and ultimately ourselves, was the publication of Rachel Carson's book *Silent Spring* in 1962. The book focused on how the widespread use of pesticides was devastating birds and other wildlife. Furthermore, space exploration reinforced perceptions of the oneness of the Earth as well as its fragility. Exploding population growth and rapid industrialization, often with reckless disregard for environmental ramifications, focused more attention on resource scarcity, deforestation, and deteriorating health standards. Nuclear weapons proliferation, especially by the United States and the Soviet Union, also helped to reinforce our vulnerability to environmental threats resulting from our activities.

Silent Spring ■ A book that focused on the negative effects of pesticides

Images of "spaceship Earth" facilitated a deeper understanding of global interdependence of environmental issues by illustrating that national boundaries are artificial and national issues are ultimately global issues. Like our example of the Boston Common, the world was increasingly being perceived as a global common. Oil pollution, because of its immediate and drastic impact on coastal areas, clearly showed the dangers of environmental disasters. When the oil tanker *Torrey Canyon* was wrecked on the coast of England and spilled about 875,000 barrels of crude oil in 1967, public opinion worldwide generated support for globalizing environmental issues. Globalization of the economy further reinforced environmental globalization by stimulating trade in endangered species, tropical hardwoods, and various metals. The production and distribution of chlorofluorocarbons (CFCs) around the world for use as a propellant in spray cans, as a refrigerant, and as cleaning solvents caused significant damage to the protective ozone layer in the Earth's upper atmosphere.[4]

Torrey Canyon ■ Oil tanker that crashed off the coast of England in 1967

International agreements were made in response to specific environmental problems. The earliest ones concentrated on protecting wildlife in Africa and in the Western Hemisphere, Pacific fur seals, and whaling. Ocean oil pollution and the proliferation of nuclear weapons became major priorities of the environmental movement after 1945. The Biosphere Conference, held in Paris in 1968, focused on how human activities—such as air and water pollution, deforestation, the drainage of wetlands, and overgrazing—affected the biosphere. The UN Conference on the Human Environment (also known as Stockholm Conference), held in Stockholm in 1972, is often viewed as the beginning of serious global cooperation on the environment. Developed countries in particular acknowledged that multilateral efforts were essential in order to adequately address transboundary environmental problems.[5] The Stockholm Conference created the United Nations Environmental Program (UNEP), an institutional framework to address the issues discussed in the conference. The 1992 UN Conference on Environment and Development (also known as the Rio Summit or the Earth Summit) and the 2002 World Summit on Sustainable Development (also known as the Johannesburg Action Plan) emphasized priorities of developing countries.

Biosphere Conference ■ Held in 1968; focused on the degradation of the environment from human activities

UN Conference on the Human Environment ■ Held in 1972; aimed at international cooperation in environmental protections

World Summit on Sustainable Development ■ Focused simultaneously on economic growth and environmental protections

States may join international agreements as a way of pressuring neighboring states into doing the same, thereby enhancing chances of widespread cooperation to protect the environment. Domestic political and economic considerations also play a role. Governments often respond to pressure from environmental activists. Industries that must comply with environmental laws in their home countries often support international agreements to prevent companies in other countries from gaining a competitive advantage.[6] Even though states recognize the need to cooperate, *political and economic considerations often weaken the effectiveness of environmental agreements*. These include disagreements between rich and poor countries about the economic implications of environmental agreements and efforts by economic interests and governments to avoid compliance.[7]

The implementation of and compliance with environmental agreements are influenced by at least four factors.[8] First *is the nature of the substances or activities that are regulated*. At the heart of many environmental debates is how international agreements will affect economic activities and the costs and benefits of complying with the agreements. Second *is the characteristics of the agreement.*

This relates to the process of reaching the agreement. Who initiates the treaty? What is required of the countries that sign it? Is the agreement vague, or does it spell out clearly the conditions for compliance? Third *is the global environment*. How major countries, international organizations—such as the World Bank, the United Nations, the World Trade Organization (WTO), and environmental NGOs—view the agreement will impact its implementation. *Fourth are domestic factors*. Ultimately, the effectiveness of an environmental agreement depends on the nature of the society in which it is being implemented.

Nongovernmental Organizations and the Environment

Older environmental groups, such as the National Wildlife Federation and the National Audubon Society, were joined by numerous other environmental organizations, many having originated on college and university campuses in the 1960s and 1970s. The Environmental Defense Fund, the Natural Resources Defense Council, Greenpeace, Environmental Action, and Friends of the Earth were among them. Scientific groups, such as the Union of Concerned Scientists and Physicians for Social Responsibility, strengthened and broadened the environmental movement. While most environmental groups operate on a local or national level and concentrate on specific problems facing particular communities, many of them have a global reach. For example, many NGOs participate in global conferences on behalf of small, ecologically vulnerable islands of the Pacific. There are also NGOs—such as the Global Climate Coalition and the Alliance for Responsible CFC Policy—that represent industries and attempt to limit the effectiveness of other environmental organizations.

Women and the Environment

Green Belt Movement
■ Kenyan movement focusing on preventing further deforestation

The connection between women and environmental issues is acknowledged by UNEP, which has held conferences on women and the environment and established a committee of senior women advisers on sustainable development. The general emphasis on the gendered nature of environmental issues arises from the leading roles women have in environmental NGOs and numerous grassroots movements worldwide. Women in Kenya organized the Green Belt Movement to prevent further deforestation and to restore the land through reforestation. Wangari Maathai, an environmentalist involved in the planting of more than 30 million trees, was awarded the Nobel Peace Prize for her work. Women's participation in environmental NGOs and at the grassroots level has resulted in *three main arguments about the connection between women and the environment*: (1) women are disproportionately disadvantaged by environmental problems, (2) gender bias is an impediment to achieving sustainable development, and (3) women's participation is vital to efforts to achieve sustainable development.[9]

Indigenous Peoples and the Environment

Global warming is melting sea ice in the Arctic Ocean, and the ice cap in Greenland is receding. It is estimated that the Arctic contains 90 billion barrels of oil and 12 trillion cubic feet of gas. That can be exploited because of thinning ice. For the

Inuit and other indigenous peoples, who comprise the vast majority of that area's population, climate change has both positive and negative consequences. Income from natural resources could make them wealthy. The loss of pack ice extends shipping, and fish stocks are increasing. On the other hand, rising sea levels are forcing many of them to leave their homes, and melting permafrost is damaging roads and runways. Furthermore, economic gains will be accompanied by the loss of some aspects of their culture.

Because the lives of indigenous peoples are intertwined with the natural environment, development in general has far-reaching consequences for them. Indigenous populations have declined sharply, and most of their land has been confiscated. Ironically, some environmentalists are so focused on protecting the animals of the forest that they contribute to the destruction of the people who have lived there for thousands of years. For example, when the Bwindi Impenetrable Forest in the Great Lakes region of East Africa was made into a national park to protect its mountain gorillas, an estimated four thousand indigenous people were expelled. Like many indigenous people throughout the world, they are poor, alcohol abuse is prevalent, and life expectancy is low. They are losing their language, religion, and culture.

Deforestation in the Amazon has long been a major global issue for environmentalists and others concerned about indigenous people. Brazil's rapid agricultural growth, in particular, and development, in general, came at an extremely high cost to the inhabitants of the Amazon. Indigenous people in Bolivia protested the construction of a Brazilian-funded road through a rainforest reserve because of the deforestation and illegal settlement it would bring. After the protesters' two-month march from their Amazon lowlands home to Bolivia's capital, Bolivian President Evo Morales, the country's first indigenous president, canceled plans for the road. Global efforts to diminish carbon emissions through forest preservation are helping indigenous peoples. Reducing Emissions from Deforestation and Degradation (REDD) programs, which pay people to preserve forests, could potentially improve the lives of indigenous peoples.[10]

Strategies Used by Nongovernmental Organizations

At the global level, NGOs must spend considerable resources to develop regimes: that is, the rules, codes of conduct, principles, and norms necessary to govern the behavior of both states and nonstate actors. Environmental NGOs that operate primarily on the global level encounter *three major impediments*. First, there is no common authority or power that can effectively force members of the global community to comply with rules. Second, the decentralized nature of international bureaucracies and their dependence on states make it difficult for NGOs to get international rules implemented. Third, global agreements and organizations are primarily produced by governments. Environmental NGOs are required in many cases to work through those governments to influence agreements and global institutions. There are *several major strategies* that environmental NGOs use to accomplish their objectives:

1. Get media coverage and publicity for their issues. Generating domestic and global public awareness and support is crucial to NGOs' efforts to persuade policymakers to take action.

regimes ■ Rules for governing state and nonstate actors

2. Share information among groups in order to educate each other on the issues, coordinate strategies and activities, and provide each other with needed support.
3. Lobby government officials and intergovernmental organizations, such as the World Bank.
4. Acquire and manage property to protect the environment.
5. Pressure companies to protect the environment.

BIODIVERSITY

biodiversity ■ The large number and diversity of organisms on Earth

Biodiversity is defined as the number and the variety of living organisms on Earth. It includes genetic diversity, species diversity, and ecosystem diversity. Crucial to biodiversity is the interdependence of species and ecosystems and how their complex relationships affect the environment. Biodiversity is concentrated in the forests of developing countries, especially Brazil, China, Colombia, Ecuador, India, Indonesia, Madagascar, Zaire, Peru, Mexico, Costa Rica, and Malaysia. Australia is the only developed country that has a large variety of species. The United States, Canada, and Europe are relatively poor in biodiversity. Biodiversity is at the heart of environmental globalization because it affects so many groups and individuals, including those interested in deforestation, agriculture, biotechnology, anthropology, pharmaceuticals, sustainable development, global trade, and ethics.

Biodiversity provides many benefits. Ecosystem functions—such as carbon exchange, watershed flows of surface and ground water, the protection and fertility of soils, and the regulation of surface temperatures and local climates—are influenced by biodiversity. Diversity lessens the vulnerability of agricultural crops to diseases and pests. This is increasingly important for large-scale, specialized agriculture. Through crossbreeding of diverse genetic stock, crops become more resistant to disease and pests. Biodiversity is especially important for medicinal and pharmaceutical product development. Preserving biodiversity is regarded as an ethical obligation. The basis of the ethical argument is that biodiversity is an intrinsic value and people should avoid destroying other species. The destruction of rain forests in Brazil, for example, directly affects biodiversity, especially since Brazil alone contains almost 25 percent of the world's plant species. Perhaps the most widespread causes of damage to biodiversity are pollution and global environmental change. Because the economic benefits derived from biodiversity, especially involving pharmaceuticals, are significant and potential benefits are even greater, governments are imposing strict controls on medicinal plants. In 2002, the Group of Allied Mega-Biodiverse Nations was created to certify the legal possession of biological material and to negotiate terms to transfer it.

Convention on Biological Diversity ■ Designed to establish an international regime to protect biodiversity

Developed countries attempted to reduce the destruction of the world's biodiversity by calling for the establishment of an international regime. Negotiations for such a regime, known as the Convention on Biological Diversity, began in 1991. Whereas the developed countries viewed genetic resources as belonging to all, as common heritage, developing countries saw these resources as national resources. The rich countries of the North wanted unimpeded access to these resources, particularly for their pharmaceutical and agricultural resources. The poor countries of the South wanted to control genetic resources to derive economic benefits from

North/South Divide ■ Refers to the large economic divide between many Northern and Southern states

them. The Convention on Biological Diversity provides for (1) national identification and monitoring of biological diversity, (2) the development of national strategies and programs for conserving biological diversity, (3) environmental assessment procedures to take into account the effects of projects on biological diversity, (4) sharing of research findings in a fair and equitable way, (5) the provision of technology for the conservation and use of genetic resources by the industrial countries, and (6) the facilitation of participation in biotechnology research by countries that provide genetic resources. The UN Climate Conference in Cancun, Mexico, in 2010 contributed to the preservation of biodiversity by providing monetary rewards for countries to preserve their forests under a program known as Reduced Emissions from Deforestation and Degradation (REDD).[11]

Endangered Species and Wildlife Protection

Many governments, environmental NGOs, and most Americans oppose whale hunting and eating whales—especially after Greenpeace's successful campaign, "Save the Whales." In Japan, however, eating whales is viewed as part of the national culture, especially by older Japanese who survived on whale meat provided by the government after World War II. Whales have received widespread attention partly because of the popularity of *Moby-Dick*, a book by Herman Melville about the whaling industry in the first half of the nineteenth century. At that time, Americans sailed the Pacific for up to four years at a time searching for whales. They returned to America with great wealth, since whales provided oil for lubricating industrial machinery and for making soap and margarine, baleen for manufacturing corsets and umbrellas, and food. Whaling was also important for making glycerin, which was an essential component in nitroglycerin that was used in manufacturing dynamite. Military competition among European countries and the outbreak of World War I created a great demand for glycerin. This, in turn, led to an expansion and intensification of whaling. The development of the harpoon cannon between 1864 and 1868 and the invention of factory ships that could process whales at sea hastened the depletion of whales.[12]

One of the earliest attempts by the international community to prevent the decline and extinction of whales, especially the widely hunted blue whale, came in 1935 when the League of Nations tried to regulate their exploitation. By 1946, the International Convention for the Regulation of Whaling, called for by nations involved in the whaling industry, established the International Whaling Commission (IWC) to protect the price of whale oil. For the most part, whales remained unprotected until 1964, when the IWC specifically advocated for the preservation of humpback whales. Blue whales were designated as a protected species a year later. The 1975 Convention on International Trade in Endangered Species of Wild Fauna and Flora (CITES) effectively prohibited trade in whale products. By 1982, the IWC had agreed to a moratorium on whaling, except whaling done by the Inuit of Alaska and Canada, whose diet and culture depended on hunting whales. An exception was also made for catching whales for scientific purposes, a provision that provides a loophole for Japan to continue harvesting a limited number of whales for consumption. In 1986, the moratorium came into effect, and in 1994, the IWC created a whaling sanctuary in the Southern Atlantic and Antarctica.[13]

IWC ■ Established to protect the price of whale oil

CITES ■ Convention prohibiting trade in whale products

However, in 2006, Japan was able to secure a majority on the IWC, a development that facilitated Japan's resumption of commercial whaling. Japan escalated its whaling activities. However, in 2011, Japan's annual whale hunt in the Antarctic Ocean was terminated early when the Sea Shepherd Conservation Society, an environmental group, prevented the Japanese from killing whales. Another major threat to whales that is receiving more attention is ships and boats. Many whales are killed or wounded in collisions with oceangoing vessels.

Dolphins, considered an endangered species, especially by the United States, are widely regarded as having human-like qualities. Environmental campaigns, movies and other media, and aquariums have strengthened the perception of dolphins as friendly creatures that must be protected. Threats to dolphins were a by-product of fishing with purse seine nets for tuna that schooled beneath the dolphins. Many dolphins drowned or were severely injured in the nets. Global environmental NGOs pressured consumers to boycott tuna that was caught in such nets. Because the United States is the world's largest market for tuna, environmentalists in America used the power of consumers to force tuna producers to adopt dolphin-safe measures for catching tuna. The Inter-American Tropical Tuna Commission (IATTC), under American leadership, adopted regulations to prevent the endangerment of dolphins, a development that has helped to protect dolphins globally.[14]

IATTC ■
Commission devoted to protecting dolphins, among other things

Sea turtles are also listed as an endangered or threatened species under the U.S. Endangered Species Act. While overfishing of turtles and harvesting their eggs continue to be serious concerns, one major threat to turtles comes from shrimp trawlers. Turtles caught in shrimp nets usually drown. To eliminate this problem, the U.S. government required shrimp trawlers to use turtle extruder devices (TEDs) on their nets. Essentially, these devices are trap doors through which turtles can escape if caught in the net. Apart from arguing that TEDs were a financial burden and that they were losing almost half of the shrimp they caught, shrimp fishers pointed out that foreign fleets did not face similar restrictions, a fact that put U.S. shrimpers at a competitive disadvantage.[15] American environmentalists ultimately succeeded in getting foreign shrimpers to comply with U.S. laws protecting turtles by agreeing with domestic shrimpers that all shrimpers should play by the same rules to ensure fair competition. Another threat to endangered turtles—especially the leatherback turtle, which can weigh up to 1,400 pounds and grow to a length of 7 feet—comes from long-line fishing. Long-line fishing involves a main line that can be as long as 30 miles. The line has branch lines that are roughly 200 feet apart and are equipped with baited hooks. Some turtles swallow the hooks or become entangled in the lines.

The African elephant, hunted mostly for ivory tusks for export, is also an endangered species, a designation that drew opposition from some countries, such as Botswana, Malawi, Mozambique, South African Zambia, and Zimbabwe. These countries had carefully managed their elephant herds and believed that restrictions on ivory exports would unfairly penalize them economically. Compared with African states that depleted their elephant herds, Botswana and the other countries had too many elephants. Other animals in peril are gorillas, chimpanzees, and rhinoceros. Roughly 80 percent of the world's go-rillas and most of its chimpanzees inhabit Gabon and the Republic of Congo. These great apes, our closest relatives, face severe threats from hunting, defor-estation, and infectious diseases. The ongoing violence and endemic poverty in Congo continue to contribute to their destruction. In China, Southeast Asia, and elsewhere, rhinoceros horns are believed to have medicinal and aphrodisiac qualities, a belief that makes them more valuable than gold. Consequently, many rhinos are killed illegally for their horns.[16] Worldwide, rare and exotic animals are threatened with extinction because of escalating exotic animal trade in them, aided by the Internet and a global network of traffickers.

DEFORESTATION

One of the principal threats to biodiversity is the accelerating rate of global deforesta-tion. The Amazon rainforest is estimated to be disappearing at the rate of 3 million acres a year. The Congo Basin—comprised of Cameroon, Gabon, the Central Afri-can Republic, Republic of Congo, the Democratic Republic of Congo (former Zaire), and Equatorial Guinea, which had the second largest tropical forests in the world—is losing about 8.9 million acres a year to deforestation. Similarly, Russia, which has roughly 22 percent of the world's forests, is depleting its natural forests. Defores-tation is also a major concern in many parts of Asia, especially in light of China's rapid economic growth and its demand for forest products.[17] Forests are essential in biodiversity and to preserve the quality of life, and life itself, for human beings. For-ests, especially large rain forests such as the Amazon, have an impact on the global climate. Air quality, water supplies, climate stability, agricultural productivity, and countless human communities are affected by deforestation. It is widely believed that protecting existing forests and planting more trees are essential to diminishing some environmental problems, such as global warming and climate change, because forests soak up between 10 and 20 percent of the heat-trapping carbon dioxide released by industrial smokestacks and automobiles.

Congo Basin ■
Tropical area in central Africa

Causes of Deforestation

The most pervasive cause of deforestation is the combination of *population pres-sures and poverty*. Throughout most of the world, poor people rely on forests for fuel, shelter, agricultural land, and grazing for their animals. The relationship between population pressure, poverty, and deforestation is demonstrated by devel-opments in Chiapas, the poorest state in Mexico. Destitute villagers in hundreds of communities in Chiapas cut down trees and burn the undergrowth to create fields for cultivation and grazing cattle. Soon after, the thin layer of topsoil is planted with corn, and the land is left to return to pasture, which is often overgrazed. The exposed soil becomes vulnerable to erosion during heavy tropical rains. Somalia, on the Horn of Africa, provides another example of how poverty accelerates de-forestation. Somalia, which lacks an effective central governmental authority to protect the environment, exports tons of charcoal to Middle Eastern countries.

Chiapas ■
The poorest state in Mexico

selective logging ■ Cutting specific trees in order to promote forest sustainability

Deforestation is also caused by the *deliberate setting of fires* by small farmers, commercial farmers, cattle ranchers, logging companies, and governments. Selective logging involves cutting down large and particular types of trees in an effort to manage exploitation of forest resources and to promote sustainability. Selective logging contributes to forest fires because as forests are thinned out, humidity decreases, and drier conditions in the forest facilitate the spread of both natural and human-made fires. The forces of *economic development* play a significant role in global deforestation. Development involves building an extensive infrastructure, which includes roads, highways, electrical plants, airports, harbors, railways, large reservoirs, and dams. Another cause of deforestation is the commercial logging practices that disregard sustainable development of forest resources. The demand for tropical hardwoods, such as mahogany and teak, is contributing to deforestation in Southeast Asia, Central America, Africa, and elsewhere in the developing world. *Government policies* have aggressively promoted deforestation in an effort to relocate people to less crowded areas in order to diminish population pressures and encourage economic development. Brazil has used this strategy. Opening up the Amazon was viewed in Brazil as important for national economic growth as well as a way to strengthen the country's strategic position in South America. Environmental protection was not a priority of the military governments that ruled Brazil. Consequently, between 1970 and 1974, the government implemented its Plan for National Integration. This plan included the construction of the Trans-Amazon Highway and offered incentives to agribusiness enterprises and landless peasants, especially from the northeast, to encourage them to settle in the Amazon.

infrastructure ■ Necessary elements of a stable society

commercial logging ■ Process disrupting sustainable development

Plan for National Integration ■ Brazil's efforts to encourage the development of the Amazon

Efforts to Prevent Deforestation

In Brazil, the transition from military rule to democracy has been accompanied by government programs aimed at halting deforestation. The Brazilian government's perception of the environment has shifted from frontier development toward environmental protection. This change is partly due to growing global awareness of the Amazon's importance to environmental health and increased global and domestic pressures for change. It is also a result of Brazil's emphasis on using scientific techniques to greatly improve agricultural production, thereby diminishing the need to cultivate more land. In 1989, the Brazilian government announced the development of its Nossa Natureza (Our Nature) Program to reduce the destruction of the Amazon rain forests. The program included (1) suspending fiscal incentives for developing forest resources, (2) limiting log exports, (3) creating national parks, and (4) increasing the emphasis on environmental protection and research. An important component of this effort was the formation of IBAMA, the federal environmental protection agency, to monitor environment problems and to enforce environmental laws. Brazil continues to implement measures to prevent deforestation. Efforts such as REDD, discussed earlier, also are helping restore forests.[18] Another example of government involvement in efforts to diminish deforestation is the agreement reached in 2000 by logging companies, the government of Gabon, and several environmental NGOs to preserve 1,900 square miles of forests that comprise Gabon's Lope Reserve. This area contains very valuable trees and the highest density of large animals, including elephants and gorillas, ever recorded in a tropical rain forest.

Nossa Natureza Program ■ Designed to reduce the destruction of the Amazon

IBAMA ■ Brazilian environmental protection agency

Gabon's Lope Reserve ■ Area in Gabon containing rich biodiversity

One of the most successful grassroots reforestation efforts is by the Green Belt Movement of Kenya. Its objectives include (1) *raising awareness* of the connection between the environment and poverty; (2) *promoting the planting of multiuse trees* to meet fuel needs, provide employment, protect the environment, and provide food for the community; and (3) *disseminating information* on environmental protection through research, seminars, and workshops.

Another approach to addressing the problem of deforestation is forest certification. The basic idea is to inform consumers about the origin of wood products and how their production affects the environment. This approach, which aims to promote eco-friendly lumber, has been championed by the Forest Stewardship Council, a coalition of environmentalists and lumber executives. The guidelines for gaining certification include complying with national laws aimed at (1) protecting forests, (2) protecting the rights of indigenous peoples, and (3) promoting economic development. Similar efforts have been made by Greenpeace in Indonesia to preserve the forests from companies such as Unilever and Kraft that produce palm oil, used in many consumer products. Palm oil production endangers wildlife and releases carbon dioxide as forests and peatlands are destroyed. Greenpeace pressures companies and their suppliers to implement environmentally sustainable practices.

forest certification ■ Required in order to protect against deforestation

Forest Stewardship Council ■ Group of environmentalists and lumber companies dedicated to protecting forests

Ocean Resources—Fishing

Concerned about proper nutrition, more people around the world—especially in Europe, Canada, and the United States—are eating more seafood. The modernization of fishing fleets has made more fish available to global markets. This modernization involves using technology such as electronic fish locators, satellite navigation, temperature depth gauges, purse-seine nets, and long-line fishing gear. More than any other food commodity, seafood crosses national boundaries daily. Most fish are exported from Africa and Southeast Asia to Europe and the United States.

Fish remained abundant throughout much of the world until relatively recently. John Cabot, the fifteenth-century explorer, claimed that cod were so abundant off the coast of Newfoundland, Canada, that he caught them simply by putting a bucket over the side of his ship. The cod fishing grounds in that area supported the fishing fleets of the United States and Canada for hundreds of years after John Cabot was there. By 1992, however, the cod had essentially disappeared. A ban on cod fishing, imposed to rejuvenate the stock, appeared to be futile. There are numerous examples of overfishing and the eventual collapse of fisheries. California's sardine industry, popularized by John Steinbeck, declined rapidly in the early 1940s and died out three decades later. Faced with declining catches of fish, communities have historically attempted to regulate fishing. Countries that share North Sea fisheries have been very aware of the dangers of overfishing and have tried to adopt measures to limit the problem. Coastal states with rich fishing grounds often clash with countries that support long-distance fishing fleets. To protect their resources, coastal states successfully pushed for the establishment of exclusive economic zones, which extend to 200 miles and over which coastal states exercise jurisdiction. These sovereign rights of coastal areas are recognized by the Law of the Sea Treaty. However, many poor countries, especially in Africa, are unable to protect their fisheries from exploitation by foreign

exclusive economic zones ■ Coastal waters exclusive to each state

Law of the Sea Treaty ■ Recognizes state rights over territorial coastal waters

commercial fishing fleets. The UN Food and Agriculture Organization Committee on Fisheries attempted to mobilize global support for reducing overcapacity in the fishing industry by adopting the International Plan for the Management of Fishing Capacity (IPMFC). But this is a nonbinding agreement. Most states have few incentives to comply with it. Another approach to protecting global fisheries is boycotting restaurants that serve fish that are being severely depleted. For example, there is growing controversy over the depletion of sharks. Many restaurants are pressured to refrain from serving shark in order to conserve those fish.[19]

IPMFC ■ FAO plan to reduce overcapacity in the fishing industry

OCEAN POLLUTION

Long perceived as an almost bottomless sink, the seas have been used as dumping grounds for centuries. Major oil spills, rapid development of coastal areas, increased use of petroleum products, the dramatic increase in shipping to meet demands for global trade, and economic globalization and the rise of leisure travel on cruise ships, among other factors, have contributed to significant increases in the pollution of the oceans by oil. Oil spills by tankers, such as the one caused by the *Exxon Valdez* in 1989 off the Alaskan Coast, often generate a sense of urgency about actions to prevent ocean pollution. The massive oil spill in the Gulf of Mexico in 2010, caused by an accident on the Deepwater Horizon rig operated by BP, attracted global attention.

Exxon Valdez ■ Oil tanker that spilled off the coast of Alaska

What are the environmental, economic, and political implications of BP's 2010 oil spill in the Gulf of Mexico, the largest oil spill in American history?

The toxic and carcinogenic properties of petroleum and the damage it causes to sea life, most of which is immobilized when soaked with oil, are the most obvious negative effects of oil spills. But the longer oil remains on the surface of the oceans, the more it blocks sunrays and oxygen essential for the health and survival of marine life. When an Ecuadorian tanker spilled 243,000 gallons of diesel and bunker fuel in the Galapagos Islands, located about 600 miles off the Pacific Coast of South America, there was global concern about the impact of the spill on the environment. Apart from the economic consequences, environmentalists, scientists, and others worried about the effects of oil pollution on the species of marine iguanas, giant tortoises, and penguins that are found nowhere else. The unusual diversity of wildlife in the Galapagos Islands was popularized by Charles Darwin, who visited the area in 1835 and developed his theory of natural selection.

Charles Darwin ■
The leading proponent of evolution theory

natural selection ■
A prevalent theory regarding the evolution of plant and animal species

Although major oil spills receive global attention, these accidents account for around 20 percent of global oil pollution at sea. Far more damaging is pollution caused by the deliberate dumping of oil used in shipping operations in the oceans. Oil tankers, container ships, and cruise ships, for example, use ballast water, which is sea water that is pumped into the bottom of the ship to keep it stable when it is not loaded with cargo. Because cargo serves as ballast, ballast water is pumped out when a ship is being loaded. Ballast water is often contaminated by oil.

The most important source of marine oil pollution is from land-based activities in which most of us engage. As your car drips oil onto the driveway, the streets, and the parking lot, you are likely to think of it as a minor inconvenience. Small amounts of oil from your outboard motorboat and jet skis are responsible for roughly 70 percent of marine pollution. These tiny amounts of oil are washed into lakes, streams, and rivers and eventually make their way to the sea, where they damage coastal ecosystems and marine life far beyond the coasts. Oil spills have influenced the development of international law on environmental pollution. The first significant international agreement aimed at reducing ocean pollution was the International Convention for the Prevention of Pollution of the Sea (ICPS) by Oil in 1954. The 1973 International Convention for the Prevention of Pollution by Ships (ICPPS) limited the amount of discharges from both land and sea for specific pollutants, including oil.

ICPS ■ First international agreement aimed at reducing ocean pollution

ICPPS ■ Limited the discharge amounts of land and sea pollutants

GLOBAL WARMING AND CLIMATE CHANGE

There is a consensus among scientists that greenhouse gases are altering the atmosphere in ways that ultimately contribute to climate change and higher temperatures. The basic assumption is that human activities are the main causes of these climatic developments. But determining human influence on global warming and climate change is complicated by a relative lack of accurate information about climate change over past centuries. Historically, climate has varied significantly. Natural forces such as volcanic eruptions can create climate changes, as was evidenced by the eruption of Mount Pinatubo in the Philippines in 1991. Ocean currents also change temperatures. Apart from greenhouse gases, factors such as deforestation, urbanization, and agricultural activities also affect the climate.

Mount Pinatubo ■
Erupted in the Philippines in 1991

When our ancestors discovered how to make fire and how to use it, they set into motion a chain of events that would ultimately alter their environment and ours. However, it was the Industrial Revolution that marked a radical step toward the current problems of global warming and climate change because of its use of massive amounts of fossil fuels—coal, oil, and natural gas. More than a hundred years ago, Svante Arrhenius, a Swedish chemist, and T. C. Chamberlain, an American geologist, independently discovered that industrialization could lead to increasing levels of carbon dioxide in the atmosphere. This could ultimately raise the atmosphere's temperature by trapping solar radiation that would otherwise be reflected back into space, creating a greenhouse effect. The U.S. government issued a report in 1965 that raised concerns about global warming and climate change. However, national security during the Cold War took precedence over more distant threats such as environmental problems. Congress, under the leadership of Representative Al Gore, held hearings in the early 1980s on global warming. In 1988, after National Aeronautics and Space Administration (NASA) scientist James Hansen told Congress that he was 99 percent certain that the greenhouse effect had been detected and that it was already changing our climate, Congress established the U.S. Global Change Research Program (USGCRP) to study human-induced climate change and stratospheric ozone depletion from industrial emissions.[20] Tables 10.1 and 10.2 show the implications of global warming and regional climate change, respectively. Unprecedented devastating floods in places such as Pakistan, Brazil, Thailand, and Australia are widely viewed as evidence of environmental consequences of climate change.

Acid rain and ozone depletion preceded global awareness and concern about global warming. Air pollution from Europe's industrial societies, especially Britain and Germany, was identified by Svante Oden, a Swedish scientist, as a leading cause of the increasing acidification of precipitation, known as acid rain, in the Scandinavian countries in the late 1960s. Acid rain caused by industrial activities in the United States was also a major concern for Canada, where more than sixteen thousand lakes were affected. Acid rain, composed of sulfur dioxide, nitrogen oxide, and volatile organic compounds, is caused primarily by burning coal. By increasing the acidity of lakes, rivers, and streams, acid rain damages animal and plant life. It has also destroyed buildings in Greece, Italy, and other parts of Europe. Ozone depletion was also identified as a serious environmental problem resulting from air pollution. The ozone layer of our atmosphere protects us from ultraviolet (UV) radiation that causes skin cancers, genetic changes in animals and plants, eye disorders, and suppression of our immune systems. Agricultural productivity and fisheries are also affected. Ozone depletion is most severe in Antarctica and the Northern Hemisphere. The major cause of ozone depletion was discovered to be CFCs, synthetic products developed by DuPont and used in a wide range of products, including air conditioning, refrigeration, foam packaging, and aerosols. CFCs, when released into the atmosphere, react with UV light to form chlorine. It is this chlorine that destroys the ozone.

Reductions in the production of greenhouse gases are widely perceived to be the solution to diminishing global warming and climate change and their effects. The Kyoto Protocol to the UN Framework Convention on Climate Change, generally known as the Kyoto Protocol, is clearly the most important global

greenhouse effect ■
Rise in Earth's temperature from greenhouse gases

USGCRP ■
Established to study ozone depletion and the greenhouse effect

acid rain ■
Toxic rain caused by industrial activities

ozone layer ■
Layer of atmosphere blocking UV radiation

CFCs ■ Synthetic products causing ozone depletion

Kyoto Protocol ■
International agreement on reducing carbon dioxide emissions

TABLE 10.1

Global Warming

Effects of Global Warming	Implications	Areas Most Affected
Floods	• Rising sea levels and heavy rains could displace millions of people and leave many areas under water.	Coastal United States, Australia, Pacific Islands, Holland, Philippines, Bangladesh, China, Mozambique, Nigeria
	• More refugees	
Heat Waves	• Increase in deaths from heatstroke, forest fires, and skin cancer	Southern Europe, United States, China, Brazil, Indonesia, Russia
Diseases	• Warmer, wetter weather could increase insect-transmitted and water-borne illnesses.	United States, Central, and South America, Africa, Asia
Coral Bleaching	• Depleted fisheries coastal flooding	Caribbean, Australia, Philippines, India
Pollution	• Coastal flooding	
Drought	• Decline of tourism	
	• More respiratory problems, cancer, lung and heart diseases	United States, Mexico, India, China, Egypt, Russia
	• Crop failure	United States, Mexico, Brazil, China, India, Africa, Middle East, Spain
	• Malnutrition	
	• Forest fires	
	• Water-related conflicts	

Sources: U.S. News and World Report 2011, "10 Ways Global Warming Could Hurt Your Health," http://health.usnews.com/health-news/ (accessed 29 April 2011); and "WWF—Impacts of global warming on corals," http://wwf.panda.org/about_our_earth/aboutcc/problems/impacts/coral_reefs/ (accessed 29 April 2011).

environmental agreement and reflects an increasing awareness of environmental globalization. But economic, scientific, and ideological disagreements have weakened the Kyoto Protocol's effectiveness. The United States, the leading producer of greenhouse gases, opposed the agreement on the grounds that the imposition of emission controls would be detrimental to the American economy. India and China are also responsible for significant shares of global carbon dioxide emissions. Developing countries that are energy exporters give *four main reasons* for opposing global efforts to reduce emissions: (1) emission controls will reduce their revenues by decreasing energy consumption, (2) imports from industrialized countries would be more expensive because of measures taken to reduce carbon dioxide emissions, (3) the development of new fuels to help cut down emissions is likely to reduce demand for their exports, and (4) oil, gas, and coal resources are

TABLE 10.2

Regional Climate Change in the United States

Region	Likely Climate Changes
Northeast	Decline in winter weather extremes; more flooding; hotter summers; changes in forest species
Southeast	Rising sea levels; disappearance of some coastal wetlands, barrier islands, and beaches; increase in water quality problems
Great Lakes	Declining water levels due to increased evaporation; increased transportation and shoreline problems due to lower water levels; warmer weather will keep shipping lanes open longer
Midwest–Great Plains	Extreme summer heat; milder winters; longer growing season; heavier rainfall; flash flooding; more droughts
Mountain West	Warmer winters; less snow; water problems; drier mountain regions; loss of mountain ecosystems
Southwest	Increased moisture; increased crop diversity; more flooding and fire risks; changes in desert ecosystem
Northwest–Alaska	Warmer water temperatures in the Pacific could cause salmon to migrate northward; more rain in summer; rising sea levels; warmer weather in Alaska will increase permafrost thawing and damage roads and buildings; warmer weather will keep shipping lanes open longer.

Sources: *guardian.co.uk*, "Carbon levels hit new peak, research shows," http://www.guardian.co.uk/environment/2011/may/31/carbon-levels-peak (accessed 31 May 2011); and "A Warming Planet Struggles to Feed Itself," *New York Times*, 5 June 2011, A1.

part of their heritage. Following the ratification of the Kyoto Protocol by more than ninety-six countries, many developing countries supported the Delhi Ministerial Declaration on Climate Change and Sustainable Development, which supports the right of poor countries to develop their own appropriate strategies to reduce carbon dioxide emissions. This position was endorsed by the United States. After meeting in Copenhagen in 2009, the United Nations Framework Convention on Climate Change was held in Cancun, Mexico, in 2010. The new agreement provides funds for developing countries to reduce emissions and deforestation under the REDD program.[21]

Table 10.3 shows carbon dioxide emissions for selected countries. The Kyoto Protocol allows countries to use market forces to reduce carbon dioxide emissions. Targets are determined for lower levels of emissions, and then permits are issued for that set level. Companies that exceed their target by not producing so much pollution can sell extra permits to companies that need to meet their targets. This approach is referred to as emissions trading, or cap-and-trade. Many European countries use this approach. Britain and Denmark, for example, trade greenhouse gases to reduce climate change. The Chicago Climate Exchange is the first attempt to decrease greenhouse gases through a market approach. Another approach, favored by the United States, is to rely primarily on forests to reduce the effects

emissions trading ■ Trading of greenhouse gases to reduce climate change

Chicago Climate Exchange ■ Attempts to decrease greenhouse gases through a market approach

TABLE 10.3

Top Twenty Countries in Carbon Dioxide Emissions (2008)

Per Capita Emissions (in tons/capita)

Country	Total Emissions (Million Metric Tons of CO_2)	Per Capita Emissions (Tons/Capita)
1. China	6534	4.91
2. United States	5833	19.18
3. Russia	1729	12.29
4. India	1495	1.31
5. Japan	1214	9.54
6. Germany	829	10.06
7. Canada	574	17.27
8. United Kingdom	572	9.38
9. South Korea	542	11.21
10. Iran	511	7.76
11. Saudi Arabia	466	16.56
12. Italy	455	7.82
13. South Africa	451	9.25
14. Mexico	445	4.04
15. Australia	437	20.82
16. Indonesia	434	1.83
17. Brazil	428	2.18
18. France	415	6.48
19. Spain	359	8.86
20. Ukraine	350	7.61

Data from Energy Information Agency 2008

Source: Union of Concerned Scientists, "Global Warming: Each Country's Share of CO_2 Emissions," http://www.ucsusa.org/global_warming/science_and_impacts/science/each-countrys-share-of-co2.html (accessed 29 April 2011).

of emissions from industries and automobiles. But the long-term effectiveness of using forests instead of taking other major steps to reduce greenhouse gases is debatable.[22]

WATER SCARCITY

At the foundation of human existence and life on Earth is water. The most common and abundant liquid in the world, water is at the heart of global environmental issues. Water, particularly potable water, is fueling conflicts globally. Increasing demands for water by the world's growing and increasingly more affluent populations threaten to create widespread shortages of freshwater. Water, in many ways, defines how we live and determines the limit of sustainable development. Imagine life without adequate water. Think of all the adjustments you would have to make just to survive. Parts of the United States—especially Arizona, Colorado, Utah, Nevada, and Wyoming—experience severe water shortages. Tensions routinely flare up between the United States and Mexico over water rights to the Rio Grande and the Colorado rivers. There are disputes between India and Pakistan over the Ganges and Brahmaputra rivers, between China and neighboring Southeast Asian states over the Mekong River, and between Egypt and Ethiopia over the Nile River. Increasing urbanization, industrialization, and the environmental problems we have discussed are likely to accelerate these problems. Southern Europe, Australia, South Korea, China, and parts of Africa are experiencing severe water shortages. India faces severe water problems that seriously threaten to undermine its economic growth and public health. Nearly one billion people do not have safe drinking water.[23]

water scarcity ■
A lack of secure, uninterrupted, long-term availability of adequate clean freshwater

Water scarcity—defined as a lack of secure, uninterrupted, and long-term availability of adequate amounts of freshwater of required quality—is becoming an important component of the broader issues of environmental and global security. As we saw in Chapter 1, security issues go beyond traditional military threats. When a country that is extremely dependent on water coming from rivers or streams in another country perceives that its supplies are threatened, it could use military force to resolve the problem. For example, when Lebanon decided to begin pumping water from the Wazzani Springs in late 2002, tensions with Israel intensified. The Wazzani Springs supply the Hasbani River, which is a tributary of the Jordan River. Israel depends on the Jordan River for water. Concerned about tensions over water erupting into war, the United States dispatched a water expert from the U.S. Department of State to try to resolve the conflict. The struggle to control water supplies is an important component of the Palestinian-Israeli conflict. Rapid population growth and more opulent lifestyles put great pressure on water in an area with some of the world's lowest supplies of water per capita. While Israel controls water supplies in Palestinian lands, and Israeli settlers in Palestinian territories have water for sprinklers and swimming pools, Palestinian water supplies are controlled by Israel and are severely restricted and polluted. In coastal areas and on islands worldwide, rising seawater, due in part to global warming, is likely to contaminate freshwater supplies. In Indonesia, Vietnam, and other parts of Southeast Asia, rising seawater is creating numerous problems, including reduced rice harvests and the relocation of millions of people.

MILITARY ACTIVITIES AND THE ENVIRONMENT

From the beginning of civilization, our ancestors have enlisted the environment in their conflicts, with destruction of the environment being the inevitable outcome. The Romans sowed salt on Carthaginian farms during the Third Punic War (149–146 B.C.), thereby destroying the land's agricultural productivity. Water supplies have been contaminated, infectious diseases inflicted on the enemy, and forests destroyed to make war and as a consequence of war. Bombs remain unexploded in fields around the world. The preoccupation with the survival of the state, to be achieved by developing lethal military weapons, relegated environmental concerns to the back burner. But growing environmental awareness and increased activism have heightened concerns about the impact of military activities on the ecosystems. Environmental damage caused by war and training for war is increasingly being taken into consideration by the U.S. military, among others.[24]

Links between military activities and the environment became a prominent issue during the Vietnam War. During the Vietnam War, many Americans were directly affected by exposure to America's use of millions of gallons of Agent Orange, a herbicide that defoliated the forests as part of a strategy designed to deprive Vietcong forces of forest cover. Decaying ordnance, nuclear wastes, chemicals, and other toxic pollutants created long-term environmental problems. The Pentagon allocates about $5 billion a year to its environmental security program, designed to protect and rehabilitate the environment. Environmentalists have launched campaigns to get the military to protect endangered species that inhabit military bases. They also succeeded in getting the U.S. Navy to abandon the Puerto Rican island of Vieques, which was used for a firing range and various military exercises. The Pacific islanders linked nuclear testing directly to environmental issues, partly because radiation on some islands forced their inhabitants to abandon them. After many years of U.S., British, and French nuclear testing in the Pacific, the islanders, together with New Zealand and Australia, created the South Pacific Nuclear Weapon Free Zone in 1985 to reduce the risk of nuclear contamination.

Numerous conflicts have created major environmental problems. During the first Persian Gulf War in 1991, retreating Iraqi soldiers ignited Kuwaiti oil fields, causing 3 to 6 million barrels of oil a day to burn and contaminate Kuwait and

Agent Orange ■
Highly toxic defoliant used by the United States in the Vietnam War

environmental security program ■
Pentagon environmental program

South Pacific Nuclear Weapon Free Zone ■
Created in 1985 to reduce the risk of nuclear contamination

What does this photo convey? Natural disasters, often overlooked by many environmentalists, have significant environmental, economic, social, and political implications. A survivor of the March 2011 Japan earthquake and tsunami salvages next to a destroyed building.

surrounding countries. Similarly, Russian soldiers deliberately ignited oil wells in Chechnya, making a large part of that area an ecological disaster zone. When North Atlantic Treaty Organization (NATO) forces bombed oil refineries, industrial plants, electrical transformers, and other parts of the Serbian infrastructure in 1999, toxins—such as polychlorinated biphenyls (PCBs), liquid mercury, and vinyl chloride monomer (VCM)—were released into the Danube River, the air, and the soil. The environmental consequences are significant and will last for a long time.

A more common and devastating environmental problem related to war is the proliferation of land mines in conflicts around the world. Land mines continue to kill long after wars end. Vietnam, Angola, Afghanistan, Mozambique, and other developing countries have abandoned forests and agricultural areas because of the dangers posed by land mines. While it is easy to plant mines, removing them is very difficult, time consuming, and dangerous. Numerous civilians are killed or injured daily in many countries by land mines laid in wars that are largely forgotten in countries not affected by them. Environmentalists have focused their attention not only on removing land mines but also on banning their production and use in wars. Their efforts resulted in the signing of the Ottawa Treaty in 1999.

Ottawa Treaty ■
Addressed the danger of land mines

The military also benefits from environmental changes. As we discussed earlier, global warming is melting pack ice in the Arctic Ocean, which enables ships to use that route for a greater part of the year. It also provides opportunities for the U.S. Navy. Russia has identified the Arctic as a place where it has both military and economic interests.[25]

CASE STUDY | The Earthquake and Tsunami in Japan

On March 11, 2011, an earthquake with a magnitude of 9.0, estimated to be as powerful as thirty thousand Hiroshima atomic bombs, struck off the northeastern coast of Japan and triggered a tsunami that caused widespread destruction estimated at a cost of $235 billion. Although environmentalists are predominantly preoccupied with damage to the environment by human activities, the earthquake and tsunami clearly underscore human vulnerability to natural forces beyond our control. This natural disaster, the most expensive in history, also demonstrates limits to solutions to environmental challenges. Japan, which invented the word "tsunami," is the best-prepared country in the world for earthquakes and tsunamis. Still, it suffered unprecedented destruction. These realities reinforce the importance of focusing on human security, discussed in Chapter 1.

Developments in Japan also illustrate that attempting to solve some environmental problems can make the world even more vulnerable to others. Nuclear power, widely viewed as a clean source of sustainable energy that would diminish dependence on polluting fossil fuels and reduce carbon dioxide in the atmosphere, reinvigorated environmental groups and others concerned about the dangers of radiation from nuclear power plants. Japan's Fukushima Daiichi nuclear power plant disaster became a major global issue partly because of the rapid expansion of the construction of nuclear power plants globally, especially in China and India, to deal with increasing energy demand.

The 1968 nuclear power disaster at Chernobyl, in Ukraine, that spread contamination across Poland, Belarus, Latvia, Lithuania, and other countries in Europe, provides a prism through which Japan's

(continued)

problems are seen. Experiences gained from this earlier environmental catastrophe prompted the Japanese government to act quickly to evacuate people closest to the nuclear power plant, to advise others to remain indoors, and to distribute potassium iodide tablets to protect residents from getting thyroid cancer. Soldiers used power shovels and other heavy construction equipment to cut through mountains of debris. Roughly one hundred thousand troops, the largest number since World War II, were mobilized to help deal with the consequences of the natural disaster. The global response to environmental problems in Japan included critical examinations of nuclear power. China, which is also vulnerable to earthquakes, reaffirmed its policy of not building nuclear power plants close to urban areas or earthquake fault lines. Germany announced a permanent phasing out of nuclear power, and the EU tested all the nuclear power plants in twenty-seven countries to ensure preparedness for emergencies such as floods, tsunamis, and terrorist attacks. Japan's problems rekindled American fears of a repeat of the Three Mile Island nuclear power accident in 1979 and eroded public support for building more nuclear power plants to enhance energy independence and reduce global warming. Americans also purchased potassium iodide capsules and called on the U.S. government to implement the law that provides for giving potassium iodide tablets to people living near nuclear power plants.

The earthquake and tsunami had significant global economic and financial consequences. The epicenter of the tsunami was Sendai-Shiogama, one of Japan's largest ports and the point from where Sony, Canon, Pioneer, and other global companies ship their products. Shipping stopped due to damaged infrastructure, including ports, roads, and railways. Automobile factories around the world experienced production problems resulting from shortages of various components made in Japan. The cost of chips used in cameras, smartphones, and computers increased dramatically. Toshiba, which manufactures about one third of

chips globally, closed some of its factories, thereby reducing production. The disaster interrupted Japan's supply chain, which severely affected many aspects of global trade. It created doubts about the just-in-time approach to business discussed in Chapter 8. Financial markets declined sharply, led by a 16 percent drop in shares on the Tokyo Stock Exchange. Huge financial losses were borne by insurance and reinsurance companies globally and by the Japanese government. China expressed concern about radiation contaminating its coastal waters and affecting marine life. The United States, South Korea, and Singapore inspected food imported from Japan for radiation. America banned imports from areas near the nuclear power plant. Combined with the turmoil in the Middle East and North Africa that increased oil prices, the natural disaster in Japan created fears of a slowdown of the fragile global economy.

This case study clearly demonstrates that human solutions to environmental problems are sometimes overwhelmed by the awesome power of nature. Roughly 10,000 miles of Japan's coastline had concrete seawalls (some as high as 40 feet), breakwaters, and other structures to protect the country from high seas, tsunamis, and typhoons. Some coastal cities installed networks of sensors that set off alarms in individual residences and automatically close floodgates. There are routine earthquake and tsunami drills. Buildings are constructed with extra steel bracing, giant rubber pads, and embedded hydraulic shock absorbers to withstand earthquakes. Following the Kobe earthquake in 1995, which killed about six thousand people, Japan invested billions of dollars developing the most advanced building technologies. Still, all of these efforts did not prevent devastation. But the damage would undoubtedly have been more massive without them.[26] Radiation from the nuclear power plant has reinvigorated debate about finding other, less dangerous, sources of sustainable clean energy and ways to reduce energy consumption. ▸

SUMMARY AND REVIEW

Environmental problems illustrate how much developments in other parts of the world can impact our lives. Environmental problems cannot be contained by arbitrary national boundaries. Environmental factors have played an important historical role in the rise and fall of great civilizations, the spread of infectious diseases, war, economic prosperity, and many other international issues. Environmental problems are intertwined with politics, economics, and culture. Despite the importance of the environment in our lives, however, movements to protect the environment are relatively new. The global environmental movement emerged principally in Western Europe, the United States, and Canada. Attention to the environment was spurred, in large part, by a tremendous population growth and rapid industrialization that took place with little regard for the serious environmental ramifications, such as deforestation and deteriorating health standards. Nuclear weapons proliferation in the United States and Soviet Union also increased concern for environmental issues.

Biodiversity is a fundamental preoccupation of environmentalists and NGOs. This is such an important issue because the destruction of some species could upset the balance of the ecosystem, resulting in the loss of other species and the alteration of the ecosystem. Biodiversity affects many groups and individuals, such as those interested in deforestation, agriculture, biotechnology, anthropology, pharmaceuticals, sustainable development, global trade, and ethics. Another major concern of environmentalists is water, the foundation for human existence. The planet's increasing population is threatening to create widespread shortages of freshwater. Roughly two thirds of freshwater consumed each year goes to irrigate farms. Compared with other environmental problems, global warming is sometimes perceived as being a less immediate issue. While there is evidence that human activities cause most climate changes, determining how much human activity influences global warming and climate change continues to be debated, partly because there is little information about climate change over past centuries. However, global warming is generally viewed as contributing to rising oceans, more destructive hurricanes, and extensive flooding.

KEY TERMS

commons   207
Chernobyl   207
environmental security   207
Mesopotamia   207
John Evelyn   208
Silent Spring   208
Torrey Canyon   209
Biosphere Conference   209
UN Conference on the Human
   Environment   209
World Summit on Sustainable
   Development   209
Green Belt Movement   210
regimes   211
biodiversity   212

Convention on Biological Diversity   212
North/South Divide   212
International Whaling Commission
   (IWC)   213
Convention on International Trade in
   Endangered Species of Wild Fauna and
   Flora (CITES)   213
Inter-American Tropical Tuna Commission
   (IATTC)   214
Congo Basin   215
Chiapas   215
selective logging   216
infrastructure   216
commercial logging   216
Plan for National Integration   216

DISCUSSION QUESTIONS

1. The global environmental movement emerged primarily in Western Europe and North America. What were some of the issues that led to the creation of this movement?
2. Because of the global nature of environmental problems, international agreements are often used to address environmental issues. What are some factors that influence these agreements?
3. Why is deforestation an important issue? Discuss the causes of deforestation and global efforts to stop it.
4. As discussed in previous chapters, revolutions in technologies have played an important role in a number of global issues. How have these developments contributed to environmental problems?
5. Discuss how environmental problems affect women and indigenous peoples.
6. What are some of the strategies that environmental NGOs use to achieve their objectives? Give examples of how these strategies have been applied.

SUGGESTED READINGS

Barker, Karen. *Privatizing Water*. Ithaca, NY: Cornell University Press, 2010. Analyzes controversies about the privatization of urban water supplies.
Byers, Michael. *Who Owns the Arctic?* Toronto: Douglas & McIntyre, 2009. With global warming melting Arctic ice, countries are scrambling to claim ownership of the area's resources.
Hufbauer, Gary Clyde, et al. *Global Warming and the World Trading System*. Washington, DC: Peterson Institute for International Economics, 2009. Efforts to reduce global warming conflict with concerns about global competitiveness.
Solomon, Steven. *Water: The Epic Struggle for Wealth, Power, and Civilization*. New York: HarperCollins, 2010. Water shortages threaten economic growth and food security and create regional conflicts.
Watts, Jonathan. *When a Billion Chinese Jump*. New York: Scribner, 2010. Focuses on how China's environmental problems contribute to global warming.

ENDNOTES

1. Neil MacFarquhar, "Islanders Fearing Climate Change Press a U.N. Debate," *New York Times*, 29 May 2009, A4.
2. John McCormick, *Reclaiming Paradise: The Global Environmental Movement* (Bloomington: Indiana University Press, 1989), vii.
3. Barbara Johnson, *Life and Death Matters: Human Rights and the Environment at the End of the Millennium* (Walnut Creek, CA: Alta Mira Press, 1997), 13–14.
4. Elizabeth Economy and Miranda A. Schreurs, "Domestic and International Linkages in Environmental Politics," in *The Internationalization of Environmental Protection*, eds. Miranda A. Schreurs and Elizabeth Economy (Cambridge: Cambridge University Press, 1997), 6.
5. Lorraine Elliott, *The Global Politics of the Environment* (New York: New York University Press, 1998), 7.
6. Scott Barrett, *Environment and Statecraft* (New York: Oxford University Press, 2006), 1–3.
7. Elliott, *The Global Politics of the Environment*, 28.
8. Harold K. Jacobson and Edith Brown Weiss, "A Framework for Analysis," in *Engaging Countries: Strengthening Compliance with the International Environmental Accords*, eds. Edith Brown Weiss and Harold K. Jacobson (Cambridge, MA: MIT Press, 1998).
9. Elliott, *The Global Politics of the Environment*, 148.
10. "Not a Small Problem," *Economist*, 25 September 2010, 11.
11. "Climate Change Diplomacy," *Economist*, 18 December 2010, 121.
12. J. R. McNeill, *Something New Under the Sun: An Environmental History the Twentieth-Century World* (New York: W. W. Norton, 2000), 241.
13. McNeill, *Something New*, 242; and Elliott, *The Global Politics of the Environment*, 135.
14. Elizabeth R. DeSombre, *Domestic Sources of International Environmental Policy* (Cambridge, MA: MIT Press, 2000), 1.
15. DeSombre, *Domestic Sources*, 64.
16. "Rhinos in South Africa," *Economist*, 20 November 2010, 55.
17. Jonathan Watts, *When a Billion Chinese Jump* (New York: Scribner, 2010).
18. "Less Smoke, Less Ire," *Economist*, 25 September 2010, 14.
19. Patricia Leigh Brown, "Soup Without Fins?" *New York Times*, 6 March 2011, A1.
20. National Research Council, *Global Environmental Change* (Washington, DC: National Academy Press, 1999), 2.
21. "Climate Change Diplomacy," *Economist*, 18 December 2010, 121.
22. Joel Kurtzman, "The Low Carbon Diet," *Foreign Affairs* 88, No. 5 (September/October 2009), 114.
23. James E. Nickum, "Hydraulic Pressures," *Foreign Affairs* 89, No. 5 (September/October 2010), 131.
24. Joshua W. Busby, *Climate Change and National Security* (New York: Council on Foreign Relations, 2008).
25. Michael Byers, *Who Owns the Arctic?* (Toronto: Douglas & McIntyre, 2009).
26. James Glanz and Norimitsu Onishi, "Japan's Strict Codes and Drills Are Seen As Life-savers." New York Times, 12 March 2011, A1.

Population and Migration

China's one-child policy was begun in 1979 to reduce population growth, but its long-term demographic and economic implications are causing many to question it. Residents of China's Guangdong Province looked at

INTRODUCTION

Population and migration issues, perhaps more than any other global problem, demonstrate the reality of globalization. Hunger, inequality, ethnic conflicts, environmental degradation, sustainable development, the treatment of women, global security, economic development, trade, poverty, democratization, human rights concerns—all aspects of globalization are intertwined with population. To a large extent, population factors will determine the future of humanity and the world. Rapid population growth is a silent threat to both human and global security, making it as grave a concern as the proliferation of weapons of mass destruction.

Demographic disparities among countries generally influence the distribution of economic, military, and political power among states. For example, France dominated continental Europe for a long time partly because of its relatively large population, although Britain used its geographic location and its navy to counter French power. America's growing population is likely to consolidate its power, whereas Europe's aging and declining population is likely to diminish its power in the global system. Russia's population decline has contributed to its loss of power globally. Population growth in the developing world is helping shift economic and political power to emerging market economy countries.[1]

Migration makes population issues an even more pressing global concern. Each wave of globalization has been accompanied by migration. The movement of capital, technology, and products across national boundaries is inseparable from the migration of people. The current period of globalization is marked by an unprecedented movement of people around the world. The creation of global institutions and the globalization of human rights and democracy have facilitated migration as well as given rise to a global human rights regime that protects migrants, independent of their nationality. This chapter focuses on population growth and its global implications. The different kinds of migrants and migrations are discussed. The role of gender in migration, rural-to-urban migration, transcontinental migration, forced migration, refugees, reform migration, and the global smuggling of immigrants are all examined. The causes of migration are as old as human civilization. After analyzing them, we will look at case studies that illustrate the dynamics of global—as opposed to regional and internal—migration. The chapter concludes with a case study of global aging and pensions.

POPULATION

overpopulation ■
Excessive population within an area that lacks enough resources for long-term sustainment

At the heart of population as a global issue is the extent to which population growth threatens the Earth's carrying capacity. Overpopulation (i.e., too many people living in an area that has inadequate resources to support them) has been a global preoccupation for centuries. Population problems must be seen in the context of consumption. In this context, the population of the developed world, which consumes much, is seen as a bigger problem for the world's resources than the population of the developing world, which consumes little. Often, population problems can be avoided if population growth remains stable, assuming that resources are also carefully managed. The rate at which the population remains relatively stable is referred to as the replacement rate. To achieve this, fertility rates must average 2.1 children per couple. Migration influences the replacement rate, population growth, and population decline.

replacement rate ■
Rate at which a population remains stable

Thomas Malthus (1766–1834), an English economist, sociologist, and pioneer in demographics, wrote *An Essay on the Principle of Population* in 1798. In it, he argued that because population increases by a geometrical ratio and food supplies increase by an arithmetical ratio, the world would have high rates of population growth and suffer from poverty and starvation. The widespread practice of family planning and technological and scientific revolutions in food production, transportation, and storage essentially rendered these dire predictions false. The invention of genetically modified crops and other agricultural scientific breakthroughs further challenge Malthus's argument. However, food shortages and higher prices, due partly to the use of corn to produce biofuels, complicate the discussion on food and population. High population growth remains a serious threat to most developing countries and, as we discussed in Chapter 9, frustrates efforts to reduce global poverty and economic inequality. Malthus was concerned about the Earth's carrying capacity. Carrying capacity refers to the maximum number of humans or animals a given area can support without creating irreversible destruction of the environment and, eventually, humans and animals themselves.

carrying capacity ■
The maximum number of humans or animals that can survive within a given area

Combined with fervent nationalism and a perception that survival itself is at stake, population pressures often result in military conflict. The Palestinian-Israeli struggle is an example of how demographic changes are perceived as determining destiny. Jews now comprise roughly 50.5 percent of the population in Israel and the Palestinian territories. By 2020, the proportion of Jews will decline to 42.1 percent, whereas the Palestinians, who now make up 44.3 percent of the population, will see their share of the population grow to 52 percent. The birthrate for Palestinians in the West Bank and Gaza is 40 for every 1,000 people. The birthrate for Palestinians in Israel is 36 per 1,000 people. Compare this with a birthrate for Jews of 18.3 per 1,000, and you will see why demographic changes are perceived as threats to Israel's security.

Population Issues in Developing Countries

Most developing countries have high population growth rates and suffer from vast differences in income. Inadequate education, low rates of contraception usage, cultural norms that value large families and male virility, the need for labor in subsistence economies, and the need to have children to support parents are some of the reasons population growth is higher in poorer countries. Most of the countries with the largest populations and the highest growth rates are in the developing world. Roughly 97 percent of the increase in the global population is occurring in Africa, Asia, the Middle East, and Latin America, with the more prosperous countries in these regions experiencing declining growth rates. Industrialized countries, on the other hand, are experiencing declining growth rates and even depopulation in some cases. Poverty is clearly a major cause of high population growth rates.

In India, more than 400 million people—roughly the combined populations of the United States and Britain—live in dire poverty and are illiterate. Nonetheless, the population in India grows by about three people a minute, or two thousand an hour, or forty-eight thousand per day. In other words, the growth of India's population each day is equivalent to that of a medium-sized American city. By 2025, India is projected to surpass China as the world's most populous country, with about 1.5 billion people, compared with China's 1.4 billion people. China and India alone account for one out of every three children added to the global population.

Problems arising from rapid population growth have influenced governments, nongovernmental organizations (NGOs), and women to take action to limit population growth. It is generally agreed that *women's level of education strongly influences fertility rates*. Education helps to determine factors that affect population growth rates, such as contraceptive usage, the age of marriage and childbearing, social status and self-perception, and employment opportunities outside of the home and residence.

An interesting development is the declining birthrates in Brazil, Mexico, Bangladesh, India, the Philippines, Iran, Vietnam, Indonesia, and Egypt, where poverty and illiteracy remain serious and pervasive problems. Even women who are less educated have become more assertive about their reproductive choices. Factors influencing this change include economic and cultural globalization, greater access to education, increasing urbanization, the declining influence of religion on women's reproductive lives, greater access to medical technologies, and the cumulative effects of satellite television and other media that stress the advantages of having fewer children. Sexism strongly influences population decisions in developing countries. In many societies, tradition supports having large families by praising the fertility of women and the virility of men. The son complex—the preference for having boys instead of girls—influences many parents worldwide to continue having children until a boy is born. Parents, especially mothers, are demeaned in many societies if they do not produce boys. In many traditional South Asian families, a boy is expected to live with his parents, be employed, inherit property, provide financial security for aging parents, and light their funeral pyres. A daughter, by contrast, is widely perceived as a financial and social liability. When she marries, her family is required, by tradition, to provide the bridegroom's family with a substantial dowry, which can be money, property, or both. Parents often incur significant debt to provide dowries. Sexism also conspires with advanced medical technology to reduce the number of girls in some countries such as India and China. With the use of ultrasound machines to determine the sex of the fetus, many parents often decide to abort female fetuses. India passed a law in 1996 prohibiting medical staff from informing parents of the gender of a fetus, but it appears to be ignored. Based on the predominance of male births, researchers estimate that up to 6 million girls were aborted in India from 2000–2010. Those practices plus female infanticide have contributed to a widening divergence in the ratio of females to males in many parts of India and China.

China's one-child policy, initiated in 1979 by Deng Xiao Ping, China's leader, to reduce its population growth is the most controversial approach to dealing with rapid population growth. China established the state family planning

sexism ■
Discrimination against an individual or group based on sex or gender classifications

son complex ■
Preference for male children

dowry ■ Financial gift given to the husband's family by the wife's family at marriage in many traditional societies

one-child policy ■
Imposed on families in China to limit population growth

bureau to formulate policies and procedures for enforcing the one-child policy. Family planning committees at the local level, a part of the Communist Party, are responsible for rewarding those who comply with the policy and punishing those who violate the one-child policy. Those who comply with it receive a monthly stipend until the child is fourteen years old and get preferential treatment when applying for housing, education, and health benefits for the child; they are also granted a pension when they are old. Those who fail to comply with the one-child policy risk the loss of benefits for the first child, jeopardize their employment with the government, and risk having their property seized. Women are often forced to be sterilized, especially after the birth of a second child. *Exceptions to the one-child policy* include the following cases: (1) if the first child has a defect; (2) in the case of a remarriage, if one partner does not have a child; (3) if couples are involved in certain jobs, such as mining; or (4) if both partners come from families with one child. Demographic and economic implications of the one-child policy are influencing more Chinese to question it.[2]

Population Issues in Developed Countries

Compared with the developing world, Europe has always had a smaller population. Among the *reasons for this disparity* are that

1. Europe was settled by humans who migrated from Africa into Asia. In other words, it started out with a smaller population.
2. Geography and climate discouraged large numbers of people from settling in Europe.
3. Confronted with overpopulation, Europe was able to conquer, colonize, and settle in North America, South America, parts of Africa, parts of Asia, Australia, and New Zealand.

The Industrial Revolution and scientific advances in agriculture made Europeans prosperous and diminished the need to have large families.

Europe is faced with the spread of subreplacement fertility regimes: that is, patterns of childbearing that would eventually result in indefinite population decline. The sharpest dip in population is in Russia. Communicable diseases, widespread environmental problems, alcohol poisoning, sexually transmitted diseases, and an abortion rate that is twice as high as live births have combined to decrease Russia's population by roughly 700,000 each year. If current demographic trends continue, Russia will see its current population of 140.4 million drop precipitously to 100 million in forty to fifty years.[3] Such long-range predictions are often highly speculative and turn out to be inaccurate. Nevertheless, it is clear that Russia is going through a population implosion. Though immigration has slowed the decline of Western Europe's populations, immigration levels are not high enough to alter the demographic realities. The United States, Canada, and Australia are actually gaining population largely due to increased immigration and rising fertility rates.

As Table 11.1 shows, by 2010 the median age in the United States reached 36.6, compared to 43.3 in Italy and 44.3 in Germany, due to the rapid growth in

subreplacement fertility regimes ■ Patterns of childbearing resulting in population decline

TABLE 11.1			
Demographic Contrasts Between Rich and Poor Countries			
Country	Median Age (years) (2010)	Total Fertility Rate (Births per Woman) (2010–2015)	Population Annual Growth Rate % (2010–2015)
Rich Countries			
Japan	44.7	1.3	−0.2
France	40.1	1.9	0.4
United States	36.6	2.0	0.9
Italy	43.3	1.4	0.2
Germany	44.3	1.3	−0.2
Poor Countries			
Bangladesh	24.5	2.2	1.3
Haiti	21.6	3.2	1.5
Nigeria	18.6	4.8	2.1
Zambia	16.8	5.3	2.4
Sierra Leone	18.2	5.0	2.3

Source: United Nations Development Programme, *Human Development Report 2010* (Basingstoke, Hampshire, UK, and New York: Palgrave Macmillan, 2010).

the number of the elderly and the subreplacement problem. Three major reasons account for Europe's aging societies:

1. Life expectancy has climbed due to medical advancements, a healthier environment, improved nutrition, and greater concerns about safety and public health.
2. The huge baby boom generation of the 1940s and 1950s is now entering middle age and moving into the old-age category.
3. Declining fertility rates, below the replacement rate, increase the proportion of the population that is old.

America's aging population, while growing, will comprise a smaller percentage of the overall population because of the number of young immigrants and higher fertility rates. Japan faces not only an aging population but also subreplacement fertility rates.

Developed countries face many challenges that require the implementation of difficult and controversial strategies. These strategies include

1. Substantially increasing immigration to offset declining fertility rates,
2. Postponing or abandoning retirement,
3. Encouraging higher fertility rates,
4. Investing more in the education of workers to increase productivity,

5. Strengthening intergenerational responsibilities within families,
6. Targeting government-paid benefits to those who need them most, and
7. Requiring workers to invest for their own retirements.

The implications of these changes are far reaching. Significant tensions within rich countries over such strategies are already evident in many European countries.

GLOBAL MIGRATION

Migration—the movement of people from one place to another—is an integral component of human behavior. Our ancestors moved out of curiosity and a sense of adventure; to find food, to search for better grazing and agricultural lands; to seek protection from adversaries; to conquer land for new settlements; and to obtain religious, political, social, and economic freedoms. Contemporary migration is rooted in the earlier periods of political, military, economic, and financial globalization that we discussed in Chapter 1. Migration includes the movement of people within a country's geographical boundaries as well as movement across national boundaries. People who migrate fall into several categories. A migrant is a person who moves from one country or area to another country or location. Migrants often move from one part of a country to another location within that country. The broad category of migrant is subdivided into refugees, displaced persons, and immigrants. Refugees are essentially migrants who live outside their country and are unable or unwilling to return because of documented cases of persecution or a well-founded fear of persecution. Historically and today, conflicts, famine, natural disasters, and political, religious, and economic oppression have been dominant factors contributing to the creation of refugees. Refugees who attempt to obtain permanent residence in the country to which they fled are referred to as asylum seekers. The immigration laws of most countries distinguish asylum seekers from other categories of migrants and generally grant them preferential treatment, in accordance with international law. A displaced person is someone who has been forced to leave his or her home because of violence, conflict, persecution, or natural disaster but has not crossed an international border. Many displaced people eventually cross national boundaries, thereby becoming refugees. An immigrant is someone who goes to a foreign country to become a permanent resident. Most migration occurs in a relatively limited geographical area, despite growing transcontinental migration (i.e., the movement of people from one continent to another).

migration ■ Movement of people from one place to another

migrant ■ A person who moves from one country or area to another country or location

refugees ■ Migrants living outside their country of origin who are unwilling or unable to return

asylum seekers ■ Refugees attempting to obtain permanent residence in the country to which they fled

displaced person ■ One who has fled his or her home but has not left the home country

immigrant ■ One who travels to a foreign country, often to become a permanent resident

transcontinental migration ■ Movement of people from one continent to another

Gender and Migration

Men are more likely than women to migrate under ordinary circumstances. There are several reasons for this. Who migrates is determined to a large extent by the requirements imposed by countries, companies, or individuals who need labor. Much of the work to be done is culturally defined as work for men. Large numbers of men from Turkey, North Africa, and the Caribbean migrated to Germany, France, and Britain, respectively, after World War II to help rebuild these countries. Men throughout the world have been recruited to work in industry, construction, and mining. Cultural norms and sex roles within sending countries also determine whether men are more likely than women to migrate. Gender roles also influence men to migrate in search of employment. Men are generally perceived as breadwinners in most countries, whereas women are viewed as being responsible for taking care of the home. Economic development and greater access to education for women change cultural views of gender roles and provide more employment opportunities for women. Demographic changes and greater employment opportunities for women in developed countries are transforming gender migration. Women migrate to rich societies to work in factories, tourism, education, hospitals, businesses, and private homes. As more women work outside the home in rich countries, more women from poor countries are hired to do domestic work.

Types of Migration

Although migration, as a contemporary global issue, is often thought of primarily as movement from developing countries to rich countries, far more common is the movement of people within countries and from one country to another within a particular geographical or cultural region. Regional migration is fueled by increasing economic opportunities in a country or group of neighboring countries. For example, people in North Africa move to Spain, France, and Italy to find employment, and people from Zimbabwe, Mozambique, Botswana, and Lesotho have migrated to South Africa to work in mining and other industries. Rural-to-urban migration is the dominant pattern of migration in both rich and poor countries. Many rural areas across the United States are losing population as residents seek better opportunities in urban areas. Much of the migration in the developing world is from rural areas to cities. Rural-to-rural migration (i.e., the movement of people from one rural area to another) is common in many parts of the world, despite the relatively limited economic opportunities found in most small towns or agricultural areas. Many migrants follow the planting, cultivation, and harvesting of various crops. Urban-to-urban migration is common in most countries. Families and individuals move from one city to another *to find employment, to pursue a college degree, or to be in a culturally dynamic area.* Urban-to-rural migration is usually designed to encourage the economic development of the countryside and to relieve population pressures on urban centers. Brazil, China, Indonesia, and Nigeria are countries that have used this strategy. Another type of migration is seasonal migration. People often move from one area to another because of the seasonal demand for labor. Agricultural industries often demand more labor at certain times of the year than at others. Harvesting fruit, sugarcane, coffee, and other crops requires intensive labor for a short period of time. Seasonal migration is also driven by other industries such as tourism.

Another type of migration is transit migration. In this case, those seeking to enter a specific country pass through another country or stay there temporarily. For example, migrants use Mexico as a transit point for illegal entry into the United States. Visiting Mexico's main immigration detention center, you see migrants from Ecuador, India, Cuba, China, Albania, Russia, Ukraine, Tanzania, Sierra Leone, Sri Lanka, Bangladesh, and other countries. Similarly, migrants attempting to enter Western Europe use countries such as Bosnia, Croatia,

regional migration ■ Movement of people within a specified region

rural-to-urban migration ■ The most dominant form of migration in both developed and developing countries

seasonal migration ■ Movement of people based on seasonal demand for labor

transit migration ■ Movement of people to one country on the way to another

Serbia, Bulgaria, Hungary, Poland, and the Czech Republic as transit points. Many migrants also stop temporarily in Europe on their way to the United States and Canada. Within Europe, France is used as a transit point for migrants attempting to enter Britain in order to take advantage of its asylum policies.

Forced and induced migration is an integral component of human history. Various minorities have been routinely expelled from countries because of political, social, ethnic, and religious differences. The Spanish crown forced Jews to leave Spain in 1492; Africans were forcibly removed from their homeland and enslaved in the Americas, the Middle East, and other parts of the world; and the Cuban and Chinese governments have used forced migration to achieve various political and economic objectives.[4] Another type of migration—one that is becoming common in an age of globalization—is return migration. For example, many American citizens retain meaningful ties with another country. Throughout history, some migrants have returned to the places they left. In the late nineteenth century, roughly a third of European migrants to the United States were returning after a few years. Immigrants from Southern Europe, particularly Italy, were most likely to return after saving enough money to build homes, start small businesses, or buy farms. This trend of migration was strengthened by the relative newness of migration from Southern Europe and by declining transportation costs and faster and more reliable means of transportation. Economic success in the new country also motivates people to return to their country of origin. India and China, for example, encourage return migration to assist economic development.[5]

forced and induced migration ■ Involuntary movement of people, often due to a government initiative

return migration ■ Movement of people back to the country from which they originally emigrated

Causes of Migration

Although the causes of migration are diverse and vary from one individual to another, demographers generally divide them into two categories: namely, push factors and pull factors.[6] Push factors are negative developments and circumstances that motivate or force people to leave their homes. These include widespread abuses of fundamental human rights, political oppression, forced resettlement programs and expulsion, high levels of violence and endemic political instability, rapid population growth, high rates of unemployment, poverty, natural and environmental disasters, the relative lack of educational and cultural opportunities, globalization, and discrimination that excludes specific groups and individuals from competition for resources and power. Pull factors are positive developments and circumstances in other areas or countries that attract people away from their homes. These include economic opportunities, higher wages, political and cultural freedom and stability, a comparatively healthy environment, educational and cultural opportunities, and family reunification.

push factors ■ Negative developments leading many people to leave their homes

pull factors ■ Positive developments inducing people to move from their homes

PUSH FACTORS

Widespread *abuses of fundamental human rights*, discussed in Chapter 3, have traditionally pushed people from their homes. The United States was settled by many individuals who were deprived of basic human rights. Many Jews, political dissidents, homosexuals, and others fled Nazi Germany because of the government's systematic and profound violations of the most basic human rights, including the right to life. During the Cold War, many Central and Eastern Europeans fled oppression in the Communist countries. Cubans migrated in large numbers when Fidel Castro came to power and imposed severe restrictions on fundamental freedom.

Forced resettlement programs and expulsion are significant push factors. Governments have both forced and encouraged people to migrate for several reasons. These include the desire

1. *To achieve cultural homogeneity.* This is particularly the case in newly independent countries that were faced with incompatible ethnic groups living in their artificially constructed boundaries. Yet the practice of achieving cultural homogeneity by expelling people perceived as different has deep historical roots. Catholic Spain expelled the Jews in the fifteenth century, and Catholic France expelled the Huguenots (i.e., French Protestants and followers of John Calvin) in the sixteenth century.

2. *To subdue a region or a people.* China's occupation of Tibet in 1950 was followed by the mass migration of Han Chinese settlers. During the Cultural Revolution (1966–1976), Mao Zedong, China's leader, sent his Red Guard storm troopers to subdue Tibet.

3. *To evict dissidents and opponents of the government.* Fidel Castro, determined to build a Communist society, influenced and coerced almost a million people to leave Cuba.

4. *To achieve foreign policy objectives.* Forced emigration is sometimes implemented as a component of broader foreign policy objectives. Governments use forced emigration to exert pressure on neighboring countries. For example, Castro has used emigration as an instrument of his foreign policy toward the United States.

5. *To achieve economic and national security objectives.* Several governments have forcibly removed people from one area of the country to another as part of an overall economic development or national security strategy.

High levels of violence and political instability are factors that push people away from home. Declining population growth rates in rich countries facilitate migration that is driven by high population growth rates in the developing world. High rates of unemployment and poverty are widely regarded as dominant and constant push factors. *Natural disasters, environmental problems, and famines* push people away from their homelands or force them to relocate within their countries.

Globalization and discrimination are also push factors. Globalization has contributed to the creation of strong economic regions within, as well as among, countries. Globalization's emphasis on economic liberalization, free trade, and diminished government involvement in the economy has resulted in the displacement of millions of small farmers in the developing world. Thousands of farmers in Mexico, unable to compete with subsidized agriculture in the United States and Europe, move to urban areas in Mexico or make the dangerous journey to the United States. Migration is often induced by governments that fail to provide adequate support for rural communities or alternative sources of employment.

Huguenots ■ French Protestants expelled from France in the sixteenth century

Han Chinese ■ China's dominant ethnic group

Cultural Revolution ■ Mao Zedong's forced implementation of Communist economy, politics, and culture in China

Mao Zedong ■ China's repressive, former Communist leader

These problems are compounded by competitive exclusion, which occurs when governments allow more land to be taken by large agroexport companies to create megafarms. This generally drives up land prices and decreases the amount of land available to small subsistence farmers. Discrimination also contributed to emigration. Successful ethnic minority groups have historically been scapegoated for problems within societies, the most obvious being the Jews in Nazi Germany. Idi Amin forced Ugandans of Asian descent to leave Uganda because of their economic success. Ethnic Chinese in Indonesia and other Asian countries have had similar experiences.

competitive exclusion ■ Process by which government allows agrocorporations to monopolize productive land

Refugees

In 2001, the European Union (EU) decided to recognize as refugees women and homosexuals fleeing violence or sexual abuse. The 1951 United Nations Geneva Convention stressed that individuals or groups persecuted on the grounds of race, religion, nationality, membership in a particular social group, and holding certain political opinions would be recognized as refugees and granted asylum. However, these categories have been expanded to reflect a growing awareness of other forms of persecution. In many ways, the interaction of economic problems, political instability, and violence makes it difficult to separate economically motivated migrants from refugees.

United Nations Geneva Convention ■ Stressed the importance of granting asylum to refugees who have been persecuted

Most governments are reluctant to accept large numbers of refugees and generally prefer to provide humanitarian assistance to displaced persons to stem the flow of refugees. Widespread refugee problems in Europe and elsewhere during and after World War II influenced the United States, Western Europe, the Soviet Union, and China to develop institutions, such as the office of the United Nations High Commissioner for Refugees (UNHCR), to help with refugees. Established in 1950, the UNHCR is funded primarily by governments, NGOs, and individuals. Because the proliferation of ethnic conflicts and natural disasters has severely restrained UNHCR's resources, other UN agencies, the International Committee of the Red Cross, and various NGOs are involved in helping refugees globally. Their task is often made even more difficult by the inability or unwillingness of some countries to separate fighters from innocent civilians in refugee camps, despite international legal guidelines for doing so. Increasingly, the UN is pressured to take measures to prevent the outbreak and escalation of ethnic conflicts, which are a major cause of the refugee problem. More countries, including the United States, favor selective humanitarian intervention (i.e., the military invasion of a country) to prevent or diminish human rights abuses that drive people away from their homes.

International Committee of the Red Cross ■ Organization involved in humanitarian operations worldwide

humanitarian intervention ■ Use of military force in defense of human rights

Numerous ethnic conflicts and civil wars in Africa have left that continent with more than 4 million refugees. In the Middle East, violence against the Kurds has not only led to the growth of Kurdish refugees in the region but also influenced many Kurds to seek refuge in Europe and North America. There are more than 500,000 Kurds in Western Europe, with Germany and France receiving most of them. Germany has about 400,000 and France has 60,000. America's invasion of Iraq in 2003 led to more than 2 million refugees and internally displaced persons. The conflict in Pakistan and Afghanistan created millions of refugees. For example, fighting in the Swat Valley in Pakistan between the Taliban and Pakistan forced nearly 3 million people to leave their homes. The Vietnam War produced a mass exodus of Vietnamese, with most of the refugees settling in the United States. As economic conditions deteriorated, and as the Communist government consolidated its power, many Vietnamese also sought refuge in neighboring countries. More than 200,000 ethnic Chinese who lived in Vietnam fled to China when conflict erupted between China and Vietnam in 1978 and 1979. Another 70,000 Vietnamese arrived in Hong Kong in small boats or were rescued from small boats by oceangoing ships on their way to Hong Kong.

The wave of protests for democracy across the Middle East and North Africa in 2011 created new refugees as people fled from Tunisia, Libya, and elsewhere to escape escalating violence, especially by Muammar Qaddafi. Violence in Côte d'Ivoire following a disputed presidential election contributed to the internal displacement of more than a million people. Globally, an estimated 27.5 million people were displaced in 2011.[7]

The Palestinian refugee problem is one of the oldest, most serious, and most intractable global refugee cases. Resolving this problem remains a central challenge to efforts to secure peace between the Israelis and Palestinians. The creation of the state of Israel in 1948 as well as wars and low-intensity conflicts between the Israelis and Arabs led to the creation of roughly 3.5 million Palestinian refugees. Many Palestinians have lived in refugee camps throughout the Arab world for more than half a century. Many of them were born and raised in

The issue of Palestinian refugees is at the heart of efforts to resolve the Palestinian-Israeli conflict. A Palestinian refugee girl walks past graffiti in the Balata refugee camp in the northern West Bank city of Nablus.

these camps, and many have also died in these camps. Between 1947 and 1948, approximately 800,000 Palestinians became refugees. The 1967 war, during which all of Palestine was occupied by Israel, created a second wave of Palestinian refugees. Roughly 400,000 Palestinians, out of a population of 2.5 million, left Palestine to seek refuge in Jordan, Lebanon, Kuwait, Syria, and other Arab countries. The civil war in Lebanon in the 1970s and 1980s and Israel's invasion of Lebanon in 1982 forced more Palestinians to become refugees again. Roughly 5.1 million Palestinians live abroad, mostly in Jordan, which has 3 million of them.[8] The United Nations Relief Works Agency for Palestinian Refugees in the Near East (UNRWA) was established in 1949 to provide relief, education, and welfare services to Palestinian refugees.

UNRWA ■ UN agency established to aid in relief, education, and welfare services for Palestinian refugees

PULL FACTORS

Pull factors are developments and circumstances that attract people to specific areas or countries. Freedom has always been a significant pull factor, both within countries and across international boundaries. Freedom, associated with cities, enticed many individuals to leave the countryside with its relative lack of freedom. *Freedom* in Britain, Holland, and the United States has served as a magnet for European migrants and, more recently, for migrants from the developing world. Religious, artistic, economic, political, and scientific freedoms remain almost irresistible pull factors, which, in turn, usually enhance the degree of freedom that existed. New York, London, Paris, Sydney, Toronto, Los Angeles, Seattle, Chicago, Miami, and Boston are vibrant and dynamic because of the freedom that characterizes them and attracts talent and financial resources from around the world.

Economic opportunities are one of the most powerful pull factors. People have historically migrated to industrial areas that offered employment and financial and entrepreneurial opportunities. Income inequality between rural and urban areas or between developing and developed countries generally induces people to migrate to seek higher income. Economic opportunities of an earlier period of globalization, between 1870 and 1910, influenced roughly 10 percent of the world's population to immigrate. Millions of Europeans migrated from poor countries to industrialized societies on the Continent and to the United States, Canada, Australia, Argentina, Brazil, and other Latin American countries. It is estimated that 12 million Chinese emigrated between 1815 and 1914, many of them from the south of China. Mexicans are motivated to migrate to the United States partly because many of them can earn much more money doing similar jobs in the United States. This is a global phenomenon. Higher wages in Britain, France, and Germany, combined with labor shortages in those countries following World War II, attracted immigrants from the Caribbean, India, Africa, and Turkey. Similarly, higher wages in the mining industry in South Africa induced people from neighboring countries to migrate to South Africa. Oil wealth and jobs in the Persian Gulf countries pulled more than 3.5 million Asians to the region. Demand for inexpensive and reliable labor contributed to the development of an Indian diaspora that covers sixty-three countries and has more than 20 million people. A diaspora is a community of people living outside their original or ancestral country.

diaspora ■ A community of people living outside their original or ancestral country

Colonization and financial globalization combined to create a very powerful pull factor between 1820 and 1920. European colonization of the Americas, Asia, and Africa was accompanied by massive flows of capital. Industrialization in Europe generated a significant supply of capital, which stimulated an expansion of industrialization overseas. Colonization enticed millions of Europeans and others to emigrate. Many of these areas had been settled long before the arrival of Europeans, a reality that often resulted in the forceful removal and even death of native populations. More than 60 million Europeans migrated to the Americas, Asia, and Eastern and Southern Africa. Demand for inexpensive labor in the European colonies led to the migration of roughly 12 million Chinese and 30 million Indians to areas conquered and colonized by Europeans. The British, who colonized India, encouraged Indians to migrate to British colonies, including Burma, Malaysia, Singapore, Australia, Fiji, Trinidad and Tobago, British Guyana, Kenya, South Africa, and Uganda. Many Indians returned to India eventually, but a significant number, estimated to be 6 million, remained abroad.[9]

Globalization is widely viewed as one of the most significant pull factors in relation to migration. Globalization, especially economic and cultural globalization, enables poor people to see prosperity in rich countries. Movies, magazines, television, and tourism contribute to promoting glamorous and desirable lifestyles in developed countries. Globalization shrinks the world, thereby making it easier for people to compare themselves not only with their immediate neighbors but also with people around the world. Globalization creates dreams that many individuals in poor countries find irresistible. Global cities enable immigrants to blend into the population and become low-wage workers in hotels, restaurants, sweatshops, homes of American families, manufacturing and retail companies, and agrobusiness.

Family reunification and cultural ties are major pull factors. In many parts of the world, people migrate to places where they know someone, which gives rise to a concentration of immigrants from a particular country or a region of a country in certain areas. For example, many early Scandinavian immigrants went primarily to the United States and settled in Midwestern agricultural states, including Minnesota, Wisconsin, Nebraska, Illinois, and Iowa. The largest group of migrants is composed of relatives of individuals who are already living in a specific country. Family reunification is a leading objective of immigration policies in several countries. In many cases, one family member will immigrate to a particular country and, once relatively economically secure, will encourage family members to join him or her. This phenomenon is known as chain migration.

Sparsely populated areas, as we have seen, provide a significant pull factor. As we mentioned earlier, European conquest and colonization of the Americas, Asia, and Africa provided opportunities for certain parts of Europe to relieve their population pressures. North America and Australia attracted millions of European emigrants. However, anthropological evidence supports the view that the Americas had vast human populations when the Europeans arrived. Today, many European countries have declining population growth, a development that is inducing the growth of both legal and illegal migration to that region. Many countries have large areas that have few inhabitants. In Brazil, for example, the vast and sparsely settled Amazon region continues to attract settlers from other parts of Brazil and

global cities ■ Cities that contain enough migrants to make them international in scope and appeal

family reunification ■ Major pull factor encouraging global migration

cultural ties ■ Major pull factor in promoting global migration

chain migration ■ Process by which one family member immigrates to a country and then encourages other family members to join him or her

other countries. Earlier we pointed out how many states in the American Midwest have been losing population. To ease this population decline, Iowa, for example, has responded by creating an immigration enterprise zone. Iowa hopes to become a priority destination for refugees and foreigners who are willing to migrate in search of economic opportunities.

Closely related to freedom and economic opportunities as pull factors is the *availability of educational and cultural opportunities*. Western Europe, Canada, and the United States have long been magnets for students, artists, and professionals from many countries. Globalization has facilitated educational and cultural exchanges to an unprecedented degree and, in the process, is creating a global community of individuals who are connected by common educational and cultural experiences. Many foreign-born students and professionals achieve great success in the United States, which encourages more students and professionals to immigrate to that country. For example, the unpopularity of careers in science among American students reinforces the demand for foreign students to study science and engineering and to become part of the science and engineering workforce in the United States.[10]

immigration enterprise zone ■ Areas created to attract immigrants due to underpopulation problems

CASE STUDIES

The following case studies provide examples of migration to specific countries. The case studies show that governments and nonstate actors regard migration and population issues as extremely important components of human, national, and global security.

The United States

More than any country in the world, the United States is known as an immigrant country. Consequently, most Americans—with the exception of Native Americans and Americans of English and African descent—are descendents of people who migrated to the United States less than three hundred years ago. The demand for labor in the United States, together with poverty, conflict, and oppression in Europe, led to the migration of millions of Europeans to America. Rapid westward expansion and the need for a growing population to develop agriculture as well as industry attracted emigrants primarily from Western and Northern Europe until the early 1900s. Agricultural problems in Scandinavia, for example, prompted Swedes, Danes, Norwegians, and Finns to emigrate and settle in agricultural states in the Midwest.[11] By 1901, most emigrants came from Southern and Eastern Europe. Chinese and Japanese immigrants came to California in the 1850s to work in the gold mines, on the railroads, and in agriculture.

The United States adopted policies that excluded Asians and restricted immigrants from non-European countries. Growing fears about America's changing ethnic composition and about competition from new arrivals among "old stock" Americans led to the passage of legislation in 1921 that initiated the national quota system, which remained in place until 1965. The national quota system was designed to preserve the ethnic or national composition of the United States as

national quota system ■ System to limit immigration into the United States

of 1920. Quotas for emigrants from any one country were calculated in terms of 1/16 of 1 percent of persons of that national origin already in the United States. There was an absolute ceiling of two thousand emigrants from the Asia-Pacific region.[12] Improved economic conditions in Europe and the abolishment of the national quota system in 1965 changed the pattern of U.S. immigration. Most of the new arrivals are from the developing world, with various groups dominating particular parts of the country. For example, Mexicans comprise the majority of new immigrants in California, Texas, and Illinois; Dominicans, Chinese, and Indians are prominent in New York; and Cubans are the leading group in Florida. Immigrants make up a large proportion of America's population, and demographic projections indicate that they will be largely responsible for the country's population growth.

Mexico's geographic proximity to the United States and historical factors combine to make the growing number of Mexican migrants in the United States a contentious issue. Many Mexicans were already living in Texas, California, Arizona, New Mexico, Utah, Nevada, and Colorado when these areas were taken by the United States from Mexico during the Mexican-American War, which lasted from 1846 to 1848. The annexation of these territories by the United States did not significantly alter migration across the newly established borders. Economic and political problems in Mexico have traditionally served as push factors, and the demand for labor and economic opportunities in the United States functioned as pull factors. For example, the demand for labor in the United States during World War II brought Mexicans to America under the Bracero Program. The Bracero Program was a set of agreements between the United States and Mexico that facilitated the migration of Mexican workers, on a temporary basis, to work principally in agriculture. The increase in legal migration under the program was accompanied by the growth of illegal immigration. From 1942 to 1952, roughly 900,000 Mexican workers entered the United States under the Bracero Program, compared with more than 2 million illegal workers during the same period. In response to economic competition as well as fears about Communists entering the country through Mexico, the United States launched Operation Wetback (from 1954 to 1959) in which hundreds of thousands of Mexicans were arrested and deported. However, by the time the Bracero Program had ended in 1964, the relationship between Mexican workers and American employers was so well established that controlling the flow of migrants across the U.S.–Mexican border was almost impossible. Emigration from Mexico, both legal and illegal, became a reality of American life. Mexican emigrants throughout the United States are employed in all sectors of the economy.

Mexican-American War ■
(1846–1848); war in which the United States seized half of Mexico's territory, which is now Texas, California, Arizona, New Mexico, Utah, Nevada, and Colorado

Bracero Program ■
Agreements between the United States and Mexico to promote the migration of Mexican workers to the United States on a temporary basis (ended in 1964)

Operation Wetback ■ U.S. operation that deported hundreds of thousands of Mexican migrants

Western Europe

The growing unification of Europe, manifested in the creation and strengthening of the EU, also enables illegal immigrants to move from one country to another once they enter a member country of the EU. Italy and Greece provide many entry points for migrants desperate to settle in Western Europe. Illegal immigrants come from North Africa, Eastern and Central Europe, the Middle East, Latin America and the Caribbean, China, Sub-Saharan Africa, India, Russia, the former Soviet Republics, and elsewhere. Variations in immigration policies among EU members make some countries more attractive than others to migrants. For example, thousands of refugees gather in France at the entrance of the English Channel tunnel waiting for an opportunity, often fatal, to hide in trains and trucks going to Britain, which has more generous refugee policies than France. Faced with stagnant economies in Portugal and Spain, many citizens left those countries for Latin America in 2011.

France   The influx of large numbers of immigrants from developing countries into France must be seen in the broader context of French colonialism and the demand for labor. France, like the United States, views its revolution as having universal significance and has developed a tradition of respecting the civil and human rights of foreigners. Its self-perception as a champion of the developing world reinforced its policy of accepting migrants from poor countries. France adopted a policy of assimilation toward its colonies in Africa, Asia, the Caribbean, and the Pacific, under which many residents of French colonies gained French citizenship and were free to migrate in France. Many Africans, Asians, and people from the Caribbean found employment in France, especially following World War I, which had such a devastating impact on the French population that the country had to import labor for its industries. World War II also created demand for labor from the colonies. Algeria's struggle for independence from France (1954–1962) resulted in hundreds of thousands of Algerians gaining asylum in France because of their support for France. More migrants from France's former colonies arrived in the 1960s to meet the labor needs of France's growing economy. The largest number of migrants came from Muslim countries—such as Algeria, Tunisia, Morocco, and Senegal—a development, as we have seen, that resulted in the large number of Muslims in France today.

As in other parts of Europe, rising immigration is fueling political and social extremism in France. Jean-Marie Le Pen, leader of the National Front party, consistently advocated ending legal immigration and deporting illegal immigrants. His daughter, Marine Le Pen, who replaced him as leader of the National Front Party in 2011, holds strong anti-Muslim views. As is the case throughout Europe, Romanies ("Gypsies"), who migrate from Bulgaria, Hungary, the Czech Republic, Romania, and Slovakia to France, face harsh discrimination. Many Romanies are viewed as being responsible for rising crime rates, street begging, and squalid shantytowns. France deported more than eight thousand Romanies to Bulgaria and Romania and cleared hundreds of illegal camps.[13] France's actions were widely criticized and compared to Nazi treatment of the Romanies, which we discussed in Chapter 3.

Germany   Unlike the United States, Canada, and Australia, Germany is not traditionally an immigrant country. Instead, Germany encouraged its citizens to immigrate to North America, Eastern Europe, Latin America, and elsewhere in order to diminish population pressures and economic problems at home. Between 1920 and 1950, almost 7 million Germans settled in the United States, many of them in

policy of assimilation ■ French policy allowing many people from its colonies to become residents and citizens of France

Jean-Marie Le Pen ■ Anti-immigration leader

Romanies in Europe face widespread poverty and discrimination.

the Midwestern agricultural states. This pattern of migration was radically altered by Germany's initiation of World War II and the devastation it experienced in that conflict. Similar to Britain and France, Germany lost so many of its citizens in the war that it was forced to import labor to help in its economic reconstruction. This was especially so after the construction of the Berlin Wall, built by the Soviet Union to divide East Germany from West Germany. The Berlin Wall effectively reduced to a trickle the flow of migrants from Communist East Germany to the more prosperous capitalist West Germany.

The growing domestic and global market for West Germany's cars, machine tools, appliances, and other manufactured products influenced the government to recruit foreign workers, primarily from Spain, Greece, Turkey, and Portugal. The government and trade unions agreed that Germans and foreigners would receive equal wages. Under the Gastarbeiter rotation system, foreign workers were regarded as guest workers who would remain in Germany for one to three years and then return to their home countries. Today, almost 3 million Turks live in Germany. The fall of the Berlin Wall in 1989 and the reunification of Germany complicated immigration issues as millions of East Germans migrated to West Germany for economic opportunities and as Germany struggled to develop the former East Germany. Unemployment became a major issue as Germany's economy weakened. Faced with the influx of migrants from Eastern Europe, the former Yugoslavia, and other countries,

Berlin Wall ■ Cold War barrier between Soviet-occupied Germany and democratic West Germany, in place 1961–1989

Gastarbeiter rotation system ■ West German plan for foreign workers to stay one to three years then return home

Germans began to perceive immigrants as economic competitors and threats to their country's cultural values.[14] These developments have been compounded by what Ralph Rotte calls "a permanent latent potential of culturally and ethnically oriented xenophobia."

SOCIAL, ECONOMIC, AND POLITICAL IMPLICATIONS OF MIGRATION

As we have seen throughout this chapter, migration has profound social economic, and political implications for both sending and receiving countries. Migration deepens cultural, economic, and political ties among countries, thereby creating an increasingly global community in which nationalism, ethnicity, and traditionalism are weakened, and broader and more complex forms of identity are emerging. Combined with other aspects of globalization such as communications, transportation, finance, and trade, migration challenges the traditional nation-state and transforms international relations.

The Impact of Migration on Sending Countries

Both gains and losses result when large numbers of people migrate. Brain drain (i.e., the migration of highly educated and trained people) is widely regarded as a serious problem and a major impediment to development in poor countries. Many doctors, nurses, teachers, and university professors leave poorer countries and rural areas for higher-paying jobs and better opportunities in neighboring countries as well as in rich industrial countries. As many as 70,000 educated and skilled Africans migrate to Western Europe, Canada, the United States, and elsewhere each year. This brain drain has significant implications for poor countries. Many medical problems in poor countries are negatively impacted by a shortage of medical personnel.

It is estimated that half of the recent graduates from the prestigious Indian Institute of Technology migrate to the United States. They are driven out by push factors such as overregulation, higher taxes, stagnant career paths, and numerous impediments to entrepreneurship. Many are attracted to the United States by better economic opportunities and a dynamic environment conducive to economic success and personal growth. The fact that most Indian immigrants speak English enables them to easily integrate into American society. It is estimated that one third of the engineers in Silicon Valley are of Indian origin. About 7 percent of Silicon Valley's high-tech firms are managed by Indians. Sabeer Bhatia, for example, founded Hotmail and sold it to Microsoft, and Vinod Khosla is a cofounder of Sun Microsystems.[15] But the migration of talented individuals is seen as detrimental to India's economic development. On the other hand, many countries have a problem of brain overflow, which is essentially an oversupply of skilled individuals. Many poor countries, such as the Philippines, India, and Egypt, have become exporters of highly educated people because of their inability to utilize their talents. Remittances (i.e., money earned abroad that is sent by migrants to their home countries) play a crucial role in the economic development of poor societies. Given

Brain drain ■
Migration of highly educated, skilled, and trained people from one country to another

brain overflow ■
When countries retain an oversupply of skilled individuals

remittances ■
Money earned abroad sent by migrants to their home countries

the fact that remittances are transferred by millions of migrants in various ways, it is extremely difficult to know how much money migrants send to their families or invest in their home countries. Remittances clearly create networks of interdependence among countries, NGOs, and individuals. Organizations such as the Inter-American Development Bank (IDB) and the U.S. Agency for International Development (USAID) have developed strategies to assist migrants in transmitting remittances more economically. This development reflects the growing economic impact of remittances on developing countries. It is estimated that remittances totaled $325 billion in 2010.[16]

The Impact of Migration on Receiving Countries

Most receiving countries are characterized by increasing cultural and ethnic diversity. Think about New York, London, Toronto, Miami, and Paris. Migration has profoundly influenced food, social relations, education, communications, art, literature, music, fashion, and architecture. Migration also raises questions about nationality. Are you a citizen? Migration challenges traditional ideas about who belongs or should belong to receiving countries. These questions are at the heart of anti-immigration nationalism and multiculturalism in Western Europe and, to a much lesser degree, in the United States. Between 2000 and 2010, the Hispanic population in the United States grew by 43 percent, compared with 5 percent for the rest of the population. Hispanics accounted for half the population growth during that period. As we discussed earlier in the chapter, population influences virtually all other domestic and global issues. Migration has transformed politics in many receiving countries, especially the United States. Because many migrants maintain links with their home societies, they influence international relations as well as the domestic politics of sending countries. Many anti-immigration nationalists view these links as threats and as a part of the broader issue of a clash of civilizations, as we will discuss in Chapter 14.

Economic issues are at the heart of migration. As fertility rates decline and the population ages in rich countries, the need for young workers becomes a priority. But many countries remain divided on the issue.[17] Migrants provide flexible workers and highly skilled professionals to labor-scarce economic sectors. They help reduce inflation by lowering prices of domestically produced goods and services, and also contribute to entitlement programs such as Social Security. On the other hand, migrants often depress local wages, put pressure on health and education services, and undermine labor rights. Simultaneously, they help create a cultural generation gap that often engenders hostility and a reluctance of the older population to allocate resources to programs for the young.

As we saw in Chapter 1, the rise and fall of great powers cannot be separated from demographics. Migration played an essential role in the rise of Holland, Britain, and the United States. Migration is giving America a demographic advantage over other developed countries where population is aging rapidly. Young migrants are crucial to America's renewal, economic growth, cultural vitality, and military power.

CASE STUDY | Global Aging and Pensions

Demographic changes have profound implications for a wide range of global issues. In many ways, population problems help determine the fate of nations and human survival. National security is affected as the proportion of younger people, who fight wars, declines, and as governments are pressured to reduce military spending in order to allocate more scarce resources to the elderly population. The broader issue of human security, discussed in Chapter 1, is becoming increasingly important as the consequences of aging populations become more acute, especially in Japan, Western Europe, the United States, China, and Canada. The proportion of people aged 60 and older in those countries comprises between 20 and 30 percent of the population, a proportion that is rapidly growing. Due to low fertility rates and the one-child policy in China, the longer people live there means there will be fewer young people to support them, thereby diminishing the traditional intergenerational contract that provided a safety net for the elderly. As large numbers of workers born during the baby boom of 1945–1965 retire, rich countries are confronting a sharp decline in the working-age population. Countries with rapidly aging populations are likely to decline economically unless they rely on immigrant workers to remain vibrant and competitive globally. As we saw in Chapter 2, great powers are usually weakened by their relative economic decline and are replaced by rising nations with growing economies. Dealing with enormous financial costs of aging populations will require even larger budget deficits and higher taxes, both of which impede economic growth and undermine the general welfare. Governments are creating huge future financial liabilities for younger taxpayers. The global financial and economic crisis and subsequent implementation of austerity measures in many rich countries focused attention on aging populations and public pensions. Japan, already facing economic stagnation and huge public expenditures to deal with its aging population, is burdened by the most expensive natural disaster in history, discussed in Chapter 10.

Pensions are expensive to provide as people are living much longer and as investments to fund their retirement are not yielding high returns and actually lost money during the global financial crisis. When the United States implemented pensions in 1935 to alleviate economic hardships in old age, the official pension age was 65 and the average life expectancy was 62. Now America's pension age has risen to 66, but people on average retire at 64 and many live for another twenty or thirty years. In America, state and local pension benefits are generally guaranteed by law. This means that even as states are facing growing budget deficits they are constitutionally required to meet their obligations to retirees. There are two main retirement plans: the *defined benefit plan*, under which retirees are paid a proportion of their final salaries (which is as high as 90 percent, in Colorado), and the *defined contribution plan*, under which employees' pensions are determined by the performance of investments they and their employers made. Many pension plans cover health insurance, which is becoming increasingly expensive as the population ages. Efforts to deal with the problems of aging and pensions by raising the retirement age (from 60 to 62, in France) were met with large protests in France, Greece, and elsewhere. Labor unions, mainly teachers and other public employees, staged extended protests in Wisconsin in 2011 to prevent the state government from weakening their collective bargaining power.

Finding solutions to problems related to aging and pensions is difficult, due partly to political pressures and the fact that those making decisions on pensions want to protect their own retirement benefits. An important part of the solution is to limit the practice of early retirement to special cases. Raising the retirement age is widely viewed as being responsible toward young people who have to support aging populations and simultaneously secure their own retirements. A later retirement age increases the number of workers as well as tax revenues. Raising the retirement age for lower-paid

(continued)

workers is generally opposed on the grounds that their jobs are strenuous and their life expectancy is shorter than that of higher-paid workers. Many countries are already implementing less expensive defined benefit plans or switching to defined contribution plans. Some countries encourage people to have more children, an idea that has been rejected in rich countries such as Singapore. A more realistic alternative is to encourage immigration to help take care of the elderly, strengthen the economy, and provide more tax revenues to fund pensions and healthcare costs. ◢

SUMMARY AND REVIEW

Migration is an important issue throughout many countries and regions of the world today. It has greatly contributed to globalization and to an increased interdependence among many countries and peoples. This chapter illustrates how population and migration issues are essentially about politics, economics, and culture. Population issues are an increasing problem in the developed and developing countries as they hinder economic growth and place great pressures on already strained populations. Underpopulation has become a major problem due to a rapid increase in aging populations throughout developed countries. In an attempt to rectify this problem, some states have attempted to increase fertility rates domestically and encourage immigration from abroad. High rates of population growth have had devastating consequences in the developed world as well. In an effort to ease overpopulation, many developing countries have resorted to strict population controls; an example is China's one-child policy. Other countries have encouraged their citizens to migrate to other states.

Migration has various forms. It can be forced or induced. Sometimes it is temporary, as when workers return to their countries of origin. Migration can be regional or transcontinental, and it can be seasonal or permanent. Many factors have contributed to increased migration. Push factors—such as environmental disasters, high unemployment, high population growth rates, state repression, and discrimination—have encouraged many to look for safer homes where they can pursue prosperous futures. Pull factors have also enticed many to migrate, seeking economic and political freedoms, a safer environment for themselves and their families, educational opportunities, and a chance to earn higher wages.

KEY TERMS

overpopulation   232
replacement rate   233
carrying capacity   233
sexism   234
son complex   234

dowry   234
one-child policy   234
subreplacement fertility regimes   235
migration   237
migrant   237

DISCUSSION QUESTIONS

1. How will the global aging and pensions problems affect you?
2. What are some of the causes, as well as negative consequences, of high and low population growth rates?
3. In what way do remittances help strengthen the ties between economies and people? Do you think remittances are a positive thing?
4. Can you identify some of the push and pull factors that traditionally lead to increased regional and global migration?
5. Discuss the economic, political, and social implications of migration for both sending and receiving countries.

SUGGESTED READINGS

Akula, Vikram. *A Fistful of Rice*. Cambridge, MA: Harvard Business Press, 2010. An autobiographical account of efforts by an American with Indian ancestry to alleviate poverty in India through microfinance.

Baily, Martin, and Jacob Kirkegaard. *U.S. Pension Reform*. Washington, DC: Peterson Institute for International Economics, 2009. Increasing longevity and low birthrates threaten the viability of public pensions in rich countries.

Dancygier, Rafaela M. *Immigration and Conflict in Europe*. Cambridge: Cambridge University Press, 2010. Discusses complex aspects of the politics of immigration, focusing on Germany and Britain.

Kapur, Davesh. *Diaspora, Development, and Democracy*. Princeton, NJ: Princeton University Press, 2010. Analyzes emigration from India and how the Indian diaspora influences India's economics, culture, and foreign policy.

ENDNOTES

1. Jack Goldstone, "The New Population Bomb," *Foreign Affairs* 89, No. 1 (January/February 2010), 33.
2. "Rethinking China's One-Child Policy," *Economist*, 21 August 2010, 31.
3. Sara Rhodin, "A Holiday and a Park Bench from Russia with Love," *New York Times*, 9 July 2008, A12.
4. David Eltis and David Richardson, *Atlas of the Transatlantic Slave Trade* (New Haven, CT: Yale University Press, 2010).
5. "Tribes Still Matter," *Economist*, 22 January 2011, 17.
6. Kimberly A. Hamilton and Kate Holder, "International Migration and Foreign Policy," *Washington Quarterly* (Spring 1996), 196.
7. "Number of Displaced People Hits Global High," *Daily Herald*, 24 March 2011, 29.
8. Michael Fischbach, *The Peace Process and Palestinian Refugee Claims* (Washington, DC: U.S. Institute of Peace Press, 2006).
9. Steve Raymer, *Images of a Journey: India in Diaspora* (Bloomington: Indiana University Press, 2008).
10. "Skilled Immigration," *Economist*, 30 October 2010, 33.
11. Hans Norman, "Swedes in North America," in *From Sweden to America*, eds. Harald Runblom and Hans Norman (Minneapolis: University of Minnesota Press, 1976), 246.
12. Henry J. Steiner and Detlev F. Vagts, *Transnational Legal Problems* (Mineola, NY: Foundation Press, 1976), 19.
13. "Romanies: A Long Road," *Economist*, 18 September 2010, 73.
14. Judy Dempsey, "Can Muslims Be True Germans?" *New York Times*, 7 March 2011, A5.
15. "How Global Leaders Tap into Diaspora Networks," *Economist*, 22 January 2011, 17.
16. "Remittances," *Economist*, 13 November 2010, 114.
17. Tamar Jacoby, "Germany's Immigration Dilemma," *Foreign Affairs* 90, No. 2 (March/April 2011), 13.

Global Crime

India's rapid economic growth has contributed to government corruption by providing more money and opportunity. For example, due to the theft of billions of dollars, facilities for the 2010 Commonwealth Games in Delhi were poorly constructed and not completed on schedule. A woman in India walked past a poster for the games.

INTRODUCTION

Global crime is intricately intertwined with revolutionary technological, financial, communications, economic, cultural, and political changes that characterize globalization, and it is increasingly difficult to separate criminal activities from legitimate global transactions. Wars and ethnic conflicts create an environment in which crime is prevalent. When armies are reduced and militias are disbanded after conflicts end, crime continues. The wars in Central America contributed to the rise of violent gangs and drug trafficking.

The disintegration of the Soviet Union contributed to the strengthening and unleashing of criminal organizations that have constructed global networks involved in drug trafficking, human trafficking, money laundering, illegal arms sales, and other criminal activities. Global crime is also linked to global poverty and inequality, failed states, global migration, growth of global cities, the expansion of free trade, rapid communications and computer technologies, and easy global financial transactions. Criminal activities of government officials facilitate global crime. This chapter examines the globalization of crime, the perpetual global drug problem, the global smuggling of migrants, contemporary slavery and human trafficking, criminal gangs and kidnapping, illegal trade in exotic animals and plants, cybercrimes, piracy, and various global responses to crime. It concludes with a case study of government corruption in India.

THE GLOBALIZATION OF CRIME

Global crime has existed with legal commerce for centuries. In fact, crime has been an integral component of human society. By diminishing the significance of geographic distance, globalization enables criminal networks to grow alongside legal global activities and to establish connections within many different countries. As we will discuss, alliances are common among criminal organizations involved in trafficking in humans, drugs, weapons, and various illicit products.

Although globalization has contributed to increased economic equality among and within nations, as Thomas Friedman argues in *The World Is Flat*, it is widely perceived as contributing to more inequality. To an unprecedented degree of poignancy, globalization heightens the awareness of the economic and social disparities between the rich and the poor within nations and between rich and poor countries. Not only do poor people perceive themselves as losers in the process of globalization, they have little incentive to adhere to rules that they perceive to be adverse to their interests. For example, convincing coca farmers in Peru, Colombia, and Bolivia that they should not participate in illegal drug production has been difficult. Similarly, small farmers in Afghanistan continue to produce poppies used to make heroin. The insatiable demand for illegal drugs in the United States, Western Europe, and elsewhere perpetuates efforts by drug traffickers to supply drugs. Although organized crime imposes excessive burdens on society, particularly the poor, many criminal groups, in order to gain political influence and legitimacy, invest in social services, athletic facilities, housing, and medical services. These areas have been largely neglected by many governments as part of the privatization process required by economic globalization. Ultimately, global crime is integrated into the fabric of these societies and enjoys significant official and unofficial protection. In some cases, weak institutional capabilities have prevented governments from reducing global crime. Consequently, there has been an unprecedented escalation in crimes such as trade in pirated goods, illegal arms, human trafficking, and illegal drugs.

The disintegration of the Soviet Union in 1991 was one of the most important developments contributing to the emergence and growth of global crime. Rapid political and economic changes in Eastern and Central European countries further enhanced opportunities for widespread criminal activities. Exploiting the weakness of the Russian government, organized criminal groups consolidated their power domestically and built strategic alliances with global criminal organizations in Latin America and the Caribbean. Russian criminal groups proliferated throughout Central Europe, in countries such as the Czech Republic, as successful revolutions against Communism ushered in social disorganization, poorly guarded national borders, free-market economies, and a willingness of young people to experiment with drugs. Furthermore, as we discussed in Chapter 1, the expansion of the European Union (EU) into Central and Eastern Europe and the removal of many national barriers to the movement of people and products facilitated the growth of criminal activities.

THE GLOBAL DRUG PROBLEM

From Shanghai to San Francisco, from London to Buenos Aires, in Christian, Jewish, Islamic, Hindu, and Buddhist societies, in small towns and big cities, and in rich and poor countries, the use of illegal drugs is a serious problem. Illegal drug use is one of the most important global issues. No society has managed to escape the consequences of the global drug trade, largely because the global drug problem is so closely intertwined with other areas of globalization. The foundations of the contemporary global drug problem were laid during an earlier period of globalization that was marked by European expansion, colonization, and trade.

The discoveries of tobacco in the Caribbean, chocolate in South America, coffee in the Middle East and Africa, and tea in Asia marked the beginning of a global trade that eventually included opium. The growth of the opium trade was influenced partly by China's huge trade advantage with Portugal, Holland, and Britain. Whereas China had silk, teas, pottery, and other items that Europeans wanted, Europe had little to trade with China, thereby creating a trade deficit in China's favor. Europeans, who had trafficked in opium in parts of Asia, decided to sell it to China in order to reduce the trade imbalances.[1] The **British East India Company**, for example, paid Asian farmers to produce opium, which was then sold to independent wholesalers. Opium cultivation in India grew steadily, and the British pressured China to import it. Chinese resistance to the importation and consumption of opium ultimately led to the Opium Wars with Britain in 1839 and 1842, in which Britain forced China to import opium, despite an already horrendous drug addiction problem in China. British military power was instrumental in the legalization of opium

British East India Company ■ British company that dominated Indian trade

Opium Wars ■ Fought so that the British could force the opium trade onto the Chinese people

in China in 1858. The Portuguese, French, Spanish, and Dutch also participated in the trade, creating opium addicts in their colonies as well as in Europe. The Spanish, for example, promoted the use of coca leaves to enable enslaved Indians to endure harsh physical labor. Miners in Peru, for example, continue to chew coca leaves before going to work. Coca leaves also are widely used legally in Bolivia. Toward the end of the nineteenth century, *the demand for opium in Europe and America was on the rise due to several factors.* These included

1. *The advancement in medical practices,* especially the discovery of morphine and heroin (both obtained from opium) and the invention of the hypodermic needle to administer them;
2. *Significant cultural and economic changes* that resulted from the Industrial Revolution, particularly the consumption of natural stimulants;
3. *The migration of Chinese,* many of whom used opium, to America and elsewhere;
4. *The growth of global trade;*
5. *The rise of mass consumption habits,* influenced by marketing and mass communication;[2] and
6. *Military conflicts,* including the U.S. Civil War, which increased the demand for drugs to diminish pain.

Globalization combined with major cultural changes worldwide—especially in the United States, Canada, and Europe—is driving the global drug trade. Most experts agree that widespread use of illegal drugs in Western societies during the 1960s and 1970s created a global demand for drugs, which in turn stimulated worldwide illegal drug production. Heroin was smuggled in from areas that cultivated opium poppies, primarily the Golden Triangle countries (Burma/Myanmar, Thailand, and Laos) and the Golden Crescent countries (Afghanistan, Pakistan, and Iran). Cocaine came primarily from Colombia, Peru, Bolivia, and other South American countries. Marijuana, now increasingly grown within consuming countries, came primarily from Mexico, Jamaica, Colombia, and Thailand. Global trafficking networks quickly developed or were expanded to produce, distribute, and sell illegal drugs. Global commerce and migration have helped to consolidate the global drug trade. For example, Mexican drug traffickers take advantage of the growing number of Mexican immigrants in U.S. cities to turn those areas into distribution centers for methamphetamine and other drugs. Industrial countries are now themselves major sources of illegal drugs. Nightclub crowds worldwide routinely use Ecstasy, a euphoria-producing psychedelic drug that was initially used in Europe around 1912 as an appetite suppressant. What's more, distinctions between legal and illegal drugs are diminishing as more people abuse prescription medications. The abuse of prescription drugs accounts for by far the largest component of the drug problem in the United States.

Golden Triangle ■
Countries that cultivate opium poppies (Burma/Myanmar, Thailand, and Laos)

Efforts to Control the Drug Problem

The reality of the global drug trade and the inability of governments to prevent drugs from entering countries have spawned essentially two different approaches to dealing with the drug problem. The first approach, the war on drugs, stresses

war on drugs ■
Stresses supply side control and harsh treatment of drug users

supply side control and harsh treatment of drug users. The second approach, *drug prevention and harm reduction*, emphasizes the need to keep drugs out of society and to treat drug abuse as a disease. The first approach is strongly embraced by the United States; the second approach is widely practiced in Europe. Before discussing these two strategies, we will briefly examine historical efforts to control the use of illegal drugs. Drug-exporting countries usually become major drug-consuming societies. As we saw earlier, European countries openly and aggressively built a global drug trade. By the beginning of the twentieth century, the widespread use of cocaine-based tonics, heroin, opium, and other narcotics in Europe, the United States, Japan, and China raised concerns about their negative impact on public morals. Religious groups, temperance societies, and others in Britain and the United States advocated ending the opium trade. As the United States expanded its power into Asia, especially after the Spanish-American War in 1898 (which resulted in the end of Spain's empire and America's acquisition of the Philippines), Americans became more concerned about drug abuse. The Philippines had many drug addicts.

Partly because of its interest in gaining greater influence in China, the United States collaborated with China to persuade other countries to participate in an international conference designed to convince drug-exporting countries to reduce their production of drugs. The conference, held in Shanghai in 1909, created the International Opium Commission. Although the twelve countries involved agreed to gradually suppress opium smoking in their territories, very little progress on controlling drugs was made. The Hague Convention of 1911 broadened the drug-fighting effort by including morphine and cocaine and committed the signatories to reducing their production and distribution of drugs. However, the Hague Convention was ineffective, partly because some countries—such as Germany, which at the time was the world's largest cocaine producer—insisted that the implementation of the treaty be made conditional on its worldwide acceptance.[3] Given the lucrativeness of drugs, few countries were willing to comply with the restrictive agreements. A turning point in the effort to control the drug trade was America's enactment of the Harrison Act in 1914, which required distributors and medical prescribers of specified drugs to be registered and pay taxes. Britain and other European countries enacted similar legislation. The League of Nations (1919) helped to consolidate drug-control efforts by stressing the development of mandatory international controls to be supervised by international organizations. The Opium Control Board was established by the League of Nations to monitor countries' compliance with international agreements on controlling drugs. The rapid spread of drug usage in the 1960s and 1970s influenced the United Nations (UN) to sponsor the International Conference on Drug Abuse and Illicit Traffic in 1987 to discuss strategies for dealing with the problem. In 1988, strongly influenced by America's emphasis on the war-on-drugs approach, the global community signed the UN Convention Against Illicit Traffic in Narcotic Drugs and Psychotropic Substances. This convention stressed sharing law enforcement evidence, providing mutual legal assistance, controlling the sale of chemicals used in producing drugs, and escalating the eradication of drug crops.[4] Founded in 1990, the UN International Drug Control Program (UNDCP) stressed the need for both demand reduction and alternative development. In 1998, the UN General Assembly Special

Hague Convention ■ Broadened the international drug-fighting effort by cracking down on morphine and cocaine

Harrison Act ■ U.S. act requiring distributors and prescribers of drugs to be registered and pay taxes

Opium Control Board ■ Established under the League of Nations to monitor countries' compliance with international drug agreements

Session on Drugs had advocated the goal of a drug-free world by 2008. Obviously, this goal has not been achieved.

Confronted with the rapid rise in drug abuse, the United States mobilized financial, law enforcement, and military resources to combat the problem. The war on drugs concentrates primarily on reducing global drug trafficking and drug use by eliminating supplies and implementing punitive drug laws. It is estimated that between 50 and 80 percent of Americans who are imprisoned have committed a drug-related offense. The United States has cooperated with governments throughout Latin America to eradicate drug crops, implement crop substitution programs, and destroy trafficking networks. In 2000, for example, the United States and Colombia launched Plan Colombia, an antidrug program that had the goal of reducing Colombia's coca crop in half by 2005. The plan involved aerial spraying, promoting crop substitution, destroying cocaine labs, and disrupting transportation routes. The United States allocated $1.3 billion to Plan Colombia. Given how lucrative the drug business is, the war on drugs has not significantly reduced the drug trade. Drug production increased in Bolivia, Mexico, Central America, and in the United States. Poverty and tradition motivate many small farmers in Latin America and Asia to grow drug crops. The money they earn from crop substitution is only a fraction of what they can earn from drug crops. Ironically, success in removing drugs from the market increases the demand for declining supplies, thereby driving up prices. This, in turn, influences people to cultivate drug crops. Corrupt law enforcement officials worldwide also undermine the war on drugs. Most importantly, the war on drugs largely ignores the demand for drugs within the United States, Europe, and elsewhere. Coca production in Colombia was not significantly reduced, despite the more than $6 billion pumped into that effort by the United States. Homicides have escalated at the U.S.-Mexico border as drug cartels fight to dominate the illegal drug trade. More than forty thousand Mexicans have been killed since 2007. The drug war and weapons sales became a major issue in U.S.-Mexican relations. In an effort to diminish violence and reduce drug sales, the United States began sending drones over Mexico to locate traffickers and follow their networks.[5] "Fast and Furious," an undercover operation by the U.S. Bureau of Alcohol, Tobacco, Firearms and Explosives, became a scandal after Americans learned that the operation, in hopes of following weapons purchased illegally in the United States to Mexican drug bosses, lost track of many weapons that were later used to commit crimes in Mexico. Also, concerned about increasing murders, many Mexicans demonstrated and called for an end to the drug war and for the legalization of drugs.

By contrast, Europeans concentrate on treating drug addiction more as a medical problem while supporting efforts to reduce drug supplies. Harm reduction approaches acknowledge the weaknesses of the war-on-drugs approach. Holland became a pioneer in implementing the harm-reduction approach. It decriminalizes possession and use of small amounts of "soft" drugs (such as marijuana), provides "safe injection rooms" so that addicts can avoid public places, distributes sterile syringes to reduce the spread of HIV and AIDS, and supports medical treatment for drug addicts.

Plan Colombia ■ U.S.-sponsored antidrug campaign implemented to eradicate Colombia's cocaine production

harm reduction approaches ■ Aim at drug prevention and drug treatment

Drug violence is escalating in Mexico. How can the United States help reduce crime there? Mexican forensic specialists work in a mass grave where they found eight bodies, murdered in drug violence.

GLOBAL SMUGGLING OF MIGRANTS

The global economic recession of 2008–2009 significantly diminished the demand for migrant workers. In fact, as we have seen, return migration is now the global trend. However, desperate people continue to be smuggled to areas where they perceive economic and social opportunities. In June 2000, British customs officials discovered the bodies of fifty-eight illegal Chinese immigrants in a sealed compartment of a Dutch-registered tomato truck. They had been smuggled into Dover after a five-hour journey across the English Channel from the Belgian port of Zeebrugge. France is also a transit point for illegal immigrants who pay global smuggling operations to get them into Britain and, in many cases, eventually to the United States and Canada.

The extensive U.S.-Mexican border provided smugglers with a relatively easy way to get migrants to the most popular destination. Increased U.S. border control activities have contributed to reduced illegal immigration. Immigrant communities along the border, the existence of criminal organizations that operate between the countries, the well-established drug trade, and the flow of people and products across the U.S.-Mexican border facilitate the successful smuggling of migrants from around the world. But the tragic deaths of nineteen migrants who were being smuggled across the border in May 2003 refocused national attention on the illegal and brutal nature of global smuggling. At least seventy-seven migrants were packed into an unconventional tractor-trailer without water for a 325-mile journey across the scorching desert. Some who survived had body temperatures as high as 105 degrees. Many migrants become victims of traffickers and drug gangs. In 2010, the Zetas, a Mexican drug-trafficking gang, killed seventy-two migrants from Central and South America when they refused to get involved in smuggling drugs into the United States.[6] An additional 145 bodies were found in ten mass graves in the same area in 2011.

Chinese global smuggling organizations are generally regarded as the most sophisticated and most brutal. Many migrants come from the Fujian province in southern China and take advantage of connections with family members and friends already established in the United States, Canada, and European countries. Chinese communities worldwide, especially those in large cities, provide extensive networks of connections that enable global smuggling operations to be efficient and lucrative. Chinese migrants pay smugglers between $30,000 and $60,000 to be transported to Europe, the United States, and Canada. They travel across many countries or across nine thousand miles of the Pacific Ocean for five weeks in unsanitary, unseaworthy ships. Many of them land in Central America and make a long and perilous journey across Mexico and into the United States, where they find employment in Chinese communities to repay their debt for being smuggled. Often, they pay an initial 10 percent of the smuggling cost, and relatives pay the rest once the migrants arrive at their destinations.[7]

CONTEMPORARY SLAVERY AND HUMAN TRAFFICKING

human trafficking ■ Forced movement of people within or between countries

contemporary slavery ■ Transporting people from one area to another, where they are subjugated to forced labor or prostitution

Human trafficking (i.e., the forced or coerced movement of people across national borders as well as within countries) is probably as old as human civilization. Throughout history, human beings have enslaved each other and forced each other to work under the most inhumane conditions, justifying this exploitation in many ways. Contemporary slavery is the transporting of victims under false pretenses from one nation, or province, to another, where they are subjugated to forced labor or prostitution.[8] Compared with the global drug trade, human trafficking receives much less attention. Nonetheless, it is a growing problem. Although the U.S. Central Intelligence Agency estimates that almost a million people worldwide are enslaved each year, including twenty thousand in the United States, it is impossible to know how many people are actually trafficked.[9]

The exponential growth in contemporary slavery and human trafficking is inseparable from increasing levels of economic and cultural globalization. Global inequality and demographic factors contribute to the rapid growth of labor migration, a development in which most countries participate. Migrants are employed to do the most strenuous and undesirable jobs in most countries, including the United States. Globalization and changing attitudes about women have led to a dramatic increase in women migrants. Many women are employed as domestic helpers in service industries and as dancers, strippers, and sex workers in the entertainment industry. This feminization of migration (i.e., the increasing percentage of women in the migrant population) complicates the human trafficking problem.[10]

feminization of migration ■ The increasing percentage of women in the migrant population

Despite the global emphasis on women and girls being trafficked for sexual exploitation, the International Labor Organization (ILO) found that of the estimated 9.5 million victims of forced labor in Asia, less than 10 percent were trafficked for commercial sexual exploitation. Globally, less than half of all trafficking victims are involved in the sex trade.[11] Women and girls are generally perceived as replaceable commodities by human traffickers. Although virtually all societies have experienced human trafficking for sexual purposes, this practice seems to be more prevalent in several Asian countries. Prior to the Russian Revolution in 1917, Russian and Eastern European women were trafficked into China and Argentina. Between the 1970s and today, there have been *four distinct waves of sexual human trafficking*, all of which are manifestations of increasing globalization. The *first wave* began in the 1970s and was primarily composed of trafficked women from Southeast Asia, particularly Thailand and the Philippines. The *second wave* started in the early 1980s and involved trafficked women mostly from Africa, especially Ghana and Nigeria. The *third wave*, from the 1980s to the 1990s, was made up of Latin Americans, with most of the women coming from Colombia, Brazil, and the Dominican Republic. The *fourth wave*, which mirrors the rapid expansion and growing complexity of globalization, is closely connected to the demise of the Soviet Union. The women are coming from Eastern and Central Europe.[12]

Although women are trafficked globally, the Netherlands, Germany, Japan, the United Arab Emirates, Israel, Greece, South Korea, Turkey, Austria, Belgium, Bosnia, the United States, and Canada are the principal destinations. Criminals collaborate to maximize their profits from human trafficking. Groups in the Russian Far East cooperate with Japanese and Korean organized crime to transport women to China, Japan, Korea, Thailand, and other countries of the Pacific Rim. Groups in the Caucasus collaborate with human traffickers in Turkey to transport women to brothels in Turkey, Cyprus, and countries in the Middle East. Women from Kazakhstan are trafficked to Bahrain, where the Muslim links of the traffickers provide women for this free-trade zone.[13]

Most trafficked women are forced into prostitution. Many young women worldwide are seduced by romantic images of the West to take risks that often result in their sexual exploitation. Poverty has usually been a major factor influencing human trafficking. Radical economic changes that accompanied the fall of Communism in the Soviet Union and the transition from a centralized economy to a market-based economy undermined economic security for many women, even as these changes provided the impetus for increased globalization. Women became more vulnerable to trafficking as they attempted to find employment in other countries to support their families.

Although trafficking across national boundaries for sexual exploitation is a significant component of global crime, most trafficked women and girls remain within their countries or regions. In India alone, for example, more than half a million girls are in brothels, more than any other country in the world. The rapid growth of sex tourism in Asia and elsewhere reinforces the sexual exploitation of women and girls within their own societies. What's more, the AIDS pandemic is influencing human traffickers to find younger women and girls, especially virgins, because customers believe they are less likely to be infected with HIV and AIDS.[14]

Fourth World Conference on Women ■ Called on governments to prevent trafficking in women

UN Protocol Against the Trafficking in Women and Children ■ Global effort in 2000 to address growing trafficking problem

Victims of Trafficking and Violence Protection Act ■ Requires the United States to prosecute human traffickers and to publish an annual report on global trafficking

The global response to human trafficking has largely been ineffective. Several efforts to address this problem have been made at both national and global levels. In 1989, the European Parliament adopted a resolution that called for tough measures to eradicate human trafficking. Meeting in Beijing at the Fourth World Conference on Women and declaring that women's rights are human rights, delegates from 189 countries unanimously adopted a platform for action, which called on governments to dismantle criminal networks engaged in trafficking women. In response to the unprecedented growth in human trafficking, the UN Protocol Against the Trafficking in Women and Children was adopted along with the UN Convention on Transnational Crime in 2000. At a world summit on organized crime in 2000 in Palermo, Italy, leaders from eighty countries signed the UN protocol. Also in 2000, a coalition of Democrats, Republicans, feminists, and evangelical Christians pressured the U.S. Congress to enact the Victims of Trafficking and Violence Protection Act to prosecute traffickers in the United States and to take action abroad against this global crime. This law recognized human trafficking as a federal crime and requires the U.S. Department of State to publish an annual report on the state of human trafficking globally.[15]

While the global community was responding to the problem of human trafficking, several countries were legalizing the sex trade, which consists predominantly of foreign women in most European countries. For example, roughly half a million women are trafficked as prostitutes in Europe every year. In Germany, three out of four sex workers are foreigners, and in the Netherlands, one out of two sex workers comes from another country. In 2000, the Netherlands legalized prostitution, which is a billion-dollar-a-year industry and represents roughly 5 percent of that country's economy. Germany legalized prostitution in 2001. The sex trade contributes approximately $4.5 billion to Germany's economy.[16] Very few traffickers are prosecuted and convicted. Furthermore, the illegal immigration status of trafficked women becomes an impediment to punishing criminals involved in trafficking. Some success in efforts to reduce human trafficking came in 2006 when John R. Miller, a senior adviser to U.S. Secretary of State Condoleezza Rice, persuaded Japan to reduce the number of entertainment visas for women from the Philippines from eighty thousand to five thousand a year.[17]

CRIMINAL GANGS AND KIDNAPPING

The same communications and technological revolutions that drive globalization also help gangs to grow. The Internet enables them to form alliances, to learn from each other, and to terrorize. Repeated exposure to cultural globalization—especially violent television programs, movies, video games, and magazines—reinforces their violent behavior. Ethnic conflicts and civil wars, combined with easy access to guns, provide fertile ground for gang violence to flourish. Aspects of globalization—especially global migration, global inequality, and fewer government-provided public services due to privatization and trade liberalization—contribute to the growth of gangs. Demographic factors also play an important role. Young people between the ages of sixteen and twenty-four tend to commit most of the crimes, especially in densely populated areas. As we discussed earlier in this chapter, poverty and the decline of social services often combine to influence parents to abandon their children, making them vulnerable to gangs. Gang violence threatens peace and security, increases political instability, weakens democratic institutions, increases human rights violations, and impedes economic development. Kidnapping is often an integral component of gang violence. Gang violence usually generates counter-violence by vigilante groups, the military, and police officers.

Foundations for rising gang violence in Central America were laid during the civil wars that devastated the region in the 1980s, driven partly by military and political rivalry between the United States and the Soviet Union. The Cold War in Central America was accompanied by widespread human rights abuses, rape, torture, extrajudicial executions, kidnappings, and drug production and trafficking. In Guatemala alone, more than two hundred thousand people were killed or missing (out of a population of 14 million) during these conflicts. Civil wars also bring with them the proliferation of weapons. As we discussed in Chapter 11, violence is a factor that pushes people to migrate. Many Central Americans came to the United States and settled in the ghettos of Los Angeles and other major American cities. Many young migrants soon became involved in street gangs, committed violent crimes, including murder, and participated in drug trafficking. When the U.S. Congress decided to enact very punitive immigration laws in 1996, noncitizens who were sentenced to a year or more in prison could be repatriated to their country of origin. Foreign-born U.S. citizens who committed felonies could lose their American citizenship and be expelled from the country after serving their sentences. Consequently, roughly twenty thousand young Central American criminals were seventy thousand gang members in Central America. Gang members recreated their violent lifestyles in Central America. Drug trafficking escalated. Central America has the world's highest murder rates. As the United States escalated its war on drugs in Colombia, drug-trafficking organizations moved into Central America and used drugs to pay gang members. Central America is a bridge between Colombia, the world's largest producer of cocaine, and Mexico, which is the transit point for the United States, the world's largest consumer of cocaine and other drugs.[18] Gang members routinely force residents of poor neighborhoods to pay what they call protection fees, demand war taxes from businesses, and often murder individuals who refuse to or cannot pay them. Rapes of young women have increased, homes are robbed, schoolchildren are turned into drug addicts, and kidnappings occur frequently. During his visit to El Salvador in 2011, President Obama pledged $200 million to reduce gang violence.

Previously, most victims of kidnappings were wealthy individuals who could arrange to pay large ransoms. Today, however, ordinary individuals are being kidnapped for a variety of reasons. Terrorists have used kidnappings as bargaining chips and to create widespread fear. Islamic terrorists in the Philippines routinely kidnap foreigners, especially Westerners, to extract money to finance terrorism. Kidnappings are an integral component of violence and drug trafficking in Colombia. Colombia is by far the world's leader in kidnappings, despite an increase in kidnappings in China. Colombia's president, Juan Manuel Santos, threatened to expel foreign companies that paid ransom to kidnappers. The Revolutionary Armed Forces of Colombia routinely kidnap prominent Colombians.[19] In Mexico, Brazil, Kenya, and other places, most kidnappings are fueled by glaring economic inequalities and poverty. These crimes are very lucrative, generating hundreds of millions of dollars each year in ransoms.

ILLEGAL TRADE IN ENDANGERED ANIMALS AND PLANTS

endangered species ■ Animals and plants vulnerable to extinction

The illegal trade in endangered species coexists with legal transactions, thereby making it difficult to ascertain the magnitude of the problem. Nevertheless, there is general agreement that many of the factors we discussed earlier about the globalization of crime combine to sustain and expand both the legal and illicit aspects of this trade. Local and individual decisions directly affect trade in endangered animals and plants. These decisions have significant global consequences. For many individuals, the trade liberalization that characterizes globalization augments perceptions that almost anything can be traded, regardless of long-term consequences for the environment. Economic inequality between conservationists in rich countries and poor people in the developing world, where most animals and plants are located, often gives rise to divergent perceptions of and approaches to illegal trade. For example, elephants are generally regarded as exotic by many residents in rich countries, but many Africans view them as threats to their safety and their crops. On the other hand, carefully managed animals and plants can play a major role in ecotourism and other aspects of economic development. Political instability and ethnic conflicts in many countries often facilitate both trade in and the destruction of many endangered animals and plants. Illicit trade fuels many conflicts. Illegal wildlife trade also raises issues such as sustainability and biological diversity. Also, imports of animals and plants sometimes contribute to problems associated with invasive species that threaten native species.

Given the global reach of traffickers in endangered animals and plants and the numerous small illegal transactions that occur daily by individuals worldwide, ascertaining the financial gains from this global crime is extremely difficult, if not impossible. While global attention was drawn to illicit trade in endangered animals by large sales of African elephant tusks to Japan and elsewhere, the expansion of legal trade and the Internet have significantly broadened this criminal activity. The most endangered species—such as tigers, Asian bears, rhinoceros, hyacinth macaws from the Amazon, Australian palm cockatoos, Saiga antelopes, and hawksbill turtles—command high prices. As we saw in Chapter 10, rhinoceros horns are more valuable than gold. Many of the highly valued illegally traded species are believed to have medicinal properties and are usually in great demand in several Asian countries. Many traditional Chinese medicines contain ingredients composed of tiger bone, bear bile, deer musk glands, and shark fins. The demand for shark fin soup is of great concern to environmentalists who believe that sharks are an endangered species. Many animals are sold for food and to pet shops worldwide. Products derived from endangered wildlife include exotic leather goods, ornaments, and tourist souvenirs. Increasing wealth, engendered by economic globalization, has also led to a growth in demand for expensive products such as caviar. As countries around the Caspian Sea attempt to conserve the sturgeon population, illegal trade in caviar has escalated. Global trade in plants and forest products is accompanied by illegal logging operations and lumber sales, especially in Southeast Asia, Central Africa, the Amazonian countries, and Russia. Millions of plants are sold illegally, and medicinal plants that are in great demand due to a global preoccupation with finding easy solutions to health problems are threatened with extinction. These include hoodia (which is used in diet pills), cistanche (a natural tonic), and the Chinese yew tree (which is believed to have cancer-fighting properties).

Concerned about animal and plant extinction, the global community responded by signing the Convention on International Trade in Endangered Species of Wild Flora and Fauna (CITES) in 1973. This convention provides a framework within which countries adopt domestic legislation to ensure that CITES is implemented at the national level. Combating illegal trade in endangered animals and plants is an integral component of efforts to strengthen wildlife management, promote sustainability, and diminish deforestation. Several nongovernmental organizations (NGOs) participate in efforts to protect endangered species, including the World Conservation Union, World Wide Fund for Nature, Fauna and Flora International, Trade Records Analysis of Flora and Fauna in Commerce, and the World Conservation Monitoring Center. CITES accords varying degrees of protection to roughly five thousand animal species and twenty-five thousand plant species. The global community has achieved significant success in its effort to protect elephants. A worldwide ban on ivory in 1989 essentially eliminated elephant poaching and led to a sharp decline in the price of ivory. Similarly, in 1992, the United States, a leading importer of parrots for pets, enacted the Wild Bird Conservation Act, which bans imports of all wild-caught threatened parrots listed in CITES. Consequently, parrot imports dropped sharply. The global community collaborates with various countries to regulate hunting certain animals in ways that promote both conservation and economic benefits. Hunters, conservationists, and local farmers are collaborating to protect Africa's wildlife.[20]

Wild Bird Conservation Act ■ Bans imports of all wild-caught threatened parrots listed in CITES

CYBERCRIMES AND PIRACY

Cybercrimes are standard crimes committed online or harmful behavior that is connected to computers. Examples of cybercrimes are fraud, pornography, smuggling, copyright and software piracy, identity theft, and extortion. The proliferation of online shopping has been a boon for cybercriminals. eBay, the biggest online marketplace, has roughly 180 million members worldwide, who are connected to the Internet, and more than 60 million items for sale at any particular moment. Both distance and anonymity conspire to render these global online shopping centers perfect places for fraudulent activities. As a marketplace that links buyers and sellers, eBay has very little control over transactions.

Cybercrimes ■ Standard crimes committed online

eBay ■ The biggest online marketplace

The essential role of computer software in global computer operations makes it a prime target for cybercriminals. So pervasive is software piracy that many ordinary individuals do not perceive stealing software as a crime, thereby further blurring the boundaries between legal and illegal behavior. Like other global crimes we have discussed, it is impossible to determine the exact value of pirated software. This crime is concentrated in Western countries, where computer technologies are most prevalent. China, with its rapid industrialization and technological growth, is also involved to a significant degree in software piracy. The estimated market for software piracy in the United States is twice as large as the market in China.

Nigerian scam ■
One of the most
common cybercrimes

The global expansion of the Internet, the widespread use of credit cards, and the growth of electronic banking combine to facilitate a wide array of fraudulent activities. The Nigerian scam is one of the most common cyberspace crimes and one of the most persistent. A Nigerian sends an e-mail asking prospective victims to assist him or her to transfer millions of recently acquired dollars out of Nigeria in exchange for a substantial part of the money. Prospective victims are instructed to deposit their own money into a specified bank account to demonstrate their honesty and willingness to cooperate. If these instructions are followed, the money and the Nigerian e-mail sender simply vanish. Credit card fraud on the Internet involves the use of stolen credit card numbers and information, such as the date of expiration and delivery address, to purchase products from virtual shopping malls and auction sites.

Despite increasingly sophisticated computer security measures, criminals are becoming adept at crashing computer systems and impeding their operation. A growing concern among governments, including the U.S. government, is that cybercriminals could be successful at penetrating security organizations and threaten vital national interests. Fore example, China and Russia focus on stealing U.S. military secrets in an effort to undermine American military superiority. The United States' vulnerabilities range from its nuclear power plants and electrical grids to the information systems of government agencies and major U.S. companies. Because countries are vulnerable to cyberattacks, they are interested in building a joint cybersecurity strategy.[21] Extortion schemes by organized criminal groups based primarily in Russia and Eastern European countries have been implemented in Australia, Britain, Canada, Thailand, the United States, and elsewhere. Criminals employ sophisticated viruses to disable computer systems. An Internet virus named Kama Sutra—named after the venerable Indian guide to eroticism—was programmed to overwrite documents, images, and compressed computer files. Aimed principally at home computers, the virus infected computers through an e-mail that promised racy pictures. Russian criminal gangs use software tools to infect thousands of personal computers in corporate and government networks with programs that steal passwords and other information.

Kama Sutra ■
A famous Internet
virus named after
the Indian guide to
eroticism

Global trade, computer technologies, and the globalization of American and European cultures have contributed to the growth of global piracy, which includes online music piracy, counterfeiting, and old-fashioned piracy on the high seas. Online music piracy and counterfeiting deal with intellectual property rights, copyrights, and patent laws. Downloading music is generally regarded as a harmless activity by those engaged in it. However, the music industry views online music piracy as theft. A Swedish court convicted four men linked to an Internet file-sharing service, *The Pirate Bay*, of violating copyright law. Each was sentenced to a year in prison and fined $3.6 million in damages. Throughout China, one can purchase inexpensive counterfeit DVDs of the most recent American movies, as well as counterfeit shoes, clothes, computer software, books, and many other products. Counterfeit prescription drugs are a major problem that threatens human security.[22]

global piracy ■
Includes online
music piracy and
counterfeiting

**intellectual property
rights** ■ Control
that people and
corporations have
over artistic, creative,
scientific, industrial,
and educational
inventions

Piracy on the high seas has reemerged as a significant threat to global shipping. It also demonstrates new threats from nonstate actors to global military powers such as the United States. Modern piracy ranges from desperately

What are the causes and implications of piracy along the Somali coast? How can it be stopped? An armed Somali pirate keeps vigil on the coastline near Hobyo, northeastern Somalia, while a Greek cargo ship, held by pirates, is anchored just off shore.

impoverished people committing petty larcenies at sea to highly organized syndicates slaughtering ships' crews to steal not only the valuable cargo but also the multimillion-dollar ships.[23] More than two thirds of piracy attacks occur in Asian waters. The Horn of Africa and the Gulf of Aden are experiencing a significant increase in piracy, along with greater American involvement in efforts to reduce it. The failure of the Somali state, the withdrawal of the Soviet and American military forces from the area with the end of the Cold War, the widespread poverty and violence in Somalia, and the ease with which cargo ships can be seized and large ransoms can be collected by small groups of men in small speed boats that are armed with grappling hooks, assault rifles, rock-propelled grenades, knives, and satellite telephones have contributed to escalating pirate attacks. When pirates seized the U.S.-flagged cargo ship, the *Maersk Alabama*, and held the captain for ransom, a U.S. Navy–guided destroyer and other warships were sent to the Somali coast. U.S. Navy Seals on the destroyer *Bainbridge* were experienced snipers. They killed the three pirates and rescued the captain, Richard Phillips, of the *Maersk Alabama*. While greater economic opportunities and political stability in Somalia could help diminish piracy, the ease with which pirates acquire wealth makes piracy attractive. Military efforts to end piracy are being tried. There are three main naval task forces in the region. Operation Atalanta is the E.U. contingent, Operation Ocean Shield is a NATO maritime group, and CTF-151 is an operation run by a coalition of twenty-five countries, headed by the United States. Countries such as China, India, Russia, Japan, and Saudi Arabia have their own naval forces along the Somali coast.[24] The United Nations Security Council passed a resolution on piracy in Somalia calling for greater efforts in apprehending and prosecuting acts of piracy and hostage-taking. Soon after that, the British government changed policy to allow British ships to carry armed guards as protection against pirates.

GLOBAL RESPONSES TO CRIME

Countries are ill equipped to effectively respond to global criminal activities. As we pointed out earlier in this chapter, globalization has been far more beneficial to nonstate actors, including smugglers, drug traffickers, and other global criminal networks, than it has been to nation-states. The hierarchical structure of countries is a liability in an increasingly decentralized, global society. Furthermore, globalization has diminished the ability of states to exercise effective jurisdiction over their territories and to regulate trade and other activities. The nature of globalization makes it difficult to determine where the crimes occurred and which country or countries have jurisdiction over them. Few governments have the resources to effectively control global crime, especially in light of reduced government budgets for public services. Furthermore, divergent views among countries about crime and different priorities render effective collaboration among states difficult to achieve.

Interpol ■ Global clearinghouse for police information that assists countries in criminal cases

The International Criminal Police Organization, commonly known as Interpol, is a global clearinghouse for police information based in France. As we have seen, global crime is proliferating so rapidly and on such a vast scale at a time when cultural attitudes are generally much more tolerant of many global criminal activities that global efforts to reduce the crimes we have discussed are significantly undermined. Nevertheless, Interpol's role in combating drug trafficking and other global crimes is important. Interpol collects and analyzes data, supports global crime investigations, organizes operational working meetings among countries, and organizes regional and global conferences on a wide range of criminal activities. Despite support from Interpol, fighting crime is essentially a local activity, and states themselves are ultimately responsible for reducing global crime. But as with many domestic crimes, states confront many serious obstacles in fighting global crime.

UN Convention Against Transnational Organized Crime ■ Global agreement aimed at reducing crime through global cooperation

Attempting to be more effective in countering global crime, 178 countries have joined Interpol. Most of these countries signed the UN Convention Against Transnational Organized Crime, a global agreement that outlaws bank secrecy, keeps prosecutors worldwide in contact by e-mail, allows international arrest warrants to be sent by e-mail, provides for videoconferences to allow witnesses to testify without having to travel around the world, and creates international witness protection programs. The challenge confronting the global community is the ability to implement these provisions. The forces of globalization are likely to give global criminals the advantage in the worldwide struggle to reduce global crime.

CASE STUDY | Government Corruption in India

Government corruption is a leading global issue, partly due to the fallout from the global financial and economic crisis, especially the resulting serious budgetary constraints in rich countries. Government corruption is the illegal use of official positions for private gain. It includes taking bribes, stealing state property, embezzling public funds, selectively and arbitrarily enforcing the law, and cooperating with criminals. Government corruption perpetuates poverty, inequality, global crime, the globalization of diseases, environmental problems, and undemocratic regimes. Endemic corruption in Afghanistan, for example, fuels terrorism, costs many lives, and undermines American and global efforts to promote democracy and assist economic and social development. Corruption creates a culture of fear, dishonesty, secrecy, cynicism, lawlessness, mistrust, and a lack of accountability. Consumers pay higher prices for almost everything as corrupt officials help create illegal monopolies in the economic sector. Government bureaucracy grows and becomes more inefficient and bribery proliferates. Official corruption filters down through society and is accepted as a way of life.

There are many reasons for government corruption. Those include basic human greed, cultural values that encourage helping relatives and friends, lack of accountability, weak and ineffective judicial systems, economic hardships for public sector employees, and the growth of global crime as a component of globalization. Rapid economic growth also is conducive to increasing government corruption. That seems to be especially the case in countries with abundant natural resources, particularly petroleum. Large sums of money donated by the global community to assist developing countries also seem to engender corruption. For example, it is estimated that more than half the money donated by the Global Fund to fight AIDS, tuberculosis, and malaria was stolen by corrupt government officials and others.[25]

India's rapid economic growth has contributed to a "season of scams" by government officials by increasing the amount of money available to steal. More than 80 percent of Indians perceive corruption to be an urgent problem, despite a long history of corruption in the country. There is an estimated $450 billion derived from illegal activities by Indians deposited in foreign bank accounts. The extent of government corruption was demonstrated by India's dismal performance in preparing to host the Commonwealth Games in Delhi in 2010. Due to the theft of billions of dollars, facilities for athletes were poorly constructed, unsanitary, and not completed on schedule. Many athletes threatened to stay away. Money is routinely stolen from programs intended to benefit the poor. For example, almost half of state fuel subsidies are stolen, amounting to roughly $2 billion a year. In Uttar Pradesh alone, more than $40 billion of food and other subsidies over a five-year period did not reach the poor due to government corruption. One of the leading cases of corruption occurred in India's telecoms industry, the world's fastest-growing market. Andimuthu Raja, the telecoms minister, refused to auction licenses. He awarded them arbitrarily and to favored companies for below market value. The government lost $40 billion. Corruption is directly affecting India's development. Foreign direct investment in India declined by 31 percent in 2010.[26]

Government corruption is widely viewed as a significant global problem, one with far-reaching implications. Consequently, there are many initiatives globally to diminish this crime. One is the proliferation of anticorruption units around the world. There is an upsurge in grassroots democracy with those who are most affected by corruption—the poor—taking measures to hold corrupt officials accountable. In India, for example, villagers perform social audits to ascertain that money is not stolen. They are helped by the rapid growth of communications technologies, which they use to

(continued)

> ### CASE STUDY | continued
>
> enhance transparency. The empowerment of the poor contributed to ending the acceptance among politicians of a culture of corruption. The opposition Bharatiya Janata Party (BJP) made government corruption a leading political issue, supported by popular anger about corruption. That forced the governing Congress Party to implement reforms that remove discretionary powers abused by politicians. Furthermore, the courts reinforce the anticorruption campaign by trying accused officials. Technology also is being used to circumvent India's largely corrupt and inefficient bureaucracy. Payments bypass bureaucrats and go directly into individuals' bank accounts. As villages gain access to broadband and government databases, they can obtain documents, assess property taxes, and pay bills online. Bids for government contracts also are made online, enabling anticorruption groups to monitor them. Global coalitions of anticorruption nonstate actors have persuaded the U.S. government to enact legislation requiring companies to disclose payments to governments. Global communications are facilitating efforts to increase transparency to reduce corruption. There also are global efforts to recover stolen assets that are in foreign secret bank accounts. ◣

SUMMARY AND REVIEW

Global criminal activities have proliferated with the rapid growth of economic, financial, technological, cultural, and other forms of globalization. Increased global migration, global inequality, the growth of global cities, the explosion of global trade, inexpensive communications, revolutions in computer technologies, and the disintegration of the Soviet Union have contributed to the spread and intensification of global crime. As we saw, global crime is intricately intertwined with politics, economics, and culture. This chapter shows how illegal activities occur alongside legal activities and how difficult they sometimes are to separate. Furthermore, there are divergent perceptions about global crimes as well as different approaches to dealing with them. Globalization has weakened states in ways that prevent them from effectively combating many global crimes. Furthermore, as the case study shows, government corruption is global crime that facilitates other criminal activities. We discussed major global crimes such as drug trafficking, human trafficking, illegal trade in endangered species, money laundering, cybercrimes, and trade in human organs. Throughout history, the world has experienced an increase in the global drug trade, accompanied by growing drug use and addiction. This global crime commands the attention of the global community, although countries adopt divergent approaches to dealing with illegal drugs. There are global responses to all of the crimes discussed. Organizations such as Interpol provide information on criminal activities and cooperate with countries in an effort to reduce global crime.

KEY TERMS

British East India Company   257
Opium Wars   257
Golden Triangle   258

war on drugs   258
Hague Convention   259
Harrison Act   259

DISCUSSION QUESTIONS

1. Discuss ways in which globalization facilitates the growth of global crime.
2. How and to what extent has globalization affected the ability of states to diminish global criminal activities?
3. Compare European and American approaches to dealing with illegal drugs. Make arguments for and against legalizing drugs.
4. Discuss the problem of government corruption.
5. Discuss the growth of piracy, and the causes, and possible ways to reduce it.
6. What can individuals do to reduce the growth of cybercrime?

SUGGESTED READINGS

Andreas, Peter, and Kelly Greenhill, eds. *Sex, Drugs, and Body Counts*. Ithaca, NY: Cornell University Press, 2010. Warns against relying on statistics on global crimes such as drugs, human trafficking, and various conflicts.

Betancourt, Ingrid. *Even Silence Has to End*. New York: Penguin Press, 2010. An autobiographical account of a Colombian senator who was kidnapped and held prisoner for six years by the Revolutionary Armed Forces of Colombia (FARC).

Chouvy, Pierre-Arnaud. *Opium*. Cambridge, MA: Harvard University Press, 2010. Examines the use of opium from prehistoric times to its use in Europe, China, and Persia today.

Eichstaedt, Peter. *Pirate State*. New York: Lawrence Hill Books, 2010. Focuses on Somalia as a failed state, the rise of Muslim fundamentalism, and reasons for piracy.

Karras, Alan. *Smuggling: Contraband and Corruption in World History*. Lanham, MD: Rowman and Littlefield, 2009. Covers smuggling from the 18th century to now and shows its connection to corrupt government officials.

ENDNOTES

1. Pierre-Arnaud Chouvy, *Opium* (Cambridge, MA: Harvard University Press, 2010).
2. Paul B. Stares, *Global Habit: The Drug Problem in a Borderless World* (Washington, DC: Brookings Institution Press, 1996), 16.
3. Stares, *Global Habit*, 17.
4. Stares, *Global Habit*, 36.
5. Ginger Thompson and Mark Mazzetti, "U.S. Drones Fly Deep in Mexico to Fight Drugs," *New York Times*, 16 March 2010, A1.

6. "People-Smuggling," *Economist*, 11 September 2010, 36.

7. Peter Andreas and Kelly Greenhhill, eds. *Sex, Drugs, and Body Counts* (Ithaca, NY: Cornell University Press, 2010).

8. Joel Brinkley, "A Modern-Day Abolitionist Battles Slavery Worldwide," *New York Times*, 4 February 2006, A4; and Kevin Bales and Zoe Trodd, eds., *To Plead Our Own Cause: Personal Stories by Today's Slaves* (Ithaca, NY: Cornell University Press, 2008).

9. Brinkley, "A Modern-Day Abolitionist," A4.

10. Suzanne Daley, "Rescuing Young Women from Traffickers," *New York Times*, 16 October 2010, A5.

11. David A. Feingold, "Human Trafficking," *Foreign Policy* 150 (September/October 2005), 26.

12. Victor Malarek, *The Natashas: Inside the Global Sex Trade* (New York: Arcade Publishing, 2004), 6; and H. Richard Friman and Simon Reich, eds., *Human Trafficking, Human Security, and the Balkans* (Pittsburgh, PA: University of Pittsburgh Press, 2008).

13. Louise Shelley, "Russian and Chinese Trafficking," in *Human Traffic and Transnational Crime*, 70.

14. Nicholas D. Kristof, "Slavery in Our Time," *New York Times*, 22 January 2006, A17.

15. Feingold, "Human Trafficking," 30.

16. Malarek, *The Natashas*, 255.

17. Brinkley, "A Modern-Day Abolitionist," A4.

18. "Organized Crime in Central America," *Economist*, 22 January 2011, 45; and Shannon O'Neil, "The Real War in Mexico," *Foreign Affairs* 88, No. 4 (July/August 2009) 67.

19. Ingrid Betancourt, *Even Silence Has to End* (New York: Penguin Press, 2010).

20. "Horns, Claws, and the Bottom Line," *Economist*, 4 September 2010, 23.

21. Ian Bremmer, "Cyberspace and Security," *Foreign Affairs* 89, No. 6 (November/December 2010), 92.

22. "Fake Drugs," *Economist*, 4 September 2010, 65.

23. Max Boot, "Pirates Then and Now," *Foreign Affairs* 88, No. 4 (July/August 2009), 94.

24. "Piracy: No Stopping Them," *Economist*, 5 February 2011, 69.

25. "Aid and Corruption," *Economist*, 19 February 2011, 65.

26. Vikas Bajaj, "Foreign Investment Ebbs in India," *New York Times*, 25 February 2011, B1.

CHAPTER 13

The Globalization of Disease

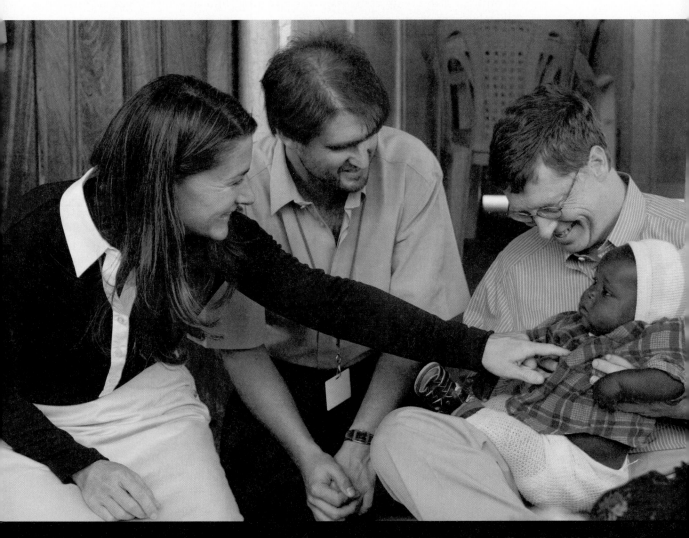

Many individuals and nongovernmental organizations (NGOs) help fight global disease. The Bill and Melinda Gates Foundation plays a key role in the war against malaria, AIDS, and other diseases. Melinda, left, and Bill Gates, right, visited a malaria intervention treatment program in Mozambique when they announced their grants totaling $168 million to fight malaria. They are pictured with a physician and a baby who was in the program.

INTRODUCTION

Globally, infectious diseases remain the leading killers of human beings. More than a quarter of all deaths today are linked to infectious diseases, with the developing world facing the brunt of the problem. Infectious diseases are intertwined with numerous global issues and are inseparable from political, economic, and cultural components of globalization. Ethnic conflicts make populations vulnerable to infectious diseases. Fighting contributes to the collapse of public services, which means that many people die from what would ordinarily be treatable diseases, such as diarrhea and respiratory infections. Conflicts also create refugees, overcrowding, and unsanitary conditions, thereby creating environments conducive to the spread of infectious diseases.

Environmental degradation and deforestation expose humans to a variety of infectious diseases. They also contribute to global warming and flooding, which facilitate the emergence of infectious diseases. Rising temperatures in winter enable germs to survive in large numbers, and flooded areas become potent breeding grounds for mosquito-related diseases and cholera. Rapid population growth and urbanization bring more people closer together and into contact with infectious diseases. Trade has long been a major facilitator of the spread of infectious diseases. Consequently, trade suffers greatly when outbreaks occur. In many ways, trade liberalization contributes to the spread of infectious diseases by reducing the role of many governments in providing essential basic health care and other services. Infectious diseases have far-reaching social, economic, demographic, security, and political consequences.

This chapter examines the globalization of infectious diseases, the concept of human security, and the nature and spread of infectious diseases. The chapter discusses global responses to the growth, persistence, and transmission of infectious diseases. It concludes with a case study of obesity as a global epidemic. The obesity epidemic is related to recent recognition of noncommunicable diseases (NCDs) including cancer, diabetes, chronic respiratory diseases, and cardiovascular diseases as a global epidemic that causes 63 percent of all deaths and increases poverty. A United Nations summit in September 2011 launched a global campaign to attack NCDs.

NCDs ■
Epidemic-level
noninfectious diseases

GLOBALIZATION OF INFECTIOUS DISEASES

The rapid spread of globalization, especially starting in the 1980s, underscored links between infectious diseases in poor countries and outbreaks of these diseases in rich countries. The most dramatic development was the discovery of HIV/AIDS in the United States, Western Europe, and other rich countries. Although perceived initially as a disease limited primarily to homosexuals, HIV/AIDS began to spread to the general population through blood transfusions, intravenous drug usage, and heterosexual practices. Furthermore, prominent people who were suffering from the disease fought to put it on both domestic and global agendas. Many of the diseases that were believed to have been eradicated in rich countries reemerged and were placed on the global agenda. Two factors explain this reemergence: (1) *growing resistance to common antibiotics* and (2) *the devastating impact of new epidemics.* The new epidemics included cholera in Latin America, particularly in Peru and Haiti; plague in India; the Ebola virus in Africa; dengue fever in Asia; West Nile virus in the United States; and bovine spongiform encephalitis (mad cow disease) in the United States and Europe.

Global Travel and Communications

Human beings are the most efficient transmitters of diseases. In the past, large proportions of populations were killed by plagues as people traveled to distant places. The Plague of Justinian, which occurred around 541 A.D., devastated Europe. In the twelfth and thirteenth centuries, the bubonic plague, known as the Black Death, killed 25 million (or one of every three) Europeans. The decimation of Native American populations by European diseases is another example of how travelers spread infectious diseases. More recently, China and other Asian countries have spawned deadly infectious diseases, which have spread quickly to the rest of the world because of travel and excellent global links. In 1968, the Hong Kong flu, originating in South China, spread from Hong Kong to other countries. About 700,000 people died worldwide. Following a devastating earthquake in 2010, Haiti faced an outbreak of cholera, which killed at least six thousand people. Unsanitary conditions helped spread the disease, however, the US Centers for Disease Control and Prevention (CDC) found evidence that strongly suggested U.N. peacekeepers from Nepal brought the deadly cholera strain to Haiti.[1]

Trade also has been a major facilitator in the globalization of infectious diseases. The bubonic plague (Black Death) was transmitted to Europe through trade with Asia. Today, the rapid expansion of trade with China exposes the world to many diseases. The global trade in agricultural products has also escalated the risk of the global transmission of diseases. Mad cow disease has become a contentious issue between the United States and Japan, for example, because of fears among the Japanese of being infected by imports of American beef.

As we saw in Chapter 10, human activities have profoundly affected the natural environment. People have migrated to areas that bring them into contact with animals and soils that play a role in the spread of infectious diseases. Furthermore, gradual increases in the Earth's temperature (i.e., global warming) are conducive to the global spread of diseases.

Ethnic conflicts, widespread violence, and wars have always contributed to the outbreak of disease and often the spread of infectious diseases. Combatants are often more likely to die from infectious diseases than from actual fighting. It is estimated that more than two thirds of the roughly 600,000 deaths in the American Civil War were caused by infectious diseases.[2] Furthermore, the movement of troops and mass migrations of civilians as a consequence of war contributed to the wider transmission of infectious diseases. During the Spanish flu pandemic of 1918–1920, many American soldiers who were transported on trains and troop ships perished. On the battlefields of Vietnam and Iraq, American troops suffered from infectious diseases, many of which are drug resistant. Endemic ethnic conflicts in Africa play a leading role in that continent's struggle with infectious diseases.

Conditions that influence people to leave one area to settle in another initiate the downward spiral leading to infectious diseases. The deterioration of health services, the destruction of infrastructure, food shortages, and the lack of proper sanitation make refugees susceptible to communicable diseases.

The poorest countries, like poor individuals, are generally more vulnerable to contracting infectious diseases. Poverty is usually a reliable incubator of disease. Overcrowding, malnutrition, inadequate medical care, and unsanitary conditions facilitate the growth and transmission of infectious diseases.

A growing problem that assists in the spread of infectious diseases is overuse and misuse of antibiotics. The increasing use of antibiotics in agricultural products has contributed to a process of pathogenic natural selection, which promotes the emergence of more virulent, resilient, resistant, and powerful disease strains

Globalization, especially cultural globalization, profoundly affects behavioral patterns worldwide. Pervasive and instant communications, television programs, movies, and the Internet facilitate the global spread of information about social practices that were once limited to smaller groups within societies. The global sex industry is an example of how changing behavior contributes to the globalization of infectious diseases such as HIV/AIDS. The spread of infectious diseases has focused attention on human security.

pathogenic natural selection ■ Process that promotes more virulent and resistant disease strains

HUMAN SECURITY AND INFECTIOUS DISEASES

As we discussed in Chapter 1, the forces of globalization have strengthened the concept and reality of global security, which stresses a common and comprehensive security. The concept of global security moves us beyond the narrow traditional view of national security with its emphasis on military force and war to emphasize the global dimensions of emerging threats and problems and the need to achieve security with others. Within the broader context of global security is the concept of human security, derived from the globalist school of thought. Human security focuses on the individual as the primary object of security. It embraces a people-centered approach of anticipating and coping with the multiple threats ordinary individuals face in an increasingly globalized society. The emergence of the concept of human security during the 1990s is attributed to *three developments*: (1) *the end of the Cold War*, which radically altered the global political and security environment; (2) *a better understanding of the everyday insecurities* experienced by the world's poor, the vast majority of the world's population; and (3) the process of globalization, which ushered in *unprecedented changes and uncertainty*, thereby influencing a reevaluation of traditional views of security.

These developments are augmented by links between health and economic development on the global agenda, especially the UN Millennium Development Goals. In fact, four of the eight Millennium Goals concentrate on health-related issues. The *globalization of infectious diseases threatens human security in several ways. First*, diseases kill far more people than wars. *Second*, disease undermines public confidence in the state, thereby eroding its legitimacy. *Third*,

global security ■ Stresses a common and comprehensive security worldwide

human security ■ Focuses on the individual as the primary object of security

UN Millennium Development Goals ■ Four of the goals concentrate on health-related issues

disease weakens the economic foundations of human security. *Fourth*, disease profoundly affects social order and stability. *Fifth*, the spread of infectious diseases contributes to regional instability. *Sixth*, disease can be used in biowarfare and bioterrorism.

INFECTIOUS DISEASES

The microbes (such as bacteria), viruses, parasites, and fungi that are the agents of infectious diseases are integral components of the natural and human environments. Throughout recorded history, our ancestors have been extremely vulnerable to, and mostly defenseless against, infectious diseases. Pathogens (i.e., organisms capable of causing disease) have routinely demolished societies. In many cases, there are outbreaks of diseases: that is, essentially localized, endemic occurrences. When infectious diseases spread to a relatively large number of people, they are classified as epidemics. Although epidemics generally impact populations worldwide, pandemics are long lasting, catastrophic, and truly global in their consequences. Two factors that have always been at the root of infectious disease threats to human populations are (1) social, economic, and environmental conditions that enable infectious diseases to exist among human hosts and (2) various means of transmission to new populations. As our ancestors developed agriculture and moved from isolated villages to more densely populated areas, they were exposed to more diseases.[3] Altering the natural environment enables microbes to infect humans. Humans are infected when they come into contact with natural hosts (i.e., organisms that carry diseases). The hosts are not negatively affected by the disease. Transmission of infectious diseases can occur within a single species or from one species to another. Humans often infect other humans. But host animals also infect humans, a transmission known as zoonosis. Infectious diseases are transmitted through air, water, direct contact with the host's bodily fluids, and sexual activity, as well as through vectors such as mosquitoes and other insects.

To better understand contemporary concerns about infectious diseases, we will discuss the problem within the framework of epidemiologic transition theory. Each transition is characterized by "a unique pattern of diseases that is ultimately related to modes of subsistence and social structure."[4] There are basically *three distinct epidemiologic transitions*. The first epidemiologic transition, as we mentioned earlier, occurred when our ancestors established agricultural communities. Think about sanitation problems in permanently settled areas and the close interaction of humans and their domesticated animals. Both of these situations provided favorable environments for the dispersal of infectious diseases. Cattle, goats, sheep, pigs, and fowl transmitted tuberculosis, anthrax, and other diseases. Large proportions of populations were routinely killed by plagues, especially as trade among communities increased and people traveled to distant places. An example of an early pandemic is the Plague of Justinian, named after the Roman emperor, which devastated Europe around 541 A.D. Increased trade and migration between Asia and Europe and the Medieval Warm Period of the twelfth and thirteenth centuries contributed to the proliferation of rats and fleas that transmitted bubonic plague. Believing that cats were witches, Europeans inadvertently helped to spread the plague by killing cats. Known as the Black Death, the bubonic plague

pathogens ■ Organisms capable of causing disease

epidemics ■ When infectious diseases spread to a large number of people

pandemics ■ Long-lasting, catastrophic global epidemics

hosts ■ Organisms that carry diseases

zoonosis ■ Transmission of diseases from host animals to humans

first epidemiologic transition ■ Related to the establishment of agricultural communities

Plague of Justinian ■ Named after the Roman emperor, it devastated Europe around 541 A.D.

Black Death ■ Bubonic plague that killed roughly 25 million people throughout Europe

killed roughly 25 million people, or one of every three Europeans.[5] Individuals who manage to survive infectious diseases acquire immunity to them but transmit them to others. For example, most Europeans survived diseases such as tuberculosis and smallpox. West Africans lived with malaria and yellow fever. However, groups that lived in isolation from Europeans or Africans became quickly infected with their diseases. Millions of Native Americans were killed by diseases brought to the Americas by Europeans.[6] Many Europeans died of malaria and yellow fever in Africa, Asia, and the Americas.

second epidemiologic transition ■ Coincided with the Industrial Revolution

The second epidemiologic transition coincided with the Industrial Revolution in Europe. Various inventions that accompanied the Industrial Revolution contributed to declining rates of infectious diseases. But overcrowding, environmental degradation, and unsanitary conditions led to the rebounding of cholera, smallpox, and tuberculosis. Developments in medical science and technology diminished epidemics, not only in Europe but also in places affected by European migration, colonization, and commercial relations. We are now experiencing the third epidemiologic transition. Just in the past three decades, we have seen an unprecedented emergence of new diseases and a reemergence of infectious diseases that were thought to have been eliminated. For example, in 2011 India experienced an outbreak of Congo fever that is passed from pigs and other animals to humans.[7] Another characteristic of this third transition is growing antimicrobial resistance, due primarily to the frequent use and misuse of antibiotics and other antimicrobials. Incomplete drug treatment for various diseases also contributes to antimicrobial resistance.

third epidemiologic transition ■ The current wave of infectious diseases

Poverty and migration help to spread diseases globally. A woman searches in trash at Mumbai, India.

INFLUENZA AND AVIAN FLU

Of all the major infectious diseases, influenza demands the unique and urgent attention of the global community because of its lethality and the speed with which it is transmitted. Of the more than fifteen hundred microbes known to cause disease in humans, influenza continues to dominate in terms of overall mortality. Every year, 5 percent to 10 percent of the American population gets the flu and about thirty-six thousand of them die. Even in normal times, an estimated 1.5 million people worldwide die from influenza infections or related complications each year.[8] Influenza, which is a viral infection of the respiratory tract, is very contagious and poses serious threats to children, the elderly, and individuals with compromised immune systems. It is estimated that three influenza pandemics in the twentieth century killed more than 50 million people. The Spanish flu pandemic of 1918–1920 is generally regarded as the most lethal plague in history, causing roughly 50 million deaths worldwide. Pandemics in 1957 and 1968, which originated in China and Hong Kong, together killed more than 2.5 million people.[9] Given the efficiency with which flu is transmitted through air, close contact is not required for people to become infected. Furthermore, it is very difficult to identify and quarantine infected people who are spreading the disease. These experiences influenced WHO to act quickly when swine flu (H1N1) was found in Mexico in 2009. WHO declared swine flu a pandemic, the United States declared a public health emergency, and Mexico essentially closed down Mexico City for five days.

Throughout the world, large commercial poultry farms, as well as the proliferation of chickens kept by families, have provided ideal conditions for the avian flu to spread. Furthermore, rapid population growth, especially in Asia, has given rise to densely populated urban areas. For example, during the 1968–1969 influenza pandemic, China had 790 million people and 12.3 million chickens and other poultry. China now has 1.3 billion people and 13 billion chickens. Poultry, pigs, and people living together or in close proximity enhance the transmission of avian flu from animals to humans. Although the avian flu (HSN1) had caused 88 deaths out of a total of 165 cases globally, transmission from human to human had not occurred. The global community feared that the virus would undergo changes enabling it to reassort (i.e., mix genes with other human influenza viruses that are also present). This process can produce an entirely new viral strain, capable of sustained human-to-human transmission

Responding to the threat of a pandemic, governments, international organizations, and nongovernmental organizations (NGOs) concentrated on quarantine and the extensive culling of birds in affected areas. European countries were advised by the Animal Production and Health Division of the UN Food and Agriculture Organization to require travelers to fill out forms detailing their travel history and the agricultural products in their possession, which is the practice in the United States. Increased checks of airline passengers and their belongings were also regarded as effective countermeasures. A major obstacle to any effective global response is the weakness of governments and poverty. As we will see, poor countries lack adequate resources to deal with routine health problems. Within rich countries, governments allocated resources to develop vaccines, primarily Tamiflu, to deal with a pandemic.

influenza ■ A contagious viral infection of the respiratory tract

Spanish flu ■ Most lethal influenza pandemic that caused 50 million deaths

reassort ■ Mutation of viruses that enhance chances of human-to-human transmission of disease

Tamiflu ■ Medicine used to treat patients infected with the avian flu

MALARIA, DENGUE, AND YELLOW FEVER

Malaria, dengue, and yellow fever are found primarily in the Tropics and are transmitted by mosquitoes. These are the most common vector-borne diseases. The spread of human settlements and various activities in forested areas have led to increased contact with mosquitoes that carry the viruses that cause these diseases. Global transportation and global warming have enabled these diseases to spread and grow outside tropical areas. Discarded tires, bottles, cans, and other containers that collect water become fertile breeding grounds for mosquitoes. Humans contract *malaria* when bitten by female mosquitoes. Malarial parasites infect red blood cells, causing chills, fever, and often death. Of the estimated 300 million to 500 million people infected with malaria each year, roughly 1.5 million die from the disease.[10] *Dengue*, a viral disease, is transmitted by mosquitoes that acquire the virus when they suck blood from an infected person, replicate the virus in their system, and transmit it to the next person they bite. Dengue is marked by fever, severe headaches, muscle and bone pain, shock, and fatal hemorrhaging. There are roughly 50 million cases of dengue infection worldwide each year.[11] *Yellow fever* is endemic in Africa, Asia, Latin America, and several Caribbean islands. It is estimated that thirty thousand people die each year of yellow fever. Symptoms include fever, muscle pain, backaches, headaches, shivering, loss of appetite, nausea, and vomiting. After a few days, most people who are infected improve and their symptoms disappear. However, approximately 15 percent of infected individuals experience a toxic phase, in which they develop jaundice, abdominal pains, bleeding, and kidney failure. Roughly half of those who enter the toxic phase die within ten to fourteen days.[12] Malaria is by far the most pervasive and deadly of these three diseases.

Malaria

Globally, Africa suffers the most from malaria. More than 90 percent of malaria deaths occur there, despite the relative ease with which the disease can be prevented and cured. In many ways, the prevalence of malaria in Africa is a manifestation of that continent's endemic poverty. Malaria was once believed to be caused by swamp air. The role that mosquitoes play in transmitting the disease was not discovered until 1898. Several factors have contributed to the increase of malaria in different parts of the world. As *population pressures* have influenced farmers to cultivate areas bordering on swamps and as agroforestry has grown, mosquitoes have multiplied and have more opportunities to infect humans. The *construction of dams and irrigation systems* for agriculture has radically altered the natural environment and provided breeding places for mosquitoes. Natural disasters, such as earthquakes, often destroy sanitation facilities, cause severe flooding, and allow standing water to accumulate in which mosquitoes breed. Finally, global warming is widely believed to be responsible for increased rainfall and higher temperatures, which can result in flooding. These environmental conditions facilitate the spread of malaria.[13]

Pregnant women and children bear the heaviest burdens. Malaria during pregnancy threatens the child's development, both in the uterus and as an infant.

Mothers who have had limited exposure to malaria parasites and therefore less immunity are extremely vulnerable during pregnancy when their immunity is generally lower. Often, malaria infections cause anemia, which often results in maternal mortality. Malaria usually causes low-birth-weight babies, brain damage, and cognitive impairment.

Efforts to eradicate malaria began in 1898, when the connection between mosquitoes and the disease was discovered. In addition to draining swamps and removing standing water from around homes, insecticides and larvicides were used. Quinine was also used to treat infections. A major breakthrough in fighting malaria came after World War II when DDT was applied. DDT was first used in 1939 as an agricultural insecticide in Switzerland. However, it was during the war that its public health applications were discovered. The allies had used DDT to control typhus epidemics. Complete eradication of malaria was achieved in places such as the United States, Southern Europe, Sri Lanka, and much of Brazil by massive DDT spraying.[14] Success in reducing malaria problems influenced the World Health Organization (WHO) to initiate its Global Malaria Campaign in 1955 to intensify the use of DDT to control malaria. However, by the 1960s malaria began to reemerge in countries that had made significant progress in eliminating it because many countries were unable to continue the highly organized and costly spray program essential for success. Furthermore, widespread use of DDT engendered resistance to it at a time when more people were becoming aware of its danger to human health and the environment. As we discussed in Chapter 10, the toxicity of pesticides was stressed by Rachel Carson in her influential book, *Silent Spring*. The WHO adopted a more comprehensive approach that included strengthening basic health services, focusing on the unique social and economic conditions in each region, and concentrating on treating malaria patients. Known as the horizontal approach, this new strategy emphasized control and containment, as opposed to complete eradication.[15] This change was due partly to limited supplies of DDT and escalating costs, as efforts to ban the use of DDT were increasingly successful. Both interest in and funding for malaria control declined during the 1970s, which enabled the disease to spread.

The globalization of infectious diseases has contributed to increased global awareness of malaria and has engendered renewed efforts to eradicate it. Furthermore, many individuals and NGOs are involved in these efforts. Rotarians worldwide have made eradicating malaria a major goal. The emphasis on bed nets was influenced by the growing ineffectiveness and health hazards of other approaches, such as indoor spraying and the use of chloroquine. Other organizations, such as the United Nations Children's Fund (UNICEF), play a leading role in providing bed nets. An insecticide-treated bed net costs around $3. However, even at that price many poor families cannot afford to purchase them. These bed nets are heavily subsidized or given away. A special initiative to eradicate malaria was launched in Zambia. Using $35 million donated by the Bill and Melinda Gates Foundation, Zambia's objective is to provide bed nets to 80 percent of its population. An additional $82 million was donated by international organizations and governments to supply the most effective malaria drugs to every public clinic and to pay for coordinated spraying programs across Zambia. Death rates from malaria have declined by around 60 percent in Zambia.[16]

Global Malaria Campaign ■ Intensified the use of DDT to control malaria

horizontal approach ■ Strategy that emphasized the control and containment, as opposed to the eradication, of malaria

Bill and Melinda Gates Foundation ■ Provides bed nets to Zambia to control the spread of malaria

TUBERCULOSIS

Links between tuberculosis and the HIV/AIDS pandemic reinvigorated global interest in diminishing the spread of tuberculosis. The combination of tuberculosis and AIDS is lethal, with each disease contributing to the rapid progress of the other. HIV weakens the immune system, making it easier for an HIV-positive person to contract tuberculosis. In Africa, the epicenter of the HIV/AIDS pandemic, HIV is the single most important factor determining the increased incidence of tuberculosis. The resurgence of tuberculosis underscores how globalization is instrumental in the transmission of infectious diseases and how increasing numbers of societies are unable to avoid the consequences. Migration from poor countries is a significant cause of the reemergence of tuberculosis in rich countries. In the United States, Sweden, Norway, Canada, Australia, Denmark, France, and other European countries, a large proportion of new cases of tuberculosis, as high as half in some countries, are found in immigrants. In fact, Mexico, the Philippines, China, India, and Vietnam—countries that are major sources of migrants to the United States—have some of the highest rates of tuberculosis in the world. High rates of illegal immigration reduce the ability of governments to screen and exclude infectious migrants. Tuberculosis is also rampant in refugee camps. For example, during the Balkan conflict (between 1992 and 1995), tuberculosis cases quadrupled. Similarly, famine and civil war throughout Africa have spawned significant growth in tuberculosis cases. Overcrowding in urban areas, rapid growth of prison populations (particularly in the United States), the rapid growth in global travel on airplanes with limited air circulation, and the global trend toward privatizing public health care systems (which generally deprives the poor of adequate medical treatment) have contributed to the reemergence of tuberculosis in affluent countries.

Balkan conflict ■ Occurred from 1992 to 1995 and contributed to the quadrupling of tuberculosis in the Balkans

The WHO estimates that someone in the world is newly infected with tuberculosis bacilli every second and that one third of the world's population is infected with tuberculosis. More than 1.7 million die from tuberculosis each year, with the highest number of deaths in Southeast Asia. However, the highest mortality rate per capita is in South Africa, due primarily to the prevalence of HIV/AIDS. In the mid–nineteenth century, tuberculosis was the leading cause of death in Europe and North America. It was a terrifying disease because it could not be prevented from spreading and it was incurable. Because it was transmitted through air, changing one's behavior provided no protection. As social, economic, and sanitary conditions improved in Europe and North America, tuberculosis began to recede. Furthermore, survivors of the disease developed greater immunity to it. The discovery of effective medicines to control tuberculosis diminished the epidemic, with wealthier countries experiencing steady declines in tuberculosis-related deaths. By 1991, pharmaceutical companies had abandoned manufacturing streptomycin, a drug commonly used to treat tuberculosis, and many developed countries sharply reduced spending on programs designed to combat the disease. Sanitariums, which had proliferated to treat tuberculosis patients, were closed, giving the perception that tuberculosis was no longer a major public concern. Although many poor areas within rich countries continue to experience cases of tuberculosis, the gap between rich and poor had created a general sense of indifference to the disease. *Four factors have contributed to tuberculosis as a global disease:*

1. Whereas tuberculosis declined in rich countries, it increased in the developing world.
2. Many policymakers and the general population in wealthy countries underestimated the degree to which their health was intertwined with that of people in other parts of the world.
3. The emergence of the HIV/AIDS pandemic rejuvenated tuberculosis, creating new concerns for wealthy countries.
4. The world was unprepared for an increase in outbreaks of multidrug-resistant tuberculosis.

Faced with the global spread of tuberculosis, various governmental organizations and NGOs rejuvenated efforts to diminish the transmission of the disease.

In 1991, the WHO introduced the DOTS strategy to control tuberculosis. This *strategy is composed of five elements*: (1) government's commitment to sustained tuberculosis control, (2) detection of tuberculosis cases through sputum smear microscopy among people with symptoms, (3) regular and uninterrupted supply of high-quality antituberculosis drugs, (4) six to eight months of regularly supervised treatment, and (5) reporting systems to monitor treatment progress and program performance. The DOTS strategy has achieved treatment success rates as high as 90 percent in some countries, a decline in the incidence of tuberculosis infections, and the prevention of an estimated 70 percent of deaths among infectious cases.

DOTS strategy ■ Introduced in 1991 by the WHO to control tuberculosis

HIV/AIDS

When AIDS was first recognized in 1981, the general assumption was that this deadly disease was essentially limited to homosexuals and West Africans. Today, however, HIV and AIDS have become a pandemic. More than 33 million people worldwide, 60 percent of them women, are infected. Roughly 2 million people die every year from AIDS. Although Africa remains the epicenter of the AIDS pandemic, home to roughly 70 percent of the people in the world who are living with HIV and experiencing 72 percent of the world's AIDS-related deaths, the disease is rapidly growing in China, India, Russia, Latin America and the Caribbean, Eastern and Central Europe, and elsewhere. It is generally accepted that HIV evolved from the simian immunodeficiency virus (SIV) found in chimpanzees in southwestern Africa. It is believed that individuals acquired the disease from exposure to blood in the process of handling the meat of a chimpanzee that carried the virus. Compared with other infectious diseases, HIV/AIDS—while devastating—is transmitted in very specific ways and is thus more controllable. The virus is passed from one individual to another through the exchange of bodily fluids during sexual intercourse, through blood transfusions, from mother to fetus, through intravenous drug use, and through other activities in which infected blood is transmitted from one person to another. Early symptoms of HIV infection include chronic fatigue or

HIV/AIDS ■ Evolved from SIV found in chimpanzees in southwestern Africa

simian immunodeficiency virus ■ Believed to be the source of HIV/AIDS

weakness, noticeable and sustained weight loss, extensive and persistent swelling of the lymph glands, routine diarrhea, and sustained deterioration of the central nervous system.

Globalization is a major factor contributing to the spread of HIV/AIDS. As global tourism continues to grow and people venture to all corners of the world, they increase their risk of contracting infectious diseases. Sex tourism, which is traveling to specific countries to participate in the local sex industry, is a potent source of infectious diseases, especially HIV/AIDS. Furthermore, as we discussed in Chapter 12, the growth in human trafficking and the sex trade in many parts of the world helps to spread HIV/AIDS. Poverty, ethnic conflicts, and wars facilitate the transmission of HIV/AIDS. And, as we will see in the case of South Africa, traditional values and perceptions of women are also important factors that assist the transmission of HIV/AIDS.

Sex tourism ■ Traveling to countries to participate in the sex industry

Africa

Southern Africa, especially South Africa, has become the epicenter of HIV/AIDS. More than 5.3 million South Africans, out of a population of 49 million, are living with the virus, making the country with the largest number of HIV/AIDS cases in the world. All aspects of South African life are affected by the pandemic. By examining South Africa, we can get a deeper understanding of the gravity of this global issue for South Africa and other developing countries.

South Africa ■ The epicenter of the global HIV/AIDS crisis

Africa is the epicenter of the AIDS pandemic, but the disease is growing around the globe. Nurses distribute free condoms during an AIDS awareness event on a street in China.

Apart from the fact that HIV/AIDS originated in Africa, several other factors have contributed to its rapid growth in South Africa. Economic, cultural, and political factors combine to make South Africa a special case. Settled by Europeans, primarily from Holland and Britain, South Africa experienced racial conflicts and endured forced racial segregation under the system of apartheid. The political and social components of apartheid provided the breeding ground for the HIV/AIDS problem. Apartheid laws required men who worked in the gold, diamond, and other mines; the factories; and all sectors of the economy to leave their families. Rural-to-urban migration occurs throughout Africa, as we discussed in Chapter 11. Under various colonial administrations, Africans were forced to leave rural areas in search of employment in urban centers, in mining, and in agriculture. The majority of these migrant workers returned home periodically. This pattern of migration was firmly rooted in South Africa and it continues. As in other parts of Africa, HIV/AIDS cases were initially concentrated along major trading routes and areas frequented by long-distance truck drivers. Bars and hotels along these routes became centers for the sex trade. The men transmit the virus to women in rural areas, making HIV/AIDS a predominantly heterosexual disease in Africa. Another factor that facilitates the spread of HIV/AIDS in South Africa is the casual, unsafe, and abusive nature of sexual relationships. Cultural attitudes and behaviors influence many South Africans to accept having multiple partners and engage in unprotected sex, rejecting the use of condoms. Traditional sexual practices (such as dry sex, which involves the use of powders and herbs to prevent vaginal lubrication) result in increased friction and greatly elevate the risk of viral transmission through internal abrasion and lesions. In a predominantly patriarchal society, women are generally perceived as being inferior to men. Women are expected to meet the sexual demands of men and are relatively passive, if not powerless, in insisting on safer practices, such as using condoms.

The costs associated with HIV/AIDS are extremely high. The virus is most prevalent among South Africans who range in age from eighteen to forty-four; it essentially destroys the most productive citizens. Education suffers as teachers die or are too sick to work. Extended families, already struggling to survive, face additional responsibility for raising orphans of relatives. More than a million children under the age of fifteen have already lost their mothers to the disease. This huge group is likely to fuel crime and other social problems. The economic implications are profound. Not only are more resources being allocated to treat and prevent HIV/AIDS; those infected with the virus are unproductive. Valuable skills are lost, and businesses often bear additional costs and inefficiencies resulting from HIV infections among employees. Agriculture also suffers, as women, who do most of the agricultural work, are unable to concentrate on providing food for their families. Finally, because HIV/AIDS is prevalent among the age groups involved in the military, South Africa's national security is undermined, and its ability to effectively participate in solving many conflicts in Africa is severely weakened.

apartheid ■ South Africa's system of rigid, legal, and racial segregation that was violently enforced

rural-to-urban migration ■ Facilitates the spread of HIV/AIDS in South Africa

dry sex ■ A practice that facilitates the transmission of AIDS

Global Responses to AIDS

Condom usage is a relatively inexpensive and effective approach to reducing the risk of infection and transmission of HIV. Governments, NGOs, and international organizations support condom distribution programs, although this practice remains controversial for some groups that stress abstinence. Given the reality of increased human sexuality, using condoms will undoubtedly be the dominant and practical approach to fighting HIV/AIDS. Thailand provides an example of how governments have integrated condom usage into an overall strategy to impede the spread of the disease. Thailand began mandatory HIV testing of high-risk individuals, such as homosexuals, commercial sex workers, and intravenous drug users. It also implemented "the 100 Percent Condom Program." The principal objectives of the program are to protect 100 percent of commercial sex acts through mandatory condom usage in brothels and to diminish the commercial sex trade through sustained educational efforts. Free condoms are distributed to the sex workers, who are instructed to use them or face several penalties. The commercial sex business is closely monitored by the government to ensure compliance.

Medical advances and a deeper understanding of HIV/AIDS—in addition to the fact that the disease was concentrated among high-risk groups—enabled rich countries to make significant progress in decreasing the transmission of the virus. Antiretroviral drug therapies, though expensive, allowed many HIV/AIDS patients to continue living relatively normal lives. Deaths from the disease have declined in most developed countries, although both HIV/AIDS and mortality rates have increased among the poor in these societies, especially among African Americans. Despite opposition by pharmaceutical companies concerned about intellectual property rights, Brazil, Argentina, Costa Rica, Cuba, and Uruguay took the unprecedented approach of providing government-subsidized antiretroviral medications to HIV/AIDS patients, thereby setting global precedents for widespread access to AIDS medications. Brazil, in particular, has made it legal for government laboratories to ignore drug patents in order to produce low-cost generic drugs to stop the spread of the disease. Brazil's aggressive strategy to control HIV infections and transmission stands in sharp contrast to the approach adopted by South Africa. Despite its massive problems with the disease, South African officials attempted to ignore them. Faced with unrelenting domestic and global pressure to confront the seriousness of its HIV/AIDS problem, the South African government eventually implemented the Comprehensive HIV/AIDS Care, Management, and Treatment Plan in 2004. This program focuses on using antiretroviral medicines to treat people, voluntary counseling, testing, and increasing the distribution of free condoms.

Although the United States has been involved in the global efforts to reduce HIV infections, a significant change in the U.S. policy was initiated by Franklin Graham, founder of Samaritan's Purse, an evangelical charity based in South Carolina. Bringing together evangelical Protestants and Catholic leaders, as well as overseas missionaries who worked in countries devastated by HIV/AIDS, Graham focused national attention on the problem. Perceptions of the disease as affecting primarily heterosexuals, as opposed to only homosexuals, enabled many conservatives to take action instead of disregarding the pandemic because they believed it was God's punishment of homosexuals. President George W. Bush, influenced by Graham and the evangelicals, announced the Emergency Plan for AIDS Relief and committed $25 billion over five years to preventing HIV infections and treating patients.[17] However, political pressure from conservatives influenced the U.S.

100 Percent Condom Program ■ Thailand's program to protect commercial sex acts through mandatory condom usage

Samaritan's Purse ■ An evangelical charity involved in fighting the spread of HIV/AIDS

government to allocate a third of the money to abstinence-promoting programs and to avoid spending money on sterile syringes and needles for intravenous drug users. Essentially, the U.S. government adopted Uganda's ABC (Abstinence, Be Faithful, and Use Condoms) program, which helped to significantly reduce the prevalence of HIV/AIDS in that country. The William J. Clinton Presidential Foundation HIV/AIDS Initiative concluded an agreement with generic drug manufacturers to lower the price of triple combination antiretroviral drug regimens to less than $140 per patient per year. The Clinton Foundation has concentrated its efforts against HIV/AIDS in Mozambique, Rwanda, Tanzania, South Africa, and several Caribbean states.

ABC Program ■ Developed in Uganda to fight HIV/AIDS; stresses abstinence, fidelity, and using condoms

The WHO and U.S. government agencies—including the U.S. Food and Drug Administration (FDA) and the Alcohol, Drug Abuse, and Mental Health Administration—convened the First International AIDS Conference in Atlanta, Georgia, in 1984. This was followed by the initiation of WHO's Special Program on HIV/AIDS in 1985, which set the objective of reducing the growth of HIV/AIDS globally and to lessen the disease's impact on the countries most seriously affected. Concerned about HIV/AIDS patients' inability to afford drugs to treat the disease, members of the World Trade Organization (WTO) ratified the Agreement on Trade-Related Aspects of Intellectual Property Rights (TRIPS) in 1994. TRIPS included a provision to allow states to waive patent protections without authorization from the patent holder in national emergencies for noncommercial use. A major breakthrough in the fight against the pandemic came in 1996 when the Joint United Nations Program on AIDS (UNAIDS) was founded. UNAIDS's main objective is to be the leading advocate for global action against HIV/AIDS. Several organizations, reflecting UNAIDS's comprehensive approach to the problem, participate in the program. These include UNICEF; the UN Development Program; the UN Population Fund; the UN Educational, Scientific, and Cultural Organization (UNESCO); the World Bank; the UN Office on Drugs and Crime; and the International Labor Organization. These organizations have been joined by the eight leading industrial countries (known as the G-8), various NGOs, and pharmaceutical companies (such as Boehringer Ingelheim, Bristol-Myers Squibb, GlaxoSmithKline, Merck, and F. Hoffmann-LaRoche). Giving in to global pressure to lower drug prices to make them accessible to the poor, pharmaceutical companies responded by discounting their antiretroviral medications and allowing countries to manufacture drugs inexpensively for patients in poor countries.

TRIPS ■ Allowed states to waive patent protections unilaterally to deal with national emergencies

UNAIDS ■ The leading advocate for global action against HIV/AIDS

SARS

SARS emerged in China's Guangdong Province in late 2002. The virus that caused SARS was transmitted from the civet cat to individuals handling and consuming the animal's meat. This highly contagious disease is spread when individuals come into contact with droplets from an infected person's coughing or sneezing. The symptoms of SARS are high fever, chills, muscle aches, and a dry cough. The vast majority of individuals infected with SARS improve without having to undergo extensive medical treatment. However, between 10 and 20 percent of those contracting the disease require breathing assistance with a mechanical ventilator for an extensive period of time. Many of them eventually die.

The transmission of the disease globally began when twelve guests in the Metropole Hotel in Hong Kong contracted it from an infected physician from Zhongshan University. Unaware of being infected, these guests carried the disease to Singapore, Vietnam, Canada, Ireland, and the United States. More than eight hundred cases of SARS worldwide are believed to have been originated with this one superspreader.[18] Global communications helped to spread the most recent information about SARS, thereby heightening global awareness of the deadly virus and generating pressure on governments, especially that of China, to take action to prevent its spread globally. Global communications also enabled the scientific community to engage in unprecedented cooperation to control the virus.

superspreader ■
Person responsible for spreading disease to a large number of individuals

Governments responded quickly. Vietnam—which had the first documented case of SARS even though SARS originated in southern China—implemented *detection-and-prevention measures* immediately. These included (1) prompt identification of people with SARS, their movements, and their contacts; (2) appropriate protection of medical personnel treating these patients; (3) isolation of suspected SARS cases; (4) exit screening of international travelers; and (5) timely and accurate reporting and sharing information with others.[19] Canada, the United States, and other countries took similar actions. The WHO also responded promptly by sending investigation teams to Guangdong, the first Chinese city that experienced SARS. Also, the WHO visited Beijing and pressured government officials to give an accurate assessment of the SARS problem and to improve its reporting system. Roughly sixty teams of public health officials and experts were recruited from the United States, Britain, Germany, France, and other countries to assist with efforts to control the spread of infections in areas affected by SARS. *Several factors contributed to this rapid global response*:

1. *Fear and Uncertainty.* The rapid spread of the disease and its lethality created a sense of urgency to respond.
2. *Stronger Leadership.* The WHO was proactive in raising global awareness and mobilizing the global response.
3. *Scientific Advances.* New scientific knowledge and techniques enabled researchers to find solutions quickly.
4. *Heightened Awareness of Biological Weapons Threat.* Concerns with terrorism and the threat of biological weapons influenced countries to act quickly to identify new infectious diseases.
5. *Concerns About Missing Another AIDS Problem.* Public health officials reacted swiftly to SARS, believing that the slow global response to HIV/AIDS allowed that disease to build up devastating momentum.[20]

The global response to SARS marks a radical departure from earlier responses to infectious diseases and has become a model for dealing with potential pandemics.

GLOBAL RESPONSES TO INFECTIOUS DISEASES

The global community has long recognized that preventing, treating, and controlling the spread of infectious diseases can be accomplished only through cooperation among individuals, NGOs, governments, and international organizations.

As early as 1851, European countries convened the International Sanitation Conference in an effort to prevent the spread of infectious diseases from developing countries to Europe, primarily through travel and trade. Significant improvements in sanitation, nutrition, and medical technology in Europe have reduced outbreaks of infectious diseases. But Europe remained vulnerable to the importation of diseases. Shortly after the United Nations was founded, the WHO was created as a specialized agency to develop international rules concerning infectious disease control. Under the International Health Regulations developed by the WHO, countries are required to report outbreaks of yellow fever, cholera, plague, and other diseases. This information is disseminated to other countries, and surveillance strategies are implemented to help prevent transmission. Countries are also required to provide safe drinking water, food, and disposal of refuse, wastewater, and other things dangerous to health at their airports and ports. International Health Regulations also require counties to provide health services, equipment, and services for isolating infected persons and for disinfecting, disinsecting, and deratting ships and aircraft.[21] The U.S. Centers for Disease Control and Prevention (CDC), based in Atlanta, Georgia, also plays a leading role in preventing and controlling the transmission of infectious diseases into the United States. Both the CDC and the WHO emphasize the importance of research and the development of medicines to prevent the emergence and spread of infectious diseases.

As we have seen, an important component of the global response to the emergence and reemergence of infectious diseases is stressing preventive measures. These include protecting and chlorinating water supplies, disposing of human feces in a sanitary manner and maintaining fly-proof latrines, paying special attention to cleanliness in food preparation and food handling, stressing the importance of frequent hand washing, and eliminating potential mosquito breeding sites. Routine preventive immunization programs have effectively reduced outbreaks of many infectious diseases. The WHO launched the "3 by 5" anti-AIDS initiative, which aimed to provide anti-AIDS drugs to 3 million people in poor countries. Of the roughly 33 million people infected with AIDS, more than 3 million received the necessary drugs.[22] In 2006, WHO launched the *universal access initiative* to bring an even greater sense of urgency and commitment to HIV prevention and treatment. The United States made a commitment to spend $15 billion on efforts to prevent and control the spread of AIDS. The Bill and Melinda Gates Foundation gave $287 million to researchers to develop an HIV vaccine in addition to their contributions to fighting malaria and other diseases. A basic challenge was persuading pharmaceutical companies to lower drug prices and to permit developing countries, such as India and Brazil, to be exempt from patent restrictions so that they could produce relatively inexpensive anti-AIDS drugs. Many major pharmaceutical companies have agreed to arrangements allowing poor countries to have access to relatively inexpensive drugs. The SARS virus, the growing concern about terrorists using biological weapons, and the emergence of avian flu contributed to a greater awareness of the globalization of infectious diseases and the need to act promptly and decisively to prevent both infections and transmission.

International Sanitation Conference ■ Effort to prevent the spread of infectious diseases from developing countries to Europe

CDC ■ U.S. organization devoted to preventing and controlling the transmission of infectious diseases into the United States

CASE STUDY | Obesity: A Global Epidemic

Obesity, long considered a problem in rich countries, is now a global epidemic. Obesity and overweight are generally defined as excessive fat accumulation that has serious health consequences. Obesity and overweight are the fifth leading cause of death globally. The World Health Organization (WHO) has warned that obesity puts populations at risk for developing noncommunicable diseases (NCDs), which have been declared a global epidemic. A United Nations (UN) summit in 2011 launched a global attack against NCDs, which it defined as cancer, diabetes, chronic respiratory diseases, and cardiovascular diseases. These often preventable diseases cause 63 percent of all deaths, frequently to people in their productive years, and account for 75 percent of all healthcare spending. The UN sees NCDs as a threat to development and an epidemic that disproportionately hits the poor and vulnerable and increases their poverty. The UN campaign has identified the major NCD risk factors, some of which are related to obesity, as unhealthy diet, physical inactivity, tobacco, and alcohol. Contrary to popular perceptions of starvation in the developing world, more people die from obesity and overweight than from being underweight. In addition to the stated NCDs, obesity is an underlying cause of infertility in women and impotence in men. Globally, obesity rates have doubled since 1980. More than 1.5 billion adults and 43 million children, mostly in the developing world, are obese or overweight. More women are obese or overweight than men worldwide. With the exception of Mexico, rich countries have the highest percentage of obese and overweight persons. The United States leads the list, with almost one third of its population obese or overweight. Mexico is a close second, with 24 percent, followed by Britain with 23 percent, Slovakia with 22.4 percent, Greece with 22 percent, and Australia with 21.7 percent.[23]

There are many causes of obesity and overweight. As part of our ancestors' evolutionary adaptation to food scarcity, human beings store calories when food is available. A gestating mother's environment directly influences her children's weight in later life. Children born to parents who did not have adequate diets during pregnancy tend to have higher rates of obesity. The children of starving mothers, anticipating starvation during their own lives, tend to hoard calories. As food remains abundant, they tend to overeat and gain weight. It also is believed that brighter lights contribute to obesity by confusing the body's biological clock, which signals when we should eat or sleep. Contemporary lifestyles deprive many individuals of adequate sleep, and an increasing amount of time is spent watching television and on the computer. Americans are not only the most overweight people on the globe; they also are the most sleep deprived and spend many hours in lighted environments.

Cultural globalization, advances in agricultural productivity that increased food supplies, declining population growth rates, and urbanization are major causes of obesity. Cultural globalization has led to the homogenization of lifestyles, diets, and an automobile culture globally. People consume foods that are high in calories and relatively low in cost. The hectic pace of life influences people to eat fast foods that have lots of sugar, fat, and salt. Those dietary habits are combined with sedentary lifestyles. Overcrowding and crime in urban areas contribute to a decline in exercise. The easy availability of high-calorie snacks and soft drinks virtually guarantees the growth of the obesity epidemic, especially as food companies find ways to get consumers to purchase their products.

Solutions to obesity and overweight are well known, though difficult to achieve in a world with constant advertising and global competition among food companies for market share. While individuals are ultimately responsible for their behavior, losing weight requires support from families and communities. Food consumption is an essential component of culture. Consequently, greater efforts must be made at a societal level to promote proper

(continued)

nutrition and smaller food portions. Global and local food companies could help by reducing the fat and sugar content of food and be more responsible in marketing products to children. By abandoning sedentary activities and increasing exercise as part of a daily routine, individuals can gradually help reduce obesity and overweight. Wellness programs in workplaces, hiking and walking trails, and communities designed to encourage walking and biking instead of driving could make a difference. Finally, working with children to make them aware of the benefits of proper nutritional and physical activity will slow down the growth of the obesity and overweight epidemic. ▲

SUMMARY AND REVIEW

This chapter discussed the globalization of infectious diseases; rapid increases in global travel, trade, and migration; growing use of illegal drugs; human trafficking for sexual purposes; rapid population growth; environmental changes; widespread poverty; and inadequate medical resources—all factors that have facilitated the global spread of infectious diseases. These diseases pose significant threats to humans as well as to global security. By discussing infectious diseases—such as influenza, avian flu, malaria, tuberculosis, HIV/AIDS, and SARS—we were able to see the social, economic, and political challenges these diseases pose and the ease with which they are spread globally. Special emphasis was given to HIV/AIDS because of its grave threats to the global society. We discussed various responses to the globalization of infectious diseases. The case of SARS demonstrates that rapid transportation and instantaneous communications have raised global awareness of how quickly infectious diseases are transmitted worldwide. The global response to SARS is widely regarded as a model for how to deal with emerging as well as current infectious diseases. Some organizations, such as the WHO, play a pivotal role in reducing the expansion of infectious diseases. NGOs as well as individuals are also actively involved in fighting pandemics. However, many governments have inadequate resources to deal with multiple infectious diseases. Furthermore, countries have different priorities. Cultural values and practices also complicate global efforts to prevent the emergence and spread of infectious diseases. This chapter also discussed the newly identified epidemics of obesity and noncommunicable diseases (NCDs), which are related to each other. Global organizations are targeting these preventable diseases that cause 63 percent of all deaths and increase poverty worldwide.

KEY TERMS

NCDs   276
pathogenic natural selection   278
global security   278
human security   278
UN Millennium Development Goals   278
pathogens   279
epidemics   279

pandemics   279
hosts   279
zoonosis   279
first epidemiologic transition   279
Plague of Justinian   279
Black Death   279
second epidemiologic transition   280

DISCUSSION QUESTIONS

1. Discuss the causes and effects of the global obesity epidemic. How does obesity relate to the global epidemic of noncommunicable diseases (NCDs)?
2. Discuss the role of the WHO in preventing the spread of infectious diseases.
3. Discuss the factors that facilitate the spread of HIV/AIDS and various efforts to deal with this pandemic.
4. Compare domestic and global approaches to malaria and tuberculosis.
5. Discuss how conflicts, global warming, and poverty contribute to the emergence and spread of infectious diseases.

SUGGESTED READINGS

Garrett, Laurie. "**The Challenge of Global Health,**" *Foreign Affairs* 86, No. 1 (January/February 2007): 14–38. The globalization of disease in general and HIV/AIDS in particular will continue to pose major threats to the global community.

Lyman, Princeton, and Stephen B. Wittels. "**No Good Deed Goes Unpunished,**" *Foreign Affairs* 89, No. 4 (July/August 2010): 74–84. The United States made a significant commitment to fighting HIV/AIDS in Africa. More U.S. assistance will limit America's influence on other issues.

Price-Smith, Andrew. *Contagion and Chaos.* Cambridge, MA: MIT Press, 2009. Discusses how diseases spread in conflict zones and become global threats.

Zacher, Mark W., and Tania J. Keefe. *The Politics of Global Health Governance.* New York: Palgrave Macmillan, 2008. Examines the history of international cooperation in relation to contagious diseases and the growth of the World Health Organization.

ENDNOTES

1. Donald G. McNeil, "Cholera's Second Fever," *New York Times*, 21 November 2010, A4.
2. Andrew Price-Smith, *Contagion and Chaos* (Cambridge, MA: MIT Press, 2009).
3. David P. Fidler, *International Law and Infectious Diseases* (Oxford: Clarendon Press, 1999), 9.
4. Ronald Barrettt et al., "Emerging and Reemerging Infectious Diseases: The Third Epidemiologic Transition," *Annual Review of Anthropology* 27 (1998), 247.

5. Paul R. Epstein, "Climate, Ecology, and Human Health," in *Plagues and Politics*, ed. Andrew T. Price-Smith (New York: Palgrave, 2001), 49.

6. Alfred W. Cosby, *The Columbian Exchange: Biological and Cultural Consequences of 1492* (Westport, CT: Greenwood Press, 1972), 37.

7. "Plagues and Livestock," *Economist*, 12 February 2011, 68.

8. Michael T. Osterbolm, "Preparing for the Next Pandemic," *Foreign Affairs* 84, No. 2 (July/August 2005), 26.

9. National Research Council, *Under the Weather: Climate, Ecosystems, and Infectious Disease* (Washington, DC: National Academies Press, 2001), 54.

10. National Research Council, *Under the Weather*, 48.

11. National Research Council, *Under the Weather*, 47.

12. World Health Organization, *Yellow Fever: Fact Sheet No. 100*, December 2001, 1.

13. Lisa Sattenspiel, "The Evolution, Transmission, and Geographic Spread of Infectious Diseases," in *The Changing Face of Disease*, eds. Nick Mascie-Taylor et al. (London: CRC Press, 2004), 44.

14. Roger Bate, "Testimony on Fighting Malaria," *Congressional Quarterly*, 13 May 2005, 3.

15. Bate, "Testimony on Fighting Malaria," 3.

16. Alun Anderson, "A Fight to the Death," *Economist*, 1 January 2011, 159.

17. Princeton Lyman and Stephen B. Wittels, "No Good Deed Goes Unpunished," *Foreign Affairs* 89, No. 4 (July/August 2010), 74.

18. Stacey Knobler et al., *Learning from SARS* (Washington, DC: National Academies Press, 2004), 6.

19. Aileen J. Plant, "SARS and Public Health," in *The New Global Threat*, eds. Tommy Koh et al. (London: World Scientific Pub. Co., 2003), 4.

20. Knobler et al., *Learning from SARS*, 260.

21. Mark W. Zacher and Tania J. Keefe. *The Politics of Global Health Governance* (New York: Palgrave Macmillan, 2008).

22. Michael Fleshman, "A Crisis in Waiting for AIDS Patients," *Africa Recovery*, April 2010, 16.

23. WHO, *Obesity and Overweight: Fact Sheet No. 311*, March 2011, 1.

Cultural Clashes and Conflict Resolution

American Marines
a nonstate actor, th

INTRODUCTION

Some groups and individuals promote globalization as a positive force to advance their own interests, whereas others perceive globalization as threatening. Global integration is increasing while, simultaneously, national cohesion is weakening as smaller groups seek increased political and cultural autonomy. Progress toward global order and security is accompanied by persistent outbreaks of violent conflicts and insecurity. Globalization challenges traditional certainties, conservative values, and parochialism; it also erodes identities based on nationality, geographic location, religion, social status, and ethnicity. Insecurity gives rise to global, international, and domestic conflicts. That these clashes occur at different levels (global, international, regional, national, and local) and often operate interdependently manifests the complexity of global society. Benjamin R. Barber, for example, envisions two possible global futures: (1) the McDonaldization or interdependence of the world and (2) a jihad (or struggle) in the name of a hundred narrowly conceived faiths against every kind of interdependence.[1] Barber's view of a jihad is essentially synonymous with ethnic conflicts. Another perspective, best articulated by Samuel P. Huntington, is that the world is divided into distinct civilizations that inevitably clash.[2] This rigid distinction among civilizations is widely rejected by scholars and policymakers.

   This chapter examines the role of culture in global conflicts, focusing on civilization clashes, international conflicts, and ethnic conflicts. It discusses efforts to resolve cultural conflicts. As the case study of the war in Afghanistan shows, America's longest war is not with another state, but is instead with a nonstate actor, the Taliban.

jihad ■ Arabic word symbolizing a religiously based inner struggle between "good" and "evil" that exists within all people

ethnic conflicts ■ Generally understood as violent clashes between or among groups within a particular country

CULTURAL INFLUENCES ON CONFLICTS

Culture and nationalism have generally been closely intertwined. In fact, culture has been synonymous with nations, races, and ethnic groups. Nations have traditionally been defined in terms of their common identity, values, customs, languages, and geographic boundaries. How nations' ethnic groups interact and resolve disagreements is determined largely by the cultural reservoirs or the lack of them. A cultural reservoir may be defined as an accumulation of goodwill and understanding that emanates from a common set of values, beliefs, attitudes, historical experiences, and racial and ethnic links. Leaders usually draw upon cultural similarities to diminish tensions and, conversely, upon cultural differences and hatreds to promote conflict.

   A distinction can be made between material culture (i.e., the tangible products of human society) and nonmaterial culture (i.e., the intangible products of society, such as values and rules of right and wrong behavior). Nonmaterial culture is the learned ideational aspects of human society.[3] In most countries, culture is generally equated with civilization. The clash-of-civilizations theory adopts this

cultural reservoir ■ An accumulation of goodwill and understanding that emanates from a common set of values, beliefs, attitudes, experiences, and racial and ethnic links

material culture ■ Tangible products of human society

nonmaterial culture ■ Intangible products of society, such as values and rules of right and wrong behavior

culture ■ A set of shared learned values, beliefs, perceptions, attitudes, modes of living, customs, and symbols

definition of culture. Culture is generally defined as a set of shared learned values, beliefs, perceptions, attitudes, modes of living, customs, and symbols.

One of the first questions we tend to ask someone who appears to be different is: Where are you from? This question, though routine, goes to the heart of identity and belonging. Do you belong to this society? Are you foreign? All societies, directly and indirectly, promote their values as positive and desirable while, simultaneously, devaluing those of other societies. This behavior is referred to as ethnocentrism. Positive images of one's society are developed and reinforced by rewards for conformity. Ken Booth, for example, contends that each society views itself as the center of the world, perceives and interprets other societies within its peculiar frame of reference, and invariably judges them to be inferior.[4] The more culturally distinct the other society is perceived to be, the more inferior it is often deemed to be and thus suitable for negative treatment. This perception is at the heart of ethnic conflicts and international wars.

ethnocentrism ■ Practice of societies promoting their values as positive and desirable while simultaneously devaluing those of other societies

CLASHING CIVILIZATIONS

According to the clash-of-civilizations perspective, global conflicts occur due to cultural differences. Although nation-states will continue to be the most powerful actors in global affairs, civilizations will be the dividing lines. A civilization is broadly defined as a cultural entity that, despite variations within it, is distinct from another civilization. For example, despite differences between Spain and Britain, they belong to the same Western civilization and are distinguished from Arab or Chinese civilizations. Huntington states "a civilization is the highest cultural grouping of people and the broadest level of cultural identity people have short of that which distinguished humans from other species. It is defined by common objective elements, such as language, history, religion, customs, institutions, and by the subjective self-identification of people."[5] From Huntington's perspective, *there are eight major civilizations:* Western, Confucian, Japanese, Islamic, Hindu, Slavic-Orthodox, Latin American, and African. The clash-of-civilizations theory stresses conflict instead of cooperation among civilizations.

civilization ■ A cultural entity that is significantly different from others

Many scholars have criticized the clash-of-civilizations perspective. For example, Fouad Ajami argues that "Huntington has found his civilization whole and intact, watertight under an eternal sky. Buried alive, as it were, during the Cold War, these civilizations rose as soon as the stone was rolled off, dusted themselves off, and proceeded to claim the loyalty of their adherents."[6] Similarly, Stanley Hoffmann criticized Huntington's concept of what constitutes a civilization as being hazy. From Hoffmann's perspective, Huntington "failed to take into account sufficiently conflicts within each so-called civilization, and he overestimated the importance of religion in the behavior of non-Western elites, who are often secularized and Westernized. Hence he could not clearly define the link between a civilization and the foreign policies of its member states."[7] Civilizational bonds have not restrained countries from competing with each other for power. Furthermore, civilizations are products of cultural cross-fertilization. Their members are complex, and the lines separating civilizations are often blurred and messy. For example, music by Haydn, Mozart, and Beethoven has Turkish origins. The Ottomans used giant war drums and cannons to frighten their enemies on the battlefield and to terrify the population in places like Vienna, Austria. Eventually, West Europeans adopted many Turkish cultural practices, including its military music for its marching bands. Haydn wrote his *Military Symphony*, and Mozart composed the piano sonata *Rondo Alla Turca* under the influence of Turkish music.[8]

Religion, a foundation of civilizations, is regarded by Huntington as essentially pure and unaffected by other religions. The mixing of religions is as old as human civilization. As Susanne Rudolph observes, "Religious communities are among the oldest of the transnationals. Sufi orders, Catholic missionaries, and Buddhist monks carried word and practice across vast spaces before those places became nation-states. Religious communities have become vigorous creators of an emergent transnational civil society."[9]

The West and the Muslim World

At the heart of the theory of the inevitability of cultural clashes between the West and the Muslim world is the assumption that the two civilizations are inherently incompatible and hostile. But Western perceptions of Islam, like perceptions in general, are rooted in selective historical memories. Cooperation and similarities between these cultures are overlooked or downplayed while historical conflicts are stressed. Despite the Muslim conquest of part of Spain in the eighth century, Muslims were largely tolerant of Jews and Christians, regarding them as Dhimmis (i.e., people of the Book who also believed in one God, the God of Abraham). The advent of the Crusades in 1096 aided the foundation for the clashes between the West and Islam. The Crusades became a potent experience that continues to influence many Muslims' perceptions of the West and their own self-perceptions. The Crusaders' brutality symbolized Western hatred not only of Muslims but also of Islam.

Dhimmis ■ People of the Book who also believe in the God of Abraham

A small number of European Christians regularly made pilgrimages to the Holy Land (then Palestine) since the fourth century without encountering systematic or widespread violence. However, in 1009, the Egyptian caliph (religious ruler) Hakim ordered the destruction of the Holy Sepulcher in Jerusalem (where Christians believed that Jesus was buried). This action engendered increased conflicts between Christian pilgrims and Muslims in Syria and Palestine. Hoping to unite European Christians, who were engaged in incessant feudal warfare against each other, and to terminate attacks on pilgrims, Pope Urban II (in 1095) called on European Christians to proclaim their faith by taking military action to force the infidels (primarily Muslims) out of Jerusalem. The First Crusade (1096–1099) represented unprecedented European cooperation as well as Europe's emergence from the Dark Ages. There were nine Crusades. The final Crusade (1271–1272) was followed by the Muslim reconquest of the last Christian stronghold in the Islamic world in 1291. Armstrong states, "The Christianity of the Angles, the Saxons, and the Franks was rudimentary. They were aggressive and martial people and they wanted an aggressive religion."[10] Crusaders, believing that Jews had killed Christ, slaughtered Jews in communities along the Rhine Valley and elsewhere on their 3,000-mile journey to fight Muslims, about whom they were largely unaware. Believing that they were "God's Chosen People," the Crusaders were unrestrained in their cruelty. When they conquered Jerusalem in 1099, "they fell on the Jewish and Muslim inhabitants with the zeal of Joshua and massacred

Pope Urban II ■ Initiated the Crusades

them with a brutality that shocked even their contemporaries."[11] The ability of the less culturally sophisticated European Christians to plunder and defile Islam's holy sites, including the Dome of the Rock in Jerusalem, has been interpreted by many Muslims as a consequence of their religious shortcomings. Contemporary Muslim grievances are often linked to the Crusades. Believing that Islam continues to be attacked by the West, many Muslims feel an obligation to engage in jihad (or struggle) against unbelievers.

Dome of the Rock ■ One of Islam's holy sites in Jerusalem

The United States and Islam

Deeply shocked by massive terrorist attacks by al-Qaeda in the United States, many Americans asked why Muslims hated them. To answer this question, many U.S. politicians, scholars, and commentators retrieved the clash-of-civilizations theory and downplayed analysis of complex causes of terrorism. President Bush declared on September 15, 2001, that "this crusade, this war on terrorism is going to take a while," thereby stunning many Muslims. For Muslims, a crusade evokes a highly emotional historical experience that laid the foundation for their interactions with the West. Furthermore, the clash-of-civilizations theory, with its assumption of a monolithic Islamic civilization, frustrated many Muslims who are aware of the diversity within the Islamic world and who also face terrorist threats from the Islamic extremists. The clash-of-civilization theme was reiterated by Bush in 2006 on the fifth anniversary of the September 11 attack when he asserted that the United States was in a struggle for civilization. Although cultural differences have contributed to conflicts between the United States and particular Muslim countries, specific national interests were by far the most important influences. The first significant clash was between a fledgling United States and the Barbary States, or North Africa (Tunisia, Algeria, Morocco, and Libya or Tripolitania). As part of its wars with Spain, the Ottoman Empire, which controlled the Barbary States, encouraged piracy against Spain. Barbary pirates enslaved Europeans and Americans and demanded tribute (payment) from European and American commercial interests. U.S. President Thomas Jefferson eventually tried to end this piracy by sending the U.S. Marines "to the shores of Tripoli" (1801–1805).

Barbary States ■ Practiced piracy against the United States; place where the United States first clashed with Muslims

The United States maintained a neutral approach to the region until the Six-Day War of 1967. As American petroleum companies became more deeply involved in the Middle East and as Britain reduced its role in the region after World War II, the United States developed closer relations with strategically important Islamic countries. Consequently, America was also increasingly perceived by many Muslims as colonial Europe's replacement. Muslims' perceptions of American indifference to Palestinian suffering as well as increasing globalization influence contemporary U.S. relations with the Muslim world. Globalization, especially American culture, both attracts and repels. Globalization reinforces connections between some Muslims and the United States while, simultaneously, undermining traditional society, compounding inequality, and generating feelings of alienation and insecurity.

The rise of militant Islam coincides with the growth of Islamic fundamentalists, whom many believe are engaged in an apocalyptic struggle with Western infidels. Some Islamic militants believe that by attacking the United States, viewed as a strong supporter of Israel, they will eventually reconquer Jerusalem from

Israel or even destroy Israel itself. But Islamic militancy is also linked to U.S. involvement in Muslim countries. For example, American actions in Iran contributed to contemporary conflicts between the West and Islam. When Iranian students discovered America's role in the 1953 overthrow of Iran's Prime Minister Mohammad Mossadeq from declassified U.S. Central Intelligence Agency documents in 1978, they engaged in mass demonstrations against the United States and the Iranian government, led by Shah Muhammad Reza. Widespread opposition to the Shah culminated in the Islamic Revolution, which forced the Shah out of Iran in 1979 and facilitated Ayatollah Khomeini's return to Iran from exile in France. American diplomats were taken hostage and demonstrators occupied the American embassy. Although secularists who supported the revolution wanted to develop democracy in Iran, the Ayatollah's followers were able to create an Islamic political system.

Ironically, peace between Egypt and Israel also fueled the emergence of extremist Islamic groups in Egypt, such as Egyptian Islamic Jihad, which was responsible for the assassination of Egypt's President Anwar Sadat in 1981. Sadat was killed because he signed the Camp David Accords with Israel and because of Egypt's close links with the United States. Egyptian Islamic Jihad was strengthened by Muslims who went to Afghanistan to fight with the mujahedeen (i.e., holy warriors) to resist Soviet occupation of that country. When the Soviets invaded Afghanistan in 1979, the United States provided military assistance to the mujahedeen. Osama bin Laden, from Saudi Arabia, also joined the mujahedeen. Assisted by veterans from Afghanistan's war, Egyptian Islamic Jihad carried out a series of bombings against U.S. targets, including American embassies in Kenya and Tanzania in 1998, and cooperated with al-Qaeda, led by bin Laden.

Sources of Muslim hatred of the United States are found within many Islamic countries. Many Arab governments are authoritarian and have used their considerable economic resources from petroleum to preserve the status quo. As we have seen, these governments now face popular uprisings. Barry Rubin argues that Muslim hatred of America is "largely the product of self-interested manipulation by groups that use anti-Americanism as a foil to distract public attention from other, far more serious problems within those societies."[12] It is generally agreed that the spread of Islamic fundamentalism is, to some extent, a product of deteriorating economic conditions, growing economic inequality, rapid population growth, rural-to-urban migration, and decline in social services, health care, and educational opportunities. Furthermore, increasing Westernization of these countries is perceived by traditionalists as undermining Islam, the foundation of their societies. America is viewed as corrupting these countries' elites and humiliating Muslims. America's invasion of Iraq, widely perceived as an effort to consolidate its power in the Middle East, has heightened Arab anti-Americanism. Widely disseminated photographs of Americans abusing Iraqi prisoners at the Abu Ghraib prison in Iraq served to confirm Muslim perceptions of the United States. The acts of brutality, sadism, and dehumanization that occurred at Abu Ghraib demonstrated to Muslims that America regarded them as culturally distant and excludable from moral considerations that govern its own society. In an effort to change these perceptions, President Barack Obama traveled to Turkey, Saudi Arabia, and Egypt. In a major speech at Cairo University, President Obama downplayed

Shah Muhammad Reza ■ Iranian leader responsible for high levels of repression committed against the Iranian people

Egyptian Islamic Jihad ■ Islamist group responsible for the 1981 assassination of Egypt's President Anwar Sadat

mujahedeen ■ Holy warriors who traveled to Afghanistan to fight the Soviet occupation

Abu Ghraib ■ Prison in Iraq where Americans abused and tortured prisoners

differences between Islam and the United States and stressed that he wanted to base American relations with Muslims on mutual respect and mutual interests.[13]

CLASHES AMONG NATIONS

Clashes among nations within the same civilization are common realities of international relations. For example, France and Britain sharpened their national identities through constant conflict with each other. Linda Colley contends that "Britain was an invention forged above all by war. Time and time again, war with France brought Britons, whether they hailed from Wales or Scotland or England, into confrontation with an obviously hostile other and encouraged them to define themselves collectively against it."[14] The consolidation of diverse cultural groupings within England, France, Spain, and Germany was an essential component of the rise of national identity and nationalism. Growing nationalism culminated in clashes with the Catholic Church and the Holy Roman Empire. This clash within Western civilization elevated states above civilizations. Following the conclusion of the Peace of Westphalia in 1648, marking the birth of the nation-state, European countries routinely engaged in wars to settle boundary disputes, underscoring not only the territoriality of states but also their preoccupation with who belongs to them. Two World Wars were not only clashes among nations but also wars among countries sharing what is seen as a common civilization.

A combination of cultural distance and threatened national interests makes international conflicts more likely, partly because negotiations with distant others are generally downplayed or rejected. Two wars between the United States and Iraq (in 1991 and 2003) demonstrate this point. Many Americans lack close relationships with Arabs, and few are knowledgeable of Arab history and culture. Few believe that they share many common cultural values with Arabs. Instead, Americans generally rely on negative stereotypes when dealing with them. The Arab oil embargo in 1973–1974 etched a negative view of Arabs in American minds, which was reinforced by the terrorist attacks on the United States. Often Arabs are perceived as dangerous, untrustworthy, immoral, undemocratic, barbaric, and primitive.[15] Iraq's leader, Saddam Hussein, reinforced these stereotypes. But American cultural values also played a significant role in conflicts with Iraq. In both wars, disputes with Iraq were framed in terms of good versus evil. The United States also viewed the wars as transformative: Saddam Hussein's destruction would bring peace and democracy to the Middle East and resolve the Palestinian-Israeli conflict.

The United States' reliance on force to resolve conflicts and its handling of international relations reinforced negative views held by the global community against it. This anti-Americanism is found among close European allies, in rich and poor countries, and in Christian as well as Islamic countries, a reality that directly challenges the clash-of-civilizations theory. Historically, countries threatened by a hegemonic power usually form alliances to balance that power, as we saw in Chapter 2. Fareed Zakaria argues that "by crudely asserting U.S. power and disregarding international institutions and alliances, the Bush administration pulled the curtain on decades of diplomacy and revealed that the United States' constraints are self-imposed."[16] From the European perspective, American power must be constrained. As Robert Jervis put it, "They fear a world in which their values and interests are served only at Washington's sufferance."[17] But great powers often experience a sense of permanent insecurity. Their quest for the illusive absolute security makes other countries feel less secure, which often engenders conflicts. By strongly supporting the UN and multilateral action to resolve disputes, the United States reduced global opposition to its overwhelming power. Conversely, America's unilateral exercise of military might created fears among Europeans and others who perceive the UN as playing an essential role in promoting global governance. Furthermore, as America grows more nationalistic, Europeans are concentrating on building European political and economic cooperation.

International conflicts that are influenced by cultural differences and divergent national interests are also prevalent in Asia. China's rapid economic expansion and growing U.S. dependence on imports from China have engendered both cooperation and conflict between the two countries. China is widely perceived as a rising power that is competing with America for global hegemony. Its strong economy attracts advanced technology from around the world, which enables it to improve its military capabilities. Japan's historical rivalry with China is reinvigorated by Japan's economic problems and the transfer of some of its manufacturing industries to China. Nationalism in both China and Japan is resurging, even as economic cooperation between them strengthens. North Korea's decision to test nuclear devices further reinforced Japan's nationalism and security concerns. But as the case study of the war in Afghanistan shows, wars among nations are rare, whereas conflicts between states and nonstate actors are increasing.

ETHNIC CONFLICTS

Horrific bloodshed in the Democratic Republic of the Congo, Rwanda, Bosnia, Sudan, Iraq, Chechnya, and elsewhere is widely publicized by the global media. The proliferation of humanitarian organizations and other nonstate actors has also helped to make the world more aware of ethnic conflicts. As our discussion of global terrorism in Chapter 5 demonstrates, European countries, such as Spain, are challenged by violent groups that claim separate ethnic identities. In fact, as Europe moves toward greater unification, minority groups—such as Catalans, Basques, Corsicans, Scots, and Flemish—are seeking more autonomy. However, most of these ethnic or nationalist groups are not violent. Although the brutality and intractability of many ethnic conflicts tend to reinforce perceptions of escalating ethnic wars, there has actually been a decline in their number. Ted Robert Gurr identifies *four regional and global forces that help to explain the decline in the number of ethnic wars:*

1. The active promotion of democratic institutions and practices that protect minority rights.
2. Engagement by the UN, regional organizations, and nongovernmental organizations (NGOs) on behalf of minority rights.
3. The virtual consensus among the global foreign policy elite in favor of reestablishing and maintaining global and regional order.
4. The costs of ethnic conflicts, which have become evident to both governing elites and rebel leaders.[18]

TABLE 14.1		
Ethnic Conflicts		
Country	**Estimated Deaths**	**Description of Conflict**
Nigeria	1 million (1966–1970)	Ibo region declared independence, calling itself Biafra.
Angola	600,000 (1975–2002)	Civil War following independence from Portugal
East Timor	307,000 (1975–2000)	Struggle for independence against Indonesian occupation
Sri Lanka	70,000 (1983–2009)	Tamils fighting the Sinhalese government for a separate state
Iraq	45,000 Kurds and Shiites (1983–1992)	Suppression of rebellion against Saddam Hussein
Sudan (Darfur)	2 million (1983–2009)	Arab/Muslim North fighting Christian and animist South
Turkey	40,000 (1984–2009)	Kurdish groups fighting for autonomy
Sierra Leone	15,000 (1992–2000)	Attempt to overthrow the government
Burundi	250,000 (1993–1999)	Tutsis and Hutus fought after the president, a Hutu, was assassinated.
Yugoslavia	400,000 (1994)	Serbs against Muslims and Croats
Rwanda	800,000 (1994)	Hutus slaughtered Tutsis and moderate Hutus.
Congo (Zaire)	5.4 million (1997)	Overthrow of Mobutu Sese Seko

While globalization contributes to cultural clashes, it also restrains them. Ethnic conflicts are much less pervasive or durable in areas that are integrated into the global economy than they are in countries that are relatively unaffected by global interdependence or regional integration.

Ethnicity and Ethnic Identity

tribalism ■ Groups of indigenous people in Africa, Asia, Latin America, and North America

Kurds ■ An ethnic group residing in Turkey, Iraq, Iran, and Syria

Tribalism, ethnicity, and ethnic nationalism are terms that are often used interchangeably. Tribalism is usually regarded as an anachronistic term that refers to groups of indigenous people. Most scholars prefer to refer to these groups as ethnic groups. Sometimes ethnic groups are across the artificially created boundaries of several countries. Ethnic groups within states as well as those that straddle national boundaries may aspire to create their own country. To achieve this, they develop a strong sense of nationalism. For example, the Kurds, an ethnic group that has nationalistic aspirations, are scattered among Turkey, Iraq, Iran, Syria, and parts of the former Soviet Union. Most ethnic groups attempt to achieve more political and cultural autonomy within the boundaries of existing states.

An ethnic group is composed of individuals who generally have a sense of common identity based on a common set of historical experiences, national sentiments, religious beliefs, geographic location, language and culture, and, in countries such as the United States, largely arbitrary racial categories. Ethnicity is a subjective perception of who belongs to a particular group. Ethnicity serves as a rallying point for mobilizing ethnic group members to compete for economic resources, positions in government and social and economic organizations, and social and religious status. An essential component of ethnicity is a strong sense of identity. Identity may be defined as a concept of the self, a selection of physical, psychological, emotional, or social attributes of particular individuals. There are different types of identity. Those include ethnic, religious, geographic, and linguistic identities. Identity provides a framework within which people construct reality and determine their positions on a wide range of issues. Members of different ethnic groups are predisposed to hold certain stereotypes about each other and to act on the basis of these assumptions.

ethnicity ■ A subjective perception of who belongs to a particular ethnic group

identity ■ A concept of oneself based on physical, psychological, emotional, or social attributes

Identity is generally about drawing sharp distinctions among groups and building boundaries that separate one group from another. It contributes to developing a feeling of "us versus them," insiders versus outsiders. We treat members of our own group differently from members of another group. Discrimination on the basis of ethnic identity is a common problem worldwide. Instead of seeing discrimination as being inherently wrong and unfair, it becomes the norm. Ethnic pluralism (i.e., ethnic diversity) is the presence of many different groups within a specific geographic boundary. *Several factors contribute to ethnic pluralism.* These include

ethnic pluralism ■ Also known as ethnic diversity

1. Conquest and annexation;
2. The decision by colonial powers to put different ethnic groups together in newly created countries;
3. The deliberate attempts by colonizers and others to divide people in order to control them; and
4. Migration.

The Causes of Ethnic Conflict

Although conflicts between ethnic groups are often perceived as the result of "ancient hatreds," most ethnic conflicts are very complex and have little to do with ancient animosities. In all societies, generational change and economic and social developments generally modify ancient hatreds. Contemporary ethnic conflicts have more immediate causes. Although the Scots and the English fought each other for centuries, these ancient hatreds do not influence them to fight today. *Most ethnic wars occur in poor countries that have weak political institutions.* Paul Collier has found that once a country achieves a per capita income similar to those of rich countries, its risk of ethnic conflict is negligible. The potential for conflict is concentrated in the poorest countries with declining economies and a heavy reliance on natural resources for a large share of national income.

Another cause of ethnic conflict is *the deliberate manipulation of negative perceptions* by leaders to mobilize group support for their own individual political, economic, and social objectives. Leaders rely on the emotional intensity and loyalty of ethnic group members. They know that distrust can be instrumental in fueling fears and that fears usually override logical, objective thinking. Consequently, despite misgivings individuals may have about engaging in or condoning violence against another group, these fears and an emotional commitment to their own group generally influence ethnic group members to follow their leaders.

Competition among groups for scarce economic resources is a major cause of ethnic violence. Growing economic disparities, resulting from economic development, may increase the fears and insecurities of those ethnic groups that are disadvantaged. On the other hand, ethnic conflict may emanate from attempts by an ethnic group to monopolize scarce resources. In Nigeria, for example, the Ibos fought to create a separate country (called Biafra) partly because of their experience with violence and discrimination and because they did not want to share their wealth from petroleum found in their region of the country. The discovery of oil in the Sudan has contributed to humanitarian crisis in Darfur and the inability of the global community to prevent the deaths of roughly 200,000 people and the displacement of more than 2 million.

Forces of globalization help to destroy boundaries essential to ethnic group solidarity and identity. Many leaders' power is threatened, a development that often influences them to promote ethnic identity more zealously. *Weak political institutions* contribute to ethnic conflicts, especially when countries are experiencing economic, cultural, and technological transformation. The inabilities of political institutions to effectively regulate change and provide mechanisms through which differences can be managed frequently contribute to ethnic violence.

Ibos ■ Ethnic group in Nigeria that tried to create a separate state (called Biafra)

A resurgence of anti-Semitism in Europe shows that developed countries are experiencing ethnic tensions. In France, a gendarme collects evidence after swastikas and other Nazi and far-right symbols were painted on tombstones at a Jewish cemetery.

Systematic and widespread frustration of human needs may culminate in outbreaks of ethnic violence. Tensions are heightened by perceptions of favoritism toward other groups, compared with disadvantages suffered by the particular ethnic group. Ethnic group members are mobilized to articulate their grievances and to seek solutions to them. In many cases, violence is seen as the most effective instrument to get the government to respond favorably to their demands. This, in turn, influences the government to respond with violence against the ethnic group. Finally, *the proliferation of automatic weapons*, especially AK-47s, is a significant contributor to ethnic conflicts around the world. While it may be argued that these weapons do not cause conflict, their availability increases the potential for deadly clashes among ethnic groups or the use of violence by ethnic groups against governments, as we discussed in Chapter 6.

Ethnic Clashes

Although ethnic violence is clearly more prevalent in poor countries, developed countries are also experiencing ethnic tensions and renewed ethnic nationalism. Since the end of the Cold War and the fall of the Berlin Wall, there has been a resurgence of anti-Semitism in Europe, especially in France. Mark Strauss states that "not since Kristallnacht, the Nazi-led pogrom [violent campaign] against German Jews in 1938, have so many European synagogues and Jewish schools been desecrated."[19] One of the oldest hatreds in Europe, anti-Semitism is strongest in Alsace, France, a region that has strong cultural ties to Germany. This traditionally German-speaking area was annexed by Germany in 1871, following the Franco-Prussian War, and remained under German control until the French conquered it in World War I. Alsace became a Nazi stronghold in the 1930s, and many Alsatians joined the Nationalist Socialist Party (Nazi Party) when Alsace was annexed by Adolf Hitler in 1940. The worst German atrocity in France against the Jews was the massacre at Oradour in Alsace in 1944. This historical affiliation with Nazism was rekindled by the rise of the National Front, an extremely conservative political movement. Both Jews and Muslims are targets of violence.

Kristallnacht ■
Nazi-led pogrom against German Jews

The growing number of Muslims in countries across Europe is perceived as a threat to cultural institutions. This perception of threat escalated with the rise of Islamic terrorism and the terrorist attacks on the United States, Spain, and Britain. But Germany, Austria, France, Britain, Spain, Italy, and other countries have been concerned about demographic changes brought about largely by Muslim immigrants. Many Europeans define their cultures in terms of Christianity, but Muslims are making Islam a part of European culture. Religious symbols, especially the Muslim headscarf, have been politicized. France, stressing the separation of church and state, has been the most aggressive European country in terms of banning headscarves in public schools.

National Front ■
Conservative French political movement that is anti-Jewish and anti-Muslim

Canada and the United States, two of the world's most ethnically diverse countries, have managed to reduce ethnic violence by bringing various ethnic minorities into the democratic process and by outlawing discrimination. Canada was confronted with separatist movements in Quebec until recently. Quebec, colonized and settled by the French, was conquered by the British in 1759. The Treaty of Paris in 1763 officially transferred Quebec from France to Britain, making it part

Treaty of Paris ■
Transferred Quebec from France to Britain in 1763

of British Canada. Many people in Quebec maintained close ties with France and nurtured French culture and language. Generational change, economic interdependence, political reforms, and increased immigration to Quebec combined to lessen nationalistic aspirations. However, the growing numbers of Muslims in Canada, as well as that country's strong commitment to multiculturalism, have created new ethnic tensions. Autonomy granted to various Native American groups has inspired other ethnic groups to seek more cultural autonomy. Muslims, for example, point to Jews and their ability to use Jewish laws to govern their communities and argue that Shari'a Law (Islamic law) should govern Muslim communities.

Ethnic conflicts in the former Yugoslavia produced widespread military confrontation in which ethnic identity literally became a matter of life and death. These conflicts also underscored how cultural links with various countries influenced both military actions and efforts to terminate the bloodshed. The Croats have historically been the most thoroughly integrated into European civilization, largely as a consequence of their domination by Austria-Hungary and Venice. Serbs identify with Eastern Orthodox countries, such as Greece and Russia, and the Muslims, though they are also Europeans and Slavic, are regarded as remnants of the Ottoman Empire and identify with Turkey and other Islamic countries. Composed of six republics—Bosnia-Herzegovina, Croatia, Macedonia, Montenegro, Serbia, and Slovenia—and the two provinces of Kosovo and Vojvodina, Yugoslavia was an artificial nation-state held together by Marshall Josip Tito's domineering personality and the League of Communists of Yugoslavia (LCY) until Tito's death in 1980 and the fall of Communism in the late 1980s. As Yugoslavia's disintegration became obvious, the Republic of Serbia intensified its efforts to arrest Yugoslavia's fragmentation and to continue Serbia's dominance. Bosnia's Serbs, led by Radovan Karadzic, favored increased centralization, whereas the Muslims and Croats opted for a loose confederation. Acting on their fears of each other and remembering historical experiences, Croats and Serbs began to dismember Bosnia. Muslims, aware that Bosnia had been divided between Croatia and Serbia prior to World War II, resisted reabsorption into those states. Serbia clearly intended to use its superior military might to fashion Greater Serbia out of Croatia and Bosnia. Slobodan Milosevic, president of Yugoslavia (who was later tried for war crimes at the International Criminal Court at the Hague), boasted that the Serbs were on the threshold of "the final solution." Milosevic died in prison in 2006.

Although Muslims and Croats engaged in their own campaigns of ethnic cleansing, the Serbs were primarily responsible for genocide and Muslims were the principal victims. After depriving Muslims of their jobs and property, the Serbs began to destroy their villages and cities and forced them to leave, thereby creating the greatest refugee crisis in Europe since World War II. Many refugees were shipped out of northern Bosnia in sealed freight trains, a practice reminiscent of Nazi Germany's treatment of the Jews. Atrocities included the massacre of villagers; the torture, rape, and killing of prisoners; the use of Muslims as human shields; and the taking of hostages. Many civilians, imprisoned in forty-five concentration camps, were executed. Serbian gunmen raped more than fifty thousand Muslim women and children as part of their program of ethnic cleansing and as a weapon of war. Echoing Nazi Germany's plan to exterminate the Jews and eliminate all traces of Jewish culture, Serb nationalists attempted to destroy the

Shari'a Law ■ Islamic law used to govern Muslim communities

Marshall Josip Tito ■ Communist leader who ruled Yugoslavia until his death in 1980

Radovan Karadzic ■ Bosnian leader who favored continued Serbian dominance of Yugoslavia

Slobodan Milosevic ■ President of Yugoslavia who was tried for war crimes at the International Criminal Court

ethnic cleansing ■ Mass, forced relocation or expulsion of one ethnic or religious group by another ethnic or religious group

What does this photo convey about ethnic conflict? A young ethnic Albanian boy carries his sister as they look through barbed wire at a refugee camp. Almost a million ethnic Albanians fled or were expelled from Kosovo.

Muslims' culture. Mosques, central to Muslims' identity and society, were principal targets. Historical monuments and libraries that were depositories for more than five centuries of Muslim culture were reduced to rubble.

Ethnic conflicts in Rwanda also demonstrate how ethnic differences are socially constructed and how deadly the consequences of policies exaggerating and emphasizing small differences can be. Genocide in Rwanda, the Congo, and Sudan illustrate that the decline in the number of ethnic conflicts globally is largely irrelevant to Africa, the continent most marginalized from globalization. As we discussed earlier, the world's poorest countries, most of which are in Africa, are the most vulnerable to prolonged and widespread ethnic violence. Africa also has a very large number of ethnic groups, many of which live together in artificially created countries. When the Germans conquered what is now Rwanda in 1899, they encountered two main groups: the **Hutus**, who comprised the majority of the population, and the **Tutsis**, a small group of cattle herders who ruled the area. Many smaller groups spoke the same language and shared the same culture. Years of intermarriage made it difficult to neatly separate them into distinct ethnic groups. The Germans relied primarily on the ruling Tutsis to help them control the territory. They designated the Tutsis as the superior group, a perception reinforced by

Hutus ■ Majority group in Rwanda who committed genocide against the minority Tutsi population

Tutsis ■ Small group of cattle herders who had ruled Rwanda under German and Belgian colonization

the Belgians who gained control of Rwanda in 1916, following Germany's defeat in World War I. Germany's and Turkey's colonies became mandates under the League of Nations. Finding it difficult to distinguish Hutus from Tutsis, the Belgians issued mandatory identity cards to all Rwandans, placing each person into a fixed ethnic category. Eventually the Tutsis, who received preferential treatment from the Belgians, believed that they were indeed superior to the Hutus. However, Belgian missionaries, believing in equality and social progress, helped disadvantaged Hutus obtain an education. Educated Hutus, facing discrimination, challenged the system that gave Tutsis significant advantages and advocated ethnic separation. In 1959, the Hutus rebelled and killed more than twenty thousand Tutsis. When Rwanda became independent in 1962, the Hutu majority gained political control.

Ethnic rivalries escalated in 1990 when the Hutus' power was challenged by the Rwanda Patriotic Front army, composed of Tutsis. To restore a measure of peace and stability, moderate Hutus agreed to share power with the Tutsis. Hutu extremists responded by killing both Tutsis and moderate Hutus. When a plane carrying Rwanda's President Juvenal Habyarimana, a Hutu, crashed on April 6, 1994, ethnic violence erupted with a force that stunned the global community. Believing that Tutsis were responsible for destroying the plane, the Hutus circulated lists of names of those favoring democracy and national reconciliation. They set up roadblocks and demanded identity cards and systematically killed Tutsis. Students were slaughtered by their teachers, neighbors killed neighbors, and clergymen participated in the genocide. In many cases, husbands killed their families and then committed suicide to avoid a more terrible death. About eight hundred thousand people were slaughtered in thirteen weeks of fighting in Rwanda. In the aftermath of this genocide, Rwandan authorities decided to outlaw ethnic identity.

RESOLVING CULTURAL CONFLICTS

In many ways, globalization was widely perceived as instrumental in creating a more harmonious world. Global markets and the promotion of democracy were believed to diminish violent clashes. Although the realization of Immanuel Kant's vision of perpetual peace seemed distant, many political scientists and others observed that democratic norms that emphasize compromise, persuasion, peaceful competition, the protection of minority rights, and so on would move the global community closer to Kant's vision. In other words, they assert that democracies rarely fight each other.[20] But, as we have seen, democracies fight countries that are not democratic, and poor, marginalized, and undemocratic countries fight each other and are often plagued with ethnic conflicts. Nevertheless, the end of the Cold War and increasing globalization contributed to a stronger global emphasis on peacefully resolving conflicts. NGOs, such as the Carter Center in Atlanta and the Crisis Management Initiative in Helsinki play leading roles in conflict resolution. Their unconventional approach to negotiation is known as Track II diplomacy. We will examine *four interrelated approaches to conflict resolution*: (1) negotiation, (2) peacekeeping (which includes humanitarian intervention), (3) peacemaking, and (4) peacebuilding.

Track II Diplomacy ■ Negotiation using non-governmental actors

Negotiation

Negotiation is back-and-forth communication to reconcile contradictory positions and conflicting interests in order to reach an agreement acceptable to the parties involved. Negotiation is principally concerned with helping your opponent make a particular decision. An important impetus for advancing proposals and making concessions and compromises is that there are common interests that can be secured through cooperation.[21] Each side must be willing to make those adjustments that are essential to reaching a compromise, thereby creating what Roger Fisher and William Ury in *Getting to Yes* call a win-win situation (where both sides gain) instead of taking a zero-sum approach (where one side wins and the other loses). But negotiation is not entirely separated from the use of coercion or violence. Most conflicts cannot be resolved by relying on either negotiation or the threat of force. Negotiations involve both carrots (inducements) and sticks (punishments).

Raymond Cohen stresses that cultural values directly influence negotiation strategies and the success of negotiations in *Negotiating Across Cultures*. When individuals, countries, and ethnic groups focus primarily on their underlying interests and objectives, they have a better chance of resolving disputes than if they allow their emotions and beliefs to dominate. Learning the other side's real interests necessitates a careful and patient probing of the needs, hopes, fears, perceptions, and cultural values that form their sense of what is threatening or vital to protecting their identity. This requires willingness on the negotiator's part to listen actively to the other side and to put himself or herself in the other side's shoes, as it were. Active listening involves trying to hear and absorb the other side's views of the facts as distinct from one's own, to seek further clarification through questioning, and to process the information received in terms of the larger context of the situation and the issues of the movement. In addition to active listening, negotiators must develop formulas or trade-offs. A trade-off is essentially an exchange to address the fears and interests of those involved. An example of a trade-off is the 1967 UN Security Council Resolution 242, which attempted to resolve the Middle East conflict by exchanging land for peace. Israel would withdraw its armed forces from territories it conquered and occupied in exchange for the Arabs' termination of belligerency against Israel and recognition of Israel's sovereignty and territorial boundaries.

Numerous barriers impede successfully negotiating cultural conflicts. Perceptions often complicate negotiations between parties that have very different cultures. Information and facts that contradict our perceptions and images of ourselves and others are usually ignored or overlooked. Stereotypes impede the negotiating process between nations and ethnic groups that are culturally distant by fostering negative interpretations of motives behind actions that could be viewed as positive developments. Public opinion is also important. If citizens or ethnic group members believe that force is an effective and desirable means of dealing with disputes, leaders are likely to consider military action against the opponent. A society or group that perceives compromise as a sign of weakness is likely to produce leaders who devalue negotiations with adversaries. Similarly, leaders and policymakers who perceive the world as hostile and conflict ridden and who believe that only military force provides real security are generally likely to reject or downplay negotiations.

carrots and sticks ■ Practice by which states rely on inducements and punishments in their relations with other states

trade-offs ■ Exchanges designed to address the interests of both groups involved in mediation

UN Security Council Resolution 242 ■ Attempted to resolve the Palestinian-Israeli conflict by exchanging land for peace

peacekeeping ■
International
intervention designed
to limit or end state
interethnic violence

R2P ■ Doctrine
of Responsibility to
Protect civilians in
conflicts

just war ■ War
fought for noble,
humanitarian
purposes

peacemaking ■
Intervention intended
to convince
combatants to reach
a political settlement
through peaceful
negotiations

arbitration ■
Negotiations under
which a third party
determines the final
settlement between
two conflicting groups

mediation ■
Process of
facilitating
communication
between combatants
in order to reach a
peaceful settlement of
disputes

facilitation ■
Cooperative,
noncoercive approach
to conflict resolution that
seeks to get conflicting
parties to acknowledge
a shared problem that
requires cooperation to
be solved

peacebuilding ■
Long-term process
of implementing
social change through
economic development,
political reforms, and
territorial compromises

Peacekeeping and Humanitarian Intervention

Increasingly, the UN and regional organizations intervene militarily to end international and interethnic violence or to prevent it from escalating. This is called peacekeeping. A principal objective is to create an environment that is conducive to both humanitarian operations and negotiations. Peacekeeping missions are generally supported by the global community as well as the combatants. Nonstate actors—such as Amnesty International, Catholic Relief Services, Oxfam, and the International Committee of the Red Cross—cooperate with the UN and regional organizations. However, as the cases of Rwanda, Bosnia, Sudan, and East Timor demonstrate, the global community is often slow in responding to ethnic conflicts. Humanitarian intervention is closely related to the doctrine of Responsibility to Protect (R2P) civilians in conflicts, as discussed in Chapter 3. The NATO intervention in Libya in 2011 against the Gadaffi regime reinforced global acceptance of the necessity for humanitarian intervention. An issue raised in humanitarian intervention is the concept of a just war. *A just war must meet certain criteria:*

1. Support a just cause,
2. Be just in intent,
3. Be of last resort,
4. Have limited objectives,
5. Be proportional,
6. Be declared by legitimate authorities, and
7. Not involve noncombatants.

Peacemaking

Peacemaking, which generally occurs after peacekeeping has made significant progress, involves the intervention of neutral third parties. Their objective is to get the combatants to reach a political settlement through negotiations. These intermediaries rely on certain methods such as arbitration, mediation, and facilitation. Arbitration refers to "binding, authoritative third-party intervention in which conflict parties agree to hand the determination of a final settlement to outsiders."[22] Mediation is a process of facilitating communication between combatants to encourage them to brainstorm, invent options for mutual gains, and try to see the other side's perception of reality and legitimate concerns, as well as help them understand difficulties that might prevent the other side from meeting their demands. Mediators generally have some leverage over parties to a conflict and are generally seen as impartial. Facilitation is a cooperative, nonhierarchal, and noncoercive approach to conflict resolution. Facilitation attempts to get those involved in conflict to see the problem as a shared problem that requires cooperation to be solved. The third party's objective is to get the adversaries to engage in joint decision making to reach a settlement that is self-sustaining.[23]

Peacebuilding

Peacebuilding is a long-term process of implementing peaceful social change through economic development and reforms, political reforms, and territorial

CASE STUDY | War in Afghanistan

War, a central component of international relations, has traditionally been fought between states. America's longest war is not with another state but is instead a war against a nonstate actor, a terrorist group. Since the beginning of the war in 2001, the United States and its allies in the U.S.-led International Security Assistance Force (ISAF), which has roughly 150,000 troops, have lost hundreds of lives each year and have spent hundreds of billions of dollars (about $7 billion a month). Suicide bombings have escalated. Despite its overwhelming military might, the United States has not defeated the Taliban, which has relied on terrorism as a strategy in this asymmetrical war. Problems within Afghanistan and declining domestic American support for the war make it unlikely that the war is winnable by 2014, when foreign troops are scheduled to be withdrawn. Calls for American withdrawal escalated after Osama bin Laden was killed by U.S. Special forces on May 1, 2011.

Afghanistan, historically at the center of the "great game" among the leading military powers for influence in Central Asia, was invaded by the Soviet Union in 1979. Responding to Soviet aggression in the larger context of the Cold War, the United States imposed ineffective sanctions against the Soviet Union and increased military support to Pakistan. The United States, regarding the Afghan resistance movement (known as the Mujahedeen, or holy warriors) as freedom fighters, provided them with military aid to counteract Soviet military superiority. Muslims from other countries, including Osama bin Laden (from Saudi Arabia), joined the Mujahedeen. The effectiveness and brutality of the Mujahedeen forced the Soviets to withdraw in 1989. Afghanistan disintegrated into a civil war during which the Taliban, which emerged from the freedom fighters, gained control of the country and provided a safe haven for bin Laden and his fighters. Bin Laden, son of a wealthy Saudi businessman, spent millions of dollars to transform Afghanistan into his own training center for global terrorists. On September 11, 2001, terrorists from Al-Qaeda, headed by bin Laden, hijacked four U.S. passenger jets loaded with fuel and used them as missiles to bomb the World Trade Center in New York and the Pentagon, the center of American military might, in Arlington, Virginia, just outside Washington, D.C.

On October 7, 2001, the United States, with British support, began *Operation Enduring Freedom* with a massive bombing campaign in Afghanistan after the Taliban refused to surrender bin Laden and to close Al-Qaeda's training bases and terrorist network. Bombs weighing 2,000 pounds and guided by lasers and GPSs were dropped on targets. Sophisticated military technologies enabled American forces to detect heat, magnetic fields, and vibrations through as much as 100 feet of solid rock. Thermobaric weapons could penetrate rock and concrete to destroy underground targets. The Predator, a pilotless reconnaissance and surveillance plane that is controlled from a remote location, was equipped with Hellfire missiles to destroy targets. Supported by the United States, the Northern Alliance (the Afghan opposition) captured Kabul and drove the Taliban from urban areas. America announced the end of major combat operations on May 1, 2003. However, driven largely by hubris and the arrogance of power, America launched a preemptive war against Iraq in March 2003, thereby diverting resources and attention away from Afghanistan and destroying the global support it had for the war against the Taliban and Al-Qaeda.

America's inability to defeat the Taliban is due in part to its failure to focus on Afghanistan's endemic weaknesses that gave rise to the Taliban. The United States and its allies did not invest enough resources in improving government institutions, the justice system, the army and police, and local governance.[26] The government, led by Hamid Karzai, is deeply corrupt. In fact, Afghanistan was ranked by Transparency International as the second most corrupt country in the world, just behind Somalia. These problems undermined U.S. military efforts.

(continued)

Recognizing that the war against a nonstate actor is unwinnable, the United States decided to withdraw its troops by 2014. Given this reality, greater emphasis must be given to empowering the Afghans to govern themselves. A major step toward this goal is focusing on *capacity development,* enhancing the capabilities and performance of civilian institutions of governance. Another solution is to support political decentralization by allowing local leaders to take greater responsibilities for their communities. In light of its vital interests in Afghanistan, America must remain engaged and continue to work with the Afghans and develop arrangements such as joint basing. This means that America would help Afghans in various military operations. Finally, there needs to be a shift away from the concept of traditional war to a comprehensive counterterrorism strategy in the Pashtun area of Afghanistan, which is a Taliban stronghold. Efforts to reach a negotiated settlement with members of the Taliban must be strengthened. Nation-building strategies could be continued in the rest of the country.[27] ◣

compromises. Peacebuilding concentrates on improving conditions for a country's population or an ethnic group's members. By making economic reform, more equal distribution of economic opportunities, and economic development leading priorities, governments of ethnically torn countries can end the cycle of conflict. Ongoing violence in Afghanistan and the civil war in Iraq are widely perceived as partly due to the failure of the United States to provide essential economic change and help people with basic human security needs. Paul Collier observes that the postconflict period is a good time to reform because vested interests are loosened up.[24] Diaspora organizations can play a major role in the economic recovery of their original countries by providing money, skills, and valuable connections. Political reforms, including transitions to democracy, and power-sharing arrangements can be helpful. However, equating holding elections with democracy is a fallacy that is usually counterproductive. Building democracy takes time. This is clearly demonstrated by the failure of U.S. efforts to promote democracy in Iraq by stressing holding elections. Power-sharing arrangements divide political power among different ethnic groups. However, unless periodic adjustments are made to reflect changing demographics, these arrangements tend to disintegrate and ethnic conflicts erupt. In Lebanon, for example, government positions and political power were divided between the Maronite Christians and Sunni Muslims. But the power-sharing arrangement was not changed to reflect the rapid growth of the Muslim population. The country was plunged into a brutal civil war from 1975 to 1990. Israel's invasion of Lebanon in 2006 weakened the Lebanese government and exacerbated tensions among the various ethnic and religious groups. Federalism (i.e., the sharing of power between the central government and states, provinces, or regions) helps to solve ethnic conflicts. Ethnic groups can enjoy a degree of autonomy while remaining within the existing country. Finally, partition (i.e., the forming of a separate and independent country from an ethnic group) is generally regarded as a last resort. Many Kurds in Iraq and Turkey have advocated creating separate states to solve ethnic conflicts. As ethnic violence escalated in Iraq, many Shiites advocated dividing the country along ethnic lines. Elections and

power-sharing arrangements ■
Division of political power among different ethnic groups

partition ■
Forming of separate and independent countries between ethnic groups

political compromises among the ethnic groups kept Iraq unified. Bitter conflicts between North Sudan and South Sudan were resolved by dividing Africa's largest state. In a referendum held in January 2011 under UN auspices, South Sudanese voted for an independent country.[25]States are extremely reluctant to agree to partition, as America's Civil War clearly demonstrates.

SUMMARY AND REVIEW

Various periods of globalization have contributed to the cross-fertilization of cultures as well as to cultural clashes. This chapter focused on how the contemporary period of globalization is creating cultural homogenization and hybridization even as scholars and others believe that the world is divided into clashing civilizations. As we have seen throughout history, most of the violent conflicts have occurred within civilizations, within regions, and among groups within the same country. We saw that culture and nationalism have often been closely intertwined. We discussed the problem of ethnocentrism as a major factor in civilizational, international, and ethnic conflicts. We challenged the dominant perspective that Western states and the Muslim world are inherently incompatible and hostile. However, the political, economic, and cultural forces of globalization heighten insecurities among states, groups, and individuals.

This chapter examined ethnic conflicts, several causes of ethnic conflicts, and some of the reasons for the decline in ethnic wars. The rising costs of ethnic conflicts, active global promotion of democracy, global concerns about human rights, and increased global efforts to find peaceful solutions to conflicts have contributed to the decline or limitation of many ethnic wars. Nevertheless, many leaders continue to manipulate ethnic differences to achieve their various objectives. Finally, we examined global and regional efforts to end conflicts. These include negotiation, peacekeeping, peacemaking, and peacebuilding.

KEY TERMS

jihad 297
ethnic conflicts 297
cultural reservoir 297
material culture 297
nonmaterial culture 297
culture 298
ethnocentrism 298
civilization 298
Dhimmis 299
Pope Urban II 299
Dome of the Rock 300
Barbary States 300
Shah Muhammad Reza 301
Egyptian Islamic Jihad 301
mujahedeen 301
Abu Ghraib 301
tribalism 304
Kurds 304

ethnicity 305
identity 305
ethnic pluralism 305
Ibos 306
Kristallnacht 307
National Front 307
Treaty of Paris 307
Shari'a law 308
Marshall Josip Tito 308
Radovan Karadzic 308
Slobodan Milosevic 308
ethnic cleansing 308
Hutus 309
Tutsis 309
Track II diplomacy 310
carrots and sticks 311
trade-offs 311
UN Security Council Resolution 242 311

DISCUSSION QUESTIONS

1. How does globalization affect ethnicity, nationalism, and cultural clashes?
2. Can you give a short background on the Hutu/Tutsi ethnic conflict that resulted in the Rwandan genocide?
3. What are the four approaches to resolving cultural conflicts discussed in this chapter?
4. What is the difference between peacekeeping, peacemaking, and peacebuilding?
5. With specific reference to U.S. relations with Muslim countries, critically evaluate Huntington's thesis on the clash of civilizations.

SUGGESTED READINGS

Bergen, Peter L. *The Longest War*. New York: Free Press, 2011. Discusses how strategic errors and America's harsh methods in the war in Iraq contributed to prolonging the war against al-Qaeda.

Evans, Gareth. *The Responsibility to Protect*. Washington, DC: Brookings Institution Press, 2008. Argues that countries have an obligation to engage in humanitarian intervention to stop gross violations of human rights.

Katzenstein, Peter J., ed. *Civilizations in World Politics*. New York: Routledge, 2009. Challenges Samuel Huntington's thesis on the "clash of civilizations." Argues that a civilization of modernity that draws on values and aspirations from the world's cultural groups is emerging.

Lebow, Richard Ned. *A Cultural Theory of International Relations*. Cambridge: Cambridge University Press, 2009. Challenges conventional thinking on international relations and focuses on the influences of individuals, psychology, and human motives on state behavior.

Lemarchand, René. *The Dynamics of Violence in Central Africa*. Philadelphia: University of Pennsylvania Press, 2008. Analysis of Hutu-Tutsi violence in Rwanda and Burundi and ongoing ethnic conflicts in the Democratic Republic of the Congo.

ENDNOTES

1. Benjamin R. Barber, *Jihad vs. McWorld* (New York: Ballantine Books, 1996), 1.
2. Samuel P. Huntington, *The Clash of Civilizations and the Remaking of World Order* (New York: Simon and Schuster, 1996).
3. Chris Jenks, *Culture* (New York: Routledge, 1993), 8.
4. Ken Booth, *Strategy and Ethnocentrism* (New York: Pergamon Press, 1990), 343.
5. Huntington, *The Clash of Civilizations*, 25.
6. Fouad Ajami, "The Summoning," *Foreign Affairs* 72, No. 4 (September/October 1993), 2.
7. Stanley Hoffmann, "Clash of Globalizations," *Foreign Affairs* 81, No. 4 (July/August 2002), 105.
8. "Invading Turks' Music Marched West," *New York Times*, 10 March 2002, A6.

9. Susanne Rudolph, "Introduction," in *Transnational Religion and Fading States*, eds. Susanne Rudolph and James Piscatori (Boulder, CO: Westview Press, 1997), 1.

10. Karen Armstrong, *A History of God* (New York: Ballantine Books), 197.

11. Armstrong, *A History of God*, 197.

12. Barry Rubin, "The Real Roots of Arab Anti-Americanism," *Foreign Affairs* 81, No. 6 (November/December 2002), 73.

13. "Excerpts from President Obama's Speech in Cairo," *New York Times*, 5 June 2009, A8.

14. Linda Colley, *Britons: Forging the Nation 1707–1837* (New Haven, CT: Yale University Press, 1992), 5.

15. Michael W. Suleiman, *The Arabs in the Mind of America* (Brattleboro, VT: Amana Books, 1988), 147.

16. Fareed Zakaria, "Hating America," *Foreign Policy* 144 (September/October 2004), 48.

17. Robert Jervis, "The Compulsive Empire," *Foreign Policy* 137 (July/August 2003), 85.

18. Ted Robert Gurr, "Ethnic Warfare on the Wane," *Foreign Affairs* 79, No. 3 (May/June 2000), 59.

19. Mark Strauss, "Antiglobalism's Jewish Problem," *Foreign Policy* 139 (November/December 2003), 58.

20. Bruce M. Russett, *Controlling the Sword: Democratic Governance of National Security* (Cambridge, MA: Harvard University Press, 1990), 121–124.

21. Roger Fisher and William Ury, *Getting to Yes: Negotiating Agreement Without Giving In* (New York: Penguin, 1983).

22. Raymond C. Taras and Rajat Ganguly, *Understanding Ethnic Conflicts* (New York: Longman, 2002), 95.

23. Taras and Ganguly, *Understanding Ethnic Conflicts*, 96.

24. Paul Collier, "The Market for Civil War," *Foreign Policy* 136 (May/June 2003), 44.

25. "South Sudan's Future," *Economist*, 5 February 2011, 57.

26. Paul D. Miller, "Finish the Job," *Foreign Affairs* 90, No. 1 (January/February 2011), 52.

27. Robert D. Blackwill, "Plan B in Afghanistan," *Foreign Affairs* 90, No. 1 (January/February 2011), 44.

PHOTO CREDITS

INDEX